# WILEY BOOKS IN THE CERTMIKE SERIES

*CompTIA ITF+ CertMike: Prepare. Practice. Pass the Test! Get Certified! Exam FC0-U61*
by Mike Chapple
(ISBN 9781119897811)

*CompTIA A+ CertMike: Prepare. Practice. Pass the Test! Get Certified! Core 1 Exam 220-1101*
by Mike Chapple and Mark Soper
(ISBN 9781119898092)

*CompTIA A+ CertMike: Prepare. Practice. Pass the Test! Get Certified! Core 2 Exam 220-1102*
by Mike Chapple and Mark Soper
(ISBN 9781119898122)

*CompTIA Network+ CertMike: Prepare. Practice. Pass the Test! Get Certified! Exam N10-008*
by Mike Chapple and Craig Zacker
(ISBN 9781119898153)

# CompTIA® A+® CertMike

**Prepare. Practice. Pass the Test! Get Certified!**
**Core 1 Exam 220-1101**

Mike Chapple
Mark Soper

SYBEX®
A Wiley Brand

*To my Aunt Jane, who has given so generously to me my entire life.*

*I owe you more than I can ever express. Thank you.*

*—Mark Soper*

# ACKNOWLEDGMENTS

*From Mike Chapple:*

This book marks the start of a new series of CertMike Test Prep books, and I'd first like to thank the people who helped shape the vision for this series. The original idea was hatched over breakfast with two very supportive editors from the Wiley team: Ken Brown and Jim Minatel. I've worked with both Jim and Ken on many books over the years, and they're both insightful industry experts who know what it takes to produce a great book.

Mark Soper did the heavy lifting of putting this book together, and I am grateful to him for lending this series his expertise on end-user support and the A+ exams.

I'd also like to extend a special thank-you to my agent, Carole Jelen of Waterside Productions. Carole is also an experienced industry pro who can deftly navigate the murky waters of publishing. Carole is the one who pushed me to create my own series.

Of course, the creation of any book involves a tremendous amount of effort from many people other than the authors. I truly appreciate the work of Adaobi Obi Tulton, the project editor. Adaobi and I have now worked together on quite a few books, and she keeps the train on the tracks! I'd also like to thank Chris Crayton, the technical editor, who provided insightful advice and gave wonderful feedback throughout the book; and Archana Pragash, production editor, who guided me through layouts, formatting, and final cleanup to produce a great book. I would also like to thank the behind-the-scenes contributors, including the graphics, production, and technical teams who make the book and companion materials into a finished product.

Finally, I would like to thank my family who supported me through the late evenings, busy weekends, and long hours that a book like this requires to write, edit, and get to press.

*From Mark Soper:*

My name is on the cover, but this book would not be a reality without the efforts of so many people behind the scenes. First, I want to thank CertMike, Mike Chapple, for the opportunity to work on this brand-new certification series. I am also deeply grateful to the editorial and production team at Wiley for all their hard work.

Many thanks to Ken Brown, acquisitions editor; Christine O'Connor, managing editor; Adaobi Obi Tulton, project editor; Chris Crayton, technical editor; Archana Pragash, production editor; Kim Wimpsett, copy editor; and everyone else at Wiley who helped to make this book a reality.

I also want to thank my family for their support and for the many technology problems they've provided me with! It's been enjoyable to fix computer problems and to teach the next generation how things work. Thanks especially to my wife, Cheryl, for smiling and nodding as we discussed tech issues during Christmas dinner.

Finally, thanks so much to Almighty God, who created everything visible and invisible, including the forces that make computers work, and for His great salvation.

# About the Authors

**Mike Chapple, Ph.D., CySA+,** is author of the best-selling *CISSP (ISC)² Certified Information Systems Security Professional Official Study Guide* (Sybex, 2021) and the *CISSP (ISC)² Official Practice Tests* (Sybex, 2021). He is an information technology professional with two decades of experience in higher education, the private sector, and government.

Mike currently is a teaching professor in the IT, Analytics, and Operations department at the University of Notre Dame's Mendoza College of Business, where he teaches undergraduate and graduate courses on cybersecurity, cloud computing, data management, and business analytics.

Before returning to Notre Dame, Mike served as executive vice president and chief information officer of the Brand Institute, a Miami-based marketing consultancy. Mike also spent four years in the information security research group at the National Security Agency (NSA) and served as an active duty intelligence officer in the U.S. Air Force.

Mike has written more than 25 books. He earned both his B.S. and Ph.D. degrees from Notre Dame in computer science and engineering. Mike also holds an M.S. in computer science from the University of Idaho and an MBA from Auburn University. Mike holds the IT Fundamentals (ITF+), Cybersecurity Analyst+ (CySA+), Data+, Security+, Certified Information Security Manager (CISM), Certified Cloud Security Professional (CCSP), and Certified Information Systems Security Professional (CISSP) certifications.

Learn more about Mike and his other security certification materials at his website, CertMike.com.

**Mark Edward Soper, MCP, CompTIA A+,** is an instructor for University of Southern Indiana's Outreach and Engagement division. He has created and taught Microsoft Windows, Excel, Word, PowerPoint, Access, Outlook, and OneNote to staff, students, community, and corporate clients for USI for more than a decade.

Mark is also the cofounder and president of Select Systems & Associates, Inc., a technology research, training, and writing organization. Mark is a world-class technology writer and trainer with an international reach, with books available in English, Spanish, Polish, French, Italian, Swedish, Russian, Chinese, and other languages. He is a proven bridge between users and technology, helping users to grasp, master, and seek new and better technologies. Mark is a 39-year tech veteran and a human tech multitool, having written or co-authored more than 40 books on CompTIA tech certifications, computer hardware and software troubleshooting, operating systems, networking, digital photography, and self-service help desk topics. Mark has also taught these and other topics across the United States.

Mark has CompTIA A+ and Microsoft MOS – Microsoft Excel 2013 certifications, and he blogs at www.markesoper.com.

# ABOUT THE TECHNICAL EDITOR

**Chris Crayton** is a technical consultant, trainer, author, and industry-leading technical editor. He has worked as a computer technology and networking instructor, information security director, network administrator, network engineer, and PC specialist. Chris has authored several print and online books on PC repair, CompTIA A+, CompTIA Security+, and Microsoft Windows. He has also served as technical editor and content contributor on numerous technical titles for several of the leading publishing companies. He holds numerous industry certifications, has been recognized with many professional and teaching awards, and has served as a state-level SkillsUSA final competition judge.

# Contents

# INTRODUCTION

If you're preparing to take the A+ Core 1 exam, you might find yourself overwhelmed with information. This exam covers a broad range of topics, and it's possible to spend weeks studying each one of them. Fortunately, that's not necessary!

As part of the CertMike Test Prep series, *CompTIA® A+® CertMike: Prepare. Practice. Pass the Test! Get Certified! Core 1 Exam 220-1101* is designed to help you focus on the specific knowledge that you'll need to pass the exam. CompTIA publishes a detailed list of exam objectives, and this book is organized around those objectives. Each chapter clearly states the single objective that it covers and then, in a few pages, covers the material you need to know about that objective.

You'll find two important things at the end of each chapter: exam essentials and review questions. The CertMike Exam Essentials distill the major points from the chapter into just a few bullet points. Reviewing these Exam Essentials is a great way to prepare yourself right before the exam. I've also recorded a free audio version of the Exam Essentials that you'll find on the book's companion website at www.wiley.com/go/sybextestprep. They're great listening when you're in the car, at the gym, or mowing the lawn!

Each chapter concludes with two practice questions that are designed to give you a taste of what it's like to take the exam. You'll find that they're written in the same style as the A+ exam questions and have detailed explanations to help you understand the correct answer. Be sure to take your time and thoroughly read these questions.

Finally, the book's website includes a full-length practice exam that you can use to assess your knowledge when you're ready to take the test. Good luck on the A+ Core 1 exam!

> **NOTE**
>
> Don't just study the questions and answers! The questions on the actual exam will be different from the practice questions included in this book. The exam is designed to test your knowledge of a concept or objective, so use this book to learn the objectives behind the questions.

# THE A+ PROGRAM

A+ is designed to be a vendor-neutral certification for those seeking to enter the information technology field. CompTIA recommends this certification for individuals who want to be problem-solvers in the world of endpoint management and technical support. These are common job roles held by A+ certified individuals:

- ▶ Help-desk technician
- ▶ Field service technician
- ▶ Associate network engineer
- ▶ Junior systems administrator

- ▶ Desktop support specialist
- ▶ System support technician
- ▶ The A+ certification is unique in that earning it requires passing two separate exams
- ▶ **A+ Core 1 (220-1101)**, which covers mobile devices, networking technology, hardware, virtualization, and cloud computing
- ▶ **A+ Core 2 (220-1102)**, which covers operating systems, security, software, and operational procedures

This book focuses on the Core 1 exam, which covers five major domains of knowledge.

- ▶ Mobile Devices
- ▶ Networking
- ▶ Hardware
- ▶ Virtualization and Cloud Computing
- ▶ Hardware and Network Troubleshooting

These five areas include a range of topics, from installing printers to configuring networks, while focusing heavily on the basic knowledge expected of IT technicians.

The A+ exam uses a combination of standard multiple-choice questions and performance-based questions (PBQs) that require you to manipulate objects on the screen. This exam is designed to be straightforward and not to trick you. If you know the material in this book, you will pass the exam.

Each exam costs $239 in the United States, with roughly equivalent prices in other locations around the globe. More details about the A+ exams and how to take it can be found at

`www.comptia.org/certifications/a#examdetails`

You'll have 90 minutes to take the exam and will be asked to answer up to 90 questions during that time period. Your exam will be scored on a scale ranging from 100 to 900, with a passing score of 675.

> **NOTE**
>
> CompTIA frequently does what is called *item seeding*, which is the practice of including unscored questions on exams. It does so to gather psychometric data, which is then used when developing new versions of the exam. Before you take the exam, you will be told that your exam may include these unscored questions. So, if you come across a question that does not appear to map to any of the exam objectives—or for that matter, does not appear to belong in the exam—it is likely a seeded question. You never really know whether a question is seeded, however, so always make your best effort to answer every question.

## Taking the Exam

Once you are fully prepared to take the exam, you can visit the CompTIA website to purchase your exam voucher.

```
store.comptia.org
```

Currently, CompTIA offers two options for taking the exam: an in-person exam at a testing center and an at-home exam that you take on your own computer.

> **TIP**
>
> This book includes a coupon that you can use to save 10 percent on your CompTIA exam registration.

### In-Person Exams

CompTIA partners with Pearson VUE's testing centers, so your next step will be to locate a testing center near you. In the United States, you can do this based on your address or your ZIP code, while non-U.S. test takers may find it easier to enter their city and country. You can search for a test center near you at the Pearson Vue website, where you will need to navigate to "Find a test center."

```
www.pearsonvue.com/comptia
```

Now that you know where you'd like to take the exam, simply set up a Pearson VUE testing account and schedule an exam on that site.

On the day of the test, take two forms of identification, and make sure to show up with plenty of time before the exam starts. Remember that you will not be able to take your notes, electronic devices (including smartphones and watches), or other materials in with you.

### At-Home Exams

CompTIA began offering online exam proctoring in 2020 in response to the coronavirus pandemic. As of the time this book went to press, the at-home testing option was still available and appears likely to continue. Candidates using this approach will take the exam at their home or office and be proctored over a webcam by a remote proctor.

Because of the rapidly changing nature of the at-home testing experience, candidates wanting to pursue this option should check the CompTIA website for the latest details.

## After the Exam

Once you have taken the exam, you will be notified of your score immediately, so you'll know if you passed the test right away. You should keep track of your score report with your exam registration records and the email address you used to register for the exam.

After you earn the A+ certification, you're required to renew your certification every three years by either earning an advanced certification, completing a CertMaster continuing education program, or earning 20 continuing education units (CEUs) over a three-year period.

Many people who earn the A+ credential use it as a stepping stone to earning other certifications in their areas of interest. Those interested in networking work toward the Network+ credential, data analytics professionals might go on to earn the Data+ certification, and the Security+ program is a gateway to a career in cybersecurity.

# WHAT DOES THIS BOOK COVER?

This book covers everything you need to know to pass the A+ Core 1 exam. It is organized into five parts, each corresponding to one of the five A+ Core 1 domains.

**Part I: Domain 1.0: Mobile Devices**

Chapter 1: Laptop Hardware

Chapter 2: Mobile Device Displays

Chapter 3: Mobile Device Ports and Accessories

Chapter 4: Mobile Device Network Connectivity and Application Support

**Part II: Domain 2.0: Networking**

Chapter 5: TCP/IP Networking

Chapter 6: TCP/IP Ports and Protocols

Chapter 7: Networking Hardware

Chapter 8: Wireless Networking Protocols

Chapter 9: Networked Host Services

Chapter 10: Installing and Configuring Networks

Chapter 11: Advanced Network Configuration

Chapter 12: Internet Connection Types

Chapter 13: Networking Tools

**Part III: Domain 3.0: Hardware**

Chapter 14: Cables and Connectors

Chapter 15: Random Access Memory (RAM)

Chapter 16: Storage Devices

Chapter 17: Motherboards

Chapter 18: Booting, CPUs, and Expansion Cards

Chapter 19: Power Supplies

Chapter 20: Printer and Multifunction Device Configuration

Chapter 21: Printer Consumable Replacement

**Part IV: Domain 4.0: Virtualization and Cloud Computing**

Chapter 22: Cloud Computing

Chapter 23: Virtualization

**Part V: Domain 5.0: Hardware and Network Troubleshooting**

Chapter 24: Troubleshooting Methodology

Chapter 25: Troubleshooting Motherboards, RAM, CPU, and Power

Chapter 26: Troubleshooting Storage

Chapter 27: Troubleshooting Video

Chapter 28: Troubleshooting Mobile Devices

Chapter 29: Troubleshooting Printers

Chapter 30: Troubleshooting Networks

## Study Guide Elements

This study guide uses a number of common elements to help you prepare.

**Exam Tips**   Throughout each chapter, I've sprinkled practical exam tips that help focus your reading on items that are particularly confusing or important for the exam.

**CertMike Exam Essentials**   The Exam Essentials focus on major exam topics and critical knowledge that you should take into the test. The Exam Essentials focus on the exam objectives provided by CompTIA.

**Practice Questions**   Two questions at the end of each chapter will help you assess your knowledge and whether you are ready to take the exam based on your knowledge of that chapter's topics.

## Additional Self-Study Tools

This book comes with a number of additional self-study tools to help you prepare for the exam. They include the following.

> **NOTE**
>
> Go to www.wiley.com/go/sybextestprep to register and gain access to this interactive online learning environment and test bank with study tools.

### Online Test Bank

Sybex's online test bank lets you prepare for taking the actual CompTIA exam with a practice exam that is included in this book. This is a great way to test your knowledge of A+ Core 1 exam objectives.

### Audio Review

I've recorded an audio review where I read each set of chapter exam essentials. This provides a helpful recap of the main material covered on the exam that you can use while you're commuting, working out, or relaxing.

# CORE 1 EXAM 220-1101 EXAM OBJECTIVES

CompTIA goes to great lengths to ensure that its certification programs accurately reflect the IT industry's best practices. It does this by establishing committees for each of its exam programs. Each committee comprises a small group of IT professionals, training providers, and publishers who are responsible for establishing the exam's baseline competency level and who determine the appropriate target-audience level.

Once these factors are determined, CompTIA shares this information with a group of hand-selected subject-matter experts (SMEs). These folks are the true brainpower behind the certification program. The SMEs review the committee's findings, refine them, and shape them into the objectives that follow this section. CompTIA calls this process a *job-task analysis* (JTA).

Finally, CompTIA conducts a survey to ensure that the objectives and weightings truly reflect job requirements. Only then can the SMEs go to work writing the hundreds of questions needed for the exam. Even so, they have to go back to the drawing board for further refinements in many cases before the exam is ready to go live in its final state. Rest assured that the content you're about to learn will serve you long after you take the exam.

CompTIA also publishes relative weightings for each of the exam's objectives. The following table lists the five A+ Core 1 objective domains and the extent to which they are represented on the exam:

| Domain | % of Exam |
|---|---|
| 1.0 Mobile Devices | 15% |
| 2.0 Networking | 20% |

| Domain | % of Exam |
|---|---|
| 3.0 Hardware | 25% |
| 4.0 Virtualization and Cloud Computing | 11% |
| 5.0 Hardware and Network Troubleshooting | 29% |

# 220-1101 CERTIFICATION EXAM OBJECTIVE MAP

| Objective | Chapter(s) |
|---|---|
| **1.0 Mobile Devices** | |
| 1.1 Given a scenario, install and configure laptop hardware and components | 1 |
| 1.2 Compare and contrast the display components of mobile devices | 2 |
| 1.3 Given a scenario, set up and configure accessories and ports of mobile devices | 3 |
| 1.4 Given a scenario, configure basic mobile-device network connectivity and application support | 4 |
| **2.0 Networking** | |
| 2.1 Compare and contrast Transmission Control Protocol (TCP) and User Datagram Protocol (UDP) ports, protocols, and their purposes | 5 and 6 |
| 2.2 Compare and contrast common networking hardware | 7 |
| 2.3 Compare and contrast protocols for wireless networking | 8 |
| 2.4 Summarize services provided by networked hosts | 9 |
| 2.5 Given a scenario, install and configure basic wired/wireless small office/home office (SOHO) networks | 10 |
| 2.6 Compare and contrast common network configuration concepts | 11 |

| Objective | Chapter(s) |
|---|---|
| 2.7 Compare and contrast Internet connection types, network types, and their features | 12 |
| 2.8 Given a scenario, use networking tools | 13 |
| **3.0 Hardware** | |
| 3.1 Explain basic cable types and their connectors, features, and purposes | 14 |
| 3.2 Given a scenario, install the appropriate RAM | 15 |
| 3.3 Given a scenario, select and install storage devices | 16 |
| 3.4 Given a scenario, install and configure motherboards, central processing units (CPUs), and add-on cards | 17 and 18 |
| 3.5 Given a scenario, install or replace the appropriate power supply | 19 |
| 3.6 Given a scenario, deploy and configure multifunction devices/printers and settings | 20 |
| 3.7 Given a scenario, install and replace printer consumables | 21 |
| **4.0 Virtualization and Cloud Computing** | |
| 4.1 Summarize cloud-computing concepts | 22 and 23 |
| 4.2 Summarize aspects of client-side virtualization | 23 |
| **5.0 Hardware and Network Troubleshooting** | |
| 5.1 Given a scenario, apply the best practice methodology to resolve problems | 24 |
| 5.2 Given a scenario, troubleshoot problems related to motherboards, RAM, CPU, and power | 25 |
| 5.3 Given a scenario, troubleshoot and diagnose problems with storage drives and RAID arrays | 26 |
| 5.4 Given a scenario, troubleshoot video, projector, and display issues | 27 |
| 5.5 Given a scenario, troubleshoot common issues with mobile devices | 28 |

| Objective | Chapter(s) |
|---|---|
| 5.6 Given a scenario, troubleshoot and resolve printer issues | 29 |
| 5.7 Given a scenario, troubleshoot problems with wired and wireless networks | 30 |

> **NOTE**
>
> Exam objectives are subject to change at any time without prior notice and at CompTIA's discretion. Please visit CompTIA's website (www.comptia.org) for the most current listing of exam objectives.

# HOW TO CONTACT THE PUBLISHER

If you believe you've found a mistake in this book, please bring it to our attention. At John Wiley & Sons, we understand how important it is to provide our customers with accurate content, but even with our best efforts an error may occur. In order to submit your possible errata, please email it to our Customer Service Team at wileysupport@wiley.com with the subject line "Possible Book Errata Submission."

# PART I

# Domain 1.0: Mobile Devices

**Chapter 1**  Laptop Hardware
**Chapter 2**  Mobile Device Displays
**Chapter 3**  Mobile Device Ports and Accessories
**Chapter 4**  Mobile Device Network Connectivity and Application Support

Mobile Devices is the first domain of CompTIA's A+ Core 1 exam. It provides the foundational knowledge that IT professionals need to work with laptops, smartphones, and other devices used by end users. This domain has four objectives.

**1.1  Given a scenario, install and configure laptop hardware and components**

**1.2  Compare and contrast the display components of mobile devices**

**1.3  Given a scenario, set up and configure accessories and ports of mobile devices**

**1.4  Given a scenario, configure basic mobile-device network connectivity and application support**

Questions from this domain make up 15 percent of the questions on the A+ Core 1 exam, so you should expect to see approximately 13 questions on your test covering the material in this part.

# CHAPTER 1

# Laptop Hardware

*Core 1 Objective 1.1: Given a scenario, install and configure laptop hardware and components.*

*Laptops* outsell other PC types, so you're more likely to be in charge of maintaining them, upgrading them, and preparing them for use.

Although laptops include the same categories of components as desktop computers, their form factors are smaller, and in many cases the performance and capacity of those components may be less than their desktop counterparts.

Laptops also include features that enhance portability and security enabling them to be used anywhere securely.

In this chapter, you will learn everything you need about A+ Certification Core 1 Objective 1.1, including the following topics:

▶ **Hardware/device replacement**
▶ **Physical privacy and security components**

## WHAT IS A LAPTOP?

A laptop is a portable computer with a built-in display that folds on top of the base unit. A laptop has the same categories of components (RAM, CPU, ports, cooling system) as a desktop computer but uses parts with smaller form factors for portability. Figure 1.1 illustrates a typical laptop, a MacBook Air.

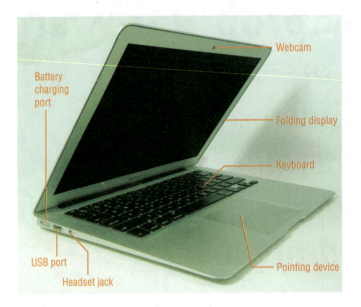

**FIGURE 1.1  A typical laptop.**

A laptop also differs from a desktop in having a built-in keyboard, camera, microphone, speakers, pointing device, battery power with an AC connection for recharging, and display. Most of these are visible in Figure 1.1.

Although laptops are much smaller and typically have smaller drive and RAM capacities than high-end desktops, laptops are capable of performing almost any job a desktop can do, from lightweight web surfing to photo and video editing and 3D gaming.

For the purposes of this chapter, convertible (2-in-1) devices that switch between conventional clamshell and tablet modes and tablets with attachable keyboards, such as Microsoft's Surface Pro series, are considered laptops.

> **EXAM TIP**
> The Core 1 exam likes to use drag-and-drop simulations for system assembly and troubleshooting, so be sure to study the equipment and troubleshooting examples in this book carefully.

# LAPTOP BATTERY POWER

Although laptops include AC adapters for recharging, most laptops are powered at least part of the time by their internal batteries. Depending upon the laptop model, the battery might be user-replaceable or require a trip to the repair shop.

Figure 1.2 shows a typical laptop battery that is user-replaceable. This battery can be removed by sliding a switch on the bottom of the unit to release the retaining mechanism.

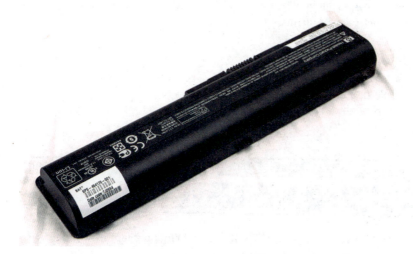

**FIGURE 1.2**  A user-replaceable battery after being removed from a laptop.

Some recent laptops require the user to remove the bottom cover to access the battery. However, ultra-thin and convertible models typically have built-in batteries that require a near-complete teardown to access them. These batteries often use a wired connection to the laptop motherboard.

Laptop batteries may be rated by watt-hours (Wh) or milliampere hours (mAh). To increase run time on battery power, use a higher-rated battery if more than one rating is available.

> **WARNING**
>
> Before replacing a battery or any other internal component, be sure to disconnect the laptop from AC power and shut down the unit.

# LAPTOP KEYBOARD AND SPECIAL LAPTOP KEYS

Laptop keyboards typically have layouts similar to desktop keyboards, although the positioning and size of arrow keys may be different, and some keyboards lack a dedicated number pad. However, the biggest difference between laptop keyboards and desktop keyboards is the presence of special laptop keys. There are no standards for the number and positions of laptop keys, so different laptops might feature different combinations of some of the following (see Figure 1.3 for an example):

- ▶ Volume controls
- ▶ Play/pause/forward/rewind media controls
- ▶ Switch to external display
- ▶ Enable/disable on-board Wi-Fi
- ▶ Display brightness
- ▶ Display contrast

**FIGURE 1.3** The top and bottom rows of a typical Windows laptop keyboard. Use the Fn key to activate the special laptop keys.

These keys are usually combined with other keys, such as function (F1–F12) keys. Switching to the secondary key assignment is done by pressing and holding the Fn key and then pressing the key. Depending upon the laptop model, the primary key assignment might be the function keys, or it might be the laptop keys.

Laptop keyboards are often more fragile than desktop keyboards and are thus easier to suffer broken keys. Replacements are model-specific. To replace a laptop keyboard, follow this basic procedure:

1. Consult the laptop's service manual to determine whether the laptop keyboard is fastened to the bottom of the laptop base. If it is, remove the necessary screws.
2. Gently remove the plastic molding around the edge of the keyboard using special case-removal tools.
3. Pry up the laptop carefully until the interface cable is visible. It is typically a flat cable.
4. Carefully disconnect the interface cable (see Figure 1.4) from the motherboard.
5. Lift the keyboard out of the system.

6. Connect the new keyboard's interface cable to the motherboard and snap the keyboard into place.
7. Replace the plastic molding around the keyboard.
8. Fasten the keyboard back into place with the necessary screws.
9. Reconnect the laptop to power and check the keyboard.

**FIGURE 1.4** **Preparing to disconnect the keyboard interface cable from a typical laptop motherboard.**

# LAPTOP RAM

*Random access memory (RAM)* is the workspace where data loaded while being processed by the CPU. Laptop computers use various types of double data rate (DDR) synchronous dynamic RAM (SDRAM) dual-inline memory modules (DIMMs) with speeds and capacities similar to the RAM used in desktop computers. However, laptop computers use a smaller RAM module form factor known as small outline DIMM (SODIMM or SO-DIMM). Current laptop models use DDR5 or DDR4 SO-DIMM, but you might encounter laptops that use older DDR3 SO-DIMM modules (see Figure 1.5).

| SODIMM Memory Module Connection Sizes |
| --- |
| DDR5 262 pins, keying notch in center |
| DDR4 288 pins, keying notch in center |
| DDR3 204 connectors (pins), keying notch to left |

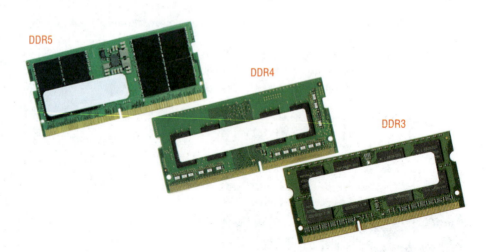

**FIGURE 1.5** From left to right, typical DDR5, DDR4, and DDR3, SO-DIMM modules.

**EXAM TIP**

When adding RAM to a laptop, be sure to determine the supported type, speeds, and sizes for the particular laptop model. Many memory vendors have online system checkers or databases you can use to find compatible modules for a given system.

Some laptops offer easy access to RAM sockets for upgrading. In the example shown in Figure 1.6, a panel on the bottom of the laptop is removed to provide access to RAM. Some laptops have separate panels for access to other user-upgradeable components such as mass storage or wireless cards, while others use a single larger panel to cover multiple components.

**FIGURE 1.6** Inserting an SODIMM module into place (left) and after it has been locked into position (right).

By contrast, other laptops require that the system be dismantled to the motherboard level to provide access to the memory modules. With systems like this, it is necessary to remove the keyboard, mass storage devices, and other components before memory can be upgraded or replaced.

The memory upgrade/installation process follows this basic outline:

1. After consulting the service manual, remove the cover or other components necessary to access the module sockets.
2. If you need to remove one or more existing modules to make room for other modules, push the spring-loaded holders out of the way until the module pops out, and carefully remove it. Place it in an anti-static bag or container.
3. Insert the new module into the connector at about a 20-degree angle and push it down so it is horizontal to the motherboard and locks into place (shown in Figure 1.6).
4. Close up the computer, reattach power, restart it, and check memory for proper operation.

# MIGRATING DATA FROM AN HDD TO AN SSD

To improve laptop performance, a popular upgrade is to replace a *hard disk drive (HDD)*, which uses magnetic platters that spin at high speeds to store data, with a *solid-state drive (SSD)*, which uses high-speed, high-capacity flash memory to store data. An important part of the process is migrating data from the HDD to the SSD. The challenge with a laptop is how to connect the SSD to the computer to allow a direct disk cloning operation.

> **NOTE**
>
> Whenever you are migrating the contents of an existing drive to a new drive, make sure the new drive has at least the same capacity as the amount of space used on the old drive.

If the new SSD uses the SATA interface (the same as the HDD it is replacing), you can insert the new SSD into a drive dock, an external 2.5-inch drive enclosure that supports SSDs, or connect it to a USB 3.x 2.5-inch SSD cable, as shown in Figure 1.7.

If the new SSD uses the M.2 interface and the laptop has both an SATA drive bay and an M.2 interface, you can install the M.2 SSD and then perform the cloning process. Figure 1.8 illustrates a system with this configuration. You can also install an SSD into an external USB enclosure for cloning.

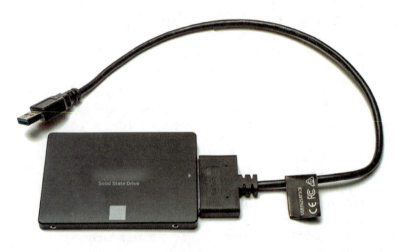

**FIGURE 1.7** Connecting an SSD to a USB 3.x adapter cable before cloning.

M.2 SSD                                SATA 2.5-in. HD

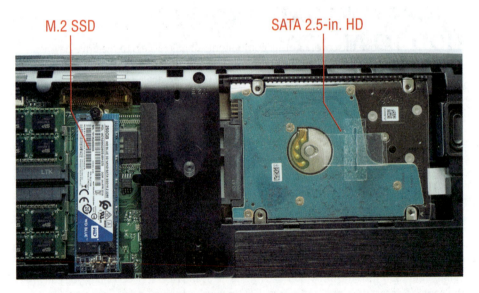

**FIGURE 1.8** A laptop with provisions for both an M.2 SSD (left) and a 2.5-inch SATA HDD (right) makes cloning simple.

The cloning process follows this basic outline:

1. After connecting or installing the new SSD, load and run the cloning software.
2. Select the existing HDD as the source drive.
3. Select the new SSD as the target drive.
4. Select disk clone as the copy option.
5. Make any option settings necessary if the drives have different capacities.
6. Run the cloning process.

   **7a.** If the new drive is replacing the old drive, shut down the system, remove the old drive, and install the new drive.

   **7b.** If the new drive can be used alongside the old drive, change the boot order in BIOS/UEFI Setup so that the new drive is the boot drive.

    **8.** Make sure the new drive boots and functions properly. If you want to reuse the old drive, reformat it after verifying the new drive contains all important files from the old drive.

# REPLACING HDDs AND SSDs

Depending upon the design of a specific laptop, the process of replacing an HDD or an SSD can require anything from removing a hatch on the bottom of the system to a near-complete teardown. The process of disassembling a system to enable access to the drive bays varies from system to system.

## Replacing an HDD

When an HDD is being removed for replacement, follow this basic procedure:

1. Remove the cover or other components to gain access to the drive bay.
2. Determine how the drive is held in place. A typical method is to use a mounting frame or rails screwed to the sides of the drive along with the drive being inserted into the SATA interface. If the drive is screwed into place, remove the screws.
3. Look for a removal tab that can be used to help disconnect the drive from the SATA interface. Gently pull the tab while pushing on the drive in the same direction (refer to Figure 1.9).
4. After the drive is disconnected from the SATA interface (Figure 1.10), gently lift the drive out of the system.

**FIGURE 1.9** **A laptop 2.5-inch SATA drive after being detached from the SATA interface.**

5. If you are replacing the HDD with an SATA SDD or a larger HDD, remove the mounting frame or rails from the sides of the drive and remove the plastic shield from the bottom of the drive (Figure 1.10). Save these parts for reuse.

**FIGURE 1.10** Removing the mounting hardware from a 2.5-inch SATA drive.

6. Attach the mounting frame or rails and plastic sheet to the new drive. Make sure these components are oriented the same way as the old drive.
7. Gently place the drive into the system and push it into the SATA connector. Reattach the drive to the chassis.
8. Close up the system and test it.

## Installing an SSD

**NOTE**

If you are installing an SSD using the M.2 interface, make sure the drive is both physically and electronically compatible with the laptop. Some older laptops use M.2 interfaces that use SATA signaling, while the current faster signaling standard is NVMe.

If the SSD uses the same SATA interface as the HDD, follow the procedure given earlier. However, if the SSD uses the M.2 interface, use this procedure instead:

1. Remove the cover or other components to gain access to the M.2 drive slot.
2. Most M.2 drives use the 2280 form factor, although most M.2 slots are also designed to hold drives and interface cards that are shorter. Remove the retaining screw from one of the mounting holes (Figure 1.11).

**FIGURE  1.11**  **An M.2 drive interface before installing an M.2 SSD.**

3. Push the gold contacts for the drive into the M.2 interface at about a 20-degree angle and lower the drive into place parallel to the motherboard.
4. Fasten the drive with the retaining screw (refer to Figure 1.11).
5. Close up the system and test it.

# WIRELESS CARDS

Almost all laptops have onboard Wi-Fi and Bluetooth interfaces for mobile connectivity, and some also feature cellular radios. Older laptops use the mini-PCIe interface (Figure 1.12), while current laptops use an M.2 interface (Figure 1.13) that is keyed for add-on cards instead of storage devices.

**EXAM TIP**

M.2 is the current standard for wireless cards. However, the M.2 connector used for wireless cards is not the same M.2 connector used for SSDs.

**FIGURE 1.12** A wireless network card using the mini-PCIe interface.

**FIGURE 1.13** A wireless network card using the M.2 interface.

Because wireless cards are built especially for certain systems, you must make sure to purchase a compatible card if the onboard wireless hardware fails or needs to be upgraded.

To gain access to a wireless card, you must shut off power to the laptop, disconnect its battery, and remove the back panel and other components.

Before removing a wireless card, make sure the antenna wires are disconnected from the existing card. Note which connection is used for a particular wire. After installing the new card, reconnect the antenna wires in the proper positions.

# PHYSICAL PRIVACY WITH BIOMETRICS

What are biometrics? *Biometrics* refers to using physical attributes such as fingerprints or face recognition to verify a user's identity.

Many laptops use some form of biometrics for additional security when logging in. These are the two most common forms of biometrics:

► Fingerprint reader
► Infrared camera for facial recognition

Windows Hello supports both of these biometrics methods. Windows Hello is configured through the Settings dialog. Some MacBook Air and Pro models support fingerprint biometrics.

To add either type of biometric support to a Windows laptop, you can plug in the appropriate device into the laptop's USB port and configure it with Windows Hello.

# PHYSICAL PRIVACY WITH NEAR-FIELD SCANNERS

What is a near-field scanner? It's a device that enables near-field communications (NFC), which enables touchless payment systems, file transfers, gaming, getting information from posters, and location-based operations.

Near-field scanners are incorporated into some recent laptop models. Because near-field scanners in mobile devices have the potential to reveal users' location and share information they might not want to share, it's important to know how to configure them.

Near-field scanners are typically defined as network devices, so the network dialog in Windows or other operating systems can be used to enable or disable them.

## CERTMIKE EXAM ESSENTIALS

► Laptop components such as RAM, mechanical and solid-state storage, and wireless adapters work similarly to those used in desktop computers, but their form factors are smaller, and the installation process can be much more difficult than with desktop computers.

► Because many different standards exist for these parts, be sure to verify installation methods and parts compatibility before you dive in.

► Laptops vary widely in their built-in components and provisions for upgrades, so researching the particular models a client is considering is key to assuring short-term and long-term satisfaction with a given laptop.

## Practice Question 1

To speed up a laptop, you have a request from a client for the following upgrades: upgrade RAM to 8GB and replacing the existing 500GB hard disk with a 1TB SSD.

Which of the following should you do FIRST before you can quote a price and timeframe for this job?

A. Price comparison for SATA and NVMe 1TB SSD.
B. Identify the location of the drive bay.
C. Review the contents of the service manual.
D. Determine amount and size of memory modules already installed.

## Practice Question 2

During the laptop RAM upgrade process (goal: 8GB per system), you determine that some of the computers have 2x2GB SODIMM RAM modules for a total of 4GB onboard, while others have 1x4GB SODIMM RAM modules for a total of 4GB onboard. All systems have two SODIMM sockets. All of the 4GB memory and 2GB memory have the same form factor (DDR3 SODIMM) and timing. There are 10 systems with 1x4GB modules, and 20 systems with 2x2GB modules. Which of the following purchases will provide 8GB of identical RAM per system without considering spares?

A. Buy 30 1x4GB modules.
B. Buy 50 1x4GB modules.
C. Buy 60 1x4GB modules.
D. Buy 10 1x4GB modules.

## Practice Question 1 Explanation

This question is asking you to identify the FIRST step of the preparation process. You should be prepared to evaluate all of the possible answer choices and find the one that is better than all of the others. Let's evaluate these choices one at a time.

1. The first suggested answer, doing a price comparison for SATA and NVMe 1TB SSD drives, may need to be determined at some point. However, until you know what the system's internal configuration is, you can't perform this step. Thus, it can't be the first step.

2. The next suggested answer, the location of the drive bay, also can't be performed until you know what the system's configuration is. Thus, it can't be the first step either.

3. The third suggested answer, reviewing the contents of the service manual, is the best answer. It should come first because it provides most of the information needed to properly cost out parts and labor for this job. For example, knowing the amount of effort needed to expose the memory slots and the drive bay helps determine labor charges. The type(s) of SSD drives the system supports (M.2 or 2.5-inch, NVMe or SATA) help provide a basis for cost-benefit storage calculations. Finally, the sizes and speeds of supported memory modules help determine whether the onboard memory can be retained or must be replaced.

4. The last suggested answer, determining the amount and size of already-installed memory modules, is important in helping to determine whether existing RAM can be reused or replaced. However, it provides no assistance in dealing with questions about mass storage.

**Correct Answer: C. Review the contents of the service manual.**

## Practice Question 2 Explanation

This question is asking you to identify the CORRECT answer by determining which systems have reusable RAM and which ones do not. You should be prepared to evaluate all of the possible answer choices and find the one that reflects a proper understanding of the numbers of modules needed. Let's evaluate these choices one at a time.

1. The first suggested answer, buy 30 1x4GB modules, provides a single module for all 30 computers. However, the systems with 2x2GB memory modules need to have both modules replaced; thus, there are not enough modules for all systems.

2. The next suggested answer is to buy 50 1x4GB modules. They will be distributed thusly: 10 will be installed in the systems that currently have 1x4GB modules, bringing them from 4GB installed to 8GB installed. All of the 2x2GB RAM modules will be removed from the 20 systems using this type of RAM. Each system will have 2x4GB of RAM installed in its place, bringing them from 4GB installed to 8GB installed. Forty modules are used for this portion of the upgrade. Thus, all 50 modules will be used, making this the correct answer.

3. The third suggested answer, buy 60 1x4GB modules, leaves 10 modules that cannot be installed in systems, because 50 is enough for the systems in question.

4. The last suggested answer, buy 10 1x4GB modules, provides only enough memory for the 10 systems with 1x4GB memory onboard. There is no memory for the systems with 2x2GB configurations.

**Correct Answer: B. Buy 50 1x4GB modules.**

# CHAPTER 2

# Mobile Device Displays

*Core 1 Objective 1.2: Compare and contrast the display components of mobile devices.*

**Laptops** and mobile devices use various types of flat-panel displays. While they look similar from a distance, their internal designs and built-in features vary widely.

In this chapter, you will learn everything you need to know about A+ Core 1 Objective 1.2, including the following topics:

► **Mobile Device Display Types**
► **Organic Light-Emitting Diode**
► **Mobile Display Components**

## MOBILE DEVICE DISPLAY TYPES

Laptops and mobile devices use two major types of displays.

► Liquid-crystal
► Organic LED (OLED)

The following sections discuss the variations available, how they differ, and what they're best used for.

## Liquid-Crystal Displays

A *liquid-crystal display (LCD)* creates shapes, colors, and text onscreen using liquid crystals.

Inside an LCD display, a backlight shines white light through a vertical polarizer and a layer of transparent transistors. These work together to control the alignment of the liquid crystals. The liquid crystals now are formed into an image. Next, the RGB color filter layer is comprised of thousands of red, green, and blue subpixels in a grid of thousands of pixels. It adds color to the image. The image is completed after passing through a horizontal polarizer to the cover glass, where the image appears (Figure 2.1).

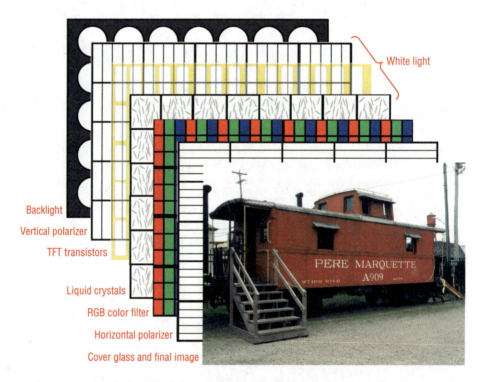

**FIGURE 2.1**  A simplified diagram of the layers in a typical LCD display.

Originally, LCDs used a mercury-based fluorescent backlight as a light source. However, this has been replaced in the last decade or so by a less-polluting light-emitting diode (LED) backlight as in Figure 2.1. For this reason, many LCD displays with LED backlights are inaccurately described as LED displays.

## Differences in LCD Display Technologies

LCD display technologies differ in several ways from each other. These include the vertical refresh rate (how quickly the screen is redrawn), the contrast ratio (the ratio of screen brightness at maximum black and bright white), the viewing angle (the angle at which the display still is readable and has acceptable contrast and color), and color quality (how many colors a display can reproduce).

The standard vertical refresh rate for most LCD displays is 60Hz (60 times a second). Some 4K displays have a 30Hz refresh rate. The higher the refresh rate, the more suitable the display is for gaming.

The wider the viewing angle, the less difference between viewing an image straight-on and from an angle. Displays with narrow viewing angles have color shift, loss of contrast, and image clarity the further away from straight-on viewing.

Color quality is also known as color gamut. Ideal is 100 percent of the total color range. The smallest color gamut is sRGB, which is suitable for gaming. Users who want to do photo or video editing will want displays that handle larger color gamuts such as Adobe RGB.

## Twisted Nematic

*Twisted nematic (TN)* is an older LCD technology. The name refers to how liquid crystals change alignment when voltage is applied. Its main advantage over newer technologies is the very high refresh rates available on some models: up to 240Hz. TN displays are less expensive than other display types, but the combination of high refresh rates and lower cost make them a good choice for gamers. TN displays have narrow viewing angles and low contrast (typically under 1000:1).

## In-Plane Switching

The most popular for general use, graphics, and presentation is called *in-plane switching (IPS)*. IPS refers to the alignment of liquid crystals when charged: they are organized in-plane (horizontally) with the layers above and below them. IPS provides superior color reproduction (wider color gamuts) and wider viewing angles than previous standards such as TN. IPS and TN have comparable contrast ratios (about 1000:1) in recent models. IPS displays support vertical refresh rates up to 144Hz, which is more than twice as fast the 60Hz refresh rates used by basic LCD displays.

## Vertical Alignment

*Vertical alignment (VA)* refers to how liquid crystals are vertically aligned when charged. VA offers higher contrast than IPS (up to 2000:1), comparable viewing angle to IPS, with color quality between IPS (best) and TN (worst). It is typically slower than IPS or TN.

# ORGANIC LIGHT-EMITTING DIODE

*Organic light-emitting diode (OLED)* displays use pixels that provide their own light, enabling individually controlled pixels that can easily been dimmed, as opposed to using a separate backlight layer as in other display technologies. OLED displays provide the highest color and image quality of all displays. However, their refresh rates are typically just 60–90Hz, which is much slower than the 120–240Hz refresh rates available on gaming-oriented displays.

The internal design of OLED is more complex than LCD displays, making them more expensive on a size-for-size basis as this is written (mid-2022). Most laptops using OLED displays sell for over $900. Most high-end smartphones use OLED displays.

> **EXAM TIP**
>
> Expect to see questions not only about the different types of displays but also which display type is best suited to a particular task.

# MOBILE DISPLAY COMPONENTS

Although laptops can use many types of display technologies, typical laptop displays of any type have most of the following components:

- ► Wi-Fi antennas
- ► Webcams
- ► Microphone
- ► Touch screen/digitizer (if the laptop has a touch screen)
- ► Inverter (if the laptop has a fluorescent backlight)

Depending upon the laptop, these components may be removable from the display panel subassembly (see Figure 2.2) or might be built into a subassembly that must be swapped if any components fail.

To gain access to these components:

1. Remove the display panel subassembly from the base unit (which contains the keyboard, I/O, and storage devices).
2. Remove the front bezel, the plastic frame covering up the antennas, webcam, microphone, and edges of the display from the display panel. This might require carefully prying the bezel from the back of the panel.

If you are working with a laptop that does not have easily removable display components, you're facing a more expensive situation. If one component fails, replacing it may require removing the original display panel subassembly and attaching a replacement display panel subassembly to the base unit.

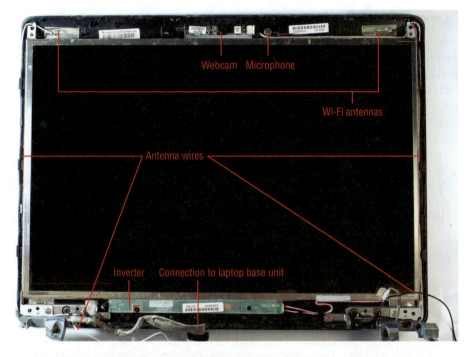

**FIGURE 2.2** An LCD panel with individually serviceable components.

> **NOTE**
>
> A frequent question that Windows laptop owners ask is, "Can a nontouch laptop be converted to a touch screen?" There is no easy answer. It depends upon whether a nontouch model and a touch-screen model use the same motherboard and the availability of touch-enabled replacement screens.

Now, let's take a closer look at the components you will find in a laptop display subassembly.

## Wi-Fi Antenna Connector/Placement

As you saw in Chapter 1, the Wi-Fi antenna wires are connected to the wireless card in a typical laptop. The wires are connected to the antennas on either side of the display panel.

If the display panel can be removed from the display subassembly, the wires are routed separately from the subassembly into the laptop base unit (refer to Figure 2.1). However, if the display panel is not designed for component-level replacement, the antenna wires are part of the display subassembly that connects to the laptop base unit.

## Camera/Webcam

Almost all laptops, tablets, and smartphones include built-in front-facing and rear-facing cameras that support video and still images. The rear-facing camera is used for video chatting and selfies.

On laptops that use a display panel with removable components, the webcam can be replaced if it fails. Its cable runs alongside one of the Wi-Fi antenna wires (refer to Figure 2.2). If the display panel is not designed for component disassembly, you'll need to replace the entire panel if a webcam or other component fails.

> **NOTE**
> If you need to replace the camera/webcam, microphone, or inverter, you might not need to remove the display panel from the base unit. On some laptops, all that is necessary is to remove the front bezel from the display panel to gain access to these components.

## Microphone

Microphones for recording audio or chatting are usually built into the top or bottom of the display panel. A typical microphone is shown next to the webcam in Figure 2.3. Depending upon the laptop, the webcam and microphone might be a single subassembly.

**FIGURE 2.3** This webcam can be easily replaced if it fails.

## Touch Screen/Digitizer

Touch screens are universal on smartphones and tablets. Many laptops and all convertible computers also feature built-in touch screens. In addition to converting touches on the display into commands, touch screens act as digitizers that can convert strokes into drawings and signatures.

> **NOTE**
>
> A convertible computer is also known as a 2-in-1 computer. These computers can be switched from standard laptop mode into tablet mode by folding down the keyboard under the screen or by detaching the keyboard. Most models with foldable keyboards can also be folded into a tent shape.

There are two major types of touch screens: capacitive and resistant. Capacitive touch screens use a combination of layers of glass and plastic with a metal conductive material. This conductive material responds to the user's touch. This is the major type used in laptops, convertibles, tablets, and smartphones. These screens can be used with bare fingers, gloves with special tips, and styluses made for touch screens. Capacitive touch screens must be replaced if damaged.

Resistive touch screens, on the other hand, have an air gap between the plastic protective layer and the metallic layer; pressing firmly makes the connection. Resistive touch screens are used in ATMs and other uses that require durability and low cost.

For more information, see www.hp.com/us-en/shop/tech-takes/how-do-touch-screens-work How Do Touch Screens Work on Laptops and Tablets? (hp.com).

## Inverter

LCD displays that use fluorescent backlights have a component called an *inverter*. The inverter provides power to the backlight, and if it fails, the LCD display becomes very dim.

The inverter is usually connected to the bottom of the display panel and frequently fails. To determine whether an inverter has failed, turn on the laptop, turn on a flashlight, and point it at the screen. If shining a light on the screen means you can now see the desktop, the inverter has failed.

To replace the inverter, check the service manual, determine the location of the inverter, and remove the bezel from the display panel. The inverter uses a small plastic connector that is easily detached from the laptop (Figure 2.4).

Inverters are used only in LCD panels that use fluorescent backlights; they are not used by LCD panels that use LED backlights or with OLED panels. Although inverters are relatively inexpensive to buy or replace, devices that use inverters are obsolete and might not be worth repairing.

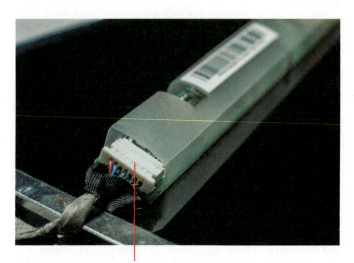

Unplug this cable and remove any screws holding
the inverter in place to remove the inverter

**FIGURE 2.4**  **Preparing to remove a failed inverter.**

## CERTMIKE EXAM ESSENTIALS

▶ Laptops and other mobile devices vary widely in the types of displays in use, and because it's seldom possible to switch to a different type of display after purchase, it's important to know the advantages, disadvantages, and pricing of each major type of display.

▶ To determine the specific details about the display used by a specific model of laptop or mobile device, be prepared to dig into the technical information provided by the vendor. Marketing documents typically don't have this level of detail.

▶ With the proliferation of thin and light laptops, the ability to service individual display components such as touch screens, webcams, microphones, and Wi-Fi antennas are less common today. In many cases, a display panel subassembly swap is necessary if any component discussed in this chapter fails. If your client needs component-level serviceability, it's essential to review the laptop's service manual before purchase.

## Practice Question 1

A client has requested your expert advice on a gaming laptop with a 15-inch display that will cost about $1,400. Which of the following screen technologies would be the BEST choice for this user?

A. OLED
B. VA
C. TN
D. IPS

## Practice Question 2

A client is generally satisfied with the thin and light laptops in use by her sales force, except that they need touch screens for more interactive presentations.

Which of the following is the BEST recommendation for this client?

A. Replace the display panels with touch-screen versions.
B. Purchase styluses for use with the existing laptops.
C. Recommend the client never buy laptops from that manufacturer again.
D. Work on a schedule for replacing laptops with touch-screen versions.

## Practice Question 1 Explanation

This question is asking you to identify the screen technology that would BEST meet the described need. This is a common format for CompTIA A+ exam questions, and you should be prepared to evaluate all of the possible answer choices and find the one that is better than all of the others. Let's evaluate these choices one at a time.

First, you should recognize that there are two key requirements in this question. The computer will be used for gaming, and it should be priced at a moderate expense level.

You can eliminate some answer choices because of their very low refresh rates.

1. Organic LED (OLED) provides the highest color and image quality of all display types. However, it is much more expensive than LCD/LED displays and is slower than other display types with a refresh rate of 60–90 Hz. This refresh rate is too slow for gaming use.

2. Vertical alignment (VA) is the slowest of the current LCD display technologies (60Hz), so it is not a good solution here because it is also too slow for gaming use. That leaves us with two possibilities: IPS and TN.

3. In-plane switching (IPS) is faster than OLED or VA display technologies (up to 144Hz) and also provides better color than VA displays. It would be a satisfactory choice for a user who wants a system for both office work and gaming, but it is not the best choice because you can find an even better option.

4. Twisted nematic (TN) is the fastest LCD display technology at up to 240Hz and is a low-cost display type, making it the best choice for a gaming laptop.

**Correct Answer: C. TN**

## Practice Question 2 Explanation

This type of scenario-based question is common on the CompTIA A+ exams, and to prepare yourself for this type of question, make sure you understand both what is theoretically possible as well as the BEST practical answer. Let's evaluate these choices one at a time to find the best recommendation to make.

1. At one time, the option of replacing display panels with touch-screen versions was feasible on some models. However, thin and light laptops don't use interchangeable display panels; the entire display assembly must be swapped. Because of the amount of time and effort needed to determine whether such a switch is possible for a given model and the possibility of system damage, this is risky and not recommended.

2. Using a stylus as an input device works only on touch-enabled displays. Because these displays are not touch-enabled, this option is useless. A stylus would not work.

3. Virtually all laptop vendors make both touch and nontouch laptop models. Firing the manufacturer doesn't solve the problem, so there is no need to permanently abandon this vendor. You just need to select hardware from your vendor of choice that meets your needs.

4. That leaves us with the option of replacing the laptops. Unless this is an urgent need, they don't all need to be replaced at once. The last option, working on a schedule to replace laptops with touch-screen versions, is the best one. Nontouch models could be repurposed for use by nonsales personnel, and the replacement touch-screen models can be configured to meet current and forthcoming requirements.

**Correct Answer: D. Work on a schedule for replacing laptops with touch-screen versions.**

# CHAPTER 3

# Mobile Device Ports and Accessories

## Core 1 Objective 1.3: Given a scenario, set up and configure accessories and ports of mobile devices.

**Laptops** and mobile devices feature a variety of expansion options, including various types of USB ports, wireless connections, and accessories.

In this chapter, you learn how to use the following to expand your laptop:

▶ Connection methods
▶ Accessories
▶ Docking station
▶ Port replicator
▶ Trackpad/drawing pad

## CONNECTION METHODS

Although laptops don't include expansion slots for add-on cards as desktop computers do, the versatility and performance of USB ports and wireless connections found in almost all laptops enable them to use a wide variety of devices.

## Universal Serial Bus

Universal Serial Bus (USB) is a series of high-speed serial connections that enable a laptop computer to connect to a wide variety of peripherals. Most laptops use USB 2.0 (480Mbps) or USB 3.0 (5Gbps) ports.

> **NOTE**
>
> Although the latest USB standard is USB 4, which runs at either 20Gbps or 40Gbps, it's going to be a while before it's widely available. On current systems, the top of the USB line is USB 3.2. It is divided into two speeds: USB 3.2 Gen 1 is the same 5Gbps standard as USB 3.0 (also known as USB 3.1 Gen 1). USB 3.2 Gen 2 runs at 10Gbps (like USB 3.1 Gen 2) and is used primarily on desktop computers. This text uses USB 3.x for all 5Gbps ports.

### USB Type-A

Most laptops use Type-A ports, which are designed to provide connections to individual peripherals such as printers, storage devices, or hubs. However, an increasing number of laptops also use Type-C ports, which are also used for connections to peripherals and hubs. Figure 3.1 illustrates both Type-A and Type-C ports on a typical late-model laptop.

HDMI A/V port
(for comparison)

USB Type-C port with
DisplayPort support

USB 3.1 Gen 1 (USB 3.0)
Type-A 5Gbps port

**FIGURE 3.1**   USB 3.1 Gen 1 Type-A and USB Type-C ports.

USB ports on laptops are typically marked with the USB symbol (a stylized fork). The stylized SS and 5 added in Figure 3.1 indicate the port is USB 3.1/3.2 Gen 1 (5Gbps). Some vendors use blue connectors for USB 3.x ports. However, some vendors simply use the original USB symbol, as in Figure 3.2 for any speed of USB port. A check of the system specifications is needed to determine the fastest USB versions supported.

USB ports are backward-compatible, so USB 3.x ports also support USB 2 and USB 1.1 devices.

**FIGURE 3.2**  **This 2015 MacBook Air's USB ports support USB 3.0 (5Gbps) but are marked with the original USB logo.**

USB Type-A ports are keyed; cables can be plugged in one way only.

For a complete list of USB versions, markings, and performance, see Chapter 14, " Cables and Connectors."

## USB Type-C

USB Type-C (also known as USB-C) is a compact form-factor version of USB. USB Type-C Power Delivery (PD) ports can also be used for charging laptops and peripherals that support USB Type-C. Unlike USB Type-A and USB Type-B ports and cables, USB Type-C is not keyed; the cables can be plugged in with either side up. USB Type-C supports connections to computers and to peripherals.

Although USB Type-C ports are often configured as USB 3.1/3.2 Gen 1 or USB 3.1/3.2 Gen 2 ports, not all devices connected to USB Type-C ports run at these speeds. For example, USB Type-C ports on smartphones and tablets run at USB 2.0 speeds (480Mbps). Not surprisingly, USB cables made for mobile device connection are USB 2.0 cables. See the "Lightning" section for an example of a USB Type-A to USB Type-C cable for smartphones and tablets.

> **NOTE**
>
> When specifying USB-C cables for a mobile device, make sure you know the performance of the USB-C ports you are connecting to and choose appropriate cables.

## MicroUSB and MiniUSB

MicroUSB ports are reduced-size versions of Type-B ports, which are used by peripherals such as flash card readers, older Android smartphones, external hard drives, and other peripherals. MiniUSB ports are larger than MicroUSB ports and are used by small USB 2.0 devices such as card readers, hubs, and external hard drives.

Figure 3.3 compares MicroUSB ports for USB 2.0 and USB 3.x devices with a MiniUSB port.

MiniUSB
(USB 2.0)    MicroUSB
(USB 2.0)    MicroUSB
(USB 3.x)

**FIGURE 3.3** MiniUSB and MicroUSB ports for USB 2.0 connections compared to a MicroUSB for USB 3.x.

To connect devices that use a MicroUSB or MiniUSB port to a laptop (or desktop) PC, a cable with a USB Type-A port at one end and the appropriate MicroUSB or MiniUSB port is used. Figure 3.4 illustrates these cables.

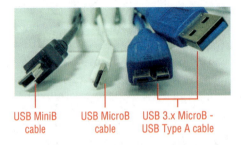

USB MiniB
cable    USB MicroB
cable    USB 3.x MicroB -
USB Type A cable

**FIGURE 3.4** MiniUSB and MicroUSB cables for USB 2.0 connections compared to a MicroUSB for USB 3.x cable.

The USB Type-A connection for the USB 3.x cable is shown in Figure 3.4; the MiniUSB and MicroUSB for USB 2.0 also have Type-A connectors not visible in this image.

> **NOTE**
> USB On-The-Go is another name for the microUSB port used on mobile devices such as older Android phones as well as rechargeable headsets. You might see references to USB On-The-Go on the exam and elsewhere.

## Lightning

Most Apple iOS devices use the proprietary Lightning port for charging and file synchronization. Like USB Type-C, Lightning ports and cables are not keyed, so they can be plugged in either way.

To connect Lightning devices to a laptop (or desktop) PC, a USB Type-A to Lightning cable is used. Figure 3.5 compares a typical USB Type-A to Lightning cable with a USB Type-A to USB Type-C cable used by some iOS devices as well as current Android mobile devices.

USB Type-A    USB Type-A    Lightning
USB Type-C

**FIGURE 3.5** USB Type-A to USB-C and USB Type-A to Lightning cables for mobile devices.

## Serial Interfaces

The DB9 connector (discussed in Chapter 14) is used by the venerable RS-232 serial port. It has long been absent from laptops, but if you need to connect to any serial device, use the appropriate USB to serial interface.

## Near-Field Communications

Near-field communication (NFC) is sometimes referred to as Touch to Connect. Originally introduced in smartphones for easy short-range data transfer and touchless payment systems, some laptops also include NFC for use in data transfer between devices or printing to NFC-enabled printers.

The Windows Device Manager lists NFC support in the Proximity devices category. Enable NFC if you want to connect to other devices using NFC. NFC is enabled or disabled with the Network menu.

See the documentation for your laptop for details on how to send or receive files using NFC.

## Bluetooth

Most laptops include Bluetooth support. Bluetooth can be used for file transfers between devices as well as interfacing with keyboards, mice, and printers. On Windows laptops, Bluetooth ports are enabled and configured through the Devices ➤ Bluetooth & Other Devices menu (Figure 3.6). On macOS laptops, use the Bluetooth status menu in the menu bar. If not visible, open the Apple menu ➤ System Preferences, and enable the Show Bluetooth option.

**F I G U R E  3 . 6**  The Bluetooth menu on a typical Windows laptop.

On laptops that don't include Bluetooth support, a Bluetooth adapter can be plugged into an unused USB port.

## Hotspot

Laptops can connect to a mobile hotspot on a smartphone or tablet by selecting the wireless network and entering the password (if required).

In Windows, you can share your laptop's Internet connection through Settings ➤ Network & Internet ➤ Mobile hotspot. Select from Wi-Fi (default) or Bluetooth, change the default network name and password, and enable the connection. Note that CompTIA refers to wireless networks as WiFi, but vendors refer to it as Wi-Fi. Figure 3.7 illustrates the Windows 10 dialog (Windows 11 is similar). Systems running macOS can share a wired Internet connection through their Wi-Fi radio.

# ACCESSORIES

Some of the most common accessories for laptops include touch pens, headsets, speakers, and webcams. The following sections discuss these.

## Touch Pens

Touch pens are designed to be used with touchscreen systems for drawing and sketching, but unlike passive styluses or finger pressure, touch pens support variable pen pressure, erasing, and other options. They are normally connected wirelessly via Bluetooth. Figure 3.8 illustrates a portion of the Pen and Windows Ink dialogs used to configure a touch pen.

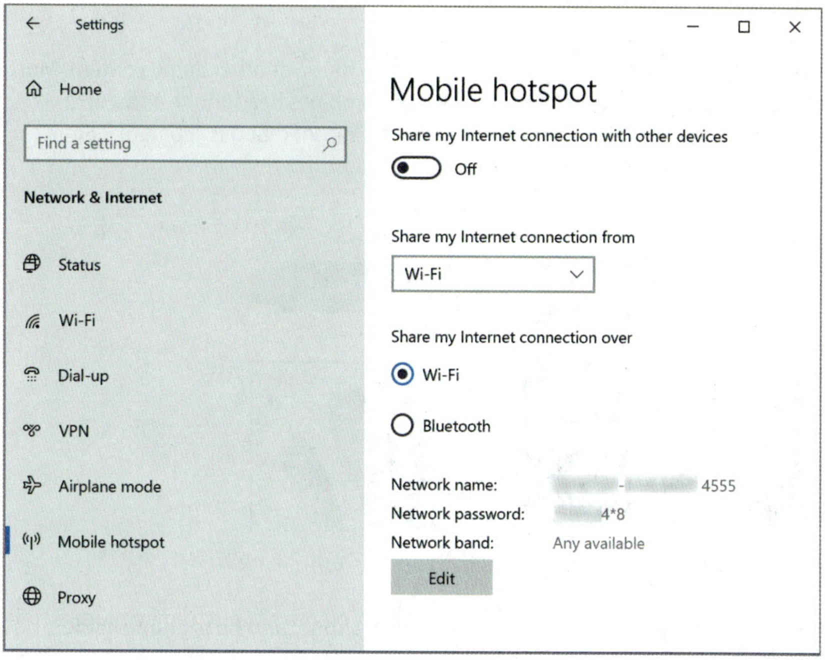

**FIGURE 3.7** Preparing to share Wi-Fi via the Windows Mobile Hotspot dialog.

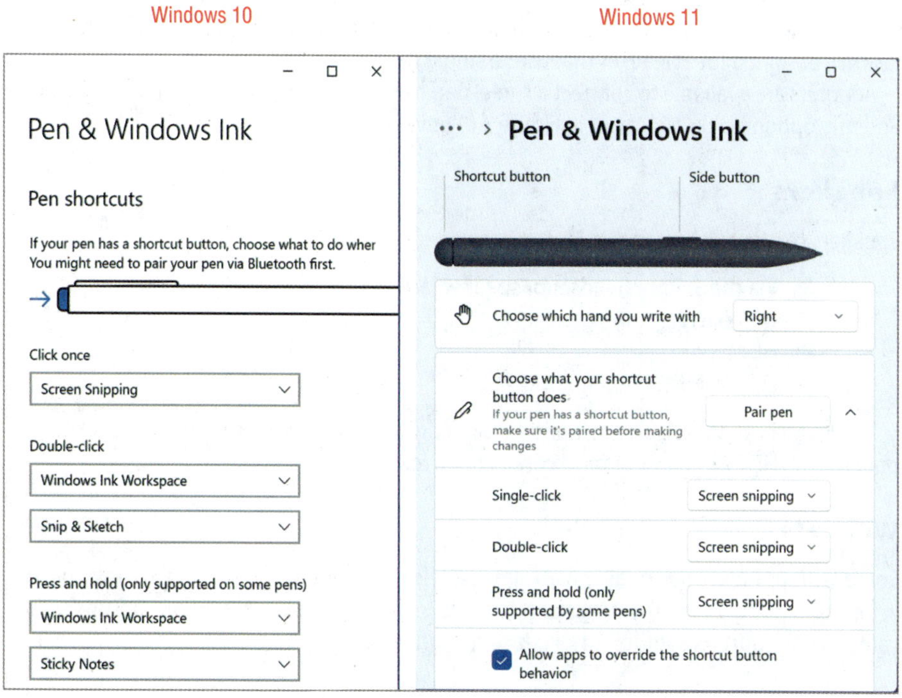

**FIGURE 3.8** Configuring shortcuts for a touch pen in Windows 10 and Windows 11.

## Headsets

Headsets are used to provide privacy when listening to music or other audio content. Most recent laptops use a single 3.5mm headset jack that combines headphone and microphone functions (Figure 3.9). However, if you prefer a headset that has separate 3.5mm speaker and headphone jacks, you need to use an adapter.

**FIGURE 3.9** Comparing laptop headset, microphone, and headphone cables, jacks, and adapter.

If your laptop has two separate 3.5mm speaker and microphone jacks, use a headset that has separate speaker and microphone plugs. However, if your laptop has a single headset jack, it's designed for a headset that uses a single plug.

Adapters are available to connect a three-ring headset to a laptop with separate speaker and microphone jacks (see inset in Figure 3.9) or vice versa.

## Speakers

Speakers can be connected to a laptop in a variety of ways.

- ▶ Via the 3.5mm headset or speaker jacks
- ▶ USB ports
- ▶ HDMI port
- ▶ DisplayPort

The HDMI port and DisplayPort options are normally used if you want to use speakers built into an HDTV or monitor or to connect to a receiver.

## Webcam

Some laptops have poor-quality webcams with low resolution and fixed focus, resulting in visually painful Zoom meetings or Microsoft Team conference calls. Some laptops' webcams lack support for Windows Hello face recognition.

Webcams with higher resolution, autofocus, and Windows Hello support can be connected via any USB 2.0 or faster port. If you want to use a webcam with macOS, be sure to check software compatibility.

# DOCKING STATIONS

A docking station enables a laptop to have access to additional ports and port types that are not built into the laptop. Docking stations were originally proprietary devices that plugged into the side, rear, or bottom of a specified model laptop.

So-called universal docking stations have largely replaced proprietary docking stations. These connect to USB 3.x ports (PC) or Thunderbolt ports (Macs) and split the high-bandwidth signal among additional ports. Typical ports available include the following:

- ▶ USB 3.x Type-A or Type-C ports
- ▶ Ethernet network port
- ▶ Thunderbolt/DisplayPort ports (Mac)
- ▶ HDMI ports (mac/PC)
- ▶ 3.5mm audio ports

Figure 3.10 illustrates three typical docking stations. The top station connects to a USB Type-C 5Gbps or faster port; the middle station is a proprietary model that connects to a Surface Pro magnetic I/O and charging port, and the bottom one connects to a Thunderbolt 2 port (similar models are made for Thunderbolt 3 and 4 ports).

**FIGURE 3.10** A variety of docking stations made for PCs (top/middle) and Macs (bottom).

# PORT REPLICATOR

Originally, port replicators were designed to provide laptops with a single connection to a monitor, USB ports, and a power supply. The idea was to prevent premature wear on individual connectors with a single proprietary connection. In practice, port replicators were smaller versions of docking stations and have been replaced by universal docking stations that connect to USB 3.x or Lightning ports.

# TRACKPAD/DRAWING PAD

Although almost all laptops have touchpads that act as mouse alternatives, trackpads that support more gestures than built-in touchpads are popular replacements. Drawing pads such as those made by Wacom and other vendors can be used as trackpads as well as for graphic arts work with photo illustration and drawing programs (Figure 3.11).

**FIGURE 3.11**   **A Wacom drawing pad suitable for use with both laptops and desktops.**

Trackpads and drawing pads are typically connected via Bluetooth, although some use a proprietary wireless USB dongle or connect to USB with a cable.

## CERTMIKE EXAM ESSENTIALS

▶ The Universal Serial Bus (USB) port is the most flexible port used on laptops. It is capable of connecting to almost any type of peripheral device. USB 3.2 Gen 1 (5Gbps) and Gen 2 (10Gbps) are the fastest and most versatile USB ports to look for. USB ports can be used to add Bluetooth, legacy serial ports, and upgraded webcams to systems.

▶ Typical laptops offer at least two wireless data-sharing options: Bluetooth and support for connections to Wi-Fi hotspots. Windows laptops can also be used to create a hotspot.

▶ Docking stations not only add additional USB ports but also provide wired Ethernet, HDMI or DisplayPort, and other types of ports to laptops via USB 3.x, Lightning, or proprietary connections.

## Practice Question 1

Your client is asking for your help in deciding between two similar laptop computers. Laptop 1 has a Type-C port according to the marketing literature, while Laptop 2 has a USB 3.1 Gen 2 Type-C port according to its marketing literature. The client needs 10Gbps speed to support an additional display and high-speed USB SSDs connected to a Type-C docking station.

Which laptop should you recommend, based on the marketing literature?

A.  You don't know how fast either laptop's USB Type-C port is, so either one will do.
B.  Laptop 1's Type-C port is faster than Laptop 2's, so you should recommend Laptop 1.
C.  Laptop 2's USB Type-C port runs at 10Gbps, but you don't know how fast Laptop 1's USB Type-C port is. Recommending Laptop 2 is the safe choice.
D.  Both laptops have the same-speed port but aren't labeled the same. Time to flip a coin?

## Practice Question 2

Your client has asked you to buy charging/sync cables for their fleet of current Android and iOS smartphones. These cables will be used with laptops that have only USB-C ports. Identify these connectors and specify which ones to look for when you are shopping.

In the following table, identify the USB-C and Lightning connectors as well as the other connectors shown. The Android charging cables will have USB-C connectors at both ends and the iOS charging cables will have a USB-C connector at one end and Lightning at the other.

The connector types are shown in the first column. Identify each connector type in the second column.

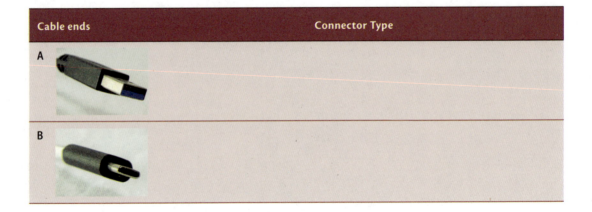

| Cable ends | Connector Type |
|---|---|
| A | |
| B | |

| Cable ends | Connector Type |
|---|---|
| C | |
| D | |

## Practice Question 1 Explanation

This question is designed to test your knowledge of the different USB standards currently on the market and how they are identified.

Let's evaluate these choices one at a time.

1. First, you are told that there isn't enough information to determine port speed for either laptop. This is true for Laptop 1, but Laptop 2's USB port has clear indications of its speed in the specific version number. There's enough information about Laptop 2, but not about Laptop 1.

2. Next, you are told that Laptop 1's Type-C port is faster than Laptop 2's. This would not be possible with the current models of USB Type-C ports. At best, both laptops might have the same port speed. A lack of information is not the way to make a recommendation!

3. The specific identification of Laptop 2's USB port as supporting USB 3.1 Gen 2 indicates it runs at 10Gbps. Because you have no details about Laptop 1's USB version, you don't know how fast it runs. Laptop 2 is the best choice for your recommendation.

4. The last option, both with the same-speed port but not labeled the same, is very unlikely. Laptops with 10Gbps USB-C performance are rare, so the vendor would make a point to mention it in their documentation and might even label the port accordingly. Put away the coin: the lack of specifics makes it likely that Laptop 1's USB Type-C port runs at 5Gbps. It's probably identified as USB 3.1 or 3.2 Gen-1.

**Correct Answer: C. Laptop 2's USB Type-C port runs at 10Gbps, but you don't know how fast Laptop 1's USB Type-C port is. Recommending Laptop 2 is the safe choice.**

## Practice Question 2 Explanation

This question is designed to test your knowledge of USB charging cable appearance and usage.

| Cable Ends | | Connector Type | Use |
| --- | --- | --- | --- |
| A | | USB MicroB for USB 2.0 | Older Android phones |
| B | | USB Type C | Current Android phones and also some laptops |

| Cable Ends | | Connector Type | Use |
| --- | --- | --- | --- |
| C | | USB Type A | Most desktops and laptops use this connector |
| D | | Lightning | Used by iOS smartphones and older iPad tablets |

Now, let's evaluate these cable connections.

1. A is USB Type-A. USB Type-A is used as the computer end for a lot of iOS and Android cables. However, the laptops you are purchasing cables for have only USB Type-C connectors, so this one won't work for either end of the connection.

2. B is USB Type-C. USB Type C-is the correct connection for the computer end. It is also the correct connection for charging the Android smartphones.

3. C is USB MicroB for USB 2.0. This was used for charging older Android smartphones. However, it can be used with current models with an adapter. This connector was never used at the computer end.

4. D is Apple's Lightning connector. It is never used at the computer end but has been used to charge Apple iPhones for years.

**Correct Answer: So, the correct connector pairing for the Android smartphones is B–B (Type-C connector at both ends). The correct connector pairing for the Apple iPhone is B–D (Type-C to Lightning).**

# Mobile Device Network Connectivity and Application Support

*Core 1 Objective 1.4 Given a scenario, configure basic mobile-device network connectivity and application support.*

**Part** of what makes mobile devices so popular is their ability to stay connected when away from the office and use apps to get work done on the go. This chapter provides you with the information you need to master Core 1 Objective 1.4, including the following topics:

▶ Wireless/cellular data network (enable/disable)
▶ Bluetooth
▶ Location services

▶ Mobile device management (MDM)/mobile application management (MAM)
▶ Mobile device synchronization

# WIRELESS/CELLULAR DATA NETWORK (ENABLE/DISABLE)

Smartphones rely on cellular data and Wi-Fi wireless connections to stay in touch anywhere. As cellular networks become faster and smarter, the functionality of those devices improves.

By default smartphones are configured to connect to cellular service. However, if you travel, you're probably familiar with Airplane mode. Airplane mode (Figure 4.1 and Figure 4.2) disables cellular but allows Wi-Fi and Bluetooth connections to continue, as they do not break airplane rules. Depending upon your phone's operating system, you may need to turn Bluetooth and/or Wi-Fi on manually when in Airplane mode.

> **TIP**
>
> When you turn on Airplane Mode on an iOS/iPadOS device, it turns off all radios except for Bluetooth. If you turn off Bluetooth while you're in Airplane Mode, your device will remember the next time you turn on Airplane Mode.

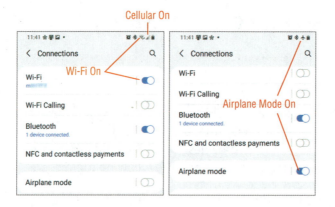

**FIGURE 4.1** Normal (left) versus Airplane mode (right) on a typical Android smartphone; Airplane mode turns off Wi-Fi and Cellular connections. (Source: Apple Inc.)

**FIGURE 4.2** Normal mode (left) on a typical iPhone (iOS) smartphone versus Airplane mode (right); Airplane mode turns off Wi-Fi and Cellular connections. (Source: Apple Inc.)

**EXAM TIP**

To prepare for the Core 1 1101 exam, be sure you know how to enable/disable wireless/cellular data connectivity using Airplane mode.

## 2G/3G/4G/5G

Smartphones are manufactured to support different versions of cellular service. The most common versions in use today are 3G, 4G, and 5G. However, some cellular services today still support 2G.

### 2G Global System for Mobile Communications vs. Code-Division Multiple Access

2G was the first digital cellular standard (original cellular phones were analog, subject to interference and garbled communications). 2G used two technologies initially: Global System for Mobile Communications (*GSM*) uses circuit switching (like landline phones) and time-sharing for multiple users. GSM was widely used in Europe. Code Division Multiple Access (*CDMA*) uses packet-switching, a network technology that supports concurrent call transmitting. CDMA was widely used in North America, Japan, Korea, and Hong Kong.

GSM supports simultaneous voice and data, while CDMA does not. CDMA voice quality is typically better than GSM. Originally, the choice between GSM or CDMA was made by the cellular provider, but more recent 2G phones support either standard. GSM phones use interchangeable SIM cards for easy switching between carriers, while CDMA phones don't.

Both GSM and CDMA versions of 2G have been phased out by most wireless carriers worldwide and in the United States.

### 3G Cellular Service

3G, unlike 2G, was designed for data networking from the ground up, using packet-switching technology. There have been a number of 3G cellular networks using different technology, including CDMA 2000 (an improved version of CDMA), Universal Mobile Tele-communications System (UMTS), and EDGE. 3G networks support web browsing, web-enabled apps, video calling, and GPS navigation. 3G has a peak speed of about 2Mbps.

By the end of 2022, 3G support was phased out by all U.S.-based cellular carriers. 3G support is also in the process of being phased out by other countries.

### 4G Cellular Service

4G cellular service is the mainstream cellular service in the United States and most other nations as this book goes to press. Compared to 3G, 4G runs at much faster speeds. The most common version of 4G in the USA is Long Term Evolution (LTE), which made it easier for networks originally using GSM and CDMA to move to 4G.

LTE is sometimes referred to as "true 4G" because it is much faster than HSPA+, which is an update to 3G technology sometimes marketed as 4G. Both LTE and HSPA+ support multiple input-multiple output (MIMO) antennas to improve transmission and receiving speed and reliability.

### 5G Cellular Service

5G cellular service is far and away the fastest cellular service available and can also be used as a replacement for wired broadband service. 5G networks use a cellular technology called New Radio (NR), which supports both 4G and 5G signals. Thus, unlike earlier transitions that saw 2G and 3G networks shut down to allow cellular frequencies and physical infrastructure to be repurposed for faster cellular networks, 4G will continue to work alongside 5G.

> **NOTE**
>
> To learn much more about current and older cellular technologies, see the Commsbrief website at `commsbrief.com`.

5G uses a large number of frequencies that offer different balances between speed and range. As with Wi-Fi and other radio frequencies, faster frequencies have shorter ranges, and slower frequencies have longer ranges.

Table 4.1 compares basic facts about 2G, 3G, 4G, and 5G cellular networks.

**TABLE 4.1** 2G-3G-4G-5G Quick Reference

| | 2G | 3G | 4G | 5G |
|---|---|---|---|---|
| **Technologies** | GSM, GPRS, CDMA, EDGE | 3G, HSPA, HSPA+, DC-HSPA+, EVDO | LTE, LTE Advanced, WiMax^ | Low-band (under 2GHz freq.) Mid-band (2-7GHz freq.) High-band (line of sight, above 7GHz)* |
| **Optimized for** | Voice, text messages | Voice and data | Voice and data | Voice and data |
| **Maximum download speeds** | Up to 384Kbps (EDGE), others are slower | 3G: 300Kbps HSPA: 7.2Mbps HSPA+: 21Mbps DC-HSPA+: 42Mbps | Up to 400Mbps (average around 40Mbps) | Up to 20Gbps (average around 100Mbps or more) |
| **Major Features** | Digital signaling Circuit switching (GSM) Packet switching (CDMA, GPRS, EDGE) | Web browsing, web-enabled apps, improved security, video calls | Greater speed, support for Wi-Fi, improved error correction | Greater speed, lower latency, greater bandwidth |
| **Status (end of 2022)** | Obsolete | Obsolescent | Current | Current |

^ WiMax has been discontinued in most worldwide markets

* See cradlepoint.com/resources/blog/what-are-the-types-of-5g for more information.

## Hotspot

If you are unable to connect your computer or tablet to a Wi-Fi network, you can still get online by using your smartphone's mobile hotspot feature, sometimes called *mobile hotspot* and *tethering*.

To get started, locate the mobile hotspot feature in your smartphone. Typically, it is part of the Connections or Wi-Fi dialog (Figure 4.3). Normally, this option turns your phone into a Wi-Fi hotspot. However, depending upon your smartphone and your carrier, you might be able to use Bluetooth.

**FIGURE 4.3** Typical hotspot settings for an Android smartphone. Tap Configure to change the SSID (network name), password, or frequency band. (Source: Apple Inc.)

Connect Wi-Fi devices by selecting the SSID for your hotspot and providing the password when prompted. On some smartphones, you can filter connections by creating a list of allowed MAC addresses; only devices whose MAC addresses are listed can use the connection.

**NOTE**

Be sure to turn off the hotspot feature when you are done using it. And, if you have a limited data plan, remember that the data used by connected devices will count against your data allowance for the current period.

## Preferred Roaming List Updates

Smartphone mobile providers periodically provide updates to the preferred roaming list (PRL); the PRL is used by CDMA wireless phones to store information used to determine the frequency bands and service providers that can be used for roving.

To determine when these updates have taken place, check the updates issued by your carrier. These updates may be listed separately or may be included in general software updates. Some carriers have a manual procedure you can follow to update the PRL, such as dialing a specific number or tapping Update PRL.

**NOTE**

Sprint was the major U.S. carrier to support manual PRL and profile updates. However, since it was absorbed by T-Mobile, which handles roving differently, manual PRL and profile updates are no longer necessary.

**EXAM TIP**

To prepare for the Core 1 1101 exam, be sure you understand the major differences between 2G, 3G, 4G, and 5G cellular services; how to set up a hotspot; and what preferred roaming list updates are used for.

# BLUETOOTH

Bluetooth is used by your smartphone or tablet to connect to headsets, car audio systems, speakers, printers, and input devices, depending upon which device types are supported by the operating system and device. The following sections discuss the Bluetooth connection process.

## Enable Bluetooth

The first step in using Bluetooth is to turn it on in your smartphone or tablet.

On a device running iOS or iPadOS, do the following:

1. Tap Settings.
2. Tap Bluetooth.
3. Drag Bluetooth to On.

On a device running Android (based on Samsung A20 running Android 11), do the following:

1. Tap Settings.
2. Tap Connections.
3. Drag Bluetooth to On.

## Enable Pairing

The next step is to enable pairing, the process of enabling your smartphone or tablet to "see" another Bluetooth device.

1. The smartphone or tablet starts scanning for devices automatically as soon as you turn on Bluetooth.
2. On iOS or iPadOS, the devices you can connect to are listed under Other Devices. On Android, devices you can connect to are listed under Available Devices.

## Find a Device for Pairing

The next step is to select a device to pair with.
On a device running iOS or iPadOS, do the following:

1. Detected devices that are not yet paired are listed in Other Devices.
2. Tap the device to add it to My Devices (Figure 4.4).

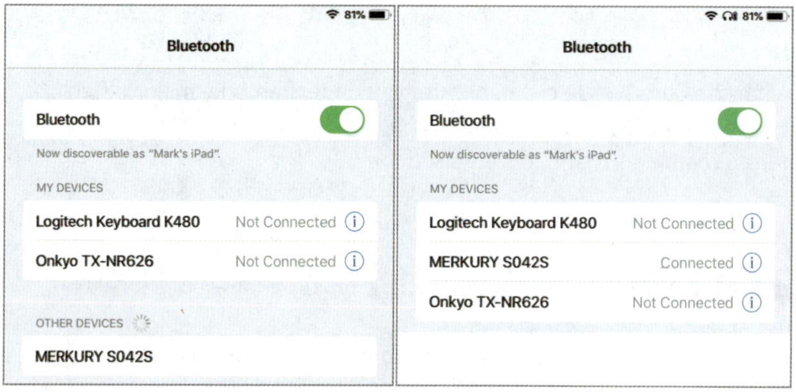

**FIGURE 4.4** Pairing with a Merkury speaker on iPadOS.
(Source: Apple Inc.)

On a device running Android:

1. Detected devices that are not yet paired are listed as Available Devices.
2. Tap the device to add it to Paired Devices.

## Enter the Appropriate PIN Code

If you need to enter a PIN code, follow the instructions on-screen (Figure 4.5).

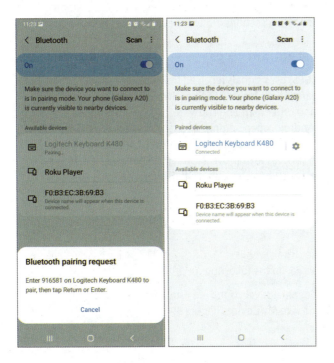

**FIGURE 4.5** Pairing with a keyboard on Android. (Source: Apple Inc.)

When the pairing process is complete, the device is listed in the My Devices category on iOS or the Paired Devices category on Android.

## Test Connectivity

Test the device for functionality. Check music playback, typing, or other functionality as needed.

## Disconnecting

Before the device can be used with a different computer or mobile device, it must be disconnected from the original host device. The easiest way to do this is to turn off Bluetooth on the host device.

> **EXAM TIP**
>
> Know the steps in the Bluetooth connection process: 1. Enable Bluetooth, 2. Enable pairing, 3. Find a device for pairing, 4. Enter the appropriate PIN code, 5. Test connectivity.

# LOCATION SERVICES

Smartphones and cellular-enabled tablets have two location services: one based on GPS and one based on cellular. The following sections discuss the differences between them.

## Global Positioning System Services

The Global Positioning System (*GPS*) uses signals received from satellites to determine the position of the GPS receiver. Smartphones include GPS receivers that are used by Google Maps, MapQuest, Apple Maps, and other mapping software.

To configure GPS services on Android, open Settings and tap Location. When Location is On, GPS services are available to mapping and other apps. When Location is Off, GPS services and Wi-Fi and Bluetooth services to improve accuracy are not available. However, Google location services can run even when Location is Off (Figure 4.6).

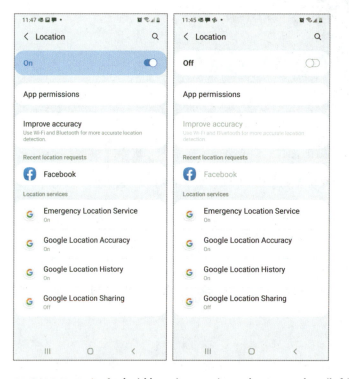

**FIGURE 4.6** Android location services when turned on (left) and off (right). (Source: Apple Inc.)

To configure GPS services on iOS, open Settings, Privacy, and Location Services. Turn off Location Services to disable GPS. However, you can leave Location Services on and configure it for specific apps.

## Cellular Location Services

Cellular location services are used along with GPS services to help make mapping and other location-dependent apps more accurate. Smartphones don't have a specific "turn off cellular location services" option under that name, but there are ways to limit tracking.

▶ Turn off your cell phone when you don't need to make or receive calls or texts, use it for navigation, and so on.

▶ On Android, turn off Location (refer to Figure 4.6).

▶ On Android, configure App Location Permissions (Figure 4.7). You can select from Allow All The time, Allow Only While Using The App, Ask Every Time, or Deny. Tap See all . . . . Permissions to see or change other permissions.

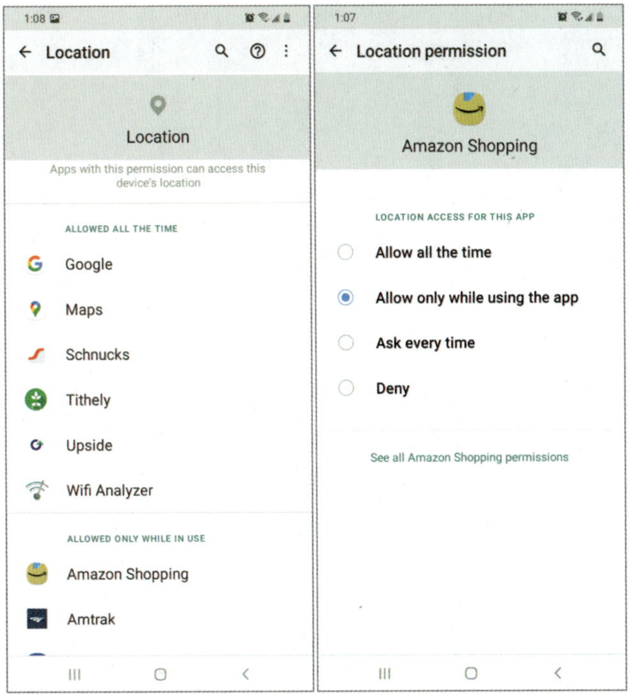

**FIGURE 4.7** Android location services when turned on (left) and off (right). (Source: Apple Inc.)

▶ On iOS, tap Settings, then Privacy, and then Location Services to turn off location services or to select location access for a specific app (Figure 4.8). You can select from Never, Ask Next Time Or When I Share, While Using the App, or Always.

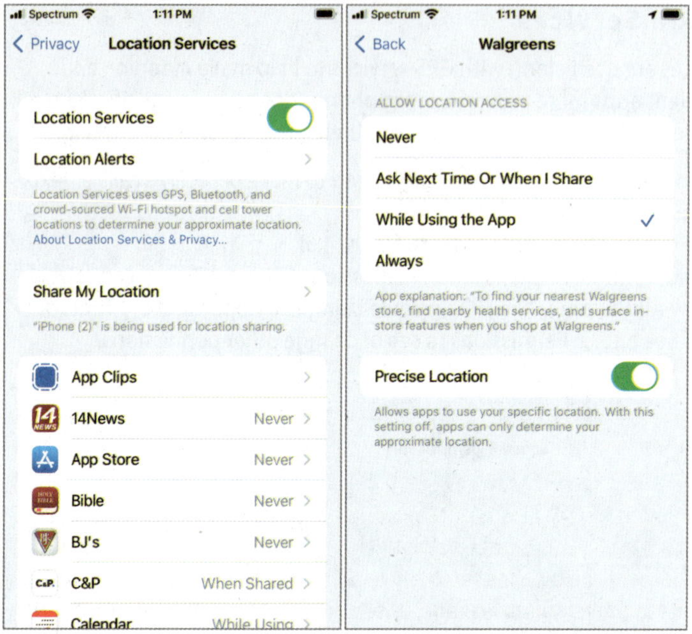

**FIGURE 4.8** iOS location services (left) and adjusting location access for a specific app (right). (Source: Apple Inc.)

**NOTE**

See www.consumerreports.org/privacy/how-to-turn-off-location-services-on-your-smartphone-a8219252827 to learn more about limiting location tracking.

**EXAM TIP**

To prepare for the Core 1 1101 exam, make sure you understand the uses for Bluetooth on mobile devices, the process of configuring it and using it to pair with devices, and how to control GPS and cellular location services on iOS and Android devices.

# MOBILE DEVICE MANAGEMENT/MOBILE APPLICATION MANAGEMENT

Whether mobile devices are company-owned or personally owned but used for company business (bring your own device, or BYOD), mobile device management (MDM) and mobile application management (MAM) are important tools many businesses use to help secure mobile devices and the data they provide access to.

## Corporate Email Configuration

Connecting to corporate email can get a bit complicated. You should know how to configure SMTP, POP3, and IMAP connections to a Microsoft Exchange or other email server.

There are settings on mobile devices where you configure incoming and outgoing email server information. For example, you would specify the POP3 server, the security type such as SSL, and the port number such as 995.

For email you should know the following ports:

- ▶ POP3 port 110/Secure port 995
- ▶ IMAP port 143/Secure port 993
- ▶ SMTP port 25/Secure port 465 or 587

To learn more about email protocols, see Chapter 6, "TCP/IP Ports and Protocols."

Email is essential to modern corporations but preventing its abuse with unauthorized content or use by unauthorized devices goes beyond what standard email clients can do.

Mobile device management can be used remotely to set up, configure, and safeguard corporate email accounts to prevent data leakage, unsecured email attachments, and other problems on both mobile and desktop devices.

> **NOTE**
>
> To explore the many types of mobile device management software and services on the market, check out www.pcmag.com/picks/the-best-mobile-device-management-mdm-solutions.

## Two-Factor Authentication

Two-factor authentication goes beyond the traditional username + password authentication to provide more security for mobile devices and data. The first factor is typically username + password, while the second factor might involve responding to an email from the resource you are attempting to use, inserting a smart card in a laptop, or entering a code generated by a website (a soft token) or an RSA code device (a hard token).

> **NOTE**
>
> To learn more about different types of two-factor authentication (2FA), see www.microsoft.com/en-us/security/business/security-101/what-is-two-factor-authentication-2fa.

## Corporate Applications

One of the potential problems with BYOD is how to deal with corporate applications on a personally owned device. Many organizations use MAM for this task.

MAM enables companies to enforce policies only on applications that use corporate data. For example, MAM permits remote wiping of an application instead of an entire mobile device in the event of a security breach or a terminated employee.

> **NOTE**
>
> To learn more about the different types of MAM applications and how they differ, see www.techtarget.com/searchmobilecomputing/definition/ mobile-application-management-MAM. To learn more about Microsoft Intune MAM, see learn.microsoft.com/en-us/mem/intune/apps/ app-management.

# MOBILE DEVICE SYNCHRONIZATION

One of the factors that makes mobile devices so useful is their ability to synchronize data with desktops so that both types of devices are working on the same data. The major methods used for mobile device synchronization include cloud-based and desktop-connected.

## Cloud-Based Synchronization

With cloud-based synchronization, data is sent from one device to cloud storage and retrieved by the other device. Cloud-based synchronization can be configured to run automatically or manually, and data can be retrieved from a web browser or a local folder configured to work with the service. The following are some examples of cloud-based synchronization:

- ▶ Apple iCloud (www.apple.com/icloud)
- ▶ Dropbox (www.dropbox.com)
- ▶ Google Drive (www.google.com)
- ▶ Microsoft OneDrive (onedrive.live.com)

To protect data, it is encrypted and secured by usernames and passwords.

## Desktop-Connected Synchronization

With desktop-connected synchronization, a USB cable is used to connect the mobile and desktop devices, and files can be transferred with drag and drop. On Windows, a mobile device can be accessed with File Explorer. With macOS Catalina (macOS 10.15 and later), Finder can be used for file transfer. With earlier versions of macOS, use iTunes.

You can also use Wi-Fi or Bluetooth for connections using a shared folder on the PC as a destination.

**NOTE**

Before you can transfer files via USB to or from a mobile device to a PC, you must confirm that your phone is set for MTP or file transfer. Watch for a prompt when you connect the device to your PC. You might need to specify on the device that the computer you are connecting to is a trusted device. For more information about connecting Android phones, see www.lifewire.com/how-to-connect-android-to-pc-4706506. For more information about connecting iPhones, see www.lifewire.com/access-iphone-files-on-pc-5180132.

## Account Setup

Mobile device synchronization is easy when you use apps made for both mobile and desktop devices that are built to work together. The following sections discuss popular apps that work together (Microsoft 365, Google Workspace, and iCloud).

**NOTE**

It's important for users to realize that mobile apps like the ones listed next rely on cloud-based storage. When an Internet connection is not available, these apps are limited in their capabilities or might not work at all.

### Microsoft 365

Microsoft 365 (formerly Office 365) can be installed in two ways on Android and iOS/iPadOS devices: a single Office Mobile app that combines Word, Excel, and PowerPoint with special mobile-centric features or separate apps (Word, Excel, PowerPoint, Outlook, OneNote, OneDrive, and others). Figure 4.9 illustrates using the Office Mobile app on an Android smartphone.

**NOTE**

To learn more about Microsoft 365 for Android, see www.microsoft.com/en-us/microsoft-365/mobile/microsoft-365-mobile-apps-for-android. To learn more about Microsoft 365 for iOS and iPad, see www.microsoft.com/en-us/microsoft-365/mobile/microsoft-365-mobile-apps-for-ios.

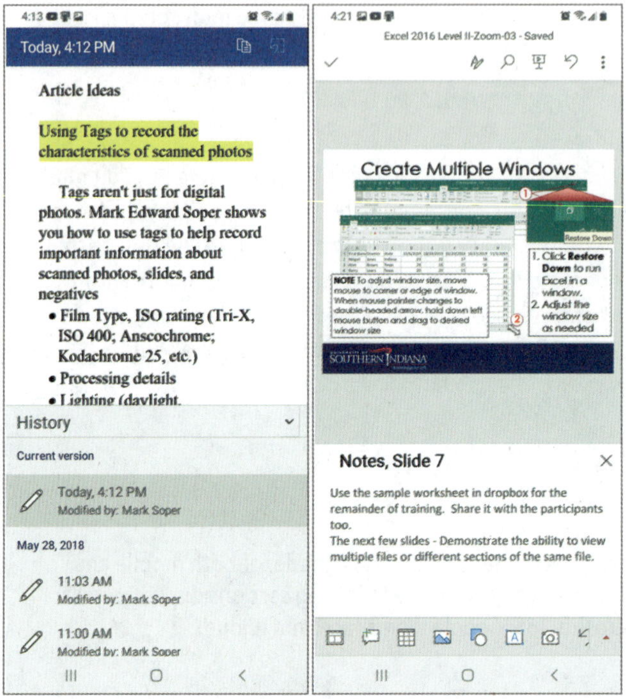

**FIGURE 4.9** Using Microsoft 365 to check the edit history of a document (left) and making changes to a presentation (right). Source: Apple Inc.

## Google Workspace

Google Workspace is the new name for Google's G Suite of collaboration apps and services. All Google Workspace plans include Gmail (email), Drive (online storage), Meet (secure video conferencing), Calendar (calendar and scheduling), Chat (individual and group chat), Jamboard (group whiteboard for real-time planning and co-authoring), Docs (word processing for teams), Sheets (spreadsheet for teams), Slides (presentations for teams), Keep (notes organizer for teams), Sites (website builder), and Forms (survey and forms builder).

> **NOTE**
>
> To learn more about Google Workspace, see `workspace.google.com/business`.

## iCloud

Apple's iCloud provides automatic synchronization for photos, files, passwords, and other data on macOS, iOS, and iPadOS devices. To configure iCloud on iOS or iPadOS, open

Settings, click your name, and use the sliders to select which apps and services will use iCloud (Figure 4.10).

**FIGURE 4.10**   Configuring iCloud on an iPad. (Source: Apple Inc.)

However, iCloud isn't just for Apple computers: it's also available for Windows (iCloud for Windows) and via the Web at www.icloud.com.

> **NOTE**
>
> To learn more about iCloud, iCloud+, iCloud.com, and iCloud for Windows, see support.apple.com/guide/icloud/welcome/icloud.

## Data to Synchronize

Many types of data can be synchronized. The following sections discuss the most common data types.

### Mail

To synchronize mail, make sure each device is configured to use the same email account, preferably IMAP, because IMAP email is stored in the cloud rather than being downloaded to each device.

### Photos

To synchronize photos, use a photo-sharing service such as iCloud, OneDrive, Google Photos (also part of Google Workspace), or Dropbox and store your photos in a folder that is configured to connect to the photo-sharing service.

### Calendar and Contacts

To synchronize calendar and contacts the easy way, use the same cloud-based calendar service on all devices. If this isn't feasible, configure your devices to sync contacts and calendar for specified accounts. On Android, open Settings, then Accounts and Backup, and then Manage Accounts. Tap an account and use the slider to select what to synchronize. On iOS and iPadOS, open Settings and then Passwords & Accounts. Tap an account and use the sliders to select what to synchronize.

### Recognizing Data Caps

If a mobile device has an unlimited data plan, there's no need to worry about data caps. However, on devices that do have cellular data caps, you need to use Wi-Fi, not cellular, to synchronize data whenever possible. There are a variety of ways to do this, including the following:

> ► Turning off automatic synchronization and using manual synchronization
> ► Turning on data saver (disables apps from using data in the background)
> ► Turning off mobile data (disables cellular data; uses Wi-Fi only)

---

**EXAM TIP**

To prepare for the Core 1 1101 exam, make sure you understand the differences between cloud-based and desktop-based synchronization, how the major mobile apps work, and the methods for synchronizing different types of mobile data.

## CERTMIKE EXAM ESSENTIALS

▶ Understanding when and why it's necessary to disable data network connections, how different cellular service standards vary, how to set up hotspots, how to pair Bluetooth with peripherals, how to disable or enable GPS and cellular location services, what mobile device management and mobile application management do, how to use two-factor authentication, and how to synchronize mobile devices with desktops are vital to understand to master this topic.

▶ Users with mobile data caps should consider upgrading to unlimited data plans to avoid running out of high-speed data or any type of data during a billing cycle.

▶ Cloud-based mobile apps and services are used for email, data synchronization, and office activities, so it's important to know how to configure, use, and troubleshoot them.

▶ Configuring location services often requires multiple configuration settings to set up the level of service you want for a particular app or service.

## Practice Question 1

Your client is using a Bluetooth speaker with two different computing devices. She calls you because after using the device with her desktop, she was unable to use it with her smartphone, but a new Bluetooth headset does work with her smartphone. Which of the following is the BEST answer as to why the user can't use her speaker with her smartphone?

A. The smartphone's Bluetooth radio has stopped working.
B. The desktop computer needs to shut off its Bluetooth radio to enable the Bluetooth device to connect with another device.
C. The speaker is turned off.
D. The Bluetooth device should be replaced under warranty.

## Practice Question 2

Your client is planning to use Google Workspace on a 45-minute flight to prepare his presentation after charging his laptop all day. The presentation will be given within a half-hour of arrival, and very little has been completed yet. Which of the following problems could make the presentation preparation difficult?

A. Running out of power
B. Airplane mode
C. Single-screen display
D. None of the above

## Practice Question 1 Explanation

This question is designed to test your real-world understanding of how Bluetooth works. Let's evaluate these choices one at a time.

1. Option A (The smartphone's Bluetooth radio has stopped working) is incorrect. If the smartphone's Bluetooth was not working, no Bluetooth device would work with it.

2. Option B (The desktop computer needs to shut off its Bluetooth radio to enable the Bluetooth device to connect with another device) is the BEST answer. You cannot connect a Bluetooth device to more than one other computer or mobile device at a time. She needs to turn off the Bluetooth radio on the desktop before connecting her Bluetooth device with her smartphone.

3. Option C (The speaker is turned off) is incorrect. Since she was using the speaker with her desktop, she knows how to turn it on and off.

4. Option D (The Bluetooth device should be replaced under warranty) is incorrect because we haven't determined that the device is at fault. Since it worked with the client's desktop, it should work with the smartphone if it is set up properly.

**Correct answer: B. The desktop computer needs to shut off its Bluetooth radio to enable the Bluetooth device to connect with another device.**

## Practice Question 2 Explanation

This question is designed to test your knowledge of mobile apps.

Let's evaluate these answers one at a time.

1. Option A (Running out of power) is incorrect. A 45-minute flight will not likely cause a mobile device to run out of power if it was adequately charged before flight time.

2. Option B (Airplane mode) is the CORRECT answer. Airplane mode blocks Internet access, and Google Workspace requires Internet access to work. A short flight might require Airplane mode to be turned on for most of the flight.

3. Option C (Single-screen display) is incorrect. Most mobile users work with a single display.

4. Option D (None of the above) is incorrect as we have already identified B, Airplane mode, as a potential problem.

**Correct answer: B. Airplane mode**

# Domain 2.0: Networking

Networking is the second domain of CompTIA's A+ Core 1 exam. It covers basic network technology used for wired and wireless network as well as the configuration of network services. This domain has eight objectives.

**2.1 Compare and contrast Transmission Control Protocol (TCP) and User Datagram Protocol (UDP) ports, protocols, and their purposes**

**2.2 Compare and contrast common networking hardware**

**2.3 Compare and contrast protocols for wireless networking**

**2.4 Summarize services provided by networked hosts**

**2.5 Given a scenario, install and configure basic wired/wireless small office/home office (SOHO) networks**

**2.6 Compare and contrast common network configuration concepts**

**2.7 Compare and contrast Internet connection types, network types, and their features**

**2.8 Given a scenario, use networking tools**

Questions from this domain make up 20 percent of the questions on the A+ Core 1 exam, so you should expect to see approximately 18 questions on your test covering the material in this part.

# CHAPTER 5

# TCP/IP Networking

*Core 1 Objective 2.1 Compare and contrast Transmission Control Protocol (TCP) and User Datagram Protocol (UDP) ports, protocols, and their purposes*

***Understanding*** networking, the connection of computers and other devices to share information from across the office to around the world, involves both hardware and software elements.

In this chapter, you will learn everything you need to know about the second half of the material covered by CompTIA A+ Core 1 Objective 2.1. The remainder of this objective is covered in Chapter 6, "TCP/IP Ports and Protocols." This chapter includes coverage of the following topics:

▶ **TCP vs. UDP**

## WHAT IS TCP/IP?

*Transmission Control Protocol/Internet Protocol (TCP/IP)* is a set of networking protocols used to connect all types of computing devices to each other, from local area networks to the Internet. TCP/IP-based networks are used in home offices, small offices, large business offices, enterprises, and the world's largest network, the Internet.

The components of TCP/IP are covered in detail in Chapter 6. In this chapter, we are focusing on the differences between the protocol families known as *Transport Control Protocol (TCP)* and *User Datagram Protocol (UDP)*, as understanding this is essential to the discussion in the Chapter 6.

# TCP VS. UDP

There are two main protocols used to move data around on TCP/IP networks: TCP and UDP. These two protocols are the workhorses of modern networks, moving data between systems. Almost every time that data is sent over the Internet or a local network, it is sent using either TCP or UDP. You need to understand the differences between the two.

*TCP* is a connection-oriented protocol. When TCP protocol is used to transmit data, the sender must receive a response from the receiver that the information was received. If the response is missing or the receiver indicates that the information isn't correct, the sender transmits the information again. TCP is like making a phone call; the call is not a success if the call isn't picked up.

On the other hand, *UDP* is a connectionless protocol. When UDP is used to transmit data, the data is sent, but there is no checking to make sure the data was received. UDP is like sending an SMS text message; there's no way to know if it arrived if the receiver doesn't reply.

Each of these approaches has their place on modern networks. Connection-oriented protocols provide guaranteed delivery of data but require extra work by networked devices, so they move a little more slowly. Connectionless protocols do move faster, but they don't provide that guaranteed delivery.

> **EXAM TIP**
>
> Be sure you understand the differences between TCP and UDP protocols and how they are used. You might encounter scenario-based questions on the exam that are very specific about configuring connections including protocol numbers (discussed in Chapter 6).

## Connection-Oriented Protocols

Let's begin by looking at a couple of examples of cases where connection-oriented approaches work best. TCP is responsible only for moving data around a network—it doesn't provide any context for what that data actually is. TCP doesn't care if it's transporting web traffic or facilitating an administrative connection to a server. Application protocols, on the other hand, are designed for specific purposes and work on top of TCP when they require connection-oriented network service.

There are many different application protocols that use TCP. Two common ones are HTTPS and SSH.

## HTTPS

*Hypertext Transfer Protocol Secure (HTTPS)* is the secure version of the HTTP protocol used by web browsers to request and receive web pages. Today, almost every website uses HTTPS instead of HTTP to provide secure, encrypted connections that are safe from eavesdropping.

When a device requests a web page using HTTPS, it must receive an acknowledgment that the website is secure before the connection can continue. Most web browsers display a closed padlock or similar icon to indicate the connection is secure (Figure 5.1)

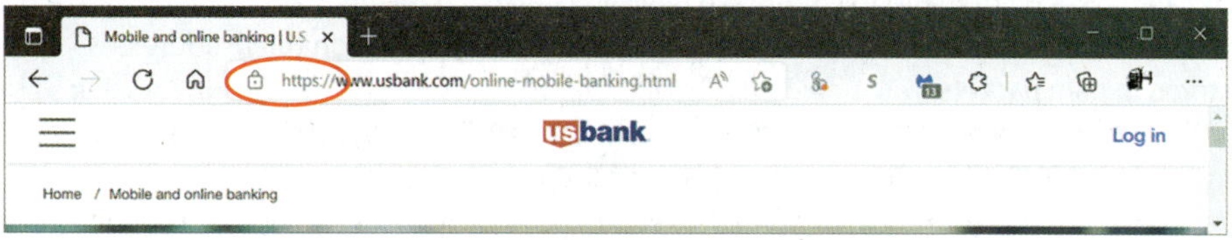

**FIGURE 5.1** **A bank website using HTTPS.**

## SSH

Secure Shell (SSH) provides for secure login to servers and other types of remote services.

SSH uses encryption to create a secure connection after a user provides standard login information during the first login. The SSH information is stored in the connecting device and is used automatically thereafter.

> **NOTE**
>
> SSH is considered a very secure protocol because it makes use of public encryption keys based on public key infrastructure (PKI) technology. SSH uses port 22 and is considered the secure replacement to the insecure Telnet protocol.

> **NOTE**
>
> Asynchronous Transfer Mode (*ATM*) is a telecom technology used for call routing, multimedia VPNs, and residential broadband networks. It uses fixed-size data packets called *cells*. ATM can coexist with data networks and requires a connection be created before a call can be made.

## Connectionless

While some protocols depend upon the guaranteed delivery of a connection-oriented protocol like TCP, other applications do not need this high level of service and can instead use the connectionless delivery offered by UDP. In cases where application protocols use UDP, they must be able to tolerate missing data either by retrying transmissions until they receive a response or by simply ignoring missing data.

There are many different UDP protocols. Let's take a closer look at a couple to understand how they work.

### DHCP

Dynamic Host Configuration Protocol (DHCP) is a protocol that assigns Internet Protocol (IP) addresses on demand to connected devices. *IP* places data into packets, adds source and destination information, and delivers network packets based on the IP addresses stored in data packets.

When a device connects to a TCP/IP network that uses DHCP, the DHCP server checks its list of available IP addresses and provides one for the device to use.

Learn more about DHCP in Chapter 9, "Networked Host Services." Learn more about IP addressing in Chapter 10, "Installing and Configuring Networks."

### Trivial File Transfer Protocol

Trivial File Transfer Protocol (TFTP) is a stripped-down version of File Transfer Protocol (FTP). It is used for the BOOTP bootstrap protocol for diskless workstations, for upgrading firmware in home network routers, and for software distribution on corporate local area networks. It uses UDP for file transfer.

---

### CERTMIKE EXAM ESSENTIALS

▶ Transmission Control Protocol/Internet Protocol (also known as TCP/IP) is a collection of rules (protocols) that enable both local and wide area networking including the Internet. Because TCP/IP is not proprietary to a single operating system or device manufacturing, it enables universal networking to any device that can connect to a network.

▶ There are two categories of protocols, those that are connection oriented and those that are connectionless.

▶ TCP/IP uses two main protocols to move data around networks. The Transmission Control Protocol (TCP) is a connection-oriented protocol that guarantees delivery of data that is sent between two systems. The User Datagram Protocol (UDP) is a connectionless protocol that does not provide guaranteed delivery but offers better efficiency than TCP.

## Practice Question 1

You are researching the electronic services offered by a bank that your company will begin using next month. You want to make sure that web-based banking users make secure connections to the bank server. Which one of the following protocols would be most appropriate for this use?

A. SSH
B. HTTP
C. HTTPS
D. FTP

## Practice Question 2

You are having a discussion with a new hire in your department. The new hire asks you this question: "Which is better, TCP or UDP?" Which of the following is the BEST answer?

A. TCP because it guarantees delivery.
B. UDP because it is faster.
C. TCP or UDP; it makes no difference.
D. TCP or UDP are both important because they do different jobs.

## Practice Question 1 Explanation

This question is designed to test your understanding of secure and insecure websites in a real-world environment.

The first answer, A (SSH), is incorrect because the question is about making a secure connection with a web browser. SSH is used for administrative connections to remote servers.

The second answer, B (HTTP), is incorrect because HTTP is not secure. This makes it a poor choice for banking or other secure web connections.

The third answer, C (HTTPS), is correct because HTTPS is secure. It is used for encrypted connections with banking and other websites that need security.

The fourth answer, D (FTP), is incorrect because FTP is used for file transfer, not for web connections.

**Correct Answer: C. HTTPS**

## Practice Question 2 Explanation

This question is designed to test your understanding of the basics of TCP/IP.

A. The first suggested answer, TCP is better because it guarantees delivery, has a kernel of truth to it. TCP does guarantee delivery because it requires a response, but that doesn't make it better. If TCP is better than UDP, why have both? This answer is incorrect.

B. The second suggested answer, UDP because it is faster, also has a basis in fact. UDP is faster because it doesn't wait for a reply. However, sometimes you need a reply before continuing. This answer is incorrect.

C. The third suggested answer, TCP or UDP; it makes no difference, has no truth to it. This ignores the differences between them and suggests the categories are arbitrary. This answer is incorrect.

D. The fourth suggested answer, TCP and UDP are both important because they do different jobs, is a great brief summation of why both are important. When you need a confirmed connection, a TCP protocol is what you use. When you just need to get information out there, a UDP protocol is right. This is the BEST answer.

**Correct Answer: D. TCP and UDP are both important because they do different jobs.**

# CHAPTER 6

# TCP/IP Ports and Protocols

*Core 1 Objective 2.1
Compare and contrast
Transmission Control
Protocol (TCP) and User
Datagram Protocol (UDP)
ports, protocols, and
their purposes.*

**TCP** and UDP ports and protocols make different parts of the Internet work properly. In this chapter, you'll learn everything you need to know about the first portion of A+ Core 1 objective 2.1, including the following topics:

▶ **Ports and protocols**

The other portions of objective 2.1 are covered in Chapter 5.

## WHAT ARE PORTS?

As you learned in Chapter 5, modern computers use the Internet Protocol (IP) to communicate on networks. IP allows a packet to reach its destination computer, identified by the IP address. On top of IP, most communications use either the Transmission Control Protocol (TCP) or the User Datagram Protocol (UDP) to deliver that packet to a particular service on the destination system. Each of these services is uniquely identified by a *port*. Think of it this way—an IP address is like a street address that identifies a specific building. A port is like an apartment number that identifies a specific location in that building.

Each computer has two sets of ports numbered from 0 to 65,534. One set of ports is for TCP communication, and the other set of ports is for UDP communication.

The services addressed by these ports each provide a function that enables connections with other devices, such as email, web browsing, IP address assignments, and more. To enable the many types of server services on each device to function, different TCP or UDP (or sometimes both) ports are used for each service.

TCP and UDP ports are assigned by an organization called the Internet Assigned Numbers Authority (IANA). In the following sections, we'll identify the services used by particular TCP and UDP ports. These ports, and others, use port numbers assigned by IANA. Port numbers from 0 to 1023 are called *well-known ports*. They have predefined uses and generally shouldn't be used for other purposes to avoid confusion.

> **EXAM TIP**
>
> There are actually 65,536 port numbers (0–65535), so what about numbers 1024 and above? Registered ports are assigned by IANA to a specific service or for ephemeral (temporary) connections, using ports ranging from 1024 to 49151. The last range, dynamic or private ports, use the port numbers ranging from 49152 to 65535. These can be used by any web service.

# PORTS AND PROTOCOLS

You need to know the following protocols and their associated ports for the CompTIA A+ Core 1 exam. They make the Internet work.

Firewalls are used to block unwanted traffic by blocking ports. Most firewalls are automatically configured to permit traffic through the well-known ports discussed in this chapter. But if a firewall is misconfigured, you would need to set up an exception (allowing traffic through) for the ports needed for a protocol.

In Chapter 5, we discussed the differences between TCP and UDP ports. While it's important to understand the differences, keep in mind that almost all of the protocols discussed in this chapter use both TCP and UDP ports.

## 20/21—File Transfer Protocol

File Transfer Protocol (*FTP*) is used to transfer files between remote sites and network devices. FTP can be used within web browsers or with command-line FTP utilities in Windows, Linux, and macOS.

FTP uses ports 20 and 21; 20 is used to send files, and 21 is used for controlling the connection.

Trivial File Transfer Protocol (*TFTP*) is a stripped-down version of File Transfer Protocol (FTP).

Neither FTP nor TFTP includes encryption or other security mechanisms, so they are not safe for use with secure applications.

## 22—Secure Shell

Secure Shell (*SSH*) is used to create a secure connection by a variety of other services such as HTTPS, Secure Copy (SCP), and SFTP, among others. SSH uses port 22.

Secure File Transfer Protocol (*SFTP*) is a version of FTP that uses SSH to secure the connection. Secure Copy (*SCP*) is a network copy command that uses SSH to secure the connection. Because both SFTP and SCP use SSH, they both also use port 22.

## 23—Telnet

Telnet creates a text-based connection to a remote device, enabling it to be controlled remotely. Telnet is an early remote access protocol, which is not at all secure. Because it is insecure, Telnet should not be used on modern networks.

Telnet uses port 23.

## 67/68—Dynamic Host Configuration Protocol

Dynamic Host Configuration Protocol (*DHCP*) is used to provide an IP address to a device that connects to a TCP/IP-based network. During the connection process, the client device sends a discovery message to the DHCP server, the server offers an address, the client requests the offered IP address, and the server sends an acknowledgment message.

DHCP uses port 67 at the server and port 68 at the client.

## 25—Simple Mail Transfer Protocol

Simple Mail Transfer Protocol *(SMTP)* is used to transport email between the sender and receiver. A client email device uses SMTP to send email to an email server. The email server uses SMTP to send the message to the destination email server.

SMTP uses port 25.

## 53—Domain Name System

Domain Name System (*DNS*) is the name for the network of domain name servers. *DNS* servers translate domain names into IP addresses. Thanks to DNS, when you enter www.wiley.com into your browser, for example, DNS translates the URL into the IP address needed to display the home page in your browser.

DNS servers may be provided automatically by a network connection, but they can also be set up manually. DNS servers are referred to by their IP addresses.

For greater security or if DNS stops working, you can flush existing records in Windows by opening a command prompt and typing **`ipconfig /flushdns`**. You can also flush DNS in macOS or Linux.

DNS uses port 53.

> **TIP**
>
> Popular choices for DNS servers are the public DNS servers managed by Google. The IPv4 public Google DNS servers are 8.8.8.8 and 8.8.4.4. Google also provides two IPv6 public DNS servers. These can be used in place of the normal DNS servers provided by your ISP.

## 80—Hypertext Transfer Protocol

Hypertext Transfer Protocol (*HTTP*) is the nonsecure protocol used by web browsers. When you see a URL such as `http://thiswebsite.net`, HTTP is the protocol used to request and receive the contents of the web page. Most websites today use the secure version, HTTPS, instead of HTTP. You'll find HTTPS covered below, under port 443.

Hypertext Markup Language (*HTML*) is a markup language that provides rules about text and image links (hypertext), how the page appears and is structured (markup), and a consistent syntax for commands (language). HTML is the basic language of web pages.

HTTP uses TCP port 80.

## 110—Post Office Protocol 3

Post Office Protocol 3 (*POP3*), as the name suggests, is used to receive email. To use POP3, the protocol must be configured on the receiver's email server and on the receiver's device.

Unlike IMAP (discussed later), POP3 stores email on the recipient's local computer or device. While this allows email to be viewed online, it also means that a user that checks POP3 email with a desktop and a mobile device will have a separate POP3 messages stored on each device received only on that device. In an era of always-on Internet and multiple device usage by most people, IMAP is a better choice.

POP3 uses port 110.

## 137–139—Network Basic Input/Output System/NetBIOS over TCP/IP

Network Basic Input/Output System (*NetBIOS*) was originally created to support software running using local area networks (LANs) before TCP/IP. NetBIOS, as such, isn't routable, so it can't be used in a modern Internet-based network like TCP/IP without some help. NetBIOS over TCP/IP (*NetBT*) enables NetBIOS-aware apps to run on TCP/IP. NetBT can be disabled if legacy apps that need it are not present on a network.

NetBIOS and NetBT uses ports 137, 138, and 139.

## 143—Internet Mail Access Protocol

Internet Mail Access Protocol (*IMAP*), as the name suggests, is used to receive email. To use IMAP, the protocol must be installed on the receiver's email server and on the receiver's device.

IMAP has largely replaced POP3 for receiving mail because IMAP stores mail on the IMAP server and supports email folders on the server, making it easy to organize messages. Thus, a user with multiple computers and mobile devices can access all of their email from any device.

IMAP uses port 143.

## 161/162—Simple Network Management Protocol

Simple Network Management Protocol (*SNMP*) is used to monitor network operation. Routers, switches, and other devices that can be monitored with SNMP are known as managed devices. They contain *agents*, software that interacts with SNMP to enable network management. A variety of network management systems use SNMP to monitor agents.

SNMP uses port 161 to send messages from the SNMP manager to agents (managed devices) and uses port 162 to receive messages indicating problems (known as *traps*) from agents.

## 389—Lightweight Directory Access Protocol

Modern networks store an immense amount of information, including usernames, passwords, email addresses, and much more. Lightweight Directory Access Protocol (*LDAP*) creates a directory of this information, enabling business applications on a network to quickly find the information they need.

LDAP should not be confused with the Microsoft proprietary Active Directory, as LDAP is vendor-neutral and can query Active Directory as well as other information stores.

LDAP uses port 389.

## 443—Hypertext Transfer Protocol Secure

Hypertext Transfer Protocol Secure (*HTTPS*) is the secure version of HTTP. HTTPS is used to create secure connections between remote servers and web browsers.

Originally used primarily for e-banking and e-commerce, the desire for greater web security has encouraged widespread use of HTTPS connections. Most browsers will automatically toggle an HTTP query to HTTPS if the URL doesn't offer an HTTP connection. HTTPS is encrypted with TLS (formerly SSL) and typically uses a closed padlock icon in the address bar to indicate a secure connection is being used.

HTTPS uses port 443.

Secure Sockets Layer (*SSL*) is the original secure transmission protocol used in web pages. SSL encrypts pages, provides a handshake process to authenticate both ends of a connection, and digitally signs data to assure data integrity.

Transport Level Security (*TLS*) is an updated and improved version of the now deprecated SSL. TLS was introduced in 1999 and provides authentication, privacy, and data integrity.

## 445—Server Message Block/Common Internet File System

Server Message Block (SMB)/Common Internet File System (CIFS) are related protocols that need to be discussed together. *SMB* is the protocol that enables file, print, and device sharing on the original Microsoft Windows networks using Windows NT 4.0 or Windows for Workgroups 3.1 in the mid-1990s. SMB was developed for use with NetBIOS and originally used port 139 just like NetBIOS itself.

SMB was modified to use TCP/IP and has been improved for greater security and flexibility. *CIFS* is Microsoft's implementation of SMB for file sharing.

The TCP/IP version of SMB/CIFS use port 445.

## 3389—Remote Desktop Protocol

Remote Desktop Protocol (RDP) is an exception to the other protocols in this chapter for a couple of reasons.

▶ RDP is a proprietary Microsoft protocol.
▶ RDP uses a reserved port rather than a well-known port.

*RDP* enables remote connections to a Windows device by using a graphical interface. The command to start Remote Desktop Protocol from the Windows Run command is `mstsc`. The name, the acronym for Microsoft Terminal Services, is left over from the time that RDP was, in fact, called Microsoft Terminal Services.

RDP uses port 3389.

## MAC Address and Address Resolution Protocol

How do networks make sure that the correct information goes to a specific device on a network? MAC and ARP team up to do the job.

A Media Access Control (*MAC*) address is a unique ID number assigned by the manufacturer to each network device, such as a network adapter card, motherboard-based network port, router (which has a MAC for its switch and a separate MAC for its connection to other networks, and so on), and others.

Address Resolution Protocol (*ARP*) keeps track of the IP addresses and the MAC addresses of devices on a network. Because IP addresses can change, ARP is essential in making sure that requests and replies are routed to the correct device.

## CERTMIKE EXAM ESSENTIALS

▶ Protocols used for file transfers, email, insecure and secure web connections, and other network and Internet tasks use Transmission Control Protocol (TCP) ports or User Datagram Protocol (UDP) ports; in most cases, both port types are used.

▶ To enable the different types of networking and Internet access to work properly, software and hardware firewalls must be configured to allow the ports used by these protocols to send and receive information.

▶ Most network and Internet protocols run automatically, and their operation is transparent to the user.

## Practice Question 1

Your client has been using POP3 email for several years when she used only a desktop computer. Now, your client has switched to IMAP, but her email client cannot connect to her email box. Her other network and Internet apps work properly. Which of the following is the MOST LIKELY reason for the problem?

A.  Her email client must be upgraded to use IMAP.

B.  She must buy a subscription to use IMAP.

C.  She must delete all of her POP3 email first.

D.  She must reconfigure her email client to use the correct ports and servers for IMAP.

## Practice Question 2

Your client has been receiving DNS errors frequently. After consulting with you and changing his DNS servers, he is still getting DNS errors on his previous lookups, but new websites are resolving (being translated from URL to IP address and opening) properly. What is the BEST suggestion to fix this problem?

A.  Reinstall the DNS server on the network.

B.  Flush the DNS cache.

C.  Stop using DNS.

D.  Switch back to the original DNS servers.

## Practice Question 1 Explanation

This question is designed to test your understanding of how different protocols work in the real world.

Let's look at the first proposed answer, her email client must be upgraded to use IMAP. Virtually all email clients have supported both protocols for many years. This is a very unlikely scenario.

How about the second answer? IMAP is a protocol, not a commercial service. Thus, this proposed answer is incorrect.

The third proposed answer, deleting all of her POP3 emails, has nothing to do with this problem. POP3 emails are typically deleted automatically from the POP3 server after being downloaded to the local email box. Thus, this proposed answer is also incorrect.

The fourth proposed answer, reconfigure her email client, is the MOST LIKELY reason. The email client must be configured to use IMAP before it can receive IMAP messages. The details are provided by the email vendor.

**Correct Answer: D (reconfigure email client to use IMAP)**

## Practice Question 2 Explanation

This question is designed to test your understanding of the basics of DNS.

The first suggested answer, reinstall the DNS server, reveals a complete misunderstanding of where DNS servers are located. They are Internet based, rather than based on a LAN. This answer is incorrect.

The second suggested answer, flush the DNS cache, addresses the most likely root cause. DNS requests are cached (stored) for reuse after they are resolved to speed up additional DNS requests for the same URL. If the information is out-of-date or corrupt, the cache would provide bad information. By flushing the cache, systems needing DNS are forced to check the newly specified DNS servers to rebuild the cache. This is the BEST answer.

The third suggested answer, stop using DNS, is impossible. DNS is essential for working with the modern Internet, in which many IP addresses are used at a particular URL. Without DNS, you would need to know which IP addresses were used by a particular website and which ones were in use at any given time. This answer is incorrect.

The fourth suggested answer, switch back to the original DNS servers is likely to make things worse rather than better. After all, right now DNS is working some of the time. This answer is incorrect.

**Correct Answer: B (flush the DNS cache)**

# CHAPTER 7

# Networking Hardware

## Core 1 Objective 2.2 Compare and contrast common networking hardware.

**Networks** of any size rely on a variety of equipment to connect PCs and devices to each other and to the Internet. This chapter helps you discover the unique functions of each network component discussed as you master Core 1 Objective 2.2

This chapter includes the following topics:

- ► **Cable modem**
- ► **Digital subscriber line**
- ► **Optical network terminal**
- ► **Routers**
- ► **Switches**
- ► **Access points**
- ► **Patch panel**
- ► **Firewall**
- ► **Power over Ethernet**
- ► **Hub**
- ► **Network interface card**
- ► **Software-defined networking**

# CABLE MODEM

A cable modem uses the same fiber-optic or coaxial networks used by cable TV providers. Depending upon the provider, users might receive a self-install kit that splits the existing cable TV service into separate TV and cable Internet services or users might need to schedule an installation of a dedicated cable Internet line.

Figure 7.1 illustrates the front and rear of a typical cable modem with bundled Voice over IP (VoIP). *VoIP* routes voice calls over cable Internet service.

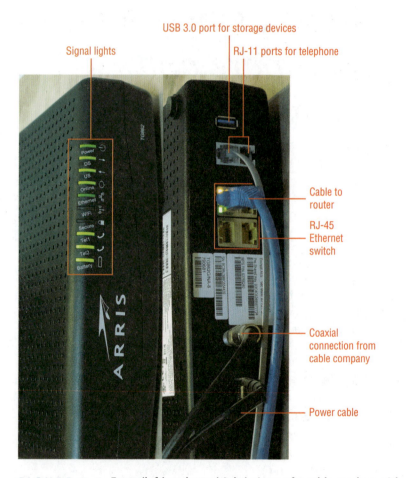

**FIGURE 7.1**  **Front (left) and rear (right) views of a cable modem with VoIP support.**

Cable Internet service is available at speeds as low as 10Mbps and speeds as high as 400Mbps or faster. Higher speeds than these offered by cable Internet companies are typically carried on fiber-optic cable into a neighborhood or directly to an individual residence or office building. See "Optical Network Terminal" later in this chapter for details.

# DIGITAL SUBSCRIBER LINE

Telecom companies such as AT&T, Verizon, and others typically offer a different type of broadband Internet known as *digital subscriber line* (DSL).

Originally, DSL used the same telephone lines used for ordinary phone service, adding high-speed digital signaling that could coexist with regular (analog) telephone services. These types of DSL are known as asynchronous DSL (ADSL) and synchronous DSL (SDSL). ADSL downloads data faster, while SDSL has the same download and upload speeds and was marketed primarily for business use.

DSL using phone lines is limited by distance (no more than 18,000 wire feet from the central office connection to the Internet to the service location) and line quality. Typical residential ADSL speeds are up to 6Mbps download and up to 0.5Mbps upload.

Faster DSL services, such as ADSL2+ (asynchronous) and VDSL2 (synchronous) may combine fiber-optic and new copper wiring. Faster speeds up to 1Gbps and beyond typically use fiber optic to get to the premises. Regardless of the service type, typical DSL modems resemble the one shown in Figure 7.2.

**FIGURE 7.2** Front (top) and rear (bottom) views of a typical DSL modem with integrated wireless router. (Source: D-Link Corporation.)

Unlike cable modems, which typically use separate wireless routers, most DSL modems include Wi-Fi wireless routers as well as four-port Ethernet switches. The easiest way to determine if a broadband modem is made for DSL or cable is to look for the WAN connection: if it's coaxial, it's made for cable; if it's RJ-11, it's made for DSL.

# OPTICAL NETWORK TERMINAL

As you learned from the discussions of cable Internet and DSL, both types of services are in the process of switching from their traditional coaxial or phone line connections to fiber-optic cable. However, unless you like to look over the shoulder of the broadband technician coming out to your location to see the upgrade to fiber, you probably won't notice anything different except for faster speed. The reason is that the connection at your location is typically made with a device known as an *optical network terminal* (ONT).

An ONT acts as a converter for fiber-optic signaling (which is light-based using photons) into the electrical impulses used by Ethernet networks. An ONT can be installed outside or inside a location and needs a power outlet. It connects to your existing Ethernet network. Figure 7.3 illustrates a typical ONT after installation in a residence.

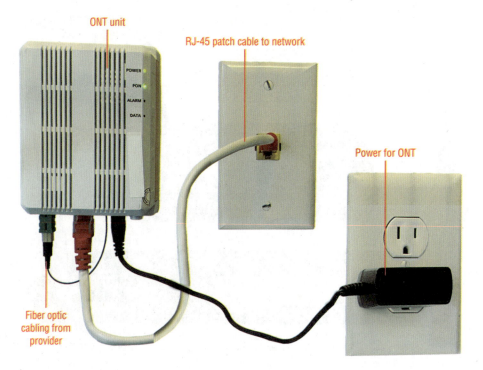

**FIGURE 7.3**  **A typical ONT connected to a home network.**

# ROUTERS

A router is a device that connects broadband Internet access to a network. It has two types of connections: a wide area network (WAN) connection to a broadband modem (the Internet), and a local area network (LAN) connection, typically a Wi-Fi access point (AP), an Ethernet switch, or both.

In addition to having two different network connections, a router has two different IP addresses: a public-facing IP address for the WAN (Internet) side, and a gateway address for the LAN (internal network) side.

Almost all routers sold for consumer and small office use today are wireless routers. Figure 7.4 illustrates the front and rear of a typical wireless router. A single RJ-45 connection runs from the router to the broadband modem. This router has a built-in four-port switch to enable other devices to use the router for Internet access. While some wireless routers have internal antennas, most have two or more external antennas that can be adjusted to provide the best-quality signal in different environments.

# SWITCHES

A switch enables multiple devices to connect to each other. Switches can be used to create a strictly local area network with no Internet access, but they are more often used in conjunction with a router to enable computers to connect with each other and the Internet.

Switches work by determining the media access control (MAC) address of each network device attached to the switch, checking the MAC origin and destination information in each data packet, and using that information to connect the origin device to the destination device. It doesn't matter whether the origin and destination devices are connected to the same switch or to another switch; if they are part of the same Ethernet network, they can connect with each other. If the destination is on a different network, the switch will look for a router to complete the connection.

There are two types of switches: managed and unmanaged. Both types of switches have multiple RJ-45 Ethernet ports, but internally they are quite different.

## Managed Switches

A managed switch includes more than just the ability to connect one device to another. A managed switch has the ability to turn a single physical network into two or more virtual LANs (VLANs). Each VLAN acts as a separate network, and this feature is often used in multi-tenant office buildings to enable each tenant to have its own secure wired network.

Other features of managed switches include enhanced security, support for advanced quality of service (QoS), support for Simple Network Management Protocol (SNMP) to enable network diagnostics and performance checking, and redundancy to provide a backup network in case the original network failed. Many managed switches also include

Power over Ethernet (PoE) to hubs, IP phones, and IP cameras so they can be located anywhere without the need for AC outlets.

USB 2.0 port

USB 3.0 port

WAN port to
broadband modem

Four-port Ethernet
RJ-45 switch

Wi-Fi antenna array

Signal lights

**F I G U R E   7 . 4**   **A typical wireless router.**

Figure 7.5 shows a typical managed switch. Managed switches often include a DB9 (serial) port or USB port along with built-in management software. Some managed switches, like the one shown here, have provision for small form-factor pluggable (SPF) modules that support fiber-optic or other types of network connectors.

USB/serial console management port

USB management port

SPF ports

Managed Ethernet switch ports

SPF fiber-optic module

**FIGURE 7.5**  A managed switch that also supports SPF modules.
(Source: NETGEAR)

## Unmanaged Switches

The switches built into broadband modems and routers are called *unmanaged switches*, as are those available separately with up to eight ports. They work well for small-office/home-office (SOHO) networks that don't need management, VLA, or PoE features. Figure 7.6 shows a typical unmanaged switch. Note the highlighted signal light legend: when both lights are on, the connection on this router is running at 1000Mbps (Gigabit) speed.

**FIGURE 7.6**  A typical unmanaged Gigabit Ethernet switch.

> **EXAM TIP**
>
> Be sure you understand the differences between managed and unmanaged switches for the Core 1 1101 A+ exam.

# ACCESS POINTS

An *access point* (AP), also known as a *wireless access point* (WAP), connects Wi-Fi devices to each other. Each access point on a wireless network has a service set identifier (SSID) that identifies it to devices. Large networks typically have multiple access points that seamlessly hand off wireless devices from one AP to another. An AP must be connected to a router to permit wireless devices to connect to the Internet.

> **TIP**
>
> Access points use the same 2.4, 5, or 6GHz radio frequencies as other Wi-Fi devices.

The wireless portion of a wireless router acts as an AP to enable wireless devices to connect to each other, to any wired devices on the same network, and to the Internet.

Because APs and wireless routers both have antennas, the easiest way to tell one from the other is to look for a WAN port. The WAN port on a router enables the router to connect to a broadband modem. An AP has an Ethernet port that can connect to a switch. If the switch is connected to a router, the AP can carry traffic to and from the Internet, but it must use a separate router.

# PATCH PANEL

A patch panel is a junction point for coaxial, twisted pair (TP), or fiber cable used in networks. Patch panels can be built into equipment racks or wiring closets. Patch panels used for RJ-45 Ethernet cable must be rated for the fastest cable used in the network; otherwise, the network will be slowed down.

The front of the patch panel uses RJ-45 connectors for short standard network cables. The back side of the patch panel has connectors where untwisted cable is pushed into place with a punchdown tool. Figure 7.7 shows the front and rear views of typical patch panels. By wiring into a patch panel, it's easier to connect the network to different devices, label cables, and maintain them.

Connection for RJ-45 patch cable

Use punchdown tool to fasten untwisted cable without connector to this side

**FIGURE 7.7** Typical front (top) and rear (bottom) views of RJ-45 Ethernet patch panels. (Source: Cable Matters Inc.)

# NETWORK INTERFACE CARD

A *network interface card* (NIC) was originally a separate card that fit into a PC's expansion slot to permit the PC to join a network. Today, almost all PCs and many laptops have built-in NICs for use with standard Ethernet networks up to 1Gbps. However, NICs are widely used in servers for faster connections, in connections to multiple networks (Figure 7.8), for use with fiber-optic cables, and as replacements in desktops for older NICs.

When purchasing a NIC for a desktop or server, check the PCIe specifications supported by the motherboard, determine the free slots, and purchase a card that fits. If you need to connect a thin light or convertible laptop that lacks an RJ-45 port to a wired network, you can use a USB 3.0/3/1/3.2 Type A or Type C-Gigabit Ethernet adapter. You can also use a USB 3.0/3/1/3.2 Type A or Type C port for a USB-Wi-Fi adapter (see Figure 7.8).

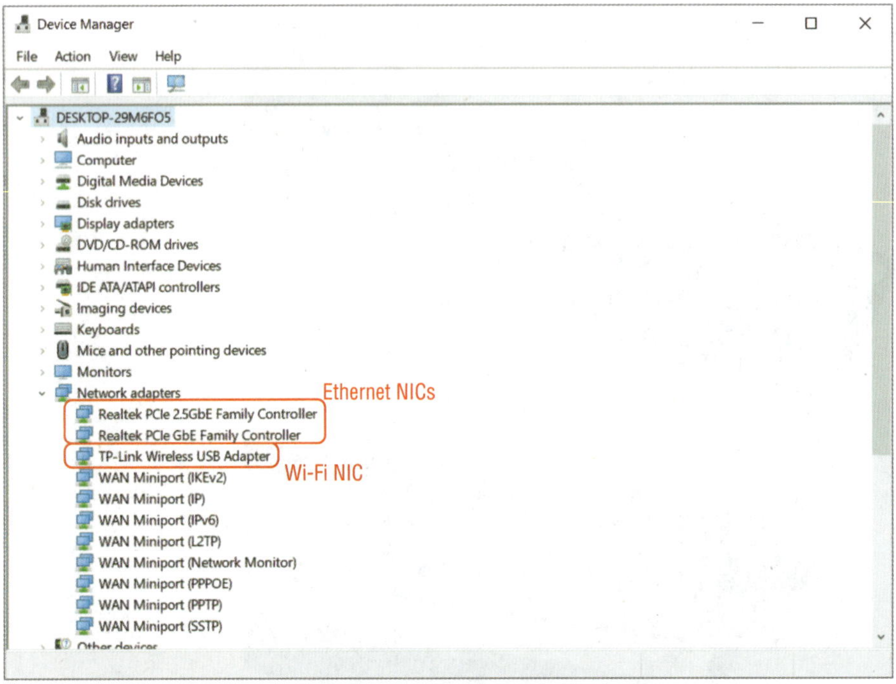

**FIGURE 7.8**  Device Manager listing two Ethernet NICs and a Wi-Fi NIC connected to a USB port.

Figure 7.9 illustrates a NIC that can be connected to two different networks. This is called a dual-homed NIC, and this type of NIC is often used in servers to permit redundant connections. In case one network fails, the server can connect to a different network.

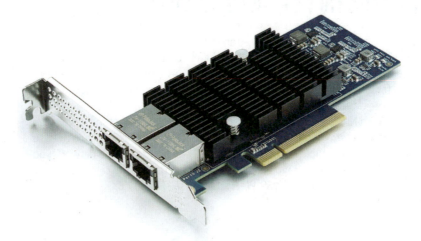

**FIGURE 7.9**  Typical dual-homed NIC that connects to two networks for redundancy. (Source: StarTech.com)

# FIREWALL

Firewalls stop unwanted network traffic and are available as software apps and hardware devices. Small-office/home-office (SOHO) networks use firewalls that are built into routers. Figure 7.10 shows a typical example of a router firewall configuration screen.

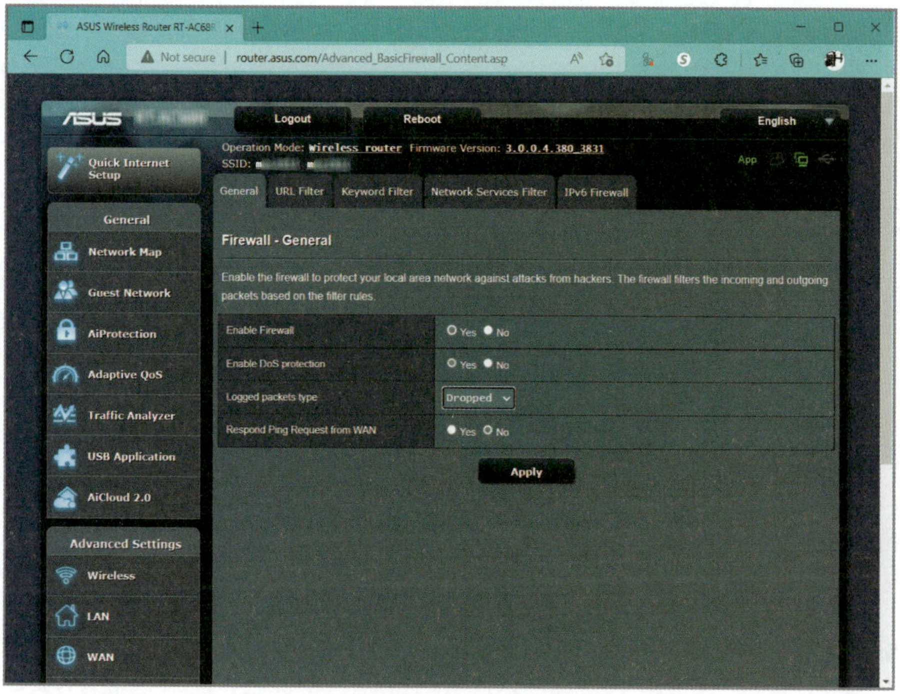

**FIGURE 7.10** A typical SOHO firewall dialog.

# POWER OVER ETHERNET

Ethernet devices require power, but in some cases, there is no power available at the best location for security and other types of Ethernet devices. The Power over Ethernet (PoE) series of standards enables standard Ethernet cables to carry data and up to 100W of power to devices. Thus, there is no need to run power and data cables separately.

Along with a PoE device, one of the following devices is needed: a PoE injector or a PoE switch.

Power sourcing equipment (PSE) refers to devices that can send PoE power and data, and powered devices (PDs) are those that use PoE power and data.

## Injectors

A PoE injector (Figure 7.11) connects to a standard AC outlet and has a pair of RJ-45 ports. The LAN port receives the unpowered Ethernet connection, while the PoE port adds power and sends power plus data to the destination device.

If you have only a few PoE devices, PoE injectors might be the most economical way to go.

Power

Data

**FIGURE 7.11** Typical 12 watt PoE injector. (Source: Tanotis.com)

## Switch

A PoE switch combines the functions of a managed or unmanaged switch with that of a PoE injector. Many variations are available, including the number of PoE and standard ports available, the amount of power available per PoE port, whether or not management functions are available, and the speeds supported for PoE ports.

Learn more about PoE switches at intellinetsolutions.com/pages/what-is-a-poe-switch-guide.

## PoE standards

The original PoE standard, 802.3af, supports up to 15.4 watts, suitable for Voice over IP and Wi-Fi signals.

PoE+, 802.3at, supports up to 30 watts, suitable for pan/tilt cameras, pocket-sized video IP phones, and alarm systems.

PoE++, 802.3bt is available in two power levels: Type 1 (60 watts) and Type 2 (100 watts). PoE++ is suitable for IP cameras, laptops, and desk-mounted video IP phones; choose Type 1 or Type 2 depending upon the power requirements of your devices.

# HUB

Before switches were common, Ethernet hubs were used to share connections. Unlike switches, which create direct MAC address to MAC address connections between devices for full-speed performance, hubs subdivide the bandwidth of the network among connected devices. For example, a four-port 100Mbps (Fast Ethernet) hub would provide only 25Mbps per device, while a four-port 100Mbps switch provides the full 100Mbps per device. Hubs also broadcast incoming traffic to all connected devices, making the connection process much slower than with switches.

Hubs have been almost completely replaced by switches, but you might encounter a few in the field. A hub is typically marked as a hub, and another way to distinguish a hub from a switch is that hubs frequently have a normal/upload button. This button enables the hub to be connected to another hub. Switches automatically stack to other switches.

# SOFTWARE-DEFINED NETWORKING

Software-defined networking (SDN) is a method of networking that logically separates network control logic from the physical devices that perform networking. SDN is typically used by organizations that have complex networks, want to improve policy control, need to improve network scalability, and want to remove vendor dependencies. SDN is also helpful in incorporating new concepts such as the Internet of Things, integrating cloud services with existing networks, working with Big Data, and improving IT mobility and consumerization.

> **TIP**
>
> To learn more about what SDN can do, see www.datacenterknowledge
> .com/archives/2016/03/31/top-five-apps-and-services-
> that-can-benefit-from-sdn.

A major advantage of SDN is its ability to provide centralized control of the network and make its condition visible outside the data center.

SDN has three components:

▶ Applications that relay network information and requests to SDN controllers
▶ SDN controllers are used to determine where network data packets are going. SDN controllers act as load balancers, sending instructions to networking devices
▶ Networking devices use the routing instructions received from the controllers

Think of SDN as being like a real-time GPS for a network, dynamically routing information according to changing traffic conditions on the network.

## CERTMIKE EXAM ESSENTIALS

▶ The major network equipment types you will encounter in a small-office/home-office (SOHO) network include cable and DSL modems, routers, switches, and network interface cards. These are the fundamental building blocks of networks at all levels.

▶ More advanced home and office networks frequently use Power over Ethernet for security and other uses and are often connected to fiber networks using optical network terminals.

▶ As you work with large office and enterprise networks, managed switches, hardware firewalls, and patch panels are the hardware components, and they may be managed as parts of a software-defined network.

## Practice Question 1

After a break-in and questions about security after working hours, your client has asked you to help add security features to their network. The client has software firewalls running on all computers and several unused Ethernet ports on outside walls. Which of the following recommendations would provide improved security? (Choose all that apply.)

A. Add power next to each Ethernet port to support cameras.
B. Use a PoE switch to provide power to cameras.
C. Add a hardware firewall to the network between the server and the Internet.
D. Add a hardware firewall to the network between the server and its clients.

## Practice Question 2

A friend of yours has asked you to help clean out a closet full of miscellaneous network hardware. Your friend is hoping to find a Gigabit Ethernet switch, a DSL modem, and an access point. Which of the following devices can your friend use? (Choose all that apply.)

A. This item is marked 10/100 Ethernet switch.
B. This item is marked 10/100/1000 Ethernet switch.
C. This item has an RJ-11 port, two antennas, and a four-port RJ-45 switch.
D. This item has an RJ-45 port and two antennas.
E. This item has an RJ-45 port and a four-port RJ-45 switch.

## Practice Question 1 Explanation

This question is designed to test your knowledge of the security-related network topics covered in this chapter. Let's evaluate these choices one at a time.

1. Option A (add power next to each Ethernet port to support cameras) is not necessary if Power over Ethernet (PoE) is used. The existing Ethernet ports can provide adequate power if PoE injectors or a PoE switch is used. This is not a good choice.

2. Option B (use a PoE switch to provide power to cameras) takes advantage of existing Ethernet networking. The standard needed to specify when purchasing the PoE switch depends on the number and type of cameras to install and other desired features. This is a good choice.

3. Option C (add a hardware firewall to the network between the server and the Internet) provides protection against undesirable network traffic. By locating it between the Internet and the server, the server and the entire network are protected. This is a good choice.

4. Option D (add a hardware firewall to the network between the server and its clients) is the right device but in the wrong location. If the server isn't protected, the rest of the network isn't protected either. This is not a good choice.

**Correct answers: B (use a PoE switch to provide power to cameras), and C (add a hardware firewall to the network between the server and the Internet)**

## Practice Question 2 Explanation

This question is designed to test your knowledge of the basic network hardware items discussed in this chapter. Let's evaluate each item to see if it fits your friend's "shopping" list.

1. Option A is a 10Mbps/100Mbps switch, commonly referred to as a Fast Ethernet switch. This is too slow, so it goes back in the parts closet.

2. Option B is 10Mbps/100Mbps/1000Mbps switch, commonly referred to as a Gigabit Ethernet switch. This is one of the items your friend wants.

3. Option C is a DSL modem. The tipoff is the presence of the RJ-11 port. This is also an item your friend wants.

4. Option D has an RJ-45 port and two antennas. The presence of antennas plus an RJ-45 port means it's an access point. Assuming it's fast enough for your friend's wireless network, this is also one your friend wants.

5. Option E is a router. The single RJ-45 port connects to a broadband cable modem, and the four RJ-45 ports mean it includes an Ethernet switch. However, it is not wireless, and it is not on the shopping list and will go back into the parts closet.

**Correct answers: B (10/100/1000 Gigabit Ethernet switch), C (DSL modem), and D (access point)**

# CHAPTER 8

# Wireless Networking Protocols

*Core 1 Objective 2.3:
Compare and contrast
protocols for wireless
networking.*

**Once** a niche curiosity, wireless networking has become a core networking technology in everything from small office/home office to enterprise environments. In this chapter, you will learn what you need to master Core 1, Objective 2.3, including the following:

▶ **Frequencies**
▶ **Channels**
▶ **Bluetooth**
▶ **802.11**
▶ **Long-range fixed wireless**
▶ **NFC**
▶ **Radio-frequency identification**

## FREQUENCIES

Wireless networking replaces network cable with radio waves on specific frequencies. Just as a car radio has separate AM and FM bands on different frequencies, Wi-Fi (often spelled as Wi-Fi on the CompTIA A+ exams) uses two different frequency bands: 2.4GHz and 5GHz. Wi-Fi frequencies are among the many radio frequencies (*RF*) that are regulated by various organizations around the world. Different types of devices are assigned different RF bands to help avoid interference.

## 2.4GHz

The 2.4GHz frequency is the more common of the two frequencies used by Wi-Fi. It is supported by almost all of the Wi-Fi standards discussed later in this chapter. It has a longer range than 5GHz. However, the 2.4GHz frequency also is used by some forms of Bluetooth wireless networking, older wireless phones, and other sources of radio frequency interference *(RFI)*, which can distort wireless signals.

## 5GHz

The 5GHz frequency is supported by about half of the Wi-Fi standards discussed later in this chapter. Because it runs at a higher frequency, 5GHz networks transmit and receive data much more quickly than 2.4GHz networks. However, their range is much shorter.

> **NOTE**
>
> The newest Wi-Fi standard to use 5GHz signaling, Wi-Fi 6 (also known as 802.11ax), is not specifically covered on the Core 1 exam. Don't confuse it with Wi-Fi 6e, which is the first Wi-Fi standard to use 6GHz signaling.

# CHANNELS

Wi-Fi's two frequency bands are sliced into a number of channels to enable different wireless local area networks (*WLANs*) to coexist nearby.

    2.4GHz channels supported worldwide are 1–11; only channels 1, 6, and 11 do not overlap with other channels. 5GHz channels supported in the US/Canada are 36, 40, 44, 48, 149, 153, 157, and 161.

> **EXAM TIP**
>
> Be sure to know the 2.4GHz and 5GHz channels for the Core 1 1101 exam. Also know the nonoverlapping 2.4GHz channels are 1, 6, and 11.

## Regulations

Regulations about allowable channels for each network band vary by nation. For example, in the United States and Canada, Wi-Fi 2.4GHz channels range from 1–11. However, in most other nations, 2.4GHz channels range from 1–13. This text covers channels 1–11.

Wi-Fi 5GHz channels are available in four groups in the United States and Canada. However, in other nations, only two or three groups of channels are permitted. This text covers all four groups of channels.

> **TIP**
>
> To learn more about Wi-Fi frequencies in different countries, see www
> `.lairdconnect.com/support/faqs/what-channels-are-`
> `supported-both-24-ghz-and-5ghz-band-most-countries`.

## 2.4GHz vs. 5GHz

Although 2.4GHz has a longer range than 5GHz, its major limitation is the narrow width of each channel and the overlapping frequencies of most channels. 2.4GHz channels are only 20Hz wide, and only channels 1, 6, and 11 do not overlap with each other (Figure 8.1). Although 2.4GHz supports channel bonding, which uses two channels at a time to send or receive data, it is not always feasible in a crowded environment with many 2.4GHz networks to use this feature. In Figure 8.1, you will notice that Channel 9 is used by two networks, although it overlaps other networks. Wireless routers and APs that are designed to dynamically scan nearby networks will select the least crowded channel. If you are manually configuring your network, using a Wi-Fi scanning app to see what channels are in use is a very good idea.

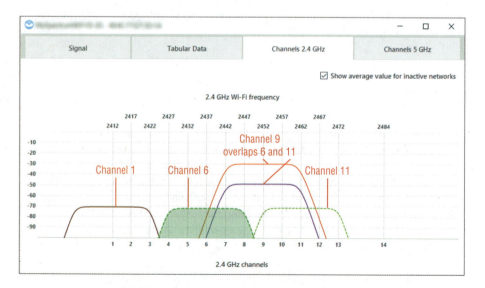

**FIGURE 8.1** Typical graph of Wi-Fi 2.4GHz networks showing how channels other than 1, 6, and 11 overlap other channels.

5GHz Wi-Fi offers many more channels to choose from than 2.4GHz. In the United States and Canada, 45 channels are available, and 24 are nonoverlapping. One of the reasons that 5GHz networks are faster is because they can easily use channel bonding for faster data than 2.4GHz (increasing the default 20Hz channel to 40 or 80Hz wide). In Figure 8.2, you can see how having more channels available enables channel bonding.

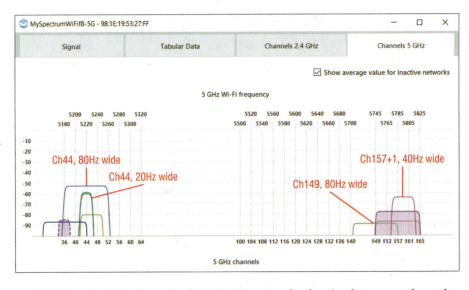

**FIGURE 8.2**   **Typical graph of Wi-Fi 5GHz networks showing how more channels help make channel bonding common.**

# 802.11

The Institute of Electrical and Electronics Engineers (*IEEE*) is an international organization responsible for developing and managing many types of electronics and network standards.

One of the families of standards managed by IEEE is 802.11, the family of wireless networking standards commonly called Wi-Fi. The Wi-Fi trademark is owned by the nonprofit Wi-Fi Alliance (www.wi-fi.org). Manufacturers may use the Wi-Fi trademark on their wireless products that are certified for Wi-Fi interoperability, so you can mix and match brands on your Wi-Fi networks.

> **EXAM TIP**
>
> Make sure you can name the different versions of Wi-Fi, the frequencies they support, and their speeds. There are likely to be several questions on the Core 1 1101 exam concerning these topics. The exam uses the term WiFi instead of Wi-Fi.

Wi-Fi has been improved many times, and although the oldest Wi-Fi standards are not widely used any more, you may encounter many different combinations of Wi-Fi hardware in the field.

## 802.11b

802.11b, the first version of Wi-Fi to support 2.4GHz channels, was first on the market. Initial versions were extremely slow, as the 11Mbps maximum connection speed was reduced by more than half when signal overhead and encryption were considered. Some vendors developed proprietary extensions of 802.11b that would run at up to 22Mbps by using two channels at the same time, a feature known as *channel bonding*. Today, 802.11b is also known as Wi-Fi 1.

## 802.11a

802.11a, the first version of Wi-Fi to support 5GHz channels, was intended to be the first one introduced. However, 802.11b beat it to market. Although 802.11a (up to 54Mbps) runs faster than 802.11b (up to 11Mbps), the higher cost of 802.11a equipment and the inability to connect to 802.11b networks made 802.11a not very popular. Some vendors developed dual-band 802.11a/b access points and wireless network cards (NICs).

Today, 802.11a is also known as Wi-Fi 2.

> **NOTE**
>
> Although both 802.11a and 802.11b are long since superseded, the two frequencies they support, dual-frequency hardware, and channel bonding, have been made standard on more recent versions.

## 802.11g

802.11g was designed to combine the speed of 802.11a (up to 54Mbps) to the popular 2.4GHz frequency band used by 802.11b. 802.11g networks are backwards-compatible with 802.11b (but not 802.11a). 802.11g is also compatible with newer Wi-Fi versions. Today, 802.11g is also known as Wi-Fi 3 (or WiFi 3).

## 802.11n

802.11n is based on 2.4GHz signaling. It supports 20 and 40MHz wide channels and multiple-input multiple-output (MIMO) signaling. MIMO enables 802.11n to send and receive both direct and reflected signals for more reliable connections (earlier versions treat reflected signals as interference). 802.11n supports speeds of up to 150Mbps with 20Hz channels and is backwards-compatible with 802.11b and g hardware. It supports up to 300Mbps with two antennas and 40Hz channels and up to 450Mbps with three antennas.

802.11n is also available in a dual-frequency version that supports both 2.4 and 5GHz channels. This hardware is often called N450 (300Mbps 5GHz and 150Mps 2.4GHz) or N600 (300Mbps signaling on both channels) when channel bonding is available. It is backward-compatible with 802.11a using 20Hz channels. Today, 802.11n is also known as Wi-Fi 4 (or WiFi 4).

> **NOTE**
> 802.11ac access points and wireless routers have built-in 802.11n support for 2.4GHz networks.

## 802.11ac (Wi-Fi 5)

802.11ac, also known as Wi-Fi 5, uses 5GHz signaling only. 802.11ac supports up to 80Hz wide channels and multiuser MIMO (MU-MIMO) for more reliable downlink connections to multiple devices at the same time. 802.11ac APs and wireless routers support different numbers of AP spatial data streams (up to four) with speeds up to 433Mbps per stream. 802.11ac devices typically include the maximum data rate for both 5GHz and 2.4GHz devices (since they also support 2.4GHz Wireless-N). For example, an AC1900 router typically provides 1300Mbps (433Mbps x 3 AC) plus 600Mbps (300Mbps 2.4GHz and 300Mbps 5GHz N) maximum data rate. The maximum throughput possible with Wi-Fi 5 is 3.5Gbps.

## 802.11ax (Wi-Fi 6)

802.11ax, also known as Wi-Fi 6, includes support for both 2.4GHz and 5GHz channels and supports up to eight AP spatial streams. Its version of MU-MIMO works in both downlink and uplink directions, and it can send and receive more data in a specified amount of time. Wi-Fi 6 also includes a feature known as BSS coloring, which helps reduce interference from other equipment on the same channel. 802.11ax APs and routers support 160Hz channels and can provide total speeds of up to 9.6 Gbps.

Table 8.1 compares the maximum throughput speed and frequencies supported by Wi-Fi 1 (802.11b) through Wi-Fi 6 (802.11ax).

**TABLE 8.1** Wi-Fi 1 Through Wi-Fi 6 Speeds and Frequencies

| Wi-Fi Version | 802.11 Version | Maximum Throughput | Frequencies Supported |
|---|---|---|---|
| Wi-Fi 1 | 802.11b | 11Mbps | 2.4 GHz |
| Wi-Fi 2 | 802.11a | 54Mbps | 5 GHz |
| Wi-Fi 3 | 802.11g | 54Mbps | 2.4 GHz |

| Wi-Fi Version | 802.11 Version | Maximum Throughput | Frequencies Supported |
|---|---|---|---|
| Wi-Fi 4 | 802.11n | 450/600Mbps | 2.4 GHz (5GHz optional) |
| Wi-Fi 5 | 802.11ac | 3.5Gbps | 5 GHz |
| Wi-Fi 6 | 802.11ax | 9.6Gbpx | 2.4GHz, 5 GHz |

**NOTE**

Wi-Fi 6e APs and routers use the new 6GHz radio band, which has no overlap with the previous 2.4 or 5GHz channel bands, and has space for seven 160Hz wide channels. It is backward-compatible with Wi-Fi 6 but provides much greater speed, lower latency, and greater capacity for larger WLANs.

Both Wi-Fi 5 and Wi-Fi 6/6e are designed to support Wireless Mesh Networking (*WMN*), which enables a wireless router to connect with two or more satellites to provide seamless coverage of a larger home or office than a single wireless router or AP can do.

# BLUETOOTH

Bluetooth is a short-range wireless standard that is designed for connections between mobile devices and PCs and between I/O devices and mobile devices or PCs. Common devices that use Bluetooth include wireless keyboards and mice, headsets, speaker systems, smart watches, automobile and other vehicles, and fitness trackers.

Bluetooth is built into most laptops, all mobile devices, and some desktop computers. For laptops and desktops lacking built-in Bluetooth, a Bluetooth-USB adapter can be plugged into a USB 2.0 or faster Bluetooth port.

Bluetooth uses pairing to make connections. To connect a Bluetooth peripheral, turn on Bluetooth on the mobile device or computer. Start the pairing process (Windows 11 version shown in Figure 8.3).

Specify Bluetooth as the device type to add and then select a device (Figure 8.4).

Enter a PIN as prompted or click a button on the device to pair the peripheral and your computer or mobile device. At the end of the process, you can use the newly connected peripheral.

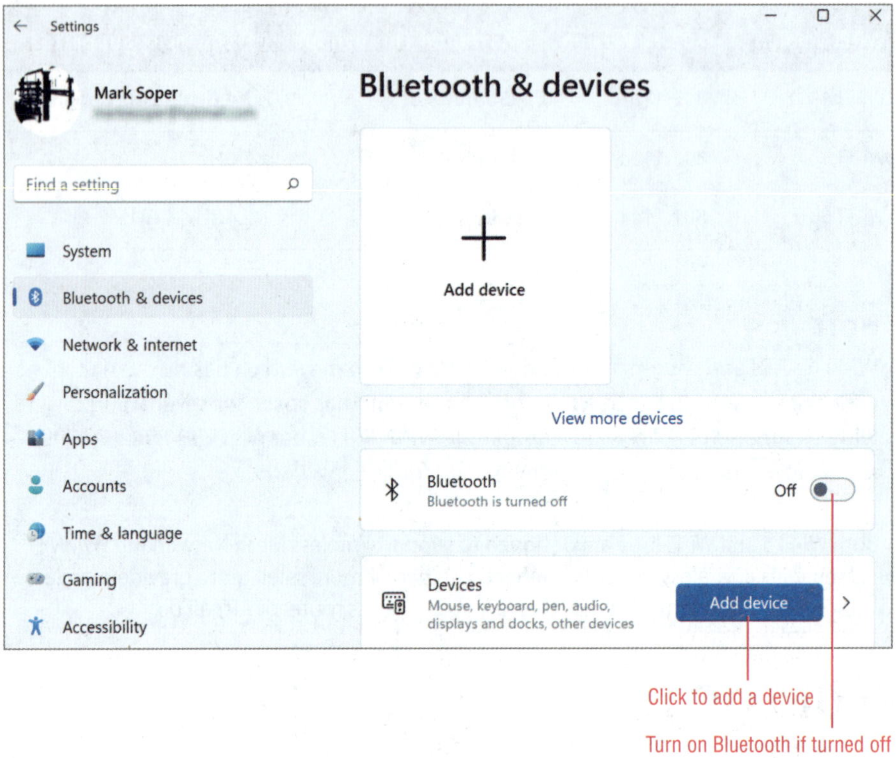

Click to add a device

Turn on Bluetooth if turned off

**FIGURE 8.3** **Enabling Bluetooth on a Windows 11 laptop.**

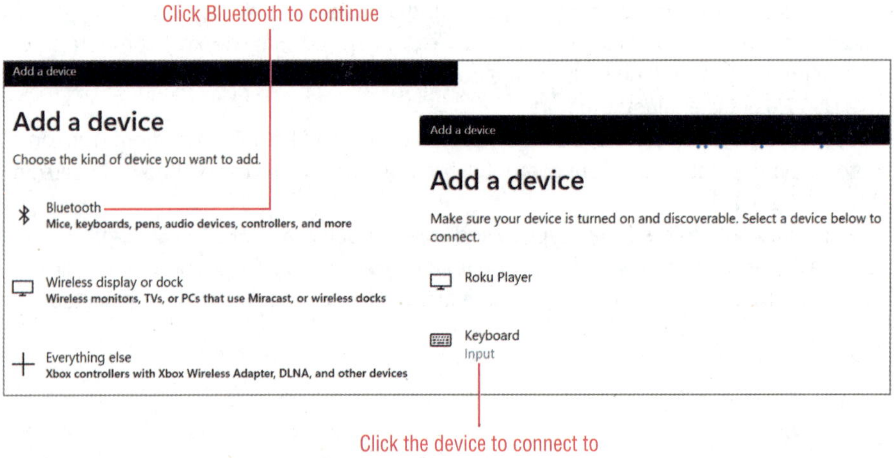

Click Bluetooth to continue

Click the device to connect to

**FIGURE 8.4** **Selecting Bluetooth as the type of device, and then select the device to add.**

**EXAM TIP**

Remember the steps in the Bluetooth pairing process:

1. Enable Bluetooth.
2. Enable pairing.
3. Find a device for pairing.
4. Enter the appropriate PIN code.
5. Test connectivity.

## Bluetooth Versions and Speeds

Bluetooth is available in versions 1.x through 5.x. 1.x offers basic Bluetooth data pairing and a range of up to 10 meters or 33 feet. It also introduced frequency-hopping to help avoid conflicts with other devices in the 2.4GHz spectrum. Newer Bluetooth versions have improved pairing speeds, improved data rates, longer ranges, and, starting in Bluetooth 4.x, improved support for low-power devices such as smart watches and fitness trackers. Bluetooth 5.x has the best audio quality so far, improved power usage, and can transmit to two devices at the same time. Previous Bluetooth versions can connect to multiple devices at the same time but transmit to them at different times.

When Bluetooth adapters and devices of different versions are paired with each other, the adapter is backwards-compatible with the devices supporting earlier versions.

# LONG-RANGE FIXED WIRELESS

Companies that need network and Internet connections between buildings where fiber broadband or fast copper connections aren't available or rural users who don't want the long latency inherent in satellite Internet use microwave wireless networking, sometimes called *long-range fixed wireless*.

## Unlicensed

Internet service providers that provide Internet access using wireless networking are typically referred to as wireless Internet service providers (WISP). Long-range fixed wireless can use the same unlicensed radio bands as Wi-Fi (2.4GHz, 5GHz, 6GHz as well as 900MHz). To avoid interference with existing wireless networks, some long-range fixed wireless use specialized hardware such as highly directional antennas (Figure 8.5) with high gain and multiple channels.

To help avoid interference from foliage and buildings, most vendors perform site surveys to determine whether a particular location is suitable, and the antennas used by a client might need to be placed on a tower or side of a multistory building. Although the month-to-month cost of a particular service might be comparable to cable or DSL, the up-front expenses for a site survey and antenna placement can add hundreds of dollars to the overall expense.

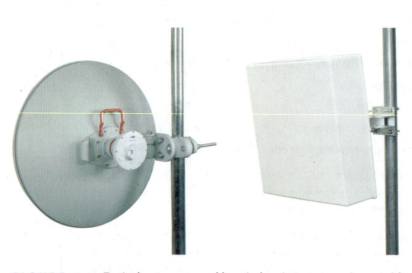

**FIGURE 8.5** Typical antennas used by wireless Internet service providers. (Source: Infinite Electronics International, Inc.)

Where 5G cellular is available, some vendors offer a plug-and-play 5G solution that uses a 5G router to connect users to the 5G cellular network.

## Licensed

Vendors who provide wireless Internet service may prefer to use licensed channels to avoid interference issues and provide better QoS. Licensed frequency bands are controlled in the United States by the Federal Communications Commission (FCC) and are assigned to various types of wireless, radio, and TV communications.

> **EXAM TIP**
>
> Licensed long-range fixed wireless provides better service than unlicensed fixed wireless.

## Power

Long-range fixed wireless transmitters and receivers must be connected to AC power. Inside the home or business being served, the router and switches or other network hardware must also be connected to AC power.

Battery backup options are available in some cases, but these will provide service for only a limited time.

## Regulatory Requirements for Wireless Power

To avoid wireless device interference with other devices using the increasingly busy spectrum, the FCC has several regulations for wireless power output. A good summary of these is available at www.air802.com/fcc-rules-and-regulations.html.

Here are some highlights:

▶ 2.4GHz point-to-point wireless signals with a 1 watt (30 dBm) transmitter cannot exceed 36 dBm or 4 watts
▶ 5GHz wireless signals support 250mW to 1 watt transmitter power, depending upon the frequency band in use

# NFC

Near field communications (*NFC*) is a very short-range wireless technology that enables devices to exchange information over a distance of 10 cm or closer.

NFC is commonly used for touchless payment transactions with services such as Apple Pay or Google Pay, but it can be used for sending and receiving messages between smartphones or other mobile devices, unlocking NFC-enabled security devices, sending print jobs with NFC-enabled printers, and so on. NFC is enabled through the Settings menu on your device.

# RADIO-FREQUENCY IDENTIFICATION

Radio-Frequency Identification (*RFID*) uses tags that are activated by radio waves. Depending upon the application, an RFID tag can trigger an alarm, be used to identify a specific user or item, and much more.

RFID tags that are used for inventory control or as anti-theft devices attached to a product or product package typically use chips that don't require on-board power; an RFID scanner's radio signal activates the chip. RFID scanners can be connected to existing smartphones, laptops, or other devices via Bluetooth or USB ports.

RFID technology used in E-Z Pass or I-Pass toll road/toll bridge payment receivers do require power and are connected to the vehicle's power system.

## CERTMIKE ESSENTIALS

▶ Wi-Fi 2.4 GHz has only three channels (1, 6, and 11) that don't interfere with each other, while Wi-Fi 5GHz has 24 nonoverlapping channels, making 5GHz much easier to deploy in areas with a lot of wireless networks already in place.

▶ Wi-Fi 802.11a, 802.11ac, and 802.11ax use 5GHz frequencies. 802.11b, 802.11g, and 802.11n use 2.4GHz frequencies. Some 802.11n hardware also supports 5GHz frequencies. 802.11ax supports both 2.4 and 5GHz frequencies.

▶ Bluetooth, NFC, and RFID have specialized uses, but cannot replace Wi-Fi because they are not designed to route Internet traffic.

## Practice Question 1

You are helping a friend set up a wireless network using a surplus 802.11n (Wi-Fi 4) router. Your friend wants to use Channel 149 because there is no wireless network using it. However, only channels 1–11 can be detected by the router. What is the reason?

A.  The router is defective and should not be used.
B.  The manufacturer must provide a special code to enable three-digit channels.
C.  802.11n routers are not required to support channels above 11.
D.  Your friend needs to attach another antenna to the wireless router.

## Practice Question 2

Your client wants to use Bluetooth interfacing for a printer, a keyboard, and a headset for listening to music. The computer doesn't have on-board Bluetooth, so purchasing and installing a USB-Bluetooth adapter is necessary. The headset recommends Bluetooth 5 or above, while the printer and keyboard don't specify a particular Bluetooth version. Which of the following is the best strategy to follow?

A.  Buy two Bluetooth adapters: Bluetooth 5.1 and an older Bluetooth version.
B.  Buy three Bluetooth adapters, one for each device.
C.  Buy a Bluetooth 5.1 adapter
D.  All of the above strategies will work equally well.

## Practice Question 1 Explanation

This question is designed to test your knowledge of the differences between 802.11 wireless networks. Let's evaluate these choices one at a time.

1. Option A (the router is defective and should not be used) is not likely. A defective router would probably not work at all. This is not a good choice.

2. Option B (the manufacturer must provide a special code to enable three-digit channels) is not true. There are no special codes needed to make channel ranges available on a wireless router. This is not the correct answer either.

3. Option C (802.11n routers are not required to support channels above 11) is the right answer. Channels from 36 up require 5GHz support. This is an optional feature of 802.11n networking; not all 802.11n hardware supports 5GHz.

4. Option D (your friend needs to attach another antenna to the wireless router) is not correct. Wireless routers include all of the antennas they will need. This is not a good choice.

**Correct answer: C. 802.11n routers are not required to support channels above 11**

## Practice Question 2 Explanation

This question is designed to test your knowledge of the basic Bluetooth features discussed in this chapter. Let's evaluate each answer to see if it's the best strategy.

1. Option A (buy two Bluetooth adapters: Bluetooth 5.1 and an older Bluetooth version): This isn't necessary. Bluetooth supports multiple devices. This is not the best answer.

2. Option B (buy three Bluetooth adapters, one for each device): Again, Bluetooth supports multiple devices, so this is also not necessary and is not the best answer.

3. Option C (buy a Bluetooth 5.1 adapter): This is the best answer. Bluetooth 5.1 will support any current and earlier Bluetooth standard and will support multiple items.

4. Option D (all of the above strategies will work equally well): This is completely false. Two of the three answers use up additional USB ports and don't improve Bluetooth support at all.

**Correct answer: C. Buy a Bluetooth 5.1 adapter**

# CHAPTER 9

# Networked Host Services

## Core 1 Objective 2.4: Summarize services provided by networked hosts.

**Network** hosts do much more than share files and printers. Depending upon the size and scope of the network, many different physical servers and server appliances are keeping the network functioning and safe and enabling it to manage complex industrial processes and work with the burgeoning Internet of Things (IoT). In this chapter, you will learn what you need to master Core 1, Objective 2.4, including the following:

▶ Server roles
▶ Internet appliances
▶ Legacy/embedded systems
▶ Internet of Things devices

## SERVER ROLES

Many different types of servers are used to manage network activities. While some of these may have the familiar tower or rackmount form factor, a lot of them are built into other devices. But whether they are discrete or combination, physical or virtual, they make the network work.

Many server roles discussed in this chapter support network protocols such as HTTP/HTTPS, SMTP, POP3, IMAP, DHCP, and DNS. To learn more about these protocols and other protocols, refer to Chapter 6, "TCP/IP Ports and Protocols."

## DNS

A DNS server converts the URL you enter into a browser or other Internet-enabled application into the actual IP address of the website you are attempting to reach. For example, if you ping Google's public website by name, you will see the DNS server translate the Google URL into the Google IP address:

1. Open the Command Prompt window.
2. Click Search, type **cmd**, and press Enter.
3. Type **ping google.com** and press Enter. You will see the current IP address for Google.com. For example, at the time of this writing, the address was 142.251.32.14.

In a normal network adapter configuration, two DNS servers are specified; a primary DNS server is used for lookups, and the secondary DNS server is used if the primary DNS server fails. DNS servers typically reside on public servers, although some network configurations route DNS requests through private gateways.

In Figure 9.2 later in this chapter, the normal Obtain DNS Server Address Automatically setting has been replaced by the Google IPv4 DNS server addresses: 8.8.8.8 and 8.8.4.4. Google also offers IPv6 DNS server addresses: 2001:4860:4860::8888 and/or 2001:4860:4860::8844. Many users prefer to specify Google DNS or other public DNS addresses because they are more reliable than the DNS servers configured by Internet service providers or other local network providers. IT administrators, on the other hand, prefer to have users access the DNS servers belonging to their organizations.

To switch to manually configured DNS addresses, follow these steps in Windows 10:

1. Click Start, then Settings, and then Network & Internet.
2. Click your network connection.
3. Click Change Adapter Options.
4. Right-click the network adapter you use and select Properties (Figure 9.1).
5. If prompted, provide the appropriate password or PIN.
6. Click Internet Protocol Version 4 (TCP/IPv4) and then Properties.
7. Click Use The Following DNS Server Addresses.
8. Enter the DNS server addresses you want (Figure 9.2).
9. Click OK.

To change IPv6 DNS addresses, click Internet Protocol Version 6 (TCP/IPv6) and then Properties in step 6 and continue with steps 7–9.

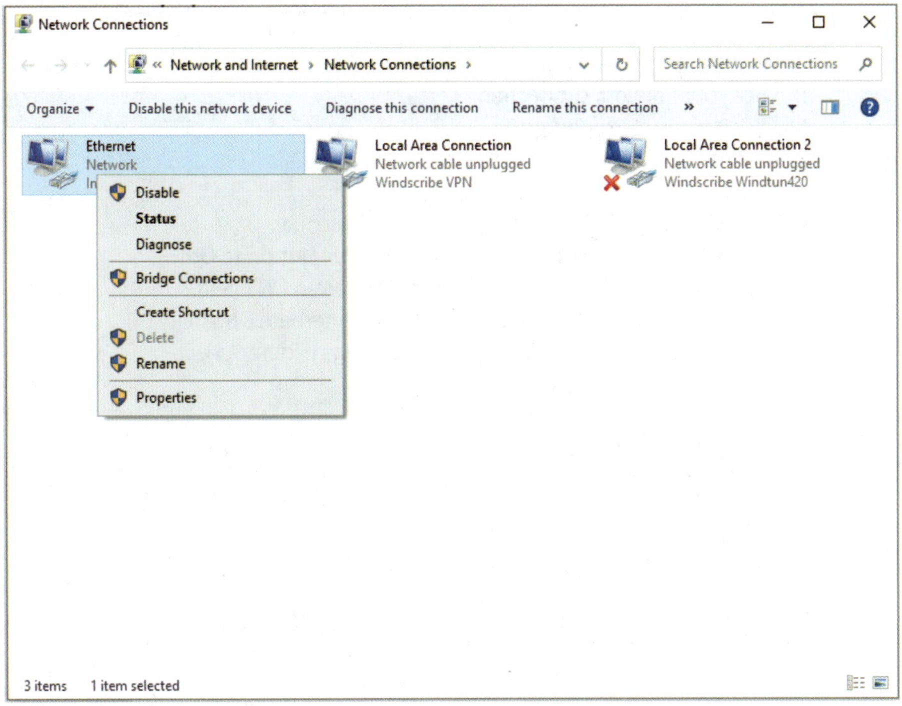

**FIGURE 9.1** Preparing to view properties for an Ethernet adapter in Windows 10. (Source: Microsoft Corporation)

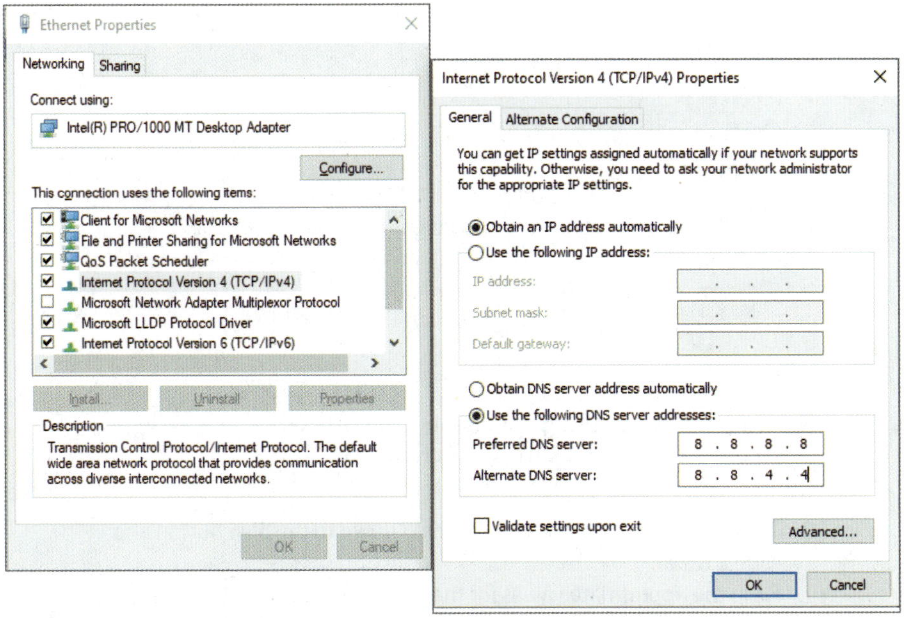

**FIGURE 9.2** Entering the Google IP v4 DNS server addresses. (Source: Microsoft Corporation)

To switch to manually configured DNS addresses, follow these steps in Windows 11:

1. Click Start, then Settings, and then Network & Internet.
2. Click your network connection.
3. Click Hardware Properties.
4. Find the DNS Server Assignment section of the dialog box and click the Edit button.
5. Open the Edit DNS Settings menu and click Manual.
6. To change the IPv4 DNS settings, drag the IPv4 button to On.
7. Enter the first DNS server address in the Preferred DNS field.
8. Enter the second DNS server address in the Alternate DNS field.
9. Do not change the default encryption settings (Figure 9.3).

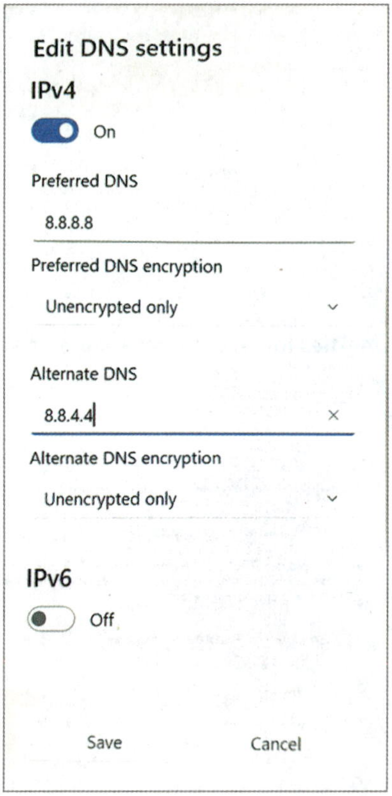

**Edit DNS settings**

**IPv4**

On

Preferred DNS

8.8.8.8

Preferred DNS encryption

Unencrypted only

Alternate DNS

8.8.4.4

Alternate DNS encryption

Unencrypted only

**IPv6**

Off

Save        Cancel

**FIGURE  9.3   Using the Google IP v4 DNS server addresses in Windows 11. (Source: Microsoft Corporation)**

10. To change the IPv6 DNS settings, scroll down to the IPv6 button and slide it to On.
11. Fill in the appropriate values for the IPv6 preferred and alternate DNS addresses.

12. Click Save.
13. Provide the appropriate password or PIN if prompted.

**EXAM TIP**

To learn more about how DNS works, see www.lifewire.com/what-is-a-dns-server-2625854.

## DHCP

A DHCP server assigns IP addresses to the network computers and devices on a network. This function is built into SOHO routers, but on large networks a dedicated DHCP server performs this task. If the DHCP server fails, devices on the network automatically assign themselves APIPA IP addresses in the 169.254.x.x range.

## Fileshare

A fileshare server (also known as a *file server*) is used to provide file storage for network devices. On a workgroup network, files and folders can be shared by any computer that has file and printer sharing enabled. Fileshare servers on domain networks might incorporate local, cloud, or a mixture of local and cloud storage.

## Print Servers

A print server distributes and manages print jobs on network-connected printers. Although dedicated print servers were once common, most networks today use multifunction servers that include print server functions. On a workgroup network, any computer with a connected printer can function as a print server by enabling file and print sharing. You can use the Print Management app (printmanagement.msc) to manage printers on a Windows Pro computer (Figure 9.4).

To learn more about print servers, see Chapter 20, "Printer and Multifunction Device Configuration."

## Mail Servers

A mail server is responsible for sending (outbound mail server) or receiving (inbound mail server) email, routing it to its destination.

- ▶ Simple Mail Transfer Protocol (SMTP) is the standard outbound email server protocol.
- ▶ Inbound email servers use either Post Office Protocol 3 (POP3) or Internet Mail Access Protocol (IMAP) protocols.

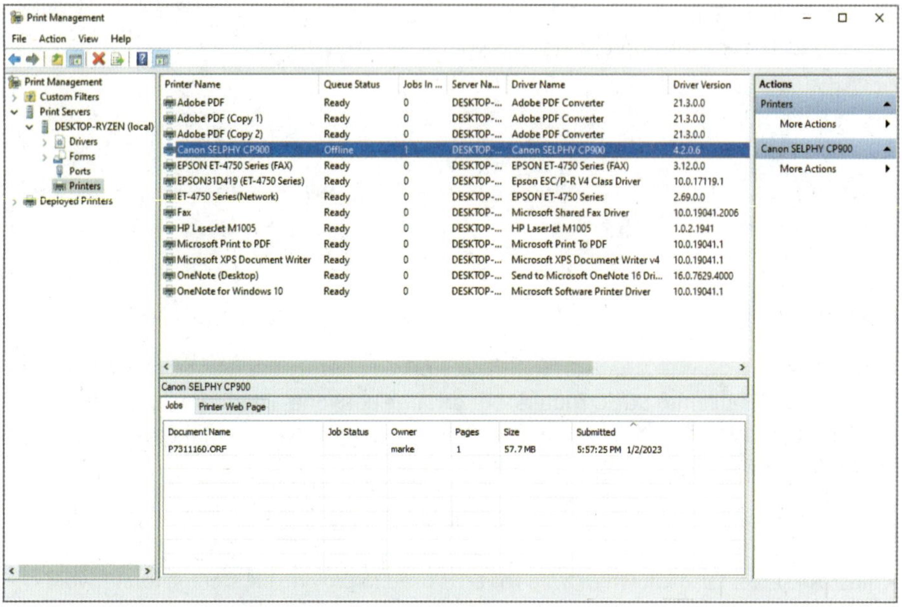

**FIGURE 9.4**   **A Print Management dialog from a Windows Pro computer. (Source: Microsoft Corporation)**

When an email client app is configured, entering the correct addresses and port numbers for the SMTP and POP3 or IMAP servers is a major part of the process. Although these protocols have standard TCP or UDP port numbers, some email providers prefer to use alternate port numbers for additional security.

> **EXAM TIP**
>
> To learn more about how email servers work, see `whatismyipaddress.com/mail-server`.

## Syslog

Syslog is short for System Logging Protocol, and a Syslog server is a server that receives system log or event messages on a network. Windows uses its own Windows Event Log, but Unix and Linux-based systems and web servers as well as network hardware (routers, switches, firewalls, and so on) use Syslog. By default, Syslog uses UDP port 514, but some devices use TCP port 1468 so message delivery can be confirmed.

Third-party Syslog servers can capture and filter messages to provide easier-to-understand information from Syslog. Windows Event Log messages can be converted into a Syslog-compatible format with third-party utilities. Systems running macOS can use third-party products that support Syslog.

**NOTE**

To learn more about how syslog works, see `www.paessler.com/it-explained/syslog`.

## Web Servers

A web server is a computer or appliance that is configured to display web pages using either HyperText Transfer Protocol (HTTP) or HTTP Secure (HTTPS). When a web server receives a request for a page, it assembles the page, which might include HTML, JavaScript, image files, Java, and other components, and sends it back to the receiver.

Many organizations use multiple web servers combined with load balancing (see "Load Balancers" later in this chapter) to avoid bottlenecks. In Windows, you can set up a web server by enabling Internet Information Services (IIS) from the Windows Features menu (Figure 9.5).

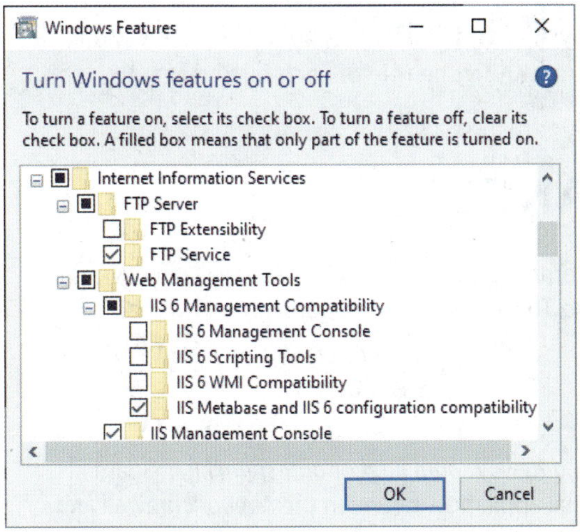

**FIGURE 9.5** Configuring Windows IIS in Windows 10 Pro. (Source: Microsoft Corporation)

**NOTE**

To learn more about how web servers work, see `www.serverwatch.com/web-servers`.

### Authentication, Authorization, and Accounting

Authentication, authorization, and accounting (*AAA*) refers to a security framework that is used to manage network users and their activity by authenticating users, authorizing them to use specific network resources, and accounting for the resource time they use.

The two major protocols used for AAA include Remote Authentication Dial-In User Service (RADIUS) used by networks that don't use Cisco network hardware, and Terminal Access Controller Access-Control System Plus (TACACS+), which supports Cisco network hardware. A third AAA protocol, Diameter, is based on RADIUS and is used primarily by cellular network providers.

RADIUS and Diameter perform all three AAA functions, while TACACS+ uses Kerberos for authentication.

> **NOTE**
>
> To learn more about how AAA functions work, see `www.fortinet.com/ resources/cyberglossary/aaa-security`.

> **EXAM TIP**
>
> DNS, DHCP, fileshare, print, mail, Syslog, and AAA servers each provide various services to networked client systems. Know the role of each for the exam!

# INTERNET APPLIANCES

A number of vendors now produce Internet appliances, which are specialized devices or services that perform specific functions. These include spam gateways, UTM, load balancers, and proxy servers.

### Spam Gateways

A spam gateway is also referred to as a *gateway spam filter* or *anti-spam filter*. Spam filters can be installed as physical or virtual appliances between the network firewall and the inbound email server, and some also work on outbound mail. They prevent unwanted emails from arriving or from being sent.

Other types of spam filters are hosted spam filters, which are cloud-based and filter email before it reaches the network, and desktop spam filters, which are used by individual users to filter email.

Spam gateways and other types of spam filters use a variety of methods to block unwanted email, including the following:

▶ Content filtering (blocks email based on sender, text in the header or body of the email, and types of attachments)

- ▶ Bayesian filtering (learns the types of email that users mark as spam to improve automatic spam detection rates)
- ▶ Rules-based filtering (blocks emails that match specified rules)
- ▶ Graylisting (blocks first email from an unknown source, but permits subsequent emails from source: blocks a lot of spam because spam is usually sent only once from a given address to a given address)

> **NOTE**
>
> To learn more about how spam gateways work, see `www.spamtitan.com/ gateway-spam-filter` and `www.socketlabs.com/blog/what-is- a-spam-filter-and-how-does-it-work`.

## Unified Threat Management

Unified Threat Management (*UTM*) refers to physical or virtual appliances that provide a wide variety of security services such as firewall, remote access and VPN, anti-malware, and intrusion protection among others to a network. A UTM is positioned at the connection between the Internet and the organization's network.

Stream-based UTMs are physical devices, and proxy UTMs use network security software along with a proxy server.

> **NOTE**
>
> To learn more about how UTM works and for its pros and cons, see `www.geeks forgeeks.org/what-is-unified-threat-management-utm` and `www.esecurityplanet.com/networks/utm-appliance`.

## Proxy Servers

A proxy server acts as a gateway between computers or devices on a network and the Internet. As it receives requests for Internet content (such as a web page), it checks to see if the content has already been requested by other computers and stored in the proxy server. In such a case, the proxy server's copy of the web page is used to fulfill the request, providing a faster response for the requesting device and less traffic to and from the Internet. A proxy server can also act as a firewall and filter, blocking prohibited content from reaching the requesting device. All devices connected to a proxy server must use the proxy server's address in their network configuration (Figure 9.6).

> **NOTE**
>
> To learn more about different types of proxy servers and how proxy servers work, see `www.fortinet.com/resources/cyberglossary/proxy- server`.

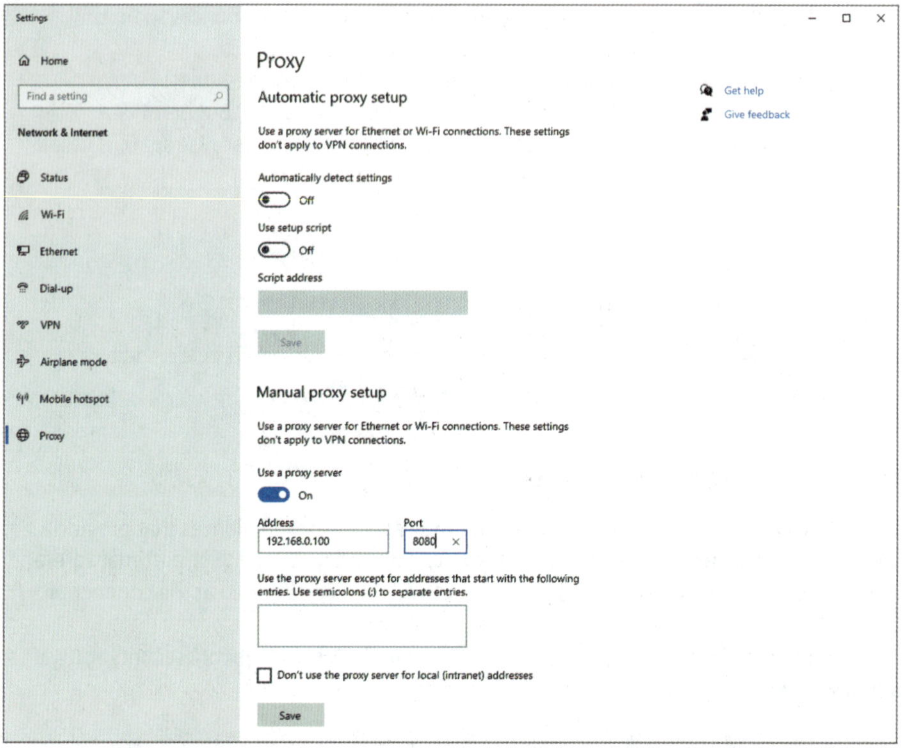

**FIGURE 9.6** Configuring a manual proxy server in Windows 10. (Source: Microsoft Corporation)

## Load Balancers

A load balancer is a network device that distributes network traffic to other devices. A typical application for a load balancer is to even out the amount of traffic to servers hosting the same content. For example, without a load balancer, Server A might wind up with two dozen client requests, while Server B might have only four or five. With a load balancer, both Server A and Server B handle similar numbers of client requests or similar amounts of traffic.

Load balancing is an example of a reverse proxy server. It intercepts incoming web traffic and routes it to a specific server. If it uses dynamic balancing, it routes it to the server with the least traffic or activity. Load balancing devices need to be placed in specific locations to improve network performance.

> **NOTE**
>
> To learn more about different types of load balancing and what it can do, see www.ictshore.com/networking-fundamentals/load-balancer.

# LEGACY/EMBEDDED SYSTEMS

Legacy and embedded systems are where older operating systems and devices are often found in organizations. For example, embedded versions of Windows 8.1 will be supported until January 2023.

Embedded systems refer to devices such as home appliances, security cameras, automotive, medical, or industrial devices such as HVAC that have their own integrated components such as RAM and/or CPU and do not necessarily require a system to control them. Some embedded systems use components that are controlled by legacy operating systems such as Windows 7. These pose a major security threat.

Industrial environments often include complex combinations of legacy and embedded systems, programmable logic controllers, and sensors. This section covers how these environments are managed.

## Supervisory Control and Data Acquisition

Supervisory Control and Data Acquisition (*SCADA*) refers to systems that are used to manage industrial control systems (ICS) hardware and software. SCADA connects hardware with software to monitor local remote processes; gathers real-time data; provides human-machine interfacing with sensors, valves, and other process components; and logs events and changes in process.

SCADA is used in food and beverage production, power production, transportation, and many other industries.

**NOTE**
For an introduction to SCADA and its uses, see `inductiveautomation`
`.com/resources/article/what-is-scada` and `scada-`
`international.com/what-is-scada`.

# INTERNET OF THINGS DEVICES

The Internet of Things (*IoT*) refers to networked devices that have embedded sensors and other technologies for capturing and exchanging information with other devices on networks, including the Internet.

IoT devices fall into many categories, from small single-board computers such as the Raspberry Pi series that are designed for easy expansion with plug-in daughterboards (known as HATs) to embedded GPS fleet tracking, smart home appliances, multivendor home control apps, farm equipment control, farm animal herd tracking, drone control, and much more.

Before rolling out IoT devices for a specific task, be sure to determine how secure they are and whether additional security functionality can be added.

---

**NOTE**

For an introduction to IoT and IoT devices, see `www.softwaretesting help.com/iot-devices`. For examples of current IoT uses in a variety of industries, see `builtin.com/internet-things/iot-examples`.

---

## CERTMIKE ESSENTIALS

▶ Some types of server roles, such as DNS, DHCP, and mail servers, require that each client must be configured with the specific settings necessary to access the service.

▶ Internet appliances such as spam gateways, UTM, and load balancers work transparently to the user, but proxy servers require each client to be configured with manual settings or provided with scripts to configure the proxy settings.

▶ Legacy and embedded systems can represent security threats if they contain unsupported operating systems or devices that are no longer supported by the vendor. Internet of Things implementations may also pose a security threat if they include devices with weak security.

## Practice Question 1

A network with multiple servers has two problems: uneven server utilization and excessive numbers of outbound requests from the network for the same Internet content. Which two of the following will help improve network performance?

A. Load balancer
B. SCADA
C. Web server
D. Proxy server

## Practice Question 2

Which of the following is most likely to include some IoT devices?

A. Fileshare server
B. SCADA
C. Spam gateway
D. Authentication, authorization, and accounting (AAA)

## Practice Question 1 Explanation

This question is designed to test your knowledge of the differences between networked host services. Let's evaluate these choices one at a time.

1. Option A (Load balancer) is correct. Adding a load balancer to the network will help make sure that the load is spread across all servers.

2. Option B (SCADA) is incorrect. SCADA refers to industrial control systems.

3. Option C (Web server) is incorrect. A web server is used to handle web content requests coming into the server. A web server does not handle outbound requests.

4. Option D (Proxy server) is correct. A proxy server stores a copy of information requested from the Internet, so if it's requested again, the proxy server can use its copy. This helps reduce excessive numbers of outbound requests for the same information.

**Correct answer: A and D. Load balancer, Proxy server**

## Practice Question 2 Explanation

This question is designed to test your knowledge of how IoT devices are used in networks. Let's evaluate each answer to see if it's the best match.

1. Option A (Fileshare server) is incorrect. Fileshare servers can provide file sharing to all types of devices, including IoT, but they are not themselves IoT devices, which capture and send information to other devices.

2. Option B (SCADA) is correct. A SCADA implementation includes a wide variety of sensors, control devices, and displays. IoT devices are a good fit for SCADA.

3. Option C (Spam gateway) is incorrect. IoT devices are designed as the starting point for data gathering, not for processing it.

4. Option D (Authentication, authorization, and accounting [AAA]) is incorrect. AAA refers to the process of authenticating users, authorizing specific users to use network resources, and accounting for the resources used. IoT devices are not used specifically for these network functions.

**Correct answer: B. SCADA**

# CHAPTER 10

# Installing and Configuring Networks

## Core 1 Objective 2.5: Given a scenario, install and configure basic wired/wireless small office/home office (SOHO) networks.

**Setting** up a network is more than installing equipment. You must also understand how devices are identified on the network. In this chapter, you will learn what you need to master Core 1, Objective 2.5, including the following:

▶ Internet Protocol addressing

## INTERNET PROTOCOL ADDRESSING

Each device on an Internet Protocol (IP) network must have an IP address, and no two devices in a specific network can have the same address. These rules might sound simple, but it takes a lot of work behind the scenes to make it happen.

## IPv4

Most networks use the IPv4 addressing scheme. Each number in an IPv4 address is called an *octet* (an eight-bit byte). There are four octets in an IPv4 address, meaning it is a 32-bit address. The numbers used in an IP address are called *dotted decimal*, converted from binary to make them easier to read. If all IPv4 devices in the world were in a single network, there could be only 4.3 billion devices total (4.3×10 to the 9th power).

### Classes A, B, and C

Originally, IPv4 addresses were divided into three groups for general use, A, B, and C. In class A, only the first octet is used for networks (net ID), and the second, third, and fourth are used for devices on the network (host ID). Class A addresses run from 0.0.0.0 to 127.255.255.255. The problem with Class A is that only 128 networks are available, but there are more than 16 million hosts (devices) in each network! This is a big imbalance of networks versus hosts.

In class B, the first and second octets are used for net IDs, and the third and fourth octets are used for host IDs. Class B addresses (128.0.0.0 to 191.255.255.255) allow 65,534 hosts and 16,384 networks. Again, this is an imbalance of networks versus hosts.

In class C, the first, second, and third octets are used for net IDs, and the fourth octet is used for host IDs. Class C addresses (192.0.0.0 to 223.255.255.255) allow 254 hosts but more than 2 million networks. A network that needs more hosts must use a class B network in the A-B-C scheme.

To enable different-sized networks from the defaults, the A-B-C scheme also uses subnet masks along with IP addresses.

Figure 10.1 illustrates how class A, B, and C networks' IP addresses and subnet masks differ.

By changing the default subnet values shown in Figure 10.1, organizations can change the default number of net IDs and host IDs. For example, take a network starting with 192.168.0.1 that has 254 hosts. For security, you want to create four networks from one and assign each network to a different department.

By changing the subnet mask from its default of 255.255.255.0 to 255.255.255.192, we increase the number of networks to four and reduce the number of hosts per network to 62. One IP address in each of the new networks is set aside for broadcasting, and one IP address in each of the new networks is the starting address. You can do the math manually or use an online calculator Figure 10.2 shows the results of using the calculator at www .calculator.net/ip-subnet-calculator.html.

The /26 at the end of the subnet is how Classless Inter-Domain Routing (CIDR) expresses a subnet. CIDR enables IP addresses to be assigned in smaller blocks than the traditional A-B-C classes create. In a CIDR IP address, the address uses the same dotted-decimal notation we saw earlier, but with a twist. The four octets are called a *prefix*, defining the first network address, but instead of a conventional subnet mask, a suffix is used to specify how may bits are in the subnet.

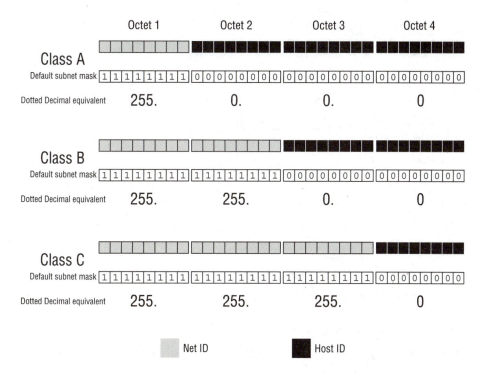

**F I G U R E   1 0 . 1**  **Class A, B, and C net ID and host ID comparison.**

In the example shown in Figure 10.2, 192.168.0.1/26, the starting IP address is 192.168.0.1, and the /26 indicates that the subnet uses 26 bits.

### Private Addresses

There are two categories of IPv4 addresses: private addresses and public addresses.

Private IP addresses are not visible to the Internet and typically have IP addresses in the 192.168.0 to 192.168.255 range. Other private IP address ranges include all IP addresses beginning with 10 (10.0.0.0 to 10.255.255.255) and addresses ranging from 172.16.0.0 to 172.31.255.255. Table 10.1 lists the reserved private IP addresses by class.

**T A B L E   1 0 . 1**  **Reserved Private IP Addresses by Class**

| Class | Private IP Address Range |
|---|---|
| Class A | 10.0.0.0 to 10.255.255.255 |
| Class B | 172.16.0.0 to 172.31.255.255 |
| Class C | 192.168.0.0 to 192.168.255.255 |

**IPv4 Subnet Calculator**

**Result**

| | |
|---|---|
| IP Address: | 192.168.0.1 |
| Network Address: | 192.168.0.0 |
| Usable Host IP Range: | 192.168.0.1 - 192.168.0.62 |
| Broadcast Address: | 192.168.0.63 |
| Total Number of Hosts: | 64 |
| Number of Usable Hosts: | 62 |
| Subnet Mask: | 255.255.255.192 |
| Wildcard Mask: | 0.0.0.63 |
| Binary Subnet Mask: | 11111111.11111111.11111111.11000000 |
| IP Class: | C |
| CIDR Notation: | /26 |
| IP Type: | Private |
| | |
| Short: | 192.168.0.1 /26 |
| Binary ID: | 11000000101010000000000000000001 |
| Integer ID: | 3232235521 |
| Hex ID: | 0xc0a80001 |
| in-addr.arpa: | 1.0.168.192.in-addr.arpa |
| IPv4 Mapped Address: | ::ffff:c0a8.01 |
| 6to4 Prefix: | 2002:c0a8.01::/48 |

**All 4 of the Possible /26 Networks for 192.168.0.\***

| Network Address | Usable Host Range | Broadcast Address: |
|---|---|---|
| 192.168.0.0 | 192.168.0.1 - 192.168.0.62 | 192.168.0.63 |
| 192.168.0.64 | 192.168.0.65 - 192.168.0.126 | 192.168.0.127 |
| 192.168.0.128 | 192.168.0.129 - 192.168.0.190 | 192.168.0.191 |
| 192.168.0.192 | 192.168.0.193 - 192.168.0.254 | 192.168.0.255 |

Network Class ○ Any   ○ A   ○ B   ⦿ C

Subnet    255.255.255.192 /26 ⌄

IP Address   192.168.0.1

**Calculate** ▶   Clear

**FIGURE 10.2** Using an online calculator to find out desired subnet values.

Use the `ipconfig /all` command in Windows or the `ifconfig` command in Linux and macOS to see the current private IP address for a computer.

**NOTE**

Many Linux distros now use the `ip` command with the address option (`ip address`) to display IP addresses on the current system instead of `ifconfig`. This command and its options are part of net-tools, a Linux tool package that is an optional feature of most Linux distros.

How do devices assigned to private IP addresses connect with the Internet? A router using a feature called Network Address Translation (NAT) does the job: the router is connected to the network using private IPv4 addresses, and when a device on that network requests an Internet resource, the router translates the private IP address into a public IP address, remembers which device asked for that resource, and sends it back to the correct device when it receives the resource from the Internet.

### Public Addresses

Public IP addresses are those that are visible to the Internet. These are assigned to companies with websites, Internet service providers (ISPs), Internet backbones, and others.

When a device on a private network connects to the Internet, the router translates its private address into a public IP address from the block of public IP addresses provided to the ISP. If you want to see the public IP address assigned to your network, you can visit a website such as `myexternalip.com` or `whatismyip.com` (Figure 10.3). Keep in mind that the public IP address will change from time to time depending upon the policies of your ISP.

**EXAM TIP**

Private addresses are used for internal networks within LANs and are not seen on the public Internet. Public addresses connect to the Internet and are visible to anyone on the Internet.

---

**My External IP address is ...**

---

**74.129.57.78**

---

**FIGURE 10.3** Seeing your public IP address with `myexternalIP.com`.

### Loopback Address for IPv4

A loopback address is an internal IP address that routes back to the local system. The IPv4 loopback address is 127.0.0.1. It is often used for testing with a command such as ping:

```
ping 127.0.0.1
```

## IPv6

Eventually, IPv6 will replace IPv4 as the standard IP addressing scheme used for networks and the Internet. IPv6 uses 128-bit IP addresses, enabling up to 340 undecillion (3.4×10 to the 38th power) addresses.

An IPv6 address is divided into eight 16-bit blocks. These blocks are converted into hexadecimal, and a colon separates each block from the next. In an Pv6 anycast address (the type of address assigned by an ISP), the first 64 bits of the address are the network portion (the first 48 to 56 bits are assigned by the ISP and the remainder are the subnet bits), and the second group of 64-bit is the host portion. See Figure 10.4.

> **TIP**
>
> In addition to anycast and loopback addresses, there are also unicast and multicast IPv6 addresses. To learn more about the different types of IPv6 addresses, see `www.ciscopress.com/articles/article .asp?p=2803866&seqNum=3`.

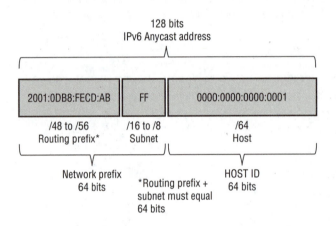

**FIGURE 10.4**  **The components of an anycast networked IPv6 address.**

Leading zeros are typically not displayed, but each block must have at least one digit. Keep in mind that hex numbering is 0–9, A–F. If an IpP6 address contains a contiguous sequence of blocks set to zero, a feature called *zero compression* is used to replace these blocks with ::, and there can only be one of these :: in an IPv6 address.

When an IPv6 device starts, it has a link-local address. This is true whether the network uses IPv6 or not. Here's a typical one (most begin with fe80):

```
fe80::b142:756b:414a:fd
```

As you can see from this example, :: has been used to replace blocks set to 0. How many? Start by counting the number of blocks listed.

```
fe80  b142  756b  414a  fd
 1     2     3     4     5
```

There are five blocks listed. Subtract five from eight (8 – 5) to get the answer, 3. The :: between fe80 and b142 replaces three blocks set to zero.

Because both Ipv4 and Ipv6 addressing schemes are in use until IPv4 is completely replaced, most devices are assigned both types of addresses. See Figure 10.5.

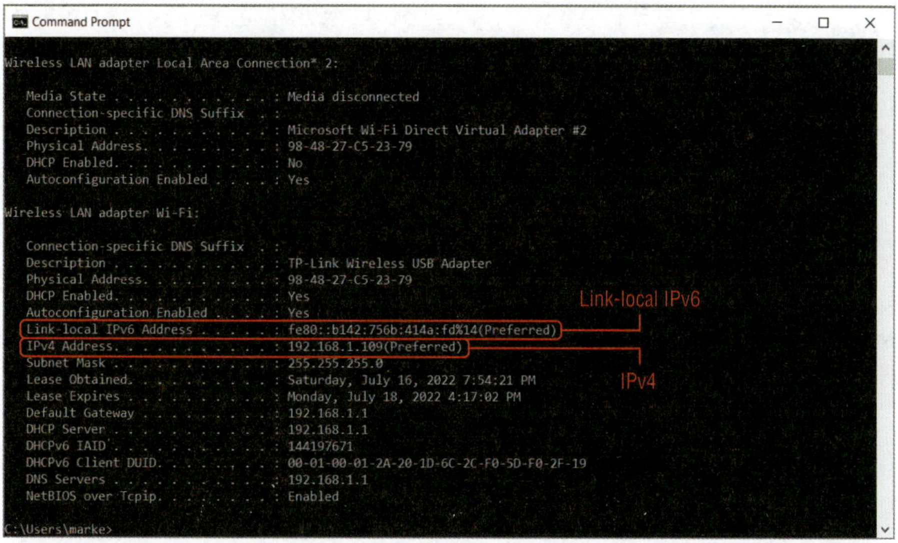

**FIGURE 10.5**   **A Wi-Fi network adapter with both IPv4 and IPv6 link-local addresses as viewed with ipconfig/add.**

## Loopback Address for IPv6

A loopback address is an internal IP address that routes back to the local system. In IPv6, the loopback address is 0:0:0:0:0:0:0:1 or ::1. It is often used for testing with a command such as ping.

```
ping ::1
```

## Static

IPv4 addresses are of two types: static and dynamic. Static IP addresses do not change; once a device (typically a server or network printer) is assigned an IP address, that address stays the same. Both public and private IP addresses can be static. Figure 10.6 illustrates configuring a Windows computer with a static IP address. Note that you must also add at least one (two are preferable) DNS servers when you use a static IP address.

A public IP address used by your router is usually dynamic (see the next section). However, if you are hosting a server, you might want to get a static address from your ISP. Check with your ISP for pricing and availability.

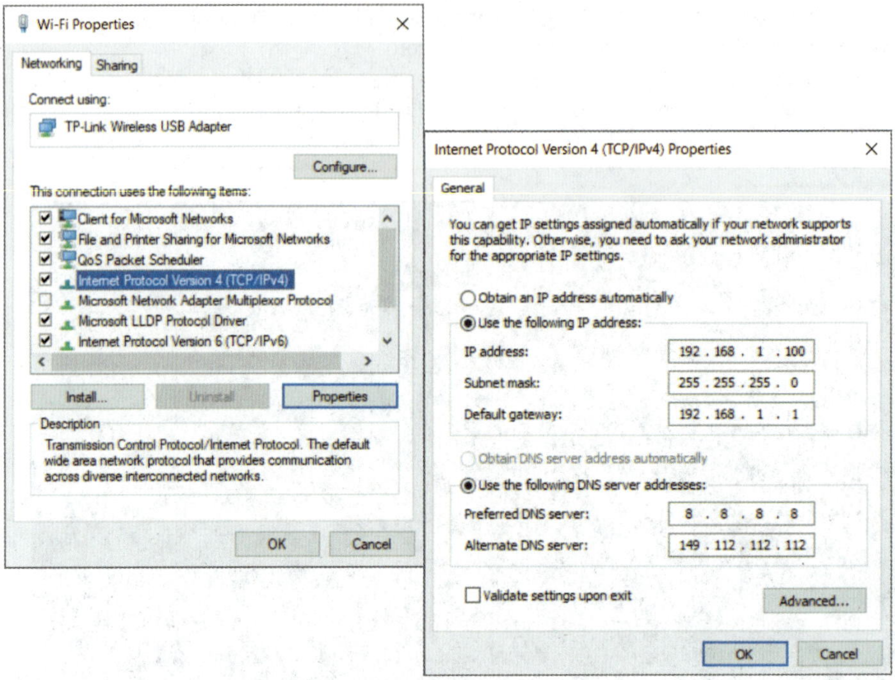

**FIGURE 10.6** Setting up a static IP address in Windows.

## Dynamic

Whether you're looking at the public IP address assigned to your router's WAN port by your ISP or the private IP address used by your PC or mobile device, it's probably dynamic. On a small network, a dynamic IP address is assigned by a DHCP server typically built into your router. Larger networks might have a dedicated DHCP server, and your ISP has a DHCP server that assigns dynamic IP addresses to routers that connect to the ISP.

If you are hosting a server on your network and prefer not to (or cannot) get a static IP address from your ISP, you can set up some of your devices with static IP addresses. That requires special router configuration to enable outside traffic to reach the server you are hosting.

## Gateway

The IP address that is assigned to the router's connection to the LAN is called the *gateway address*. The gateway allows access to outside networks such as the Internet. The DHCP server in the router assigns IP addresses according to the gateway address.

For example, a common gateway address on a private network is 192.168.0.1. The other computers on the network would be assigned (via DHCP or manually) to addresses ranging from 192.168.0.2 to 192.168.0.254 (0 and 255 are reserved values).

The default gateway IP address can sometimes be changed in the router's configuration.

## Automatic Private IP Addressing

In a typical IP network, most or all devices are given their IP addresses by a DHCP server. However, if the devices cannot connect to a DHCP server, they can still work as a local (non-routable and therefore no Internet access) area network. In Windows, this is referred to as Automatic Private IP Addressing (*APIPA*). Any computer that normally gets an IP address from DHCP uses its form of APIPA if DHCP doesn't provide an IP address. APIPA automatically assigns an IP address in the range of 169.254.0.1 to 169.254.255.254 (65,534 total addresses) with a subnet mask of 255.255.0.0 to each affected computer. In Windows, every five minutes, computers using APIPA check to see if the DHCP server is running and will get a DHCP-assigned address when the DHCP server comes back online.

MacOS and Linux also support this feature. MacOS calls it Bonjour or Zeroconf support, and Linux calls it avahi.

APIPA addresses can't be routable, so there's no Internet access until the DHCP server comes back online. However, LAN functions like printing and file sharing can still work.

## CERTMIKE ESSENTIALS

▶ Understanding the addressing methods used by Internet Protocol v4 (IPv4) requires you to have a grasp of Class A, Class B, and Class C networking as well as the newer CIDR method of setting up addresses and subnet masks.

▶ IPv4 requires the use of subnet masking and CIDR to help overcome its limitations on network size and number of hosts caused by its 32-bit address space, while IPv6's 128-bit address space is basically unlimited.

▶ Private addresses and public addresses are both used by IPv4 networks and the router used to connect networks to the Internet uses Network Address Translation to enable private networks to connect to the public Internet.

## Practice Question 1

Your client has been reading about the advantages of IPv6 and wants to start using it. However, when she runs `ipconfig /all`, she sees only an IPv6 address that starts with fe80, and when she checks her public IP address, it only shows an IPv4 address. What is the reason? Select the best answer from the following:

A. fe80 indicates that IPv6 has failed.

B. A link-local address can't join an IPv6 network.

C. The ISP doesn't support IPv6 yet.

D. She needs to upgrade her network card drivers.

## Practice Question 2

A co-worker has just lost Internet connectivity. However, he can still open folders on the network and print to the multifunction printer/scanner/copier/finisher device down the hallway. You ask him to run `ipconfig /all` to see the current IP address, and it comes up as 169.254.255.6. Which of the following best explains what is going on?

A. The network is broken.

B. The company didn't pay its ISP this month.

C. The DNS server has failed.

D. The DHCP server has failed.

## Practice Question 1 Explanation

This question is designed to test your knowledge of the fundamentals of how IPv6 works. Let's evaluate these answers one at a time.

1. Option A (fe80 indicates that IPv6 has failed) is not correct. All devices are assigned a link-local address when IPv6 drivers are present.

2. Option B (a link-local address can't join an IPv6 network) is incorrect. All IPv6-compatible devices have a link-local address.

3. Option C (the ISP doesn't support IPv6 yet) is correct. Once the ISP supports IPv6, a public IPv6 address will be assigned and IPv6 servers will be visible in `ipconfig /all`.

4. Option D (she needs to upgrade her network card drivers) is incorrect. The presence of a link-local IPv6 address in `ipconfig /all` indicates the network card has IPv6 drivers already.

**Correct answer: C. The ISP doesn't support IPv6 yet.**

## Practice Question 2 Explanation

This question is designed to test your knowledge of how networks react when certain components stop working. Let's evaluate each answer to see if it provides a good explanation.

1. Option A (the network is broken) is not accurate. The network still provides local network services like printing and folder access. The problem is beyond the local network.

2. Option B (the company didn't pay its ISP this month) is very unlikely. There would have been discussions about changing providers or making other moves.

3. Option C (the DNS server has failed). This answer recognizes the problem is not with the local network, but in the event of a DNS failure, it would still be possible to specify IP addresses to reach specific servers. This is not correct.

4. Option D (the DHCP server has failed) is the best answer. The DHCP server failure is proven by the computer using an APIPA address. Once the DHCP server (whether it's in a router or a separate server) starts working, this problem should be resolved.

**Correct answer: D. The DHCP server has failed.**

# CHAPTER 11

# Advanced Network Configuration

## Core 1 Objective 2.6: Compare and contrast common network configuration concepts.

**Networks** rely on specialized servers to translate IP addresses into URLs, and vice versa, and to assign IP addresses on networks. Networks also use specialized virtual methods to improve security. In this chapter, you will learn what you need to master Core 1, Objective 2.6, including the following:

▶ DNS
▶ DHCP
▶ Virtual LAN
▶ Virtual private network

## DNS

A DNS server performs a variety of functions on a network, including translating friendly URLs like www.wiley.com into IP addresses, providing the URLs of the mail servers that receive email addresses for a particular domain name, and storing text and machine-readable data, including spam management, for a particular domain name.

Learn more about DNS and DHCP ports in Chapter 6, "TCP/IP Ports and Protocols," and DNS and DHCP server roles in Chapter 9, "Networked Host Services."

> **TIP**
>
> Learn more about DNS record types at `www.cloudflare.com/learning/dns/dns-records`. To learn how to use `nslookup` in Windows from the command line to see DNS records, see `learn.microsoft.com/en-us/answers/questions/65182/how-to-find-all-possible-dns-records-for-a-server.html` and `www.comparitech.com/net-admin/nslookup-check-dns-records`. To learn how to use the Linux `dig` command to see DNS records, see `www.howtouselinux.com/post/linux-command-use-dig-to-query-dns`.

## Address

The most recognized feature of a DNS server is its function of translating URLs into IP addresses. It can perform this function because it stores information about domains and their IP addresses. These are stored in two types of records: A and AAAA.

### A

An A record points a friendly URL to the IPv4 address used by the URL's domain. For example, an A record would be used to point `google.com` to Google's host IP address 74.125.224.147. Some websites have more than one A record to allow load balancing.

### AAAA

An *AAAA* record performs the same function as an A record, but for the IPv6 address of a particular domain.

## Mail Exchange

A mail exchange (*MX*) record stores the mail exchange information, including the SMTP mail server and its priority, for a particular domain.

## Text

A text (TXT) record is used for a variety of purposes, the most common of which are spam management (following section) and identification of the owner of the domain.

> **EXAM TIP**
>
> Make sure you know the differences between A, AAAA, MX, and TXT DNS record types for the exam.

## Spam Management

TXT records typically include a number of records designed to help block spam. These include DKIM, SPF, and DMARK.

## DomainKeys Identified Mail

DomainKeys Identified Mail (*DKIM*) has two components: a DKIM record stored in the TXT portion of the domain's DNS record and a DKIM header attached to all email coming from that specific domain. Email lacking matching DKIM information is rejected as spam.

To see examples of DKIM and the servers that use this type of record, see `www.cloudflare.com/learning/dns/dns-records/dns-dkim-record`.

## Sender Policy Framework

Sender Policy Framework (*SPF*) records the authorized email-sending servers in a particular domain. It can also identify email spoofers.

The SPF line in the `microsoft.com` DNS TXT record looks like the following as this book went to press:

```
"v=spf1 include:_spf-a.microsoft.com include:_spf-b.microsoft
.com include:_spf-c.microsoft.com include:_spf-ssg-a.msft.net
include:spf-a.hotmail.com include:_spf1-meo.microsoft.com -all"
```

The `include` statements list the email servers authorized to send email on behalf of `microsoft.com`.

> **TIP**
> To look at additional examples of SPF, see `www.cloudflare.com/learning/dns/dns-records/dns-spf-record`.

## Domain-Based Message Authentication, Reporting, and Conformance

Domain-based Message Authentication, Reporting, and Conformance (*DMARC*) authenticates email messages by determining what to do if a message fails the SPF and DKIM checks. DMARC could mark the message as spam, quarantine it, or not deliver it.

To look at an example of DMARC, see `www.cloudflare.com/learning/dns/dns-records/dns-dmarc-record`.

> **EXAM TIP**
> DKIM, SPF, and DMARC are used to verify senders of emails and ensure they are who they claim to be.

# DHCP

A Dynamic Host Configuration Protocol (*DHCP*) server assigns IP addresses to hosts on its network. DHCP servers are built into typical SOHO routers or on larger networks can be a function of a server operating system like Windows Server. DHCP is also used to assign a broadband device like a cable modem an IP address.

> **TIP**
>
> DHCP uses a process called Discover, Offer, Request, Acknowledge (DORA) to assign an IP address to a host. Learn more at `ipwithease.com/ understanding-dora-process-in-dhcp`.

The DHCP server is set up with a range of IP addresses it can provide to connected hosts (computers, mobile devices, printers, scanners, etc.) and provides these addresses on a first-come, first-served basis. Addresses assigned by DHCP are known as dynamic IP addresses because they are assigned for a limited period of time, so they can change over time.

When a router connects to the public Internet, it has only a single address, although it might be providing Internet access to dozens of devices on a local network. The router uses a feature called Network Address Translation (*NAT*) to enable all of the devices on the local network to share a single public IP address. A router using NAT keeps track of which device made a request from the Internet and routes the response to the correct device.

## Leases

A DHCP server-assigned IP address is sometimes referred to as an *IP address lease*. Like a vehicle or building lease, it is good for only a specified amount of time. To determine the amount of time your IP address is leased for, use `ipconfig /all` from the command prompt in Windows and look for "lease obtained" and "lease expired" for your active connection (Figure 11.1).

## Reservations

A lease reservation converts a DHCP lease into a static IP address. For example, an enterprise network might set up a DHCP lease reservation for a shared printer so that users can always locate and use the printer, regardless of whether their own devices' IP addresses change.

Windows Server can perform this function through its DHCP Management Console. On non-Server editions of Windows, a static IP address is configured through the IPv4 or IPv6 properties for the active network adapter.

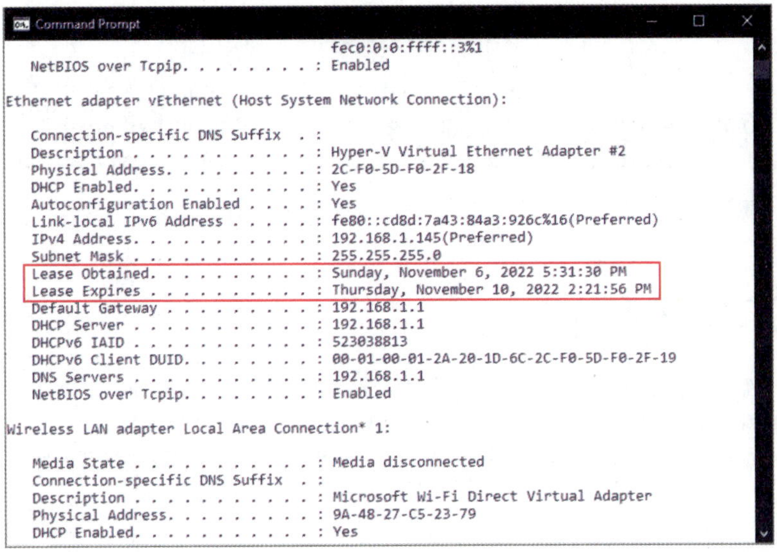
Command Prompt
fec0:0:0:ffff::3%1
NetBIOS over Tcpip. . . . . . . . : Enabled
Ethernet adapter vEthernet (Host System Network Connection):
Connection-specific DNS Suffix . :
Description . . . . . . . . . . . : Hyper-V Virtual Ethernet Adapter #2
Physical Address. . . . . . . . . : 2C-F0-5D-F0-2F-18
DHCP Enabled. . . . . . . . . . . : Yes
Autoconfiguration Enabled . . . . : Yes
Link-local IPv6 Address . . . . . : fe80::cd8d:7a43:84a3:926c%16(Preferred)
IPv4 Address. . . . . . . . . . . : 192.168.1.145(Preferred)
Subnet Mask . . . . . . . . . . . : 255.255.255.0
Lease Obtained. . . . . . . . . . : Sunday, November 6, 2022 5:31:30 PM
Lease Expires . . . . . . . . . . : Thursday, November 10, 2022 2:21:56 PM
Default Gateway . . . . . . . . . : 192.168.1.1
DHCP Server . . . . . . . . . . . : 192.168.1.1
DHCPv6 IAID . . . . . . . . . . . : 523038813
DHCPv6 Client DUID. . . . . . . . : 00-01-00-01-2A-20-1D-6C-2C-F0-5D-F0-2F-19
DNS Servers . . . . . . . . . . . : 192.168.1.1
NetBIOS over Tcpip. . . . . . . . : Enabled
Wireless LAN adapter Local Area Connection* 1:
Media State . . . . . . . . . . . : Media disconnected
Connection-specific DNS Suffix . :
Description . . . . . . . . . . . : Microsoft Wi-Fi Direct Virtual Adapter
Physical Address. . . . . . . . . : 9A-48-27-C5-23-79
DHCP Enabled. . . . . . . . . . . : Yes

**FIGURE 11.1** A typical lease obtained and lease expires report from `ipconfig /all`. (Source: Microsoft Corporation)

## Scope

DHCP scope refers to the IP address range available for a DHCP server to assign to clients. If your DHCP server is configured by Windows Server, use its DHCP Management Console to configure it. If your DHCP server is built into your router, use the router configuration dialog to make this change (Figure 11.2).

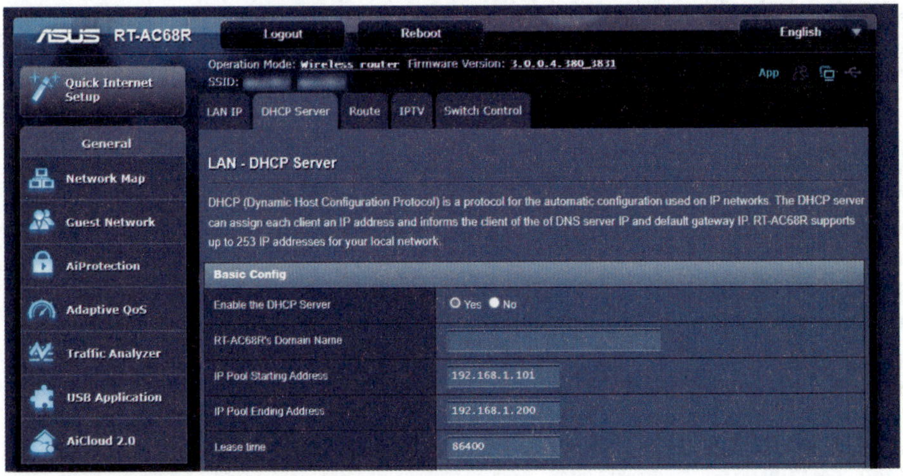
RT-AC68R
Logout
Reboot
English
Operation Mode: Wireless router Firmware Version: 3.0.0.4.380_3831
SSID:
App
Quick Internet Setup
LAN IP
DHCP Server
Route
IPTV
Switch Control
General
Network Map
Guest Network
AiProtection
Adaptive QoS
Traffic Analyzer
USB Application
AiCloud 2.0
LAN - DHCP Server
DHCP (Dynamic Host Configuration Protocol) is a protocol for the automatic configuration used on IP networks. The DHCP server can assign each client an IP address and informs the client of the of DNS server IP and default gateway IP. RT-AC68R supports up to 253 IP addresses for your local network.
Basic Config
Enable the DHCP Server
Yes No
RT-AC68R's Domain Name
IP Pool Starting Address
192.168.1.101
IP Pool Ending Address
192.168.1.200
Lease time
86400

**FIGURE 11.2** Adjust the size of the IP Address pool and its starting and ending addresses to adjust the DHCP scope on a typical wireless router. (Source: ASUSTeK Computer Inc.)

> **EXAM TIP**
>
> A DHCP lease is the amount of time a client system can use an IP address. A DHCP reservation is a specifically reserved IP address within a DHCP pool of addresses. A DHCP scope is a specific group or pool of IP addresses that a DHCP server draws from when assigning IP addresses.

# VIRTUAL LAN

A virtual LAN (*VLAN*) can be created on a managed switch. A VLAN is a group of switch ports configured to act as a logical network. This allows a single physical switch to appear as multiple separate networks. For example, on a 24-port smart switch, eight ports could be assigned to network A and 16 ports could be assigned to network B.

> **TIP**
>
> Learn more about VLANs and how they can be used at `www.lifewire.com/virtual-local-area-network-817357`.

Each VLAN can be part of the same organization, providing better organization, improvements in performance, and increased security. VLANs can also be used to enable a single switch to handle networks belonging to different organizations.

> **EXAM TIP**
>
> A VLAN is a logical network created on ports in a managed switch to provide additional security and other benefits.

# VIRTUAL PRIVATE NETWORK

A virtual private network (*VPN*) uses end-to-end encryption to conceal your network traffic and IP address from other network users on a public network. A VPN works on desktop, laptop, or mobile devices. It enables you to perform e-commerce activities such as shopping and banking securely, even from an unsecured Wi-Fi connection in a coffee shop or hotel. It also enables you to bypass territory-based limitations ("this content is not available in your country") by allowing you to choose to run your connection through a different country's servers. Windows has support for configuring VPNs in Settings ➢ Network & Internet ➢ VPN.

**EXAM TIP**

A VPN provides a secure tunnel through a public network such as the Internet using end-to-end encryption.

## CERTMIKE ESSENTIALS

▶ DNS servers do much more than translate URLs into IP addresses, including managing email connections and blocking spam.

▶ DHCP servers are used by most networks to automatically provide IP addresses, on both private networks and connections between routers and the Internet.

▶ Virtual LANs enable a single switch to service multiple networks, and virtual private networks provide secure connections when public Wi-Fi connections would otherwise make your connection vulnerable.

## Practice Question 1

Your client has decided to create a second network in her office building for "hoteling" clients who show up occasionally to avoid potential security risks for her own company's network. Which of the following should you recommend to do this?

A. Virtual private network
B. Router
C. Virtual LAN
D. DHCP

## Practice Question 2

Your client has been having a lot of problems with email spam and bots. Which of the following DNS records need to be changed to help fight these threats?

A. DHCP lease
B. TXT record
C. A record
D. AAAA record

## Practice Question 1 Explanation

This question is designed to test your knowledge of the network features discussed in this chapter. Let's evaluate these answers one at a time.

1. Option A (Virtual private network) is incorrect. A VPN is designed to provide a secure connection over unsecured networks. That is a different issue.

2. Option B (Router) is a given for any network with Internet access. A router is already present, but that isn't the issue here.

3. Option C (Virtual LAN) is the correct answer. A virtual LAN enables a single managed switch to service two or more networks, keeping their traffic separate.

4. Option D (DHCP) is incorrect. DHCP is a standard feature of almost all networks, and the issue here isn't network addressing but network security.

**Correct answer: C. Virtual LAN**

## Practice Question 2 Explanation

This question is designed to test your knowledge of DNS records. Let's look at each answer.

1. Option A (DHCP lease) is incorrect, because DHCP lease is a function of a DHCP server, which is not a part of a DNS record.

2. Option B (TXT record) is correct because TXT records can be used to store a variety of anti-spam records, including DKIM, SPF, and DMARC.

3. Option C (A record) is incorrect because it is the IPv4 information about the domain.

4. Option D (AAAA record) is incorrect because it is the IPv6 information about the domain.

**Correct answer: B. TXT record**

# CHAPTER 12

# Internet Connection Types

*Core 1 Objective 2.7: Compare and contrast Internet connection types, network types, and their features.*

**As** you work with networks, you are likely to encounter a variety of Internet connections and network types. In this chapter, you will learn what you need to master Core 1, Objective 2.7, including the following:

▶ **Internet connection types**
▶ **Network types**

## INTERNET CONNECTION TYPES

An Internet service provider (*ISP*) is a company that provides Internet access to its customers. ISPs can use a variety of methods to connect their clients to the Internet. Some use multiple methods as older, slower methods are replaced by faster methods.

## Satellite

Satellite Internet providers, such as HughesNet and Viasat, use dish antennas similar to satellite TV antennas (Figure 12.1) to receive and transmit signals between geosynchronous satellites and computers.

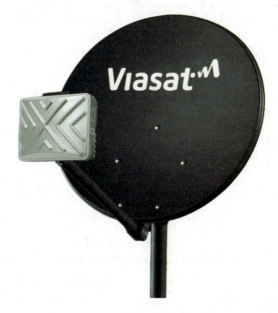

**FIGURE 12.1** Typical Viasat dish for geosynchronous satellite Internet service. (Source: Viasat, Inc.)

Geosynchronous satellites are positioned above the earth's equator at about 22,000 miles (about 35,000 kilometers) up. Geosynchronous means that the satellites are in the same position in the sky at all times. To make a connection, your location must have an unobstructed view of the southern sky (Northern Hemisphere) or northern sky (Southern Hemisphere). This may require that the satellite antenna be located on the upper story of a building or on a tower to avoid trees or buildings.

Starlink, operated by SpaceX, is the latest satellite Internet service, but it uses low-earth-orbit satellites that form a mesh network. This permits optional mobile satellite Internet and much greater speeds for upload, download, and latency than with geosynchronous satellite Internet.

Table 12.1 compares residential satellite ISPs. The information is accurate as of mid-2022.

**TABLE  12.1  Residential Satellite Internet Service Provider Comparison**

| Satellite Internet Service Provider | Download Speeds | Upload Speeds | Latency Range | High-Speed Data per Month |
|---|---|---|---|---|
| HughesNet | 25Mbps | 3Mbps | 500–800ms | 15–75GB |
| Viasat | 12–30Mbps | 3Mbps | 500–800ms | 40–300GB |
| Starlink | 50–250Mbps | 10–20Mbps | 20–40ms | Unlimited |

To connect the satellite dish to your home network, a device called a *satellite modem* is used. Usually, a satellite modem also includes a wireless router. Installation costs and equipment rental versus purchase plans vary by vendor.

> **NOTE**
>
> *Latency* refers to how quickly a network device will respond to a request for data. The shorter the latency, the more suitable a connection is for gaming or video chatting. The very long latency provided by geosynchronous satellite Internet services makes them unsuitable for these uses.

## Fiber

The fastest Internet speeds are available from fiber-optic ISPs. With most services offering speeds up to 1000Mbps (1Gbps) and some reaching 2 Gbps or faster, fiber is the best choice for users who need plenty of download speed and upload speed (which is often the same as download speed).

Fiber is available from some companies that also offer cable or DSL Internet as well as companies that offer only fiber connections. Fiber is not as widely available as cable, DSL, hotspot, or wireless Internet service providers, but fiber is available in many parts of the US and beyond. Rural areas and small towns usually lack fiber options.

## Cable

Cable Internet is typically the second-fastest Internet service available in an average market. Traditional cable Internet service uses the same RG-6 or other coaxial cable used for TV to connect to a cable modem in your home. If a single TV/Internet connection is provided, a cable splitter is used to separate cable TV from cable Internet.

However, many cable Internet vendors are now offering partial or complete fiber-optic services. Fiber-optic service can be brought to a neighborhood, and coax can be used to bring service to individual locations. Some cable Internet vendors provide service up to 1Gbps.

Cable, unlike fiber, usually has much faster download than upload speeds. For example, a 400Mbps service from a major cable Internet vendor has a 20Mbps upload speed. The same vendor's 1Gbps download speed has an upload speed of only 35Mbps. If you need upload speed comparable to download speed, consider fiber if available in your area.

## DSL

Digital subscriber line (DSL) is a very slow Internet service. Originally provided by AT&T and other telephone companies, DSL runs a digital signal over high-quality phone lines to reach very modest service speeds of up to 15Mbps (Verizon). AT&T has discontinued its DSL service in favor of various speeds of fiber.

Some forms of DSL, VDSL and VDSL2, use fiber-optic cable to the neighborhood and connect to the traditional telephone network to carry the signal the rest of the way. These services can reach download speeds of up to 200Mbps but have much slower upload speeds.

DSL is rapidly fading away because most areas also offer much faster cable or fiber Internet service at comparable pricing. DSL is faster than geosynchronous satellite, but it's getting harder and harder to find.

## Cellular

With cellular Internet service, the user simply plugs in a cellular hotspot in a central location and in a few minutes is enjoying a fast connection. There is no need for specific cabling or installation. While cellular Internet service has been offered for several years with 4G LTE networks, it has become much faster with the advent of 5G networks. Cellular hotspots made for 5G service normally have built-in access points and switches so both Wi-Fi wireless and wired Ethernet devices can use the Internet. Cellular Internet services are offered by many of the major wireless carriers, but unlike the mobile plans, cellular Internet services typically don't have data caps.

Although 5G services offer speeds "up to" 1Gbps, actual download speeds with many plans are around 300Mbps, with upload speeds of around 50Mbps. These speeds are comparable to mid-range cable Internet or low-end fiber.

## Wireless Internet Service Provider

Wireless Internet service provider (WISP) is a category of Internet service that fills in the coverage gaps of other ISPs. A usual WISP service is shown in Figure 12.2. A *WISP* uses a base station that is connected to the Internet. The base station uses directional wireless signals to connect to a relay station or directly to the customer. The use of relay stations helps increase the service area of a WISP.

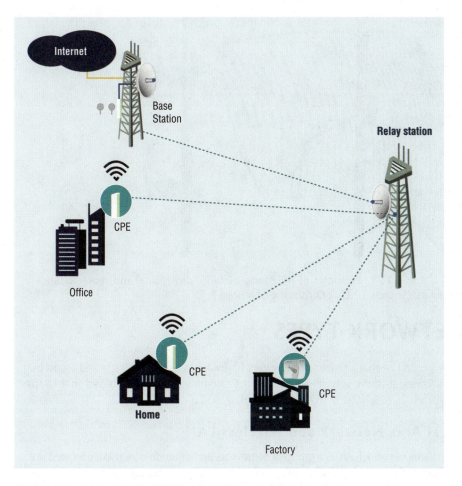

**F I G U R E   1 2 . 2**   **Typical WISP using a base and relay station.**

A WISP provides fixed wireless Internet service, which is popular in rural areas where cable, fiber, or DSL may not be readily available.

Depending upon the speed desired and the distance between the base or relay station and the customer location, customer premises equipment (CPE), (a term used for the equipment used to receive Internet service) might use a directional antenna mounted outdoors or a smaller antenna for use indoors or outdoors. Figure 12.3 shows examples of both types.

The speeds available with WISP vary according to the distance between the base or relay station and the CPE and the type of antenna used.

**FIGURE 12.3** Examples of WISP long-distance directional and short-distance antennas. (Source: TP-Link Corporation Limited.)

# NETWORK TYPES

Networks can be characterized both by their hardware as well as their size and scope. In the following sections, you will learn about the categories of networks based on their size and scope.

### Local Area Network and Wireless LAN

A local area network (*LAN*) is a group of computers and other devices usually located in a small area: a house, a small office, or a single building. The computers all connect via network cable to one or more switches and to a router for access to the Internet. A LAN can be as small as two devices or as large as several dozen devices.

A wireless LAN (WLAN) is a LAN in which the connections between devices are made with Wi-Fi. Although the term *hybrid LAN* is not commonly used, it describes a mixture of wired and wireless technology. For example, the connections made between desktop computers can use network cable, but the connections made to laptop or mobile devices would use Wi-Fi.

Most LANs in small-office/home-office (SOHO) settings are effectively hybrid LANs. However, the term LAN is normally used for any type of local area network, regardless of how the devices are connected.

### Metropolitan Area Network

A metropolitan area network (*MAN*) is a network of networks in the same locality that use direct high-speed connections to connect the networks. For example, a college campus has two satellite facilities a few blocks away from the main campus. The campus has a number of LANs, and each satellite facility has a number of LANs. The connections on the main campus and in each facility can be made with copper, fiber, or wireless connections. The MAN can use fiber or WISP connections between locations.

Figure 12.4 illustrates the differences in size and scope between a LAN and a MAN.

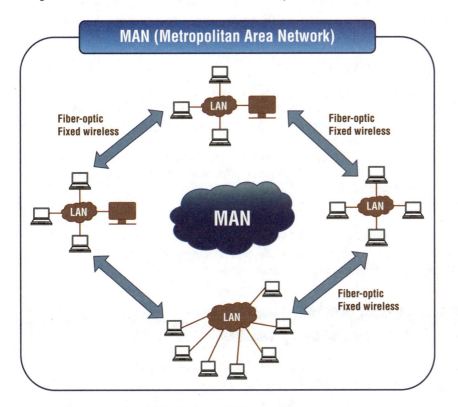

**FIGURE 12.4**  Typical MAN versus LAN comparison.

## Wide Area Network

A wide area network (*WAN*) is a group of two or more LANs or MANs over a large geographic area that are connected to each other seamlessly. For example, a financial institution's home office, branch offices, and ATMs are in different cities, countries, or continents. However, by being connected with a WAN, they appear to be on the same network. The financial institution would use fiber, networking, and wireless connections to build the WAN. Each LAN would require a router to connect to each other.

The ultimate example of a WAN is the Internet, which is comprised of a network of networks.

## Personal Area Network

A personal area network (PAN) is a small, often temporary, computer network used to connect smartphones, tablets, and other small personal computing devices and accessories using Bluetooth.

A PAN is created when a user pairs a headset with a phone, a wireless keyboard with a desktop or laptop computer, and so on. The pairing process helps prevent unknown devices or computers from joining a PAN.

## Storage Area Network

A storage area network (SAN) is a network separate from the normal LAN or MAN that is used strictly for storage. Unlike network-attached storage (NAS), which locates drives or RAID arrays on the same network as PCs and mobile devices, SAN storage, because it's on a separate network, can be accessed by any server connected to the SAN.

Because a SAN is on a network, if the most direct access to the storage devices on the SAN is affected by a network attack or slowdown, a different route to the SAN devices can be used to prevent downtime.

A SAN can use either of the following interfaces: Fibre Channel (which uses fiber optic and can provide speeds of up to 128Gbps at distances up to 10Km or 6 miles) or iSCSI, which can run over standard Ethernet networks. Fibre Channel is faster and more reliable than iSCSI, but iSCSI is much cheaper and more flexible because it uses Ethernet. Both Fibre Channel and iSCSI use switches to connect to the network and to servers.

### CERTMIKE ESSENTIALS

▶ Internet service providers offer a wide range of download and upload speeds in their product lines. Customers who need very fast upload and download speeds should consider fiber, while other services usually have much faster download than upload speeds.

▶ Generally speaking, fiber offers the fastest download speeds, followed closely by cable and by 5G cellular. Digital subscriber line (DSL) is significantly slower where available, but is still a better choice than satellite. Fixed wireless ISPs (WISPs) offer a wide range of speeds, so it's important to check with available providers.

▶ Standard and wireless local area networks (LANs) are the smallest building block of networks. Metropolitan area networks (MANs) include multiple LANs in a city. Wide area networks connect multiple LANs and MANs across a nation or across the world. Personal area networks (PANs) use Bluetooth to connect peripherals to devices over very short distances. Storage area networks (SANs) can coexist with networks of any size because they run on separate network hardware and software.

## Practice Question 1

Your client has decided it's time to connect networks in satellite offices around the city. Which of the following are necessary to make this happen?

A. Using a WISP to set up the connection
B. Adding a SAN for storage
C. Using a PAN to connect the computers
D. All of the above

## Practice Question 2

A client of yours has moved to a rural area and has asked for your assistance in selecting a broadband provider. The maximum budget per month is $100, the customer needs fast speeds for gaming and video chatting, and the customer expects to download up to 150GB of data per month. The available options include the following:

A. WISP #1 (50Mbps download, unlimited data) $75/month
B. Satellite Internet (30Mbps download, 100GB high-speed data) $100/month
C. Cellular LTE service (25Mbps download, unlimited data) $60/month
D. WISP #2 (75Mbps download, unlimited data) $90/month
E. Based on these factors, as well as what you know about the service types, which would you recommend?

## Practice Question 1 Explanation

This question is designed to test your knowledge of the basic types of networks discussed in this chapter. Let's evaluate these answers one at a time.

1. Option A (using a WISP to set up the connection) is a great answer. The WISP will determine what types of wireless connection will best suit the city's environment.

2. Option B (add a SAN for storage) is not necessary. Adding a SAN requires the setup of a completely separate network and adds a great deal of complexity to the job.

3. Option C (using a PAN to connect the computers) misunderstands what a PAN is used for. A PAN is used to connect mobile devices and computers to peripherals. To connect computers to each other, a LAN (wired, wireless, or hybrid) should be used.

4. Option D (all of the above) is incorrect because two of the answers have already been ruled out.

**Correct answer: A. Using a WISP to set up the connection**

## Practice Question 2 Explanation

This question is designed to test your ability to comparison shop for Internet service providers based on price, speeds, and known features. Let's evaluate each service.

1. Option A (WISP #1 50Mbps download, unlimited data at $75/month): This is a possible choice because of unlimited data and fast latency inherent in WISP Internet.

2. Option B (satellite Internet, 30Mbps download, 100GB high speed data, $100/month): This is not a good choice because of the slowdowns in downloading beyond 100GB per month, the slow download speed for all data, and the very slow latency.

3. Option C (Cellular LTE service, 25Mbps download, unlimited data, $60/month): This is a better choice than B, but A is twice as fast.

4. Option D (WISP #2, 75Mbps download, unlimited data, $90/month): This is the best choice because of its download speed (the fastest of all), unlimited data, and fast latency inherent in WISP Internet.

**Correct answer: D. WISP #2, 75Mbps download, unlimited data, $90/month**

# CHAPTER 13

# Networking Tools

## Core 1 Objective 2.8: Given a scenario, use networking tools.

**Whether** you're building, configuring, maintaining, or troubleshooting a network, you'll need to be familiar with network tools and what they do.

In this chapter, you'll learn what you need to know about Core 1 Objective 2.8, including the following:

► **Crimper**
► **Cable stripper**
► **Wi-Fi analyzer**
► **Toner probe**
► **Punchdown tool**
► **Cable tester**
► **Loopback plug**
► **Network tap**

## WHAT ARE NETWORK TOOLS USED FOR?

Network tools are, for the most part, pieces of equipment or software that are used to build or test wired or wireless networks. A Wi-Fi analyzer, for example, can be a piece of equipment or an app on a mobile device.

> **NOTE**
>
> CompTIA uses refers to wireless networks as Wi-Fi. However, the actual trademark is WiFi.

# CRIMPER

A *crimper* is a tool that is used to attach connectors to either coaxial or twisted-pair (TP) cable. Crimpers squeeze the connector to make a secure connection with the coaxial (coax) cable or TP wire pairs.

Crimpers are available for RJ-45 (Ethernet), RJ-11 (phone cable), and coax (RG-6, RG6QS, RG-59). Some crimpers can handle both RJ-45 and RJ-11 (Figure 13.1).

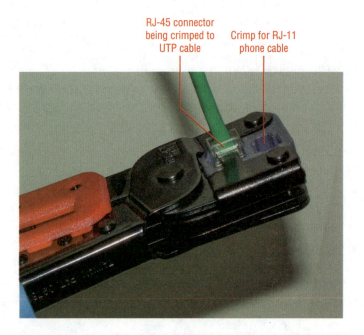

RJ-45 connector being crimped to UTP cable

Crimp for RJ-11 phone cable

**FIGURE 13.1** A crimper designed for RJ-45 and RJ-11 cable.

Manual crimpers rely on the strength of the user's hands, while ratcheted crimpers provide more power for crimping and are recommended for larger jobs. Be sure to choose a crimper made for the cable and connector types you use. Some have interchangeable dies to support a wider range of cables and connectors.

# CABLE STRIPPER

When you build a TP cable, you must strip the jacket off each wire with a *cable stripper* before you can pair them and insert them into an RJ-45 connector. Some cable strippers automatically adjust to cable thickness, but the more common models have different sizes of strippers you select manually (Figure 13.2).

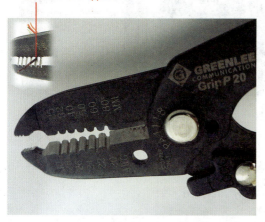

**FIGURE 13.2** **Stripping the jacket off a 22 AWG UTP wire.**

# WI-FI ANALYZER

A Wi-Fi analyzer is a device that can detect Wi-Fi networks, determine signal strength, and perform diagnostic routines to help improve network performance and reliability. Hardware-based analyzers (Figure 13.3) cost hundreds of dollars or more but are worth the price for those building, maintaining, or optimizing large wireless networks.

If your needs are simpler, such as detecting existing wireless networks and their signal strength so you can use a less-crowded frequency, you can use low-cost or free analyzers for smartphones, laptops, or tablets to detect 2.4 and 5GHz Wi-Fi networks and signal strength (Figure 13.4).

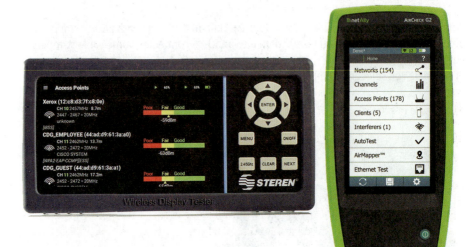

**FIGURE 13.3** Typical hand-held Wi-Fi analyzers.

# TONER PROBE

A *toner probe* (sometimes referred to as a *tone and probe* or *tone generator and probe*) is used to find a particular coax or TP cable in a wiring closet. Figure 13.5 illustrates a typical toner probe.

Connect the toner (tone generator) to a cable or wire and turn it on. Go to the wiring closet and use the probe to locate the source of the tone, which is the specific wire with the tone generator connected.

# CABLE TESTER

A *cable tester* is used to test the connectivity of a particular TP or coax cable. To test connectivity, connect one end of the cable to the tester, make sure the other end is connected to a network switch or NIC card, and run the test. Some testers made for RJ-45 can also test the cable's support for different speeds, crossover cable operation (one end T568B and the other end T568A), and more. The tester shown in Figure 13.6 supports both RJ-45 Ethernet and coaxial cables and tests each wire in a TP cable.

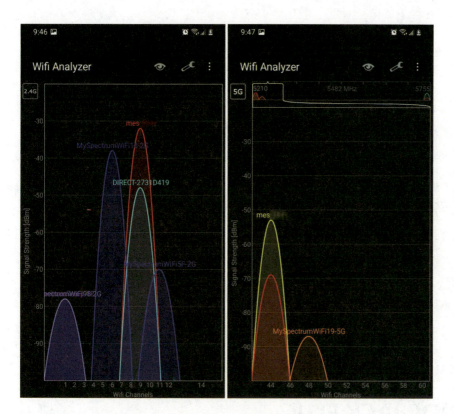

**FIGURE 13.4** Viewing nearby 2.4GHz (left) and 5GHz (right) Wi-Fi networks with the Wi-Fi Analyzer app on an Android smartphone.

**FIGURE 13.5** Typical toner probe.

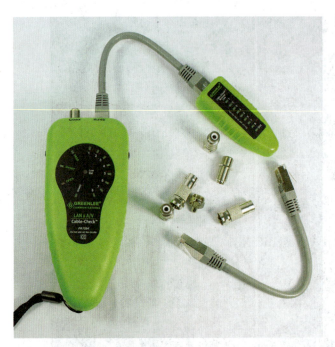

**FIGURE 13.6** A typical cable tester preparing to test a short Ethernet cable.

# LOOPBACK PLUG

A *loopback plug* connects the transmit lines of a cable to its receive lines. You can then test the cable for connectivity. Some NICs include support for a loopback test, as do many self-contained cable testers. Loopback plugs are available for RJ-45 TP cable (Figure 13.7), fiber optic, USB, and legacy serial and parallel ports.

**FIGURE 13.7** A typical RJ-45 loopback plug.

# NETWORK TAP

A *network tap* (more properly spelled TAP) is a device that monitors network traffic. On a simple network tap (Figure 13.8), you plug a cable carrying traffic into the A port and the port carrying traffic beyond the tap into the B port. Plug a cable and an analysis device into the Monitor port, which copies the traffic going through the network tap.

**F I G U R E   1 3 . 8**  **A typical network TAP.**

A network tap is invisible to network users, as it has no IP address or MAC address.

**NOTE**
TAP variously is short for "traffic access point" or "test access point."

## CERTMIKE EXAM ESSENTIALS

▶ Network tools fall into two categories: those that are used to build a network and those that are used to maintain and troubleshoot a network. Depending upon the type of network you work with, different mixes of network tools will be needed.

▶ The tools you need to build a wired network include a cable stripper, crimper, and punchdown tool. To maintain and troubleshoot a wired network, your toolkit should include a cable tester, loopback plug, network tap, and toner probe.

▶ A Wi-Fi analyzer app finds existing Wi-Fi networks so a new network can be configured to use wireless frequencies and channels that are not overloaded. If you have a hybrid (wired/wireless) network, consider having all of the tools covered in this chapter.

## Practice Question 1

Your client is asking for your recommendations for troubleshooting the company network. The company network is using a mixture of wired and wireless clients, and cabling is provided and maintained by the building management. Which of the following network tools should be recommended? (Choose all that apply.)

A. Loopback plug
B. Network tap
C. Wi-Fi analyzer
D. Crimper

## Practice Question 2

A different client is planning to replace its obsolete CAT5 cable with CAT6 cable and has purchased a spool of the cable. Which of the following items does this client also need to purchase for this job? (Choose all that apply.)

A. CAT6 connectors
B. Coax crimper
C. TP crimper
D. Coax wire stripper

## Practice Question 1 Explanation

This question is designed to test your knowledge of network tools to prepare for a real-world problem.

Let's evaluate these choices one at a time.

1. The first suggestion, loopback plug, would be appropriate if the company was responsible for its cabling. The building management should have this tool because they are responsible for cabling. So, this item does not belong on the shopping list.

2. The second suggestion, network tap, has many uses in managing a network, including security and performance. This is a good choice for your client's shopping list.

3. The third suggestion, Wi-Fi analyzer, is useful for setting up and maintaining a wireless network. Since the company, rather than the building, is responsible for the wireless network, this should also be on the shopping list.

4. The last suggestion, crimper, is a good item for organizations to have that build or maintain cables. Your client isn't responsible for the wired infrastructure, so they don't need this item either.

**Correct answers: B (network tap) and C (Wi-Fi analyzer)**

## Practice Question 2 Explanation

This question is designed to test your knowledge of network tools used for cable building.

Let's evaluate these choices one at a time.

1. The first suggestion, CAT6 connectors, is exactly what is needed for CAT6 cable. Don't mix cable and connector types.

2. The second suggestion, coax crimper, is the wrong tool for the job. A crimper is needed to connect the connectors to the cable, but it needs to be a crimper for RJ-45 TP cable, not coax. This choice is incorrect.

3. The third suggestion, TP crimper, is just what is needed to join the CAT6 connector to the CAT6 cable. CAT6 is a type of twisted-pair cabling.

4. The last option, coax wire stripper, would be correct if CAT6 cable was coaxial. It is not (it is TP), so this is the wrong answer. Instead, a TP stripper is needed.

**Correct answers: A (CAT 6 connectors) and C (TP crimper)**

# Domain 3.0: Hardware

Hardware is the third domain of CompTIA's A+ Core 1 exam. In this domain, you'll learn about the various types of hardware used in IT environments. These include the internal components of a computer: RAM, storage, motherboards, CPUs, and power supplies, as well as the use of printers, multifunction devices, cables, and connectors. This domain has seven objectives.

**3.1  Explain basic cable types and their connectors, features, and purposes**

**3.2  Given a scenario, install the appropriate RAM**

**3.3  Given a scenario, select and install storage devices**

**3.4  Given a scenario, install and configure motherboards, central processing units (CPUs), and add-on cards**

**3.5  Given a scenario, install or replace the appropriate power supply**

**3.6  Given a scenario, deploy and configure multifunction devices/ printers and settings**

**3.7  Given a scenario, install and replace printer consumables**

Questions from this domain make up 25 percent of the questions on the A+ Core 1 exam, so you should expect to see approximately 23 questions on your test covering the material in this part.

# CHAPTER 14

# Cables and Connectors

## *Core 1 Objective 3.1: Explain basic cable types and their connectors, features, and purposes.*

**Both** desktop and laptop computers rely on a wide variety of cables and connectors to interface with networks, peripherals, monitors and projectors, and hard drives.

In this chapter, you'll learn what you need to know about Core 1 Objective 3.1, including the following:

▶ **Network cables**
▶ **Peripheral cables**
▶ **Video cables**
▶ **Hard drive cables for both internal and external drives**
▶ **Adapters**
▶ **Connector types**

## NETWORK CABLES

Network cables include any cable that is used to connect a PC or other device to other network components, such as routers, switches, cable, DSL, or fiber-optic internet services. Network cables are divided into two broad categories: those made of copper wiring and those using fiber optics.

## Copper

Copper network cables are used for local connections between PCs as well as for inbound/outbound Internet connections. The following sections provide important details about these cables:

▶ **Twisted pair:** The most common type of copper cabling dividing into categories of 5, 5e, 6, and 6a
▶ **Plenum, STP:** Variations on standard twisted-pair cabling
▶ **Coaxial:** Cabling that uses a solid copper strand and is similar to cable TV wiring

Figure 14.1 compares a typical twisted-pair (TP) network cable to a coaxial network cable.

**FIGURE 14.1** TP cable (top) and coaxial cable (bottom).

### Twisted Pair

Twisted-pair (TP) cabling, which uses four wire pairs of thin wires (see Figure 14.3), is used for local area network (LAN) cabling between NICs, switches, and routers. The most common type of TP cabling is unshielded twisted-pair (*UTP*), whose four wire pairs have no insulation against electromagnetic interference (EMI).

There are four widely used standards, known as Category or CAT, for twisted-pair network cabling. Table 14.1 lists them and their uses.

**TABLE 14.1**  CAT5-5e-6-6a Specifications

| CAT | Maximum Data Transmission Rate | Frequency | Maximum Distance Per Segment | Recommended For |
|---|---|---|---|---|
| 5 | 100Mbps | 100MHz | 100 meters (328 feet) | 10/100BaseT (Fast Ethernet) |
| 5e | 1000Mbps (1Gbps) | 100MHz | 100 meters (328 feet) | 10/100/1000BaseT (Fast/Gigabit Ethernet) |
| 6 6 | 1000Mbps (1Gbps) | 250MHz | 100 meters (328 feet) | 10/100/1000BaseT (Fast/Gigabit Ethernet) |
|  | 10000Mbps (10Gbps) |  | 55 meters (180 feet) | 10/100/1000BaseT  10G Ethernet at short distances |
| 6a | 10000Mbps (10Gbps) | 500MHz | 100 meters (328 feet) | 10/100/1000/10GBaseT |

**EXAM TIP**

You may be asked to recommend the best TP category for a particular network type. Although both CAT5e and CAT6 support Gigabit Ethernet, CAT6 is a better choice because of higher frequency and better protection against crosstalk (interference between wire pairs). CAT6 and 6a both support 10G Ethernet, but CAT6a is a better choice because of higher frequency and longer distances supported.

Most TP cables are labeled with the CAT/Category type, which is helpful if you are examining installed network cable and want to see what network speeds are supported. See Figure 14.2.

**FIGURE 14.2**  CAT5e (top) and CAT6 (bottom) cable labels.

**Plenum**    Standard TP cables, also called *riser cables* because they are suitable for vertical cable runs, have a polyvinyl chloride (PVC) jacket around the wire pairs, which, if burned, produces a highly toxic smoke. For this reason, standard TP cables are not recommended for cable runs in a plenum, which is a space used for HVAC air circulation such as air ducts or air returns.

Plenum cabling, typically marked CMP (communications plenum), uses a different type of wire jacket that does not produce toxic smoke when burned.

**T568A/T568B**    There are two standards for arranging the wire pairs in a TP cable. The EIA/TIA T568B standard is the de facto standard for TP network cables, but some are wired using the EIA/TIA T568A standard. Whichever standard you follow, make sure both ends of a cable use the same wire pairing.

These standards are listed in Table 14.2. The wire pairs are as seen from the top of the RJ45 network connector (the opposite side from the locking clip). See Figure 14.3.

**T A B L E  1 4 . 2**  **EIA/TIA T568A and T568B Wiring Standards**

| Wiring Standard | Pair 1 | | Pair 2 | | Pair 3 | | Pair 4 | |
|---|---|---|---|---|---|---|---|---|
| T568B | Pin 1 | Orange/ white stripe | Pin 3 | Green/ white stripe | Pin 5 | Blue/ white stripe | Pin 7 | Brown/ white stripe |
|  | Pin 2 | Orange | Pin 4 | Blue | Pin 6 | Green | Pin 8 | Brown |
| T568A | Pin 1 | Green/ white stripe | Pin 3 | Orange/ white stripe | Pin 5 | Blue/ white stripe | Pin 7 | Brown/ white stripe |
|  | Pin 2 | Green | Pin 4 | Blue | Pin 6 | Orange | Pin 8 | Brown |

**Shielded Twisted Pair**    Standard UTP cable has no protection against external interference. Elevators, fluorescent lights, electric motors, and wired alarm systems are some of the causes of interference with networks using UTP cable. When interference sources are nearby, you can use shielded twisted pair (*STP*) cable in place of STP cable. STP cable has a metal shield around the TP wires and has a ground wire.

It is available in riser and plenum grades and in the same CAT standards as UTP cable. It is more expensive, slightly thicker, and less flexible than UTP cable. Figure 14.4 compares a typical UTP (left) and STP cable (right).

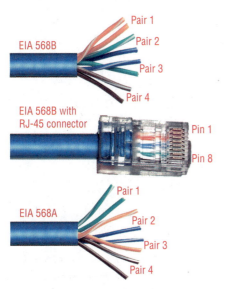

EIA 568B

Pair 1
Pair 2
Pair 3
Pair 4

EIA 568B with
RJ-45 connector

Pin 1
Pin 8

EIA 568A

Pair 1
Pair 2
Pair 3
Pair 4

**FIGURE 14.3**  **EIA/TIA T568B and T568A wire pairings and an assembled UTP cable using the EIA/TIA T568B standard.**

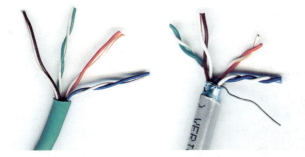

**FIGURE 14.4**  **UTP versus STP cable.**

**UTP/STP Connectors**    UTP and STP cables use what are commonly referred to as RJ45 connectors. *RJ45* connectors have eight contacts, one each for the wires inside of TP cable, and a locking clip on one side. All of the connectors are clear so you can see the wire pairs through the top of the connector, as in Figure 14.3. STP connectors have metal sides for better protection.

RJ45 connectors are designed to lock into the RJ45 jack on a network adapter, router, or cable modem. To protect the locking tab on the bottom of the connector from damage, many cables use a protective boot, clip, or wings. Figure 14.5 illustrates typical UTP and STP RJ45 connectors with protected locking tabs.

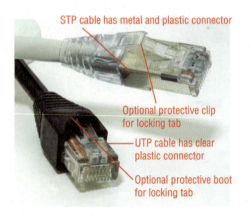

FIGURE 14.5 UTP and STP connectors.

Punchdown Connectors    A *punchdown* (also referred to as a *punch down*) connector is used to terminate RJ45 cable. It is also referred to as an *Ethernet keystone jack*. Typical uses include wall plates for connections to patch cables and in wiring closets.

A punchdown tool is used to insert the wire pairs into the back of a punchdown connector. Figure 14.6 shows a punchdown tool and connector.

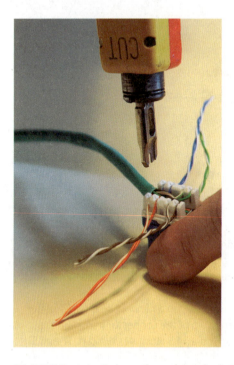

FIGURE 14.6 Inserting wire pairs into a punchdown connector with a punchdown tool.

## RJ11 Connectors and Cables

An *RJ11* connector is used for telephone cables. It resembles an RJ45 connector but is smaller, supporting two wires (single-line telephone) or four wires (two-line telephone).

Figure 14.7 compares typical RJ45 and RJ11 cables.

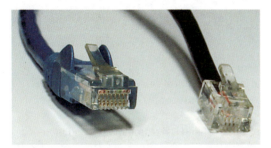

**FIGURE 14.7**   **A typical RJ45 cable with protective wings over its locking tab (left) and a typical RJ11 cable (right).**

### Coaxial

Coaxial cables are used for cable Internet connections, going from the outside service location and connecting to the cable modem in the home or office. Coaxial cables use Type F connectors that are threaded.

The recommended coaxial cable type is RG6. It has wire mesh and foil layers between the outer jacket and the plastic cladding around the copper core. Figure 14.8 shows the interior of an RG6 cable and its connector.

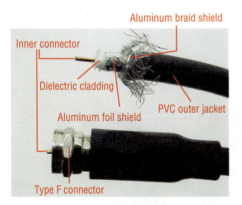

**FIGURE 14.8**   **RG6 coax cable connector and interior.**

**EXAM TIP**

All coaxial cables can interconnect with each other, but using RG59 cable for cable Internet can cause poor network connections. RG59, used for HDTV antennas and cable TV installs, is thinner than RG6 and has only a single layer of shielding. RG6QS is quad-shielded for better protection against interference than RG6.

## Optical

Copper cables transmit data with electrical impulses. Optical cables transmit data with light particles (photons) at much faster speeds than most copper network cables.

**Fiber Cable and Connections**    Fiber-optic cabling is becoming more and more common in home and business broadband with the rise of gigabit and faster service levels. Fiber-optic cables typically terminate in a fiber terminal inside your home or garage. The fiber terminal has an Ethernet (RJ45) port to connect to your home network.

Fiber can transmit data in only one direction, so fiber-optic connections need a pair of cables, one for each direction.

The common fiber-optic cable types you need to be able to recognize are as follows:

▶ Lucent connector (*LC*): Smaller than other common connectors for easier installation in cramped locations; uses a push-pull latching mechanism
▶ Straight tip (*ST*): Less common than LC or SC; uses a bayonet-type locking mechanism
▶ Subscriber connector (*SC*): Most common connector; uses a locking tab for latching

Figure 14.9 shows all three types.

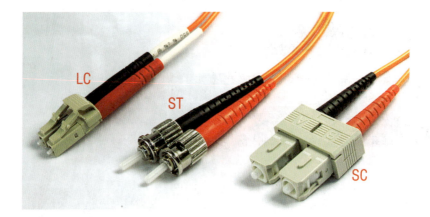

**F I G U R E   1 4 . 9   Bidirectional fiber-optic cables.**

# PERIPHERAL CABLES AND CONNECTORS

The most common types of peripheral cables are USB 2.0, USB 3.0, and USB Type-C, but you are also likely to encounter Thunderbolt cables, especially with Macintosh computers and some high-performance PCs. Serial ports are used primarily for interfacing with control devices and specialized telecom equipment.

## USB 2.0

USB 2.0 is a four-wire serial connection that runs at up to 480Mbps. Desktop computers use USB 2.0 ports for low-speed peripherals such as keyboards, mice, printers, scanners, and multifunction devices. Typical USB 2.0 cables for these devices use the Type A connector for the USB ports on the computer or USB hub and the Type B connector at the other end for the device connection. Refer to Figure 14.10 for USB 2.0 cables, Figure 14.11 for Type-A ports, and Figure 14.12 for Type-B ports.

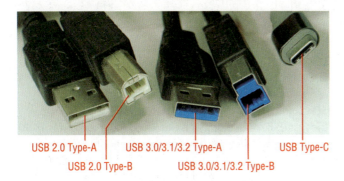

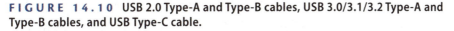

USB 2.0 Type-A    USB 3.0/3.1/3.2 Type-A      USB Type-C

USB 2.0 Type-B    USB 3.0/3.1/3.2 Type-B

**FIGURE 14.10**  USB 2.0 Type-A and Type-B cables, USB 3.0/3.1/3.2 Type-A and Type-B cables, and USB Type-C cable.

## USB 3.0/3.1/3.2

USB 3.0 is an eight-wire serial connection that runs at up to 5Gbps. Desktop computers use USB 3.0 ports for high-speed peripherals such as SSDs, external hard drives, and flash drives as well as USB 3.0 hubs. USB 3.0 ports are backward-compatible with USB 2.0 devices. Recent systems call USB 3.0 ports USB 3.1 Gen 1 or USB 3.1 Gen 1. For USB 3.0/3.1/3.2 cables, refer to Figure 14.10. Refer to Figure 14.11 for Type-A ports, and refer to Figure 14.12 for Type-B ports.

USB 3.1 Gen 2 ports run at 10Gbps. USB 3.2 has replaced USB 3.0/3.1, and 5Gbps USB ports are now called USB 3.2 Gen 1 ports. 10Gbps USB ports are now called USB 3.2 Gen 2. USB 3.2 Gen 2×2 ports run at 20Gbps, but use only Type-C cables. See Table 14.3 for details.

**TABLE 14.3**   USB 3.0/3.1/3.2 Speeds and Port/Cable Types

| USB Speeds/ Versions | 5Gbps | 10Gbps | 20Gbps |
|---|---|---|---|
| USB 3.0 | Supported | No | No |
| USB 3.1 | Gen 1 | Gen 2 | No |
| USB 3.2 | Gen 1 | Gen 2 | Gen 2×2 |
| USB Cable Types Supported | | | |
| 3.0 Type-A | Yes | Yes | No |
| 3.0 Type-B | Yes | Yes | No |
| Type-C | Yes | Yes | Yes |

Because of the high speeds provided by USB 3.1/3.2 (5Gbps or faster) ports, they support adapters for Gigabit Ethernet, 3D graphics, and legacy ports such as serial, parallel, and SCSI.

## USB Type-C

USB Type-C (also known as USB-C and USB Type C) is unusual because it supports several different USB standards. It is the first USB connector that is not keyed (refer to Figures 14.10 and 14.11), connects to both computers and devices, and supports speeds ranging from USB 2.0 (for smartphone and tablet charging) up through USB 3.2 Gen 2×2 and USB 4. Because USB Type-C supports many speeds, you must check the specifications for a particular device's USB Type C port to determine its speed.

> **NOTE**
>
> The latest version of USB is USB 4.0, which uses Thunderbolt 4 connectors (same form factor as USB Type-C) and will run 40Gbps with 40Gbps-rated cables.

**FIGURE 14.11**   USB 2.0, 3.0, and 3.1 Gen 2 Type-A ports and a USB 3.1 Gen 2 Type-C port on a typical desktop computer port cluster.

**NOTE**

Some USB 2.0 devices use the smaller mini-B or micro-B (also known as USB On-The Go) connectors. Some USB 3.0 devices use the smaller micro-B connector. See Chapter 3 for illustrations of these ports and cables.

**FIGURE 14.12** USB 2.0 and USB 3.0 Type-B ports.

## Serial

The DB9 cable and connector shown in Figure 14.13 are used by the RS-232 serial port. At one time, this port was widely used for printers, dial-up modems, mice, pen plotters, and other types of peripherals. RS-232 is used today primarily for control of industrial equipment, configuration of enterprise-grade network equipment, and control of headless servers (headless = no monitor or keyboard).

Most modern systems lack built-in RS-232 ports, but USB to RS-232 adapters or PCIe RS-232 add-on cards enable interfacing with serial devices. RS-422 and RS-485 are newer, faster serial standards that can also be connected by means of USB adapters or PCIe add-on cards.

## Thunderbolt

Thunderbolt is a series of high-speed peripheral interfaces originally developed by Apple and Intel to support power, data, video, and audio in a single cable. Some high-performance PCs have Thunderbolt support, but Thunderbolt is more often found on Macs. Originally, only PCs with Intel processors could have Thunderbolt ports, but a few systems running AMD processors also support Thunderbolt.

There are four different versions of Thunderbolt, using two different connectors (see Figure 14.14).

**FIGURE 14.13** DB9F RS-232 serial cable with thumbscrews and DB9M RS-232 serial port.

▶ Thunderbolt 1 runs at 10Gbps and uses the same physical connector as a Mini-DisplayPort (mDP) connector, but marked with a stylized thunderbolt icon.
▶ Thunderbolt 2 runs at 20Gbps and uses the same connector as Thunderbolt 1.
▶ Thunderbolt 3 runs at 30Gbps and uses the same physical connector as USB-C; however, a connector supporting Thunderbolt is marked with a stylized thunderbolt icon.
▶ Thunderbolt 4 runs at 40Gbps and uses the same connector as Thunderbolt 3.

**FIGURE 14.14** Thunderbolt 1/2 cable (left) compared to a USB Type-C (same form factor as Thunderbolt 3/4) cable (right),

See Chapter 3 for illustrations of mDP, Thunderbolt 2, and USB-C ports.

# VIDEO CABLES AND CONNECTORS

Video cables and connectors are among the most confusing interfaces used by PCs today. Don't be surprised if you find that a typical system might have two or three different interfaces available for a display. Knowing what each one is best for is vital for configuring and updating systems.

## Video Graphics Array

Video Graphics Array (*VGA*) is an analog video standard that supports up to 16.7 million colors and resolutions up to 2048×1536.

The VGA port is a DB15F port at the computer, and most monitors used for VGA have a detachable cable with the same connector. The VGA cable has a DB15M connector with thumbscrews. See Figure 14.15. Although VGA has been replaced by newer standards, most of them can be adapted to VGA so you can continue to use VGA monitors and HDTVs.

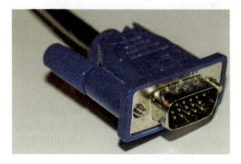

**F I G U R E   1 4 . 1 5**  **VGA cable.**

## Digital Visual Interface

Digital Visual Interface (*DVI*) is a complex video standard to describe. DVI is available in digital-only versions (*DVI-D*), digital/analog versions (DVI-I), and analog versions (DVI-A). DVI supports color depths similar to VGA and resolutions up to 2560×1600 in its dual-link version.

The most common types are DVI-D and DVI-I. DVI can also be adapted to HDMI and DisplayPort's digital video signals.

All DVI ports and cables use thumbscrews. DVI-D ports have a horizontal slot to the right of the pin grid, while DVI-I ports have both horizontal and vertical slots as well as four holes around the slots. These are visible in Figure 14.16, along with miniHDMI, HDMI, and VGA ports.

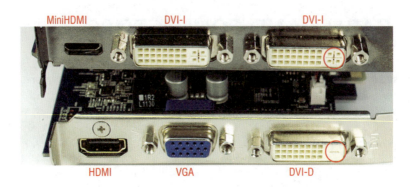

**FIGURE 14.16** **Two graphics cards with DVI, HDMI, VGA, and other ports.**

DVI dual-link cables and DVI-I to VGA adapters support up to 2560×1600 resolution. DVI single-link cables and DVI-I to VGA adapters are missing pins and limit resolution to 1920×1200.

## High-Definition Multimedia Interface

Although the High-Definition Multimedia Interface (*HDMI*) is a much smaller connector than DVI, it carries both video and audio signals in digital form.

HDMI, originally developed for HDTVs, is available in many versions, with newer versions supporting higher resolutions up to 8K and improved audio and video standards, but all use the same physical HDMI port and cable connections (refer to Figure 14.16). The smaller mini-HDMI (also shown in Figure 14.16) and microHDMI ports are rare.

Figure 14.17 illustrates typical HDMI, miniHDMI, DisplayPort, and miniDisplayPort cables/adapters.

**FIGURE 14.17** **HDMI and DisplayPort cable variations.**

If you are unable to get the desired resolution, 3D support, or support for HDR video with an HDMI hookup, verify that the A/V output and monitor support the features. Then, upgrade to a newer HDMI cable (the latest version is 2.1); the newest cables are backward-compatible with older standards.

HDMI can be adapted to VGA, DVI, and DisplayPort.

## DisplayPort

DisplayPort (DP) is the chief rival to HDMI on high-performance 3D graphics cards. Like HDMI, DP supports high-speed, high-resolution audio and video output (up to 8K) and can support other standards with passive or active (powered) adapters.

DP differs from HDMI in the use of packetized data (DP was developed by PC and chip-makers), no changes in cables as DP standards change, and the ability to be daisy-chained (starting with DP version 1.2). A single DP connection can support multiple displays if the displays have DP output as well as DP input. Daisy-chaining is supported by Microsoft Windows. Figure 14.18 compares typical DP ports to HDMI.

HDMI                    DP

**FIGURE  14.18   HDMI and DP ports on a typical 3D graphics card.**

MiniDP (mDP) is a smaller form factor originally developed by Apple but freely available to all PC vendors; it supports all DP versions and features and can use simple adapters to make DP to mDP connections. Many displays that support DP also have mDP ports, and mDP ports are also used on 3D graphics cards to save space (Figure 14.19).

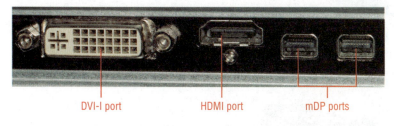

DVI-I port              HDMI port              mDP ports

**FIGURE  14.19   mDP ports on a typical 3D graphics card.**

# HARD DRIVE CABLES AND CONNECTORS

Although there are four standards listed for hard drive cables and connectors, the most common one is Serial Advanced Technology Attachment (SATA). However, older systems might use eSATA, IDE, or SCSI. Here's what they look like and how they work.

Learn more about hard drive and other storage devices in Chapter 16, "Storage Devices."

## Serial Advanced Technology Attachment

Serial Advanced Technology Attachment (*SATA*) is a high-speed serial replacement for IDE (see later in this chapter). Instead of using parallel signals that limit cable length and can cause reliability issues as in IDE, SATA uses high-speed serial signaling.

All versions of SATA use the same form factor for data and power cables. However, cables made for SATA Revision 3 are typically marked 6Gbps.

Original SATA cables simply push into place, but right-angle and locking-tab data cable versions are common. Figure 14.20 shows standard SATA power and data cables and connectors on a typical SATA drive. Note that power and data cables and connectors use an L-shaped cross section to prevent incorrect installation.

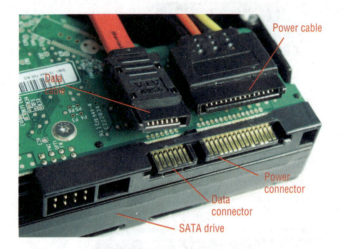

**FIGURE 14.20** **SATA data and power cables and drive connectors.**

Figure 14.21 compares right-angle 6Gbps SATA cables with external SATA (eSATA) cables.

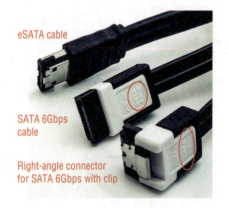

**FIGURE 14.21** **SATA and eSATA cables.**

## External SATA

External SATA (*eSATA*) enables external drives to use the high-speed SATA interface. The eSATA cable (see Figure 14.21) is heavier than the SATA cable but carries the same signals. In fact, a low-cost expansion card bracket can be used to convert motherboard SATA ports into eSATA ports.

Learn more about SATA and eSATA motherboard host adapters in Chapter 17, "Motherboards."

## Integrated Drive Electronics

The predecessor to SATA was Integrated Drive Electronics (*IDE*). The IDE interface has always used a two-row 20-pin connector on both the motherboard host adapter (or add-on card) and drives. IDE data cables have two drive connectors, so a single host adapter can control two drives.

Originally, the IDE cable had 40 wires, but Ultra DMA and later versions switched to a cable that used 80 narrower wires to improve reliability at faster speeds (up to 133MBps transfer rate). Figure 14.22 illustrates an IDE/PATA host adapter and 80-wire cable on a motherboard that also has SATA ports.

**FIGURE 14.22** Installed IDE cable (top) and IDE port (bottom).

IDE drives use the four-wire Molex power connector (Figure 14.23).

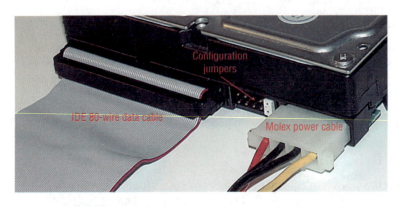

**F I G U R E   1 4 . 2 3**   **IDE drive with an 80-wire data cable, configuration jumpers, and Molex power cable.**

## Small Computer System Interface

The Small Computer System Interface (*SCSI*) once dominated fast drive and peripheral interfacing on high-performance PCs. SCSI devices connect to a single host adapter that can communicate with multiple devices in a daisy-chain. Each device has a separate Device ID, and the end of the daisy chain must be terminated. External SCSI devices such as scanners and drives use large round cables, while internal SCSI devices use ribbon cables.

Narrow SCSI host adapters support up to seven devices and use 50-pin or 50-wire cables. Wide SCSI host adapters support up to 15 devices and use 68-pin or 68-wire cables. Figure 14.24 shows two Internal SCSI cables, 50-pin and 68-pin.

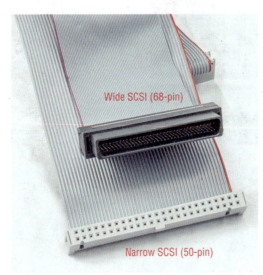

**F I G U R E   1 4 . 2 4**   **SCSI 50-pin and 68-pin ribbon cables for internal drives.**

On PCs, SCSI has been replaced by USB for external devices and SATA for internal storage. On servers, SCSI has been replaced by SATA and SAS (Serial Attached SCSI [Small Computer System Interface]) for storage.

## CERTMIKE EXAM ESSENTIALS

▶ Network, peripheral, video, and storage technologies have frequently changed, and understanding their physical and performance characteristics is an important factor in being a successful computer technician.

▶ Slower cable standards can cause performance bottlenecks when used with devices that support faster speeds. Be sure to match device and cable standards or use faster cables than required to make upgrades easier.

▶ Legacy devices need not be abandoned if adapters can be used to enable them to work with modern systems.

## Practice Question 1

Your client has asked you to add a second 4K display to a PC. The PC currently connects to the first 4K display with DisplayPort (DP). The new 4K display has DP-in, DP-out, and HDMI ports. The PC has a single Display-Port and two HDMI ports.

The cable run between the PC and the existing display is 50 feet, and the new display will be located directly beside the existing display. The second display is already paid for, but you need to select the connection type. The budget for the connection is $50. Which of the following is the BEST recommendation for making this work?

A.  Buy a 60-foot 4K HDMI cable to allow sufficient slack.
B.  Daisy-chain the second 4K display to the first 4K display with DP or mDP cables.
C.  Daisy-chain the second 4K display to the first 4K display with HDMI.
D.  Inform the client that you need to purchase a second graphics card and cable.

## Practice Question 2

Your company has had a cable failure on an existing 100BaseT (Fast Ethernet) network segment. Plans are to upgrade this segment to Gigabit Ethernet in the next 12 months. Keeping both current and future needs in mind, which of the following is the BEST solution?

A.  Replace the current cable with a CAT5 cable now and run CAT5e alongside it for future use.
B.  Replace the current cable with a CAT5e cable.
C.  Replace the current cable with an RG6QS cable.
D.  Replace the current cable with a CAT6 cable.

## Practice Question 1 Explanation

This question is designed to test your knowledge of the different video connectors and their capabilities to solve a real-world problem.

Let's evaluate these choices one at a time.

1. The first option, buying a 60-foot cable, costs too much, ranging from $75 to $100, plus installation.

2. The second option, daisy-chaining the second 4K display to the first one, is the best because it uses the daisy-chain feature of DP/mDP. The cable needed will be less than $20, and no installation through walls, etc., is necessary.

3. The third option, daisy-chaining the displays with HDMI, isn't technically possible, as HDMI doesn't support daisy-chaining.

4. The last option, buying a second graphics card and cable, is unnecessary. All that needs to be added to existing hardware is a short DP or mDP cable.

**Correct Answer: B (daisy-chaining displays using DP/mDP)**

## Practice Question 2 Explanation

This question is designed to test your knowledge of different network cables and their capabilities to solve a real-world problem.

Let's evaluate these choices one at a time.

1. The first option, CAT5 now and CAT 5e later, is unnecessary. CAT5 is limited to 100Mbps (Fast Ethernet) and CAT5e supports both Fast and Gigabit Ethernet, so there's no need to have two cable runs.

2. The second option, use CAT5e now, will support both Fast and Gigabit Ethernet, but CAT5e is not the best choice for Gigabit Ethernet.

3. The third option, use RG6QS cable, would require additional hardware as coaxial cable and UTP cable must use converters to "talk" to each other. This is unnecessary and not cost-effective.

4. The last option is the BEST. CAT6 supports Fast and Gigabit Ethernet and provides a better-quality signal. It's ready for current and future needs because it can also support a short 10G segment.

**Correct answer: D (replace current cable with CAT6)**

# CHAPTER 15

# Random Access Memory (RAM)

## *Core 1 Objective 3.2: Given a scenario, install the appropriate RAM.*

**In** any type of computer, random access memory (RAM) is the temporary workspace where programs are loaded and data is processed before being output or stored. Increasing the amount of RAM in a system is one of the best ways to improve its performance.

In this chapter, you will learn everything you need to know about A+ Certification Core 1 Objective 3.2, including the following topics:

▶ RAM types
▶ Single-channel
▶ Dual-channel
▶ Triple-channel
▶ Quad-channel

## RAM TYPES

We usually think of RAM in terms of its physical form, memory chips, and the memory modules where they are installed. However, one type of RAM doesn't use memory modules at all, while memory modules that look similar can have significant differences in the types of memory installed on them. The following sections give you the facts you need.

Dynamic RAM, or *DRAM*, is the type of RAM used in memory modules. Dynamic means that memory must be frequently refreshed with a new charge of electricity or the contents of RAM will be lost.

Originally, computers used individual memory chips installed directly on the motherboard. However, starting in the mid-1980s, some computers began to use single-inline memory modules, or SIMMs. A *SIMM* contains two or more memory chips soldered to the module and gets its name from using a single-row inline connector on the bottom of the module. The connector, which snaps into a socket on the motherboard, has leads on both sides, but the front side's connectors are repeated on the rear.

To boost RAM performance during the memory chip and SIMM eras, a second type of RAM was installed on some high-performance computers. *Static RAM (SRAM)* is bulkier than DRAM but is much faster because it doesn't require refreshing as often as DRAM. It is used as part of the memory circuit between the CPU and DRAM as a cache: by holding a copy of the contents of DRAM, the CPU can retrieve data it wants to reuse from SRAM faster than always going to DRAM. For many years, SRAM caches have been built into CPUs instead of being installed on the motherboard.

## Virtual RAM

Despite the name, virtual RAM isn't really RAM at all. It refers to the use of hard drive space as a substitute for RAM. If an application or process doesn't have enough RAM, the operating system "borrows" the additional amount of space needed from available hard disk space. The amount is "paid back" by being released when the additional space is no longer needed.

This process is automatic unless you want to manually set the paging file size. When the operating system uses virtual RAM, the system slows down. To avoid using slow virtual RAM, install more physical RAM.

## Memory Module Types

Computers use one of two types of memory modules, Dual Inline Memory Modules and Small Outline Dual Inline Memory Modules. The following sections discuss their major features.

### Dual Inline Memory Modules

A Dual Inline Memory Module (DIMM) is the standard memory module type used in desktop computers. DIMM modules have different contacts on the front and rear sides of the module. Each DIMM has a 64-bit data bus, which matches the data bus width of 64-bit processors.

**Installing DIMMs**    DDR-family modules slide into place vertically and are held in place by a clip at one end (DD4/5) or by clips at both ends (DDR3 and older). To avoid excessive flexing of the motherboard, you should install memory on a new build before installing the motherboard in the case. Here's how:

1. Wear an ESD wrist strap and ground it to metal in the work area.
2. Place the board on an antistatic surface.

3. Flip open the retaining clip(s) for the slot you are using.
4. After consulting the motherboard manual, align the first module to install over the slot, keying notch, and retaining clips (DDR3) or retaining clip and slot guide (DDR4/5); see Figure 15.1.
5. Gently push down until the retaining clip(s) flip up and the module's leads no longer are visible. Use even pressure (both thumbs work well).

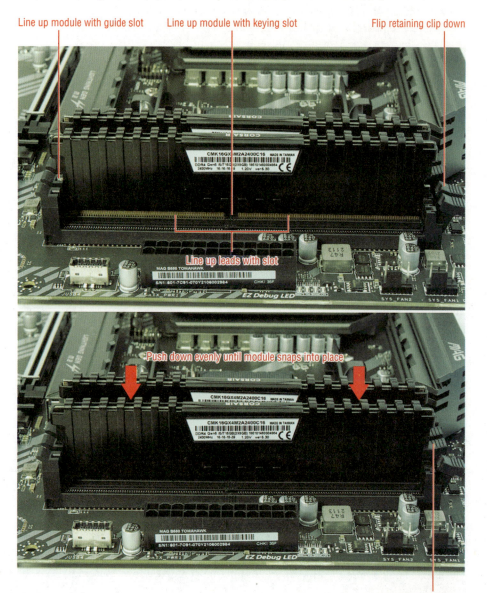

**FIGURE 15.1** Installing a DDR4 DIMM on a motherboard.

### Small Outline Dual Inline Memory Module

Small Outline Dual Inline Memory Module (SODIMM) memory modules are used in laptops as well as some all-in-one desktop computers and on a few Mini-ITX motherboards. The *SODIMM* modules are reduced-size versions of the dual-inline memory module (*DIMM*). DIMM modules are used by desktop computers and servers. Both module types have memory chips mounted on a flat circuit board that clips into a slot on the motherboard. DIMM and SODIMM have different leads on each side of the module.

Figure 15.2 compares a typical DDR4 SODIMM to a DDR4 DIMM module.

**FIGURE 15.2   A typical DDR4 SODIMM (top) compared to a DDR DIMM (bottom).**

Learn more about SODIMM modules in Chapter 1, "Laptop Hardware."

## Memory Speed

Memory speeds are based on two major factors: the memory technology used and the clock speed of the memory chips. All memory in current use is based on double-data-rate designs. Double Data Rate (*DDR*) memory refers to a family of memory that performs two data transfers per clock cycle. Various types of DDR memory have been used by computers since the first DDR modules were introduced more than 20 years ago.

The systems an A+ technician are most likely to encounter use DDR3, DDR4, or DDR5 memory, all covered in the following sections.

> **EXAM TIP**
>
> Vendor-specific memory evaluation apps are very helpful in determining installed and compatible RAM upgrades for almost any Windows system.

## Double Data Rate 3

The type of DDR memory you are likely to encounter on computers built from about 2007 to 2015 is Double Data Rate 3 (DDR3). DDR3 uses lower voltage than its predecessor (1.5V in standard, 1.35V in DDR3L versions) to enable faster transfers and faster speed than with its predecessors. DDR3 DIMMs have 240 pins with a left-offset keying notch. DDR3 SODIMMs have 204 pins with a left-offset keying notch.

DDR3 DIMMs differ in size (GB), data transfer rate (MB per second) memory clock speed, voltage used (don't use DDR3 modules in a system that uses low-power DDR3L modules), and by transfer per clock cycle. Typical module sizes range from 1GB to 16GB per module. DDR3 memory is also known as PC3 (standard voltage) or PC3L (low-voltage).

> **NOTE**
>
> Mac-compatible memory is not the same as standard memory. Macs use buffered memory, while PCs use unbuffered memory. Mix them up, and you'll have unreliable computers! This applies to any memory technology including DDR4 and DDR5.

Table 15.1 lists some of the common DDR3 speeds. You don't need to memorize this list; just learn how to distinguish DDR3 from other module types.

**TABLE 15.1** Common DDR3 Speeds

| Module ID | Memory ID | Peak Data Transfer Rate (MB/Sec) | Transfer per Clock Cycle (MT/Sec) |
|-----------|-----------|----------------------------------|-----------------------------------|
| DDR3-1866 | PC3-14900 | 14900 | 1866 |
| DDR3-1600 | PC3-12800 | 12800 | 1600 |
| DDR3L-1600* | PC3L-12800 | | |
| DDR3-1333 | PC3-10600 | 10600 | 1333 |
| DDR3L-1333* | PC3L-10600 | | |
| DDR3-1066 | PC3-8500 | 8500 | 1066 |
| DDR3L-1066* | PC3L-8500 | | |

* DDR3 indicates the module is a standard voltage DDR3 module; DDR3L indicates the module is a low-voltage DDR3L module; both types are available in DIMM and SODIMM form factors.

## Double Data Rate 4

The type of DDR memory you are likely to encounter in almost all current systems (2015-present) is Double Data Rate 4 (DDR4). DDR4 uses only 1.2V of power, has higher capacity (modules range in size from 2-32GB per module), and offers faster performance than DDR3. DDR4 memory is also known as PC4.

DDR4 DIMMs have 288 pins, and both sets of pins have a curved edge for easier insertion. DDR4 SODIMMs have 266 pins and a keying notch slightly offset to the right. Figure 15.3 compares a DDR3 with a DDR4 DIMM.

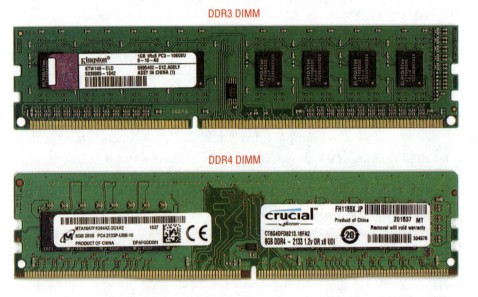

**FIGURE 15.3** A typical DDR3 DIMM (top) compared to a DDR4 DIMM (bottom).

DDR4 DIMM and SODIMM modules differ in memory size (GB), in speed, and by module throughput. Typical DDR4 module sizes range from 4GB to 32GB.

Table 15.2 lists some of the common DDR4 speeds. You don't need to memorize this list; just learn how to distinguish DDR4 from other module types.

> **NOTE**
>
> With any memory technology, pairing slower memory with faster processors can slow down a system. See your system or motherboard documentation for recommended combinations.

**TABLE 15.2**  Common DDR4 Speeds

| Module ID | Memory ID | Peak Data Transfer Rate (MB/Sec) | Transfer per Clock Cycle (MT/Sec) |
|---|---|---|---|
| DDR4-3600 | PC4-28800 | 28800 | 3600 |
| DDR4-3200 | PC4-25600 | 25600 | 3200 |
| DDR4-2666 | PC4-21300 | 21300 | 2666 |

**NOTE**

When buying high-performance memory for gaming, CAD, or graphic arts with any type of memory module, there's another factor to look for: the column-address-strobe (CAS) latency value (also called CL). The smaller the number, the faster the module can switch addresses and the better the performance. Timing numbers are often listed like this example from a fast DDR4 module: 15-15-15-35. The first number is the CL value; you pay more for a smaller CL value with otherwise similar modules.

## Double Data Rate 5

The first systems to use Double Data Rate 5 (DDR5) memory are available as this book goes to press. DDR5 uses only 1.1V of power, has higher capacity (modules expected to reach 128GB), and offers faster performance than DDR4, along with built-in error correction (discussed later in this chapter) and built-in power management. DDR5 memory is also known as PC5.

DDR5 DIMMs have 288 pins, and both sets of leads have a curved edge for easier insertion. Although DDR5 DIMMs look similar to DDR4, they are not interchangeable. DDR5 SODIMMs have 262 pins and a keying notch slightly offset to the left.

DDR5 DIMM and SODIMM modules differ in memory size (GB), in speed, and by module throughput.

Current DDR5 module sizes range from 8GB to 32GB, but higher capacities are on the way.

Table 15.3 lists some of the common DDR5 speeds. You don't need to memorize this list; just learn how to distinguish DDR5 from other module types.

**TABLE 15.3**  Common DDR5 Speeds

| Module ID | Memory ID | Peak Data Transfer Rate (MB/Sec) | Transfer per Clock Cycle (MT/Sec) |
|---|---|---|---|
| DDR5-6000 | PC5-48000 | 48000 | 6000 |
| DDR5-5600 | PC5-44800 | 44800 | 5600 |
| DDR5-4800 | PC5-38400 | 38400 | 4800 |

**FIGURE 15.4**  A typical DDR5 DIMM (top) compared to a DDR5 SODIMM (bottom).

### Error Correction Code RAM

Memory is organized in groups of eight bits (1 byte). Very early PCs used a ninth parity bit to check the accuracy of the data in the eight data bits. However, parity checking could display, but not fix, memory errors.

A later development of parity checking is error correction code (ECC) RAM, which uses the parity bit along with extra circuitry to correct single-bit memory errors. ECC RAM also requires that the chipset have ECC support enabled. Most desktop computers do not support ECC.

ECC RDIMM RAM is registered ECC memory; it has additional circuitry to improve reliability on large modules. Be sure to determine if a system that uses ECC RAM needs registered modules.

ECC is used primarily by servers. However, DDR5 DIMMs and SODIMMs include a type of ECC that helps make memory more reliable and does not require specific BIOS/UEFI settings.

## MEMORY CONFIGURATION

To achieve the best memory access performance with a given desktop or server system, you must make sure you are using identical modules in certain sockets. That is because most systems support multichannel memory access, as discussed in the following sections.

### Single-Channel RAM

At a minimum, a 64-bit processor must address memory in 64-bit wide channels. This corresponds to the 64-bit wide data pathway of DIMMs and SODIMMs. Using a single DIMM, using a mixture of DIMMs of different sizes, or installing a pair of DIMMs in two separate channels puts your system into single-channel RAM mode. If your system is designed to support dual-channel operation, using only a single DIMM or two or more DIMMs single-channel mode slows down your system.

Figure 15.5 illustrates a system with two identical DIMMs installed. Without consulting the instruction manual or looking for marking on the board, we don't know if these modules are installed for best performance.

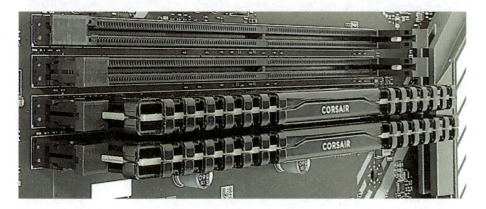

**FIGURE  15.5**  A pair of identical DIMMs installed on a DDR4 motherboard.

## Dual-Channel

Systems with one or more pairs of memory sockets typically have at least two 64-bit wide memory controllers. If you install two identical modules in the correct memory slots, your system will automatically switch to dual-channel memory access, accessing both modules as if they were a single 128-bit wide memory module. This can significantly improve frame rates in 3D games and speed up other types of applications. Most desktop systems support dual-channel memory configuration.

> **EXAM TIP**
>
> You may encounter questions about which memory and memory slots to use for dual-channel operation. Be sure to read the question carefully to determine which slots are paired and which memory modules are identical.

Here's a typical example:

You have four DDR4 memory modules. Two are 8GB, one is a slower 4GB, and one is a faster 16GB. The motherboard has two pairs of slots: DIMM A2 and DIMM B2 are one pair, and DIMM A1 and DIMM B1 are another pair. For best performance, use the A2/B2 slots first with identical modules and set the other modules aside. Figure 15.6 shows the same motherboard used in Figure 15.5. However, in this view, we can see the board markings, which indicate that you use the second (A2) and fourth slots (B2) for the first channel. This installation provides faster performance.

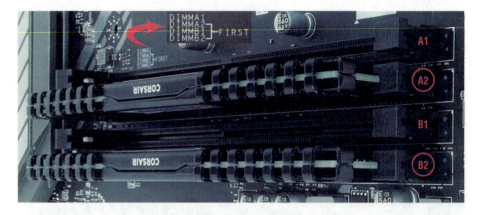

**FIGURE 15.6** Use identical modules in memory slots A2 and B2 for dual-channel performance per the motherboard markings.

### Triple-Channel

Several years ago, some motherboards were manufactured with four or six memory slots for use with processors that had triple-channel memory controllers.

By installing three identical modules in the same-color memory slots, these systems run in triple-channel mode, which is even faster than dual-channel mode. Some motherboards for these processors have only four slots, but three of them were marked for use with identical modules.

### Quad-Channel

Some servers support quad-channel memory. For fastest performance, install four identical (same size and speed) modules into their memory sockets.

If the server has more than four memory sockets, consult the instruction manual for the system or motherboard for memory configuration information.

## CERTMIKE EXAM ESSENTIALS

▶ Standard-size and laptop-size memory modules may have different physical form factors, but their speeds, capacities, and CL timings are similar.

▶ The memory controller in the CPU determines the technology, sizes, and speeds of memory that a given motherboard supports.

▶ Installing a matched pair of slower memory in dual-channel mode often provides better performance than a single faster module with the same capacity. For example, two 8GB modules installed in dual-channel mode provide better performance than a single 16GB module, even if the 16GB module is faster.

## Practice Question 1

Your client is asking for your help in selecting memory upgrades for their desktop computers. All of the computers use DDR4 memory, but there are four different models in the fleet. The Internet connection at the client site is out for a few days, which is why the upgrade has been scheduled.

Of the following strategies, which can best help you determine the upgrades that are necessary?

A. Open one system at random and check its memory size, type, and configuration.
B. Watch all of the computers when they start up and look for memory size information.
C. Open up one system of each model and check its configuration.
D. Run `MSInfo32.exe` on each system.

## Practice Question 2

Your client has asked you to perform a custom desktop build using, as much as possible, leftover parts from previous system upgrades that took place in 2020 or earlier. Some of the parts you can choose from include

▶ A motherboard with 240-pin memory slots and an installed AMD CPU

▶ A motherboard with 288-pin memory slots and an installed 7th generation Intel CPU

▶ Two matched DDR3 4GB modules

▶ Three DDR4 modules, two 8GB, and one 4GB

Which of the following builds are most likely to work from the facts listed?

A. 240-pin motherboard with all DDR4 modules
B. 288-pin motherboard with any or all DDR4 modules
C. 288-pin motherboard with pair of DDR3 modules
D. 240-pin motherboard with pair of DDR3 modules

## Practice Question 1 Explanation

This question is designed to test your ability to deal with a less-than-perfect situation. If the Internet were working, you could download and run vendor-specific or third-party memory detection utilities. Without that option, your options are more limited.

Let's evaluate these choices one at a time.

1. Option A is to open a system at random and check its configuration. Because there are four different models, this isn't very useful for evaluating the fleet. It's not the best answer.

2. Option B, watching startup information for memory sizing, was a good suggestion back in the early 2000s. Today's systems typically don't display this information on startup. This is not the best answer either.

3. Option C, to open up one of each model and check its configuration, is the best of those suggested. It provides a starting point for determining possible upgrades.

4. Option D, running MSInfo32.exe, doesn't provide the level of detail needed. It reports CPU type and speed, and memory size, but doesn't provide module-level information. It's not the best answer either.

**Correct Answer: C. Open up one system of each model and check its configuration.**

## Practice Question 2 Explanation

This question is designed to test your ability to apply your memory knowledge to a real-world scenario, a common feature of CompTIA A+ Certification exams.

Let's evaluate these choices one at a time.

1. Option A, a 240-pin motherboard with all DDR4 modules, is impossible. DDR4 modules have 288 pins and can't fit on the motherboard.

2. Option B, the 288-pin motherboard with any or all DDR4 modules, is a winner. DDR4 uses 288 pin memory sockets, and a 288-pin board dating from 2020 or earlier has to be a board ready for DDR4. It's the best choice

3. Option C, a 288-pin motherboard with DDR3 modules, won't work. 240 doesn't fit into 288, or vice versa.

4. Option D, a 240-pin motherboard with a pair of DDR3 modules, might work. However, if you keep in mind that DDR2 and DDR3 modules are both 240-pin interfaces, you must look at the board to determine whether it uses DDR2 or DDR3 memory. We can't be certain from the information we have.

**Correct Answer: B. 288-pin motherboard with any or all DDR4 modules.**

# CHAPTER 16

# Storage Devices

## Core 1 Objective 3.3: Given a scenario, select and install storage devices.

**Laptops** and desktops alike depend upon a variety of storage devices for use by their operating systems, as temporary storage, and as permanent data storage.

In this chapter, you will learn everything you need to know about CompTIA A+ Certification Core 1 Objective 3.3, including the following topics:

▶ **Hard drives**
▶ **SSDs**
▶ **Drive configurations**
▶ **Removable storage**

## HARD DRIVES

The term *hard drive* refers to the large-capacity onboard storage found in either desktop or laptop computers. Magnetic hard drives are also known as *hard disk drives* (*HDDs*). HDDs have one or more magnetized platters mounted on a spindle and spin at high speeds past read/write heads (see Figure 16.1).

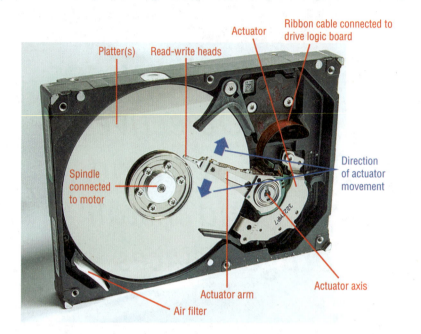

Actuator

Ribbon cable connected to drive logic board

Platter(s)   Read-write heads

Direction of actuator movement

Spindle connected to motor

Actuator axis

Actuator arm

Air filter

**FIGURE 16.1** A typical 3.5-in HDD with its top cover removed.

## Speeds

The speed at which the magnetic media spins has a great deal to do with drive performance and its suitability for a specific task. Table 16.1 compares the common speeds found in recent internal HDDs and what each speed is best used for.

> **NOTE**
>
> 3.5-inch form-factor drives are used in desktop computers. 2.5-inch form-factor drives are used in laptop as well as desktop computers.

**TABLE 16.1** HDD Speeds and Recommended Uses

| Speed | Form factors | Interface | Best Use |
| --- | --- | --- | --- |
| 5,400rpm | 2.5 in, 3.5 in | SATA | General computing |
| 7,200rpm | 2.5 in, 3.5 in | SATA | High-performance PCs; NAS; enterprise network storage |
| | 3.5 in | SAS | Enterprise network storage |

| Speed | Form factors | Interface | Best Use |
|-------|-------------|-----------|----------|
| 10,000rpm | 3.5 in | SATA | High-performance PCs |
| | 2.5 in, 3.5 in | SAS SCSI* | Enterprise network storage |
| 15,000rpm | 2.5 in, 3.5 in | SAS SCSI* | Enterprise network storage |

rpm=revolutions per minute

SATA=Serial Advanced Technology Attachment

NAS=Network Attached Storage

SAS=Serial Attached SCSI

SCSI=Small Computer System Interface (parallel)

* Parallel SCSI drives have capacities of 300GB or less, making them suitable primarily for maintaining legacy network storage

Small Computer System Interface (*SCSI*) is a series of standards for connecting multiple devices (HDDs, tape drives, printers, scanners, and others) to a single host adapter. SCSI devices use parallel connections.

Serial Attached SCSI (*SAS*) is a modern version of SCSI that uses high-speed serial connections while continuing to use SCSI protocols. SATA drives can be connected to SAS ports.

> **NOTE**
>
> Drives of a particular speed and capacity can vary greatly in price. For example, drives built for use in NAS devices or for enterprise network storage are designed to have much longer lifespans than those made for use in PCs and have higher costs in consequence. When shopping for drives for a specific intended use, such as surveillance, RAID arrays, and gaming, consider drives made for the specific task.

## HDD Form Factors

In computers, *form factor* refers to the physical shape and dimensions of a component such as a hard drive, power supply, or motherboard. There are two form factors used in HDDs.

- ▶ 2.5-inch drives
- ▶ 3.5-inch drives

The dimensions refer to their width (see Figure 16.2). Each size is optimized for different uses. Let's take a closer look, focusing on SATA (internal) and USB (external) interface drives.

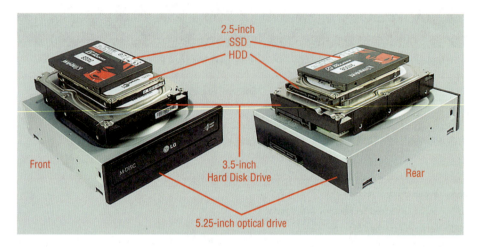

**FIGURE 16.2** Typical SATA drives in order by size, smallest to largest dimensions.

### 3.5-inch

3.5-inch drives are optimized for use in desktop computers and high-capacity USB external drives.

▶ 3.5-inch HDDs fit into standard-sized drive bays without needing adapters.
▶ 3.5-inch drives have capacities ranging up to 20TB as of this writing.
▶ 3.5-inch drives in the 7,200rpm speed range are widely available at reasonable prices.

However, there are some downsides to this form factor.

▶ 3.5-inch HDDs in USB drive enclosures must have AC power.
▶ 3.5-inch HDDs use more power than 2.5-inch drives and produce more heat.
▶ 3.5-inch HDDs take up more space inside the case than 2.5-inch drives.
▶ 3.5-inch HDDs are also bulkier when used in USB external drives.

### 2.5-inch

2.5-inch drives are optimized for use in laptop computers and for mobility.

▶ 2.5-inch HDDs can be installed in smaller drive bays that use less space inside a case than 3.5-inch drives.
▶ 2.5-inch HDDs fit inside laptops.
▶ 2.5-inch HDDs in USB external drives are bus-powered via the USB cable; no AC adapter needed.
▶ 2.5-inch HDDs use much less power than 3.5-inch HDDs and produce much less heat.

What are the downsides to 2.5-inch drives? Consider these:

▶ 2.5-inch SATA HDDs have capacities up to only 5TB as of this writing.
▶ 2.5-inch drives in the 7,200rpm speed range have smaller capacities than slower drives.

To sum up, for speed and capacity, 3.5-inch drives rule! For mobility and versatility in both desktop and laptop installations, 2.5-inch drives are winners.

## Installing an HDD in a Desktop

To install an SATA HDD in a desktop, follow these steps:

1. Shut off power to the system and unplug it.
2. Open the right-side panel (as viewed from the rear) to reveal the drive bays.
3. Locate the 3.5-in or 2.5-in drive bays as appropriate.
4. If necessary, remove the mounting cage from the system.
5. If a drive uses mounting rails or a mounting frame, attach the drive to the rails or frame.
6. Connect an SATA data cable to a motherboard SATA port.
7. Locate an unused SATA power cable connector.
8. Attach SATA data and power cables to the drive.
9. Insert the drive into an empty bay in the system or drive cage and fasten it into place with drive screws (Figure 16.3).
10. If the drive is in a cage, remount the cage in the system.
11. Close the side panel.
12. Restore power to the system and turn it on.
13. Go into the BIOS/UEFI firmware setup screen and make sure the drive is detected and configured properly (AHCI for non-RAID, RAID for RAID array).

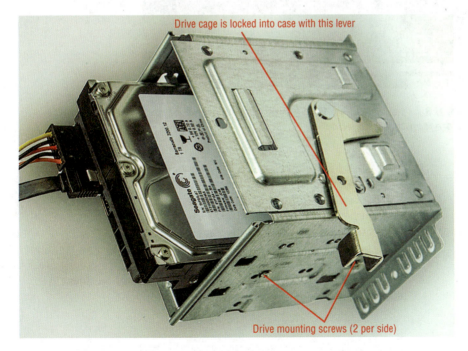

**F I G U R E  1 6 . 3**  **A typical 3.5-inch HDD mounted in a drive cage.**

## Installing an HDD in a Laptop

HDDs used in laptops use the 2.5-inch form factor.

To install an HDD in a laptop, follow these steps:

1. Check instructions for preparing the laptop for upgrades and follow them.
2. Shut off power to the system and unplug it.
3. Open the system and locate the drive bay.
4. Remove or disconnect the battery if possible.
5. Unscrew bolts holding the drive in place (if any).
6. Remove the drive from the SATA interface (Figure 16.4).

**FIGURE 16.4** **Pulling the SATA drive away from the laptop's SATA connector before replacing it.**

7. Remove the existing drive.
8. Remove the mounting frame from the existing drive.
9. Place the new drive into the mounting frame and fasten it to the frame.
10. Install the new drive where the old drive was connected; push the drive into place until it connects with the SATA port (Figure 16.5) .
11. Reattach or reinstall the battery.
12. Start up the system.
13. Go into the BIOS/UEFI firmware setup screen and make sure the drive is detected.

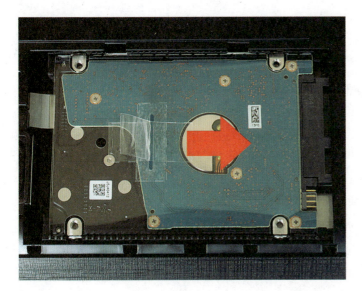

**FIGURE 16.5** Pulling the replacement SATA drive into the laptop's SATA connector.

# SSDs

Solid-state drives (*SSDs*) use high-speed, high-capacity nonvolatile memory, typically NAND, and are designed for use as a system or data drive in place of HDDs. SSDs have largely replaced HDDs as system drives in laptops. SSDs are also used as system drives in midrange and high-end desktop computers.

Solid-state drives have much faster boot times, faster read speeds, and faster write speeds than HDDs. However, SSDs are more expensive per gigabyte, so HDDs continue to be useful for data storage. Consequently, many systems use SSDs for boot drives and HDDs for data drives.

## SSD Form Factors

SSDs are available in three form factors.

- ▶ SATA
- ▶ M.2
- ▶ mSATA

Let's learn about the differences among them next.

### SATA

SATA SSD drives connect to the same power and data cables as SATA HDDs but use smaller 2.5-inch drive bays (adapters enable these drives to fit into 3.5-inch drive bays as well). These drives are faster than SATA HDDs, but the M.2 form factor (next section) drives are much faster than any SATA interface drive.

### M.2

M.2 drives, originally known as *next-generation form factor* (NGFF) drives, are about the same size as a memory module but have contacts on one end instead of on one side. An M.2 drive slides into a small surface-mounted connector on a laptop (or desktop) motherboard and is held in place by a set screw at the opposite end of the drive.

M.2 drives are available in various form factors, the most common of which are as follows:

2280 (22mm wide, 80mm long)

2242 (22mm wide, 42mm long)

2230 (22mm wide, 30mm long)

M.2 is an interface that is also used by various types of communication cards, and the M.2 interface connectors on motherboards are keyed according to the device types they accept. M.2 drives use either SATA or NVMe communications interfaces. Figure 16.6 compares an M.2 SSD card with a wireless M.2 card.

**FIGURE 16.6** **M.2 SSD drive compared with an M.2 wireless card.**

## mSATA

The predecessor to the M.2 drive was the mini-SATA (mSATA) drive. Compared to M.2 drives, mSATA drives are wider, have two mounting screw holes, and have smaller capacities (up to about 1GB). This type of drive has speeds comparable to other SATA SSDs. Although mSATA drives are currently still on the market, desktops and laptops that use it were never common and have been discontinued.

## Communications Interfaces

SSDs use three different communications interfaces.

▶ SATA
▶ Non-volatile Memory Express (NVMe)
▶ Peripheral Component Interconnect Express (PCIe)

Let's take a closer look at each.

## SATA

Serial ATA (*SATA*) is a high-speed serial interface that is based on ATA logic. AT Attachment (*ATA*) is a series of standards for HDD and other types of mass storage devices. PATA and SATA are based on ATA. SATA is used only for storage devices. SATA connections are supported by two types of physical drive interfaces: SATA and M.2.

SATA interfacing is the only interface available for SSD drives connected to the SATA interfaces used on desktop and laptop drives. However, SATA is also used on older and low-end SSDs that connect via the M.2 connector (refer to Figure 16.7).

SATA SSDs are about three times faster than SATA HDDs using SATA 6Gbps interfacing.

## Non-volatile Memory Express

Non-volatile Memory Express (*NVMe*) drives use *PCIe* lanes to connect with the rest of the computer instead of SATA communications. The maximum number of PCIe lanes that an NVMe drive connects via M.2 is four, but depending upon the motherboard chipset and system configuration, some systems might only provide two PCIe lanes per M.2 slot.

PCI Express (*PCIe*) is a high-speed interface that consists of multiple lanes between motherboard devices. PCIe is provided by both the CPU and by most modern chipsets. The most common versions today are PCIe v3 and PCIe v4.

M.2 interfaces that support NVMe drives can also support SATA drives. However, an M.2 interface made only for SATA drives cannot use NVMe drives.

The faster the PCIe version (v4 is fastest) supported by the M.2 slot, the faster that NVMe can run. On systems that have more than one M.2 slot, check the PCIe lanes and PCIe version supported by each slot and use the fastest slot and largest number of lanes for best drive performance.

How much faster is NVMe than SATA? A typical NVMe drive connected to PCIe v4 using four lanes can transfer data at a rate up to 5000MBps! PCIe v3 uses four lanes up to 3500MBps. SATA SSDs can't exceed 600MBps. M.2 drives are labeled as NVMe or SSD, and the connector can vary as well (Figure 16.7).

**FIGURE 16.7** These M.2 NVMe drives (center and bottom) use the M key connector, while this M.2 SATA drive (top) uses the B+M key connector.

### EXAM TIP

An M.2 drive with a B+M connector can be either SATA or NVMe. An M.2 drive with an M connector must be NVMe. An M.2 drive with a B connector must only be SATA.

### Peripheral Component Interconnect Express

For desktop computers that have Peripheral Component Interconnect Express (PCIe) slots but lack M.2 slots, a third interfacing option is available: M.2 NVMe SSDs mounted on PCIe cards. Originally, these cards were produced with preinstalled SSDs, but a number of manufacturers now sell cards that can be user-populated.

Cards vary in capacity from one to four M.2 SSDs. The size of the physical connector ranges from PCIe x4 to PCIe x16, but the number of PCIe lanes might vary. PCIe-attached SSDs will run at the same speed as SSDs mounted into a same-specification M.2 NVMe slot.

Cards that are designed to support M.2 SATA as well as NVMe drives use an SATA cable to carry SATA signals to an open SATA port on the motherboard.

# DRIVE CONFIGURATION

Drive configuration settings are performed through the BIOS/UEFI firmware configuration settings. The most important consideration for both HDD and SSD drives is the Redundant Array of Independent (or Inexpensive) Drives (*RAID*). RAID refers to a standardized way to use two or more drives as a single logical unit (array) to improve performance or data safety.

## Redundant Array of Independent Disks

There are many levels of Redundant Array of Independent Disks (RAID), but the most common ones are RAID 0, RAID 1, RAID 5, and RAID 10. It is possible to use drives of different sizes in any RAID array, but if you do, drives that are larger will have only part of their capacity used. Best practice is to use drives of identical capacity, layout, and performance; basically, use two, three, or four drives of the same brand and model number.

### RAID 0

Despite the common name, RAID 0, also known as disk striping, does *not* provide any data redundancy at all. RAID 0 uses two drives and copies part of the data to the first drive and the remainder to the second drive in the array. Because RAID 0 stripes the data across two drives, a RAID 0 array provides much faster data reads than a single drive of the same type. However, if either drive fails, all data stored in the array is lost. Think of RAID 0 as "Zero RAID" in terms of data safety!

   The size of a RAID 0 array using identical drives is the total size of the individual drives. A RAID 0 array using two 2TB drives has a capacity of 4TB.

### RAID 1

RAID 1, also known as disk mirroring, is the lowest level of RAID to actually provide redundancy. RAID 1 uses two drives and writes the same data to both drives in the array. RAID 1 is slower than RAID 0, but if either drive fails, the array can be rebuilt from the contents of the surviving drive.

   The size of a RAID 1 array using identical drives is one-half of the individual drives' total size. A RAID 1 array using two 2TB drives has a capacity of 2TB.

### RAID 5

RAID 5, also known as disk striping with parity, provides faster read performance than RAID 1 along with protection against the failure of a single drive. Data and parity information used to rebuild the array are stored across all drives. RAID 5 requires a minimum of three drives but can also be configured with more drives.

   The size of a RAID 5 array using identical drives depends upon two factors: the size of each drive and the number of drives. The more drives in the array, the greater the usable space:

> ▶ Three identical drives means the array size is about 2/3 of total drive capacity.
> ▶ Four identical drives means the array size is about 3/4 of total drive capacity.

For example, a RAID 5 array with three 2TB drives has a capacity of 4TB, and a RAID 5 array with four 2TB drives has a capacity of 6TB.

### RAID 10

RAID 10 combines data mirroring with data striping for fast performance, data protection, and, compared to RAID 5, much faster array rebuilding in case of a single drive failure. RAID 10 requires four identical drives that are arranged in two RAID 1 pairs, with RAID 0 striping across both pairs of drives.

The size of a RAID 10 array using identical drives is one-half of the individual drives' total size. For example, a RAID 10 array using four 2TB drives is 4TB.

> **EXAM TIP**
>
> RAID 0 and RAID 1 are supported by the most recent SATA host adapters on motherboards. Many also support RAID 10, but RAID 5 requires an add-on RAID card.

### Installing RAID Arrays

Drives in a RAID array are installed normally. The difference is that after the drives are installed, the RAID functions are set up in the system BIOS or UEFI firmware RAID dialog or by running the setup utility provided with an add-on RAID card. The details vary according to the motherboard or add-on card RAID feature. Figure 16.8 shows a typical RAID configuration utility dialog box.

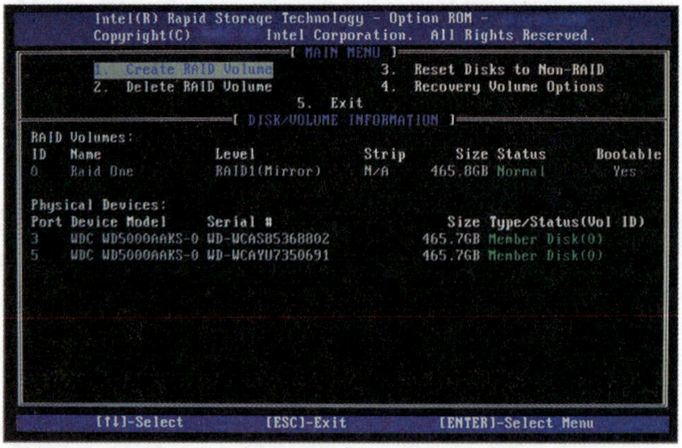

**FIGURE 16.8** A RAID 1 (mirrored) array configured on a system using an Intel chipset. (Source: Microsoft Corporation)

The contents of all drives are deleted during the setup process, and the array is treated as a single drive letter in Windows or a single volume in Linux or macOS.

**NOTE**

There are many YouTube videos showing the process. A good one especially for users with Intel chipsets is OC3D TV's "How to set up a RAID array on your motherboard" at www.youtube.com/watch?v=rgo0OPSw9_E.

# REMOVABLE STORAGE

There are three types of removable storage that are commonly used, and you need to know how they work and how to install them for the CompTIA A+ Core 1 certification exam:

▶ Flash drives
▶ Memory cards
▶ Optical drives

## Flash Drives

Flash drives contain flash memory (which retains data when power is turned off) and a memory controller inside a shell that has a USB connector (USB 2.0, 3.x, or USB Type-C). Some drives use a retractable or swivel-top design to protect the connector, while some drives use a removable cap. Figure 16.9 shows the outside and inside of a typical 64GB USB 3.0 flash drive with a retractable design.

**FIGURE 16.9 Inside the shell of a typical 64GB flash drive.**

To install a flash drive, simply plug it into a USB port on your computer. Windows, macOS, and most Linux distributions will display the contents of the drive automatically.

**EXAM TIP**

If a flash drive is not automatically recognized in Linux, you can use the autofs utility. If it is not automatically recognized in macOS, open Finder and enable the Show External disks option in the Preferences menu.

To remove a flash drive safely in Windows, close File Explorer or other processes using the drive, open the Safely Remove Hardware and Eject Media menu in the taskbar, and click Eject (drive). When a status box indicates the drive is safe to remove, remove it.

To remove a flash drive safely in macOS, close any processes using the drive, right-click the drive icon, and select Eject Drive, or open a new Finder window, select the drive, and click Eject (drivename) from the File menu in Finder.

To remove a flash drive safely in Linux, see the documentation with your distro or desktop. Procedures vary.

**TIP**

USB flash drives are often blocked in enterprise environments to protect against malware threats or data theft. USB flash drives can be blocked by network or local security policy settings, by disabling USB in BIOS/UEFI settings, or by disabling AutoPlay in operating system settings.

## Memory Cards

Like USB flash drives, memory cards contain flash memory and a memory controller. The difference is that instead of a USB connector, memory cards have an edge connector enabling them to be inserted into a smartphone, digital camera, or other device with a compatible card slot.

The most common family of memory cards in use today is the Secure Digital (SD), available in full-size and micro versions (a mini version is rare). Full-size SD card slots can also read/write microSD cards by means of an adapter (refer to Figure 16.10).

SD and microSD cards come in three size ranges; SDXC slots also support SDHC and SD, and SDHC slots also support SD.

- ► SD (up to 2 GB)
- ► SDHC (4-32GB)
- ► SDXC (64GB-1TB or larger)

Drive speeds are measured in several ways including speed class (stylized C from C2-C10), Ultra Speed Class (U1, U3), and Video Speed Class (V10-V90). A1 cards are best for smartphones, tablets, and Chromebooks. Some digital cameras can transfer data faster when using A2 cards.

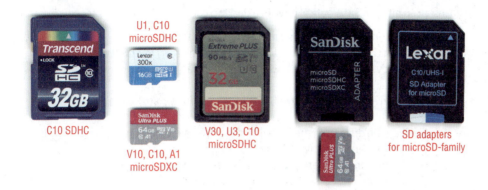

U1, C10
microSDHC

C10 SDHC

V10, C10, A1
microSDXC

V30, U3, C10
microSDHC

SD adapters
for microSD-family

**F I G U R E   1 6 . 1 0**   **SD and microSD cards and adapters with different speed markings.**

Cards marked C10 are suitable for high-speed still photography and standard resolution video. Cards marked with U1 or U3 are designed for HD video, as are cards marked with V10. Cards marked with V30 or higher are designed for 4K to 8K video. Many cards have more than one marking, which can indicate their age or their suitability for various tasks (Figure 16.10).

To install a memory card, simply plug it into a card reader built into your computer or connected to a USB port on your computer. Windows, macOS, and most Linux distributions will display the contents of the drive automatically.

To remove a memory card safely, see the tips in the "Flash Drives" section.

## Optical Drives

Internal optical drives, once common in both laptop and desktop computers, have been largely left out of recent designs. However, they can be added to 5.25-inch drive bays on desktop computers, and external versions can always be connected to both types of computers via USB ports. Optical drives remain useful for installing software, for running utility programs, and for backups of small amounts of data.

Compact Disc (*CD*) is the oldest optical storage medium, designed originally for music (74 minutes, 80 minutes), but also can be used to store computer data. DVD and BD drives can also use CD media.

Compact Disc File System (CDFS) is the file system used for CD and CD-R (recordable CD) media. It provides a standardized way to read, write, and replace older files with newer files.

Internal optical drives used the IDE/PATA interface, but in the last decade, SATA interface optical drives have replaced them.

The most common type of optical drives can read and write to DVD and CD media; external versions connect to USB 2.0 ports. Some Blu-ray internal and external drives are also available and connect to USB 3.0 ports.

To install an internal SATA optical drive in a desktop computer, follow this procedure:

1. Shut off power to the system and unplug it.
2. Open the right-side panel (as viewed from the rear) to reveal the drive bays.
3. Remove the cover over the 5.25-inch drive bay you want to use for the optical drive.
4. If a drive uses mounting rails or a mounting frame, attach the drive to the rails or frame.
5. Slide the drive from the front into the drive bay. Make sure the media tray is to the front and the drive is mounted upright.
6. Connect an SATA data cable to a motherboard SATA port.
7. Locate an unused SATA power cable connector.
8. Attach SATA data and power cables to the drive (Figure 16.11).
9. Fasten it into place.
10. Close the side panel.
11. Restore power to the system and turn it on.
12. Go into the BIOS/UEFI firmware setup screen and make sure the drive is detected and configured properly.

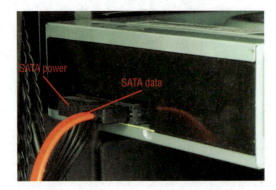

**FIGURE 16.11** Typical SATA optical drive installed in a 5.25-inch drive bay.

## CERTMIKE EXAM ESSENTIALS

▶ Know the hard disk drive (HDD) speeds including 5,400, 7,200, 10,000, and 15,000 RPM (revolutions per minute) and form factors including 2.5 and 3.5 inch.

▶ Recognize the solid-state drive (SSD) communications interfaces and form factors including NVMe, SATA, and PCIe with form factors M.2 and mSATA.

▶ All three types of removable storage (flash drives, memory cards, or optical media) can be used for data transfer between devices, but flash drives are the only type that does not require additional hardware.

## Practice Question 1

You have the following 2TB drives:

1. 7200 RPM SATA
2. SSD SATA 2.5-inch
3. SSD SATA M.2
4. SSD NVMe M.2

You have three desktop systems:

▶ System X has an available SATA host adapter on the motherboard

▶ System Y has an available M.2 interface with an M key

▶ System Z has an available M.2 interface with a B key

Which drive provides the best performance in System X? _____

Which drive provides the best performance in System Y? _____

Which drive provides the best performance in System Z? _____

## Practice Question 2

1. You have 10 systems that need RAID drive installations. Five of these support RAID 0 and 1 only, while the other five support RAID 0, 1, and 10. To provide maximum safety and best performance for all systems and provide RAID array sizes of at least 4TB each, how many identical drives are needed? How large should each drive be? Do not calculate for spares, as they are provided for in a separate budget. Choose the BEST answer from the following possibilities.

▶ 30 drives, 4TB each

▶ 40 drives, 8TB each

▶ 30 drives, 2TB each

▶ 20 drives, 3TB each

## Practice Question 1 Explanation

First, let's consider System X. System X has only an SATA port. That means options 3 and 4, both of which require an M.2 interface, can't work. That narrows down the possible answers to 1 and 2. 1 is an HDD, and 2 is an SSD. Even the slowest SSD is about 3X faster than a typical HDD, so 2 is the best answer for System X.

Next, let's consider System Y. System Y has an M.2 interface with an M key, so options 1 and 2 are eliminated. An M key is used for M.2 drives that use the NVMe interface. NVMe is much faster than SATA, so option 4 is the best choice for System Y.

Finally, we must provide the best drive for System Z. Like System Y, options 1 and 2 are eliminated because our system has an available M.2 interface. However, a B key M.2 interface doesn't support the NVMe drives. It supports the slower SATA M.2 SSD drives. Thus, option 3 is the best choice for System Z.

**Correct Answers:**

**System X: Option 2 (SSD SATA 2.5-inch)**

**System Y: Option 4 (SSD NVMe M.2**

**System Z: Option 3 (SSD SATA M.2)**

## Practice Question 2 Explanation

This question is designed to test your understanding of RAID levels and how RAID array sizes are calculated.

Option A, 30 drives at 4TB each, works out like this. RAID 0 provides no data security for any systems, so it can be dismissed for all calculations. RAID 1, which uses two identical drives and provides a mirror of one drive to another for data safety, is supported by five systems, so 10 drives are required. RAID 10, supported by five systems, is safer and faster than RAID 1 and requires four identical drives per system. Thus, 20 drives are needed. The total identical drives needed are 30 (10+20). To achieve a RAID array of 4TB in RAID 1, each drive must be 4TB. Four 4TB drives in a RAID 10 array actually create an 8TB array, but that's acceptable.

Option B, 40 drives at 8TB each, works out this way. There would be 10 unused drives, the RAID 1 array size is 8TB, and the RAID 10 array is 16TB. It exceeds the number of drives and the array size needed, so it's more expensive than needed.

Option C, 30 drives at 2TB each, calculates out this way. The number of drives provides enough for each array. However, the RAID 1 arrays are only 2TB, and the RAID 10 arrays are 4TB. The RAID 10 arrays meet the specifications, but not the RAID 1 arrays.

Option D, 20 drives at 3TB each, doesn't include enough drives to take care of both the RAID 1 and RAID 10 systems. If the drives were used only for RAID 10 arrays, each array would be 6TB, but if 10 more drives were purchased to provide enough drives for the RAID 1 systems, the RAID 1 arrays would be only 3TB each.

**Correct Answer: A. 30 drives, 4TB each**

# CHAPTER 17

# Motherboards
## Core 1 Objective 3.4 (Part 1) Given a scenario, install and configure motherboards.

*Motherboards* are the foundation for both desktop and laptop computers. Everything that connects to a computer connects either directly or indirectly to the motherboard. In this chapter, you learn what you need to know about the motherboard portion of Core 1 Objective 3.4 (the CPU and add-on cards portions of this objective are covered in Chapter 18). These include the following:

▶ Motherboard form factors
▶ Motherboard connector types
▶ Motherboard compatibility
▶ Cooling

## MOTHERBOARD FORM FACTORS

Desktop motherboards are available in several form factors, the most important of which are ATX, microATX, and mini-ITX. The following sections discuss their features.

### Advanced Technology eXtended

Most desktop motherboards are based on the Advanced Technology eXtended (*ATX*) standard. These motherboards all feature a rear port cluster for input/output (I/O) ports such as USB, network, audio, and others, up to seven expansion slots that run parallel to the short side of the motherboard, four or more memory sockets near the CPU, and a case that opens from the left side (as viewed from the front). A full-size ATX motherboard is up to 12 inches wide and 9.6 inches tall.

MicroATX (mATX) motherboards are smaller versions of ATX (no more than 9.6 inches tall and 9.6 inches wide) with no more than four expansion slots. Figure 17.1 compares the dimensions and major components of late-model ATX and mATX motherboards.

> **EXAM NOTE**
>
> ATX and mATX motherboards should not be confused with the short-lived BTX motherboard design. BTX has its expansion slots running along the right side of the motherboard, has memory on the left side of the motherboard, and locates the processor between the expansion slots and memory to improve airflow. It is not compatible with ATX and has been obsolete for many years.

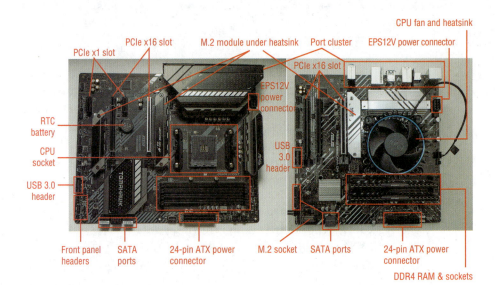

**FIGURE 17.1** Typical ATX motherboard (left) and microATX motherboard (right).

## ATX and microATX Port Clusters

ATX and microATX motherboards feature port clusters at the rear of the motherboard. The details of a port cluster vary according to the ports built into the motherboard. In general, ATX motherboards have more ports than microATX motherboards because they have more room for ports and components.

Figure 17.2 illustrates two typical port clusters from recent ATX and microATX mother-boards. The ATX port cluster is from a motherboard that uses a built-in I/O shield. The micro-ATX port cluster is from a motherboard that uses the more-typical removable I/O shield (not installed).

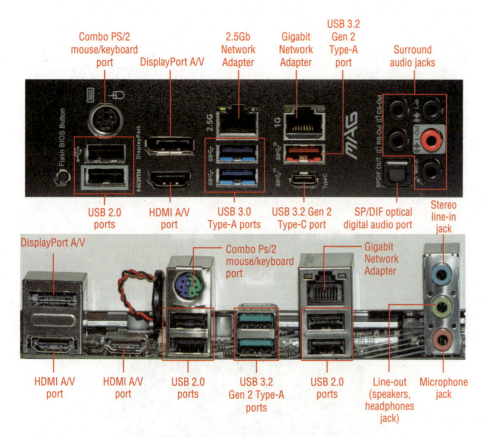

**F I G U R E   1 7 . 2   Typical ATX port cluster (top) and microATX port cluster (bottom).**

To learn more about the technologies used in typical motherboard ports, see Chapter 14, "Cables and Connectors." For more about USB Type-C ports, see Chapter 3, "Mobile Device Ports and Accessories."

## Information Technology eXtended

The Information Technology eXtended (*ITX*) motherboard form factor was introduced by VIA Technologies in March 2001 for use with their low-power C3 processor and chipsets. These motherboards were originally designed for set-top box and home entertainment small form-factor PCs. The original ITX motherboard was never used in production PCs, but the first mini-ITX (a smaller version of ITX) form-factor motherboards were released in November 2001.

Mini-ITX motherboards are 6.7 × 6.7 inches and may have either integrated processors (see Figure 17.3) or socketed processors from a variety of vendors, including Intel and AMD, as well as VIA Technologies. Mini-ITX motherboards have port clusters similar to micro-ATX and have a single expansion slot (typically PCIe ×16 in recent versions). Most use full-size DIMMs, but a few use SO-DIMMs. Mini-ITX motherboards can fit into ATX or microATX cases as well as mini-ITX cases.

Mini-ITX and its smaller siblings (Pico-ITX and Nano-ITX) are most typically used for home theater and embedded applications, but those with socketed AMD or Intel processors and PCIe ×16 slots can be used for small-form-factor gaming systems.

**FIGURE 17.3**  A typical mini-ITX motherboard optimized for home theater uses.

# MOTHERBOARD CONNECTOR TYPES

Motherboards have many connector types. They are used for add-on cards, internal ports, connections for external ports, fans, case features, and mass storage. The following sections discuss these features.

## Peripheral Component Interconnect

The Peripheral Component Interconnect (PCI) slot was introduced in 1992 as a multipurpose connector for many different types of add-on cards. Over the years, this 32-bit slot running at 33MHz (Figure 17.4) was used for network, video, audio, I/O, and hard disk host adapter cards.

Intel stopped supporting the PCI bus on desktop motherboards in 2012, and AMD stopped supporting the PCI bus on desktop motherboards in 2014.

Some industrial PCs and older servers also use the 66MHz 32-bit PCI slot or the PCI-X 64-bit slot. Some vendors offer PCIe cards with PCI slots built in to enable use of older cards in current systems.

## PCI Express

PCI Express (PCIe or PCIE) was introduced in 2003 and gradually replaced PCI slots. PCIe slots are available in four widths, based on the number of lanes used (Table 17.1). PCIe has been released in six versions, each newer version being about double the speed of the previous version. PCIe slots and versions on a given system depend upon the CPU and chipset it uses. See Figure 17.4 for a comparison of PCIe ×1 and ×16 and PCI slots and cards (these are the most common sizes).

**NOTE**

Speeds shown in Table 17.1 are unidirectional, but PCIe supports full-duplex (bidirectional) transfers.

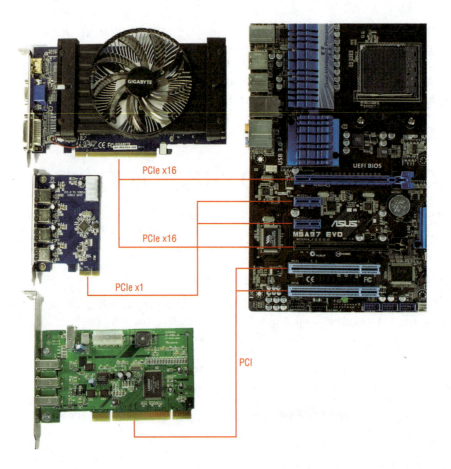

**FIGURE 17.4** PCI card and PCI slots compared to PCIe ×16 and ×1 slots.

**TABLE 17.1** PCIe Slots and Versions

| PCIe Slot Type | v1 Speed | v2 Speed | v3 Speed | v4 Speed | v5 Speed | v6 Speed |
|---|---|---|---|---|---|---|
| ×1 | 250MB/sec | 500MB/sec | 1GB/sec | 2GB/sec | 4GB/sec | 8GB/sec |
| ×4 | 1GB/sec | 2GB/sec | 4GB/sec | 8GB/sec | 16GB/sec | 32GB/sec |
| ×8 | 2GB/sec | 4GB/sec | 8GB/sec | 16GB/sec | 32GB/sec | 64GB/sec |
| ×16 | 4GB/sec | 8GB/sec | 16GB/sec | 32GB/sec | 64GB/sec | 128GB/sec |

×=PCIe lane, pronounced "by" as in "PCIe by 1, PCIe by 4," etc.

PCIe slots are backward-compatible in two ways: wider slots can use narrower cards (for example, an ×4 slot can use an ×1 card), and newer versions of PCIe can use cards made for older versions (and vice versa). When there's a mismatch of versions, the older version's speeds and features are supported. Some motherboards have two or more slots that use the x16 connector. However, the additional slots might actually support only x4 or x8 transfer rates. These are designed for multi-GPU gaming applications such as NVIDIA SLI or AMD CrossFire technology.

> **EXAM TIP**
>
> Given a scenario, be able to identify PCIe x16 and PCIe x1 expansion slots on the motherboard.

## Power Connectors

Motherboards use a 24-pin ATX power connector to provide 3.3V, 5V, and 12V DC power for expansion slots, PCIe video cards, SATA and other storage devices, and small motors such as case and CPU fans; Recent systems also use an eight-pin EPS12V connector to provide power for the CPU's voltage regulator, while older systems use a four-pin 12V ATX12V connector for this purpose. The 24-pin ATX and 8-pin EPS12V power connectors are highlighted in Figure 17.1, and the details are shown in Figure 17.5.

**F I G U R E   1 7 . 5**   **24-pin ATX (left) and 8-pin EPS12V (right) power connectors compared.**

> **EXAM TIP**
>
> Know that motherboards use a 24-pin ATX power connector to provide 3.3V, 5V, and 12V DC power for expansion slots and other components.

## SATA

Serial ATA (SATA) host adapters are used for hard disk drives (HDDs), for solid-state drives (SSDs), and for optical drives. Some motherboards have upward-facing SATA ports, while others have forward-facing ports or a mixture. Figure 17.6 compares typical front-mounted and top-mounted SATA ports. All SATA ports, regardless of speeds supported, use the same connector.

**F I G U R E   1 7 . 6**  Front-mounted (left) and top-mounted SATA ports from two different motherboards.

## eSATA

External SATA (eSATA) was built into some motherboards before USB 3.0 was introduced and continued to be used for a while afterward. The eSATA port enables the SATA interface to be used by external drives. However, because most eSATA ports run at only 1.5Gbps or 3Gbps and eSATA requires AC power, USB 3.0, which runs at 5Gbps and can provide power to 2.5-inch-wide drives, rapidly replaced eSATA.

SATA internal ports can be converted to eSATA with an inexpensive adapter cable for use with eSATA docks and drives. Figure 17.7 shows eSATA and USB 3.0 ports in an older ATX port cluster compared to a SATA-eSATA cable adapter.

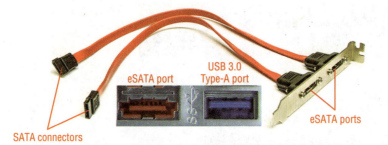

**F I G U R E   1 7 . 7**  eSATA port (left inset), USB 3.0 port (right inset), and SATA-eSATA adapter cable.

## Headers

Headers are used to attach cables that are built into the front or top of a desktop case, fans, and additional ports that are mounted on card brackets. Typical headers include front-panel cables for the power switch and signal lights, audio jacks, USB 2.0, USB 3.x, and USB Type-C ports; CPU and case fans; legacy ports (LPT and COM); and TPM modules. Some motherboards also include LED lighting headers. See Figures 17.8 and 17.9.

USB 2.0                USB 2.0                    USB 3.0              Front-Panel          Front-Panel

**FIGURE 17.8** Typical headers for USB 2.0, USB 3.0, and front-panel cables.

**FIGURE 17.9** Typical headers for four-pin CPU fan (left) and three-pin system (case) fans (right).

## M.2

Many recent systems include slots for M.2 SSDs, with most supporting either SATA or NVMe interfacing. Originally, these slots were open, but many high-performance systems now use covers that incorporate thermal interface material to prevent heat buildup. Figure 17.10 illustrates a gaming motherboard with a cover over its M.2 slot.

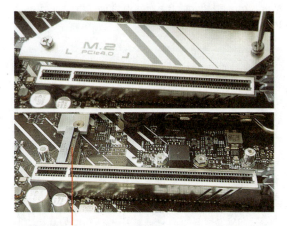

M.2 connector

**FIGURE 17.10** Removing the cover over an M.2 slot in preparation for installing an M.2 SSD.

> **EXAM TIP**
> For the Core 1 1101 exam, make sure you understand the differences between PCI and PCIe slots, the different types of motherboard power connectors and what they do, and the differences between SATA, eSATA, and M.2 mass storage connectors.

# MOTHERBOARD COMPATIBILITY

Motherboards differ in many ways from each other. Motherboards are made for processors from either AMD or Intel, and they are optimized for servers, for two or more server or workstation processors, and for desktop or mobile uses. These topics are covered in the following sections.

## CPU Sockets

When selecting a motherboard, the first question most users ask is, "What processors does it support?" Motherboards that support Intel or AMD processors use different processor sockets and have other differences depending upon the processor families they support.

### Advanced Micro Devices, Inc.

Recent and current models of AMD desktop processors use various models of the pin grid array (PGA) socket. With this type of processor socket, holes in the socket connect to pins in the rear of the socket. A clamping lever is moved to lock the pins in place after the processor is lowered into the socket (Figure 17.11).

> **NOTE**
> For a quick visual breakdown of the various AMD PGA sockets and the processors they support, see www.buildcomputers.net/amd-cpu-socket.html.

**FIGURE 17.11** Installing an AMD PGA processor.

> **NOTE**
>
> As this book went to press, AMD released its first mainstream desktop CPU socket using LGA technology, AM5 (also known as LGA 1718), along with the launch of its Ryzen 7000 processors. To learn more about LGA, see "Intel," next.

## Intel

Intel processors, in contrast to AMD, have used Land Grid Array (LGA) sockets for a number of years. LGA sockets use spring-loaded lands in the processor socket to touch contacts on the backside of the processor. LGA processors are locked in place by a frame around all four sides of the processor (Figure 17.12).

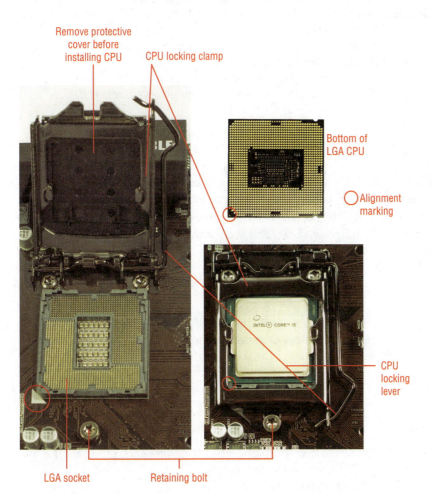

**FIGURE 17.12** **Installing an Intel LGA processor.**
(Source: jan nakhonkae / Adobe Stock)

## Multisocket

Multisocket motherboards have two or more processor sockets. Most multisocket motherboards are designed for servers, but some workstation motherboards also use multisocket designs. Multisocket motherboards, combined with multicore and multithreading processors, enable systems to multitask many more jobs than any single-processor system.

## Server

Server motherboards have several differences from desktop motherboards, including the following:

▶ Support for server CPUs such as Intel Xeon and AMD Opteron or EPYC
▶ Support for ECC or Registered RAM for greater reliability
▶ More memory sockets (most have at least eight), compared to four or less on most desktop motherboards
▶ PCIe x8 rather than PCIe x1 slots for I/O cards
▶ More SATA host adapters (eight or more)
▶ Two or more gigabit or faster Ethernet network adapters
▶ Available in tower, rackmount, and other form factors including Extended ATX (EATX)

> **NOTE**
>
> Supermicro is one of the world's leaders in server and workstation motherboards. See many types of motherboards, including multisocket models, at `www.supermicro.com/en/products/motherboards/server-boards` and `www.supermicro.com/en/products/motherboards/workstation-boards`.

## Desktop

Desktop motherboards typically use the ATX, microATX, or mini-ITX form factors. For details, see the "Advanced Technology eXtended" and "Information Technology eXtended" sections earlier in this chapter.

## Mobile

Mobile motherboards are used in laptops. Compared to desktop motherboards, mobile motherboards differ in many ways. Typical differences include:

▶ Surface-mounted lower-wattage (and lower-performance) processors that use heat pipes and a built-in fan for cooling
▶ SO-DIMM memory modules instead of DIMMs

▶ A single 2.5-inch drive bay and/or one or two M.2 slots for mass storage
▶ Integrated LCD display and keyboard
▶ M.2 slot for WLAN

Figure 17.13 illustrates a motherboard from a Dell touch-screen laptop.

**FIGURE 17.13**  **A late-model Dell touch-screen laptop motherboard.**

**NOTE**

Tablets and smartphones also have motherboards (also called *logic boards*), but these are much smaller and use a system-on-a-chip (SoC) design that builds the CPU, graphics, memory controller, and other components into a single chip. Perform an image search with your browser to see motherboards for a specific tablet or smartphone.

**EXAM TIP**

For the Core 1 1101 exam, make sure you understand the differences between the desktop, server, multiprocessor, and mobile motherboards and why AMD and Intel motherboards cannot use each other's CPUs.

# COOLING

Overheated motherboard components lead to instability, system crashes, and sometimes fatal damage. Heat sinks, fans, thermal paste/pads, and liquid cooling are the major ways used to keep CPUs, RAM, and GPUs cool for reliable operation.

## Heat Sink

A heat sink attaches to the top of a processor, radiating heat away from the processor through its metal fins. Almost all heat sinks use the heat sink fan design (also known as *active heat sink*), which places a fan above the heat sink to further improve cooling. A few motherboards with low-wattage CPUs use passive heat sinks, such as the one shown earlier in the chapter in Figure 17.3.

Although copper has better thermal transfer properties than aluminum, most heat sinks are made of aluminum, while some use a combination of a copper base and aluminum fins.

## Fans

Cooling fans are found in several locations in a typical desktop or server computer.

Almost all power supplies have at least one cooling fan to blow hot air out of the power supply, while many recent models also feature a bottom-mounted cooling fan to draw cool air from the outside past the power supply's components.

> **TIP**
>
> If you are installing a power supply with a bottom-mounted fan, make sure the fan on the bottom of the power supply is facing an opening in the case. If the case doesn't have an opening for the fan, turn the power supply so it faces upward and add an additional fan to the case so the power supply can be cooled more efficiently. Or, consider replacing the case with a modern design that has a bottom air vent for the power supply fan.

As mentioned in the previous section, heat sink fans for processors incorporate at least one fan that blows across the heat sink fins. Figure 17.14 shows late-model Intel and AMD active heat sinks sold with processors. The Intel heat sink fan has a copper base with aluminum fins, while the AMD heat sink fan is all aluminum. Both heat sink fans have preapplied thermal pads.

Most cases have one or more fans to improve air flow. Typical locations are the front and top of the case. Almost all video cards have one or more fans that cool video memory and the GPU. Figure 17.15 illustrates a mid-range AMD PCIe ×16 video card with two fans. Look through the fan blades to see the cooling fins and copper heat pipes that bring heat from the GPU and RAM to the fans.

**FIGURE 17.14** Top and bottom views of an AMD heat sink fan (left) and an Intel heat sink fan (right).

## Thermal Paste/Pads

To assure the best possible heat transfer between the bottom of a heat sink or heat sink fan and the top of a CPU, thermal paste or thermal pads are used. This material has sometimes been referred to as *phase-change material*. OEM heat sink fans included with processors have thermal pads preapplied (refer to Figure 17.14), but you can also buy thermal paste in tubes for use with separately purchased heat sink fans or if you need to remove and reinstall a heat sink fan.

**FIGURE 17.15** A typical PCIe video card with two fans for cooling the GPU and video RAM.

Be sure to remove any protective cover over the preapplied thermal pads before installing a heat sink fan. If you are reinstalling a heat sink fan, remove any old thermal paste or pads from the heat sink fan and CPU with 100 percent isopropyl alcohol before applying new thermal paste. Follow the manufacturer's directions for applying thermal paste.

Be sure to use the clamp or screws supplied with the heat sink fan to lock it in place and assure lasting contact between the heat sink fan and the CPU.

## Liquid

Liquid cooling for CPUs and GPUs enables extreme overclocking, as it is more effective than air cooling at much higher than normal clock speeds. Liquid cooling can be built into a case or can be retrofitted into standard cases that are designed to handle the large radiators needed.

To use liquid cooling for a CPU, the normal heat sink fan is removed, and a cooling block is attached in its place. The radiator has a pump connected to it to circulate the cooling liquid. To use liquid cooling for a GPU, the fan and cooling assembly must be removed from the video card, and a cooling block made for the GPU is attached to it. The cooling block also connects to a radiator with a pump.

See Figure 25.7 in Chapter 25, "Troubleshooting Motherboards, RAM, CPU, and Power," for an example of a CPU liquid cooling system.

> **EXAM TIP**
>
> For the Core 1 1101 exam, make sure you understand the differences between heat sinks, heat sink fans for CPUs, other locations for fans (power supply, case, GPU), thermal paste/pads, liquid cooling, and when to use each type.

## CERTMIKE EXAM ESSENTIALS

Modern desktop computers rely on PCIe, SATA, and M.2 interfaces, so make sure that whatever motherboard form factor you choose, you have enough of these interfaces for the job the computer needs to perform.

Desktop and server motherboards have some features in common, but server motherboards typically have more expansion slots, have more SATA ports, and come in many different form factors.

Adding cooling fans to a case is a low-cost way to improve system cooling.

## Practice Question 1

Your client has located several computer components in a closet and wants you to build a PC using these parts:

▶ AMD CPU

▶ Desktop motherboard with a 2017-vintage LGA CPU socket

▶ PCI video card

Which of the following is the most accurate answer to your client's request?

A. The PCI card will plug into the motherboard.
B. An adapter is needed to enable the CPU to work in the motherboard.
C. These parts can work in a single PC.
D. These parts must be used in separate PCs.

## Practice Question 2

Your client needs to add four large-capacity external drives to a media development PC. The drives are USB 3.2 Gen 1 and Gen 2 hard disk drives and SSDs. When the drives were plugged into a USB 3.2 Gen 2 hub, the drives were too slow because they were sharing a single USB controller chip. You recommend a USB 3.2 Gen 2 card with four separate USB controllers (one for each port). However, this card is a PCIe ×4 card, and the computer has a PCIe ×8 and a PCIe ×1 slot available. What should you do?

A. See if a PCIe ×8 card is available.
B. See if a PCIe ×1 card is available.
C. Use the PCIe ×8 slot for the x4 card.
D. Tell the client to get a new motherboard that includes a PCIe ×4 slot.

## Practice Question 1 Explanation

This question is designed to test your real-world understanding of motherboard compatibility. Let's evaluate these choices one at a time.

1. Option A (The PCI card will plug into the motherboard) is incorrect. Both Intel and AMD stopped supporting PCI cards in desktop computers well before 2017.

2. Option B (An adapter is needed to enable the CPU to work in the motherboard) is incorrect. PGA and LGA CPUs and sockets use completely different internal and external designs because PGA CPUs are made by AMD, and LGA CPUs are made by Intel.

3. Option C (These parts will work in a single PC) is incorrect. The CPU, motherboard, and PCI card can't work together because they are not compatible.

4. Option D (These parts must be used in separate PCs) is the correct answer. They can be used as spare parts but not in the same PC.

### Correct Answer: D. These parts must be used in separate PCs

## Practice Question 2 Explanation

This question is designed to test your ability to understand how PCIe slots work.

Let's evaluate these answers one at a time.

1. Option A (See if a PCIe ×8 card is available) is incorrect. It is not necessary to look for a PCIe ×8 card because a PCIe ×4 card can be used in a PCIe slot with more lanes.

2. Option B (See if a PCIe ×1 card is available) is incorrect. A PCIe ×1 cannot support multiple USB 3.2 Gen 2 controllers.

3. Option C (Use the PCIe ×8 slot for the x4 card) is correct. PCIe slots are compatible with cards with the same number or fewer lanes. Thus, a PCIe ×8 slot works with ×8, ×4, and ×1 cards.

4. Option D (Tell the client to get a new motherboard that includes a PCIe ×4 slot) is incorrect. The PCIe ×8 slot will work fine. There is no need to replace the motherboard.

### Correct Answer: C. Use the PCIe ×8 slot for the x4 card.

# CHAPTER 18

# Booting, CPUs, and Expansion Cards

*Core 1 Objective 3.4 Given a scenario, install and configure motherboards, central processing units (CPUs), and add-on cards.*

**Desktop** computer support requires technicians to be familiar with how to configure boot, fan, and security settings in BIOS/UEFI firmware settings; how to set up encryption; the differences in CPU architecture; and how to install expansion cards. In this chapter, you will learn what you need to know about portions of Core 1 Objective 3.4 (see Chapter 17 for the remainder of Objective 3.4), including the following:

▶ Basic Input/Output System and Unified Extensible Firmware Interface settings
▶ Encryption
▶ CPU architecture
▶ Expansion cards

# BASIC INPUT/OUTPUT SYSTEM AND UNIFIED EXTENSIBLE FIRMWARE INTERFACE SETTINGS

The Basic Input/Output System (BIOS) is a 16-bit read-only memory (ROM) chip used on PC motherboards to test the system at startup (Power On Self-Test) and to hold a configuration program used to store settings for the CPU, memory, drives, and other onboard components. Because of advances in system design, the BIOS has been replaced by the Unified Extensible Firmware Interface (*UEFI*), which provides support for 32-bit firmware, support for drives bigger than 2TB, an optional GUI interface, and built-in networking for easier configuration.

UEFI performs all of the tasks that traditional BIOS does, plus adds many additional features. Most of the essential settings used to configure a computer are supported by BIOS or UEFI, so the term BIOS/UEFI settings is used by CompTIA as well as this text.

To access BIOS/UEFI firmware if Secure Boot is not enabled, press the key visible at startup if the full-screen logo display option is also disabled (Figure 18.1).

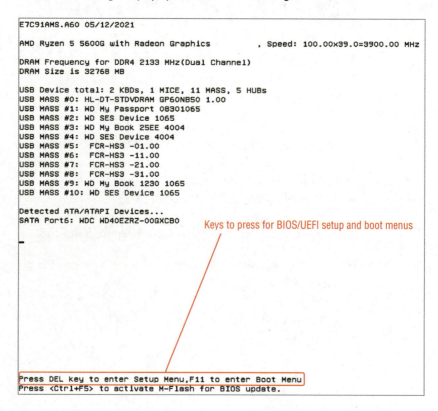

```
E7C91AMS.A60 05/12/2021

AMD Ryzen 5 5600G with Radeon Graphics           , Speed: 100.00x39.0=3900.00 MHz

DRAM Frequency for DDR4 2133 MHz(Dual Channel)
DRAM Size is 32768 MB

USB Device total: 2 KBDs, 1 MICE, 11 MASS, 5 HUBs
USB MASS #0: HL-DT-STDVDRAM GP60NB50 1.00
USB MASS #1: WD My Passport 08301065
USB MASS #2: WD SES Device 1065
USB MASS #3: WD My Book 25EE 4004
USB MASS #4: WD SES Device 4004
USB MASS #5:  FCR-HS3 -01.00
USB MASS #6:  FCR-HS3 -11.00
USB MASS #7:  FCR-HS3 -21.00
USB MASS #8:  FCR-HS3 -31.00
USB MASS #9: WD My Book 1230 1065
USB MASS #10: WD SES Device 1065

Detected ATA/ATAPI Devices...
SATA Port6: WDC WD40EZRZ-00GXCB0

_
```

Keys to press for BIOS/UEFI setup and boot menus

```
Press DEL key to enter Setup Menu,F11 to enter Boot Menu
Press <Ctrl+F5> to activate M-Flash for BIOS update.
```

**FIGURE 18.1** When the full-screen logo option is disabled in BIOS/UEFI firmware, you can see the keys to press for setup and for the boot menu.

To access the UEFI firmware if Secure Boot is enabled and you are running Windows 10, select Start ➤ Settings ➤ Update & Security ➤ Recovery ➤ Restart Now.

On Windows 11, select Start ➤ Settings ➤ System ➤ Recovery ➤ Restart Now ➤ Restart Now.

After Windows 10/11 restarts, select Troubleshoot ➤ Advanced Options ➤ UEFI Firmware Settings.

### EXAM TIP

Be sure you know how to access UEFI firmware settings from the startup screen and on Windows 10 and 11. Also, be familiar with configuring boot options, USB permissions, Trusted Platform Module, Secure Boot, and encryption features. Finally, know the differences between x64/x86 and ARM.

## Boot Options

Boot options determine which drives will be checked for operating system startup files, in what order, and are a core function of BIOS/UEFI settings. In addition to normal settings, many BIOS/UEFI settings also offer a boot override menu that is useful for temporarily changing the boot drive. This is handy for running USB or disc-based diagnostics. Figure 18.2 illustrates a typical boot options menu.

**FIGURE 18.2  Boot options menu.**

> **TIP**
>
> If you want to temporarily change the boot drive so you can boot from a diagnostic USB drive or optical disc, use boot override. Using boot override doesn't change the normal boot settings.

## USB Permissions

USB permissions, which are used to configure how onboard USB ports work, vary a great deal from system to system. Some systems offer the ability to enable or disable individual USB ports, as in Figure 18.3.

> **TIP**
>
> Blocking or disabling unnecessary USB ports is considered an important USB security option as it helps prevent malware infections.

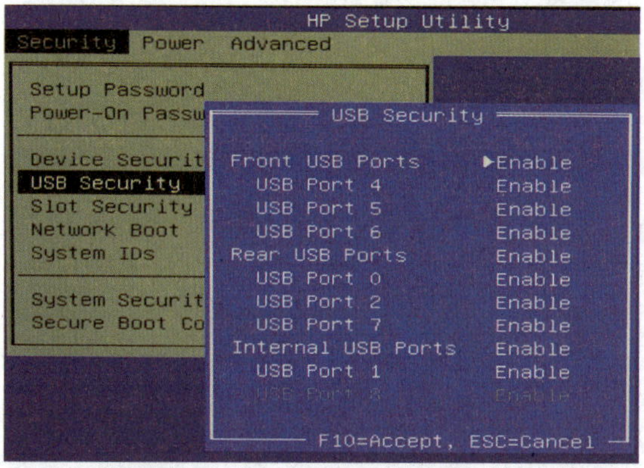

**FIGURE 18.3** **Enabling or disabling individual USB ports is an option available on some systems.**

Others support a feature called USB Legacy mode (Figure 18.4). USB Legacy mode, when enabled, supports USB ports during system startup before the USB drivers in the operating system have been loaded. If you use USB mice and keyboards, this should be enabled.

The XHCI Hand Off feature also shown in Figure 18.4 should be enabled if you are installing operating systems that lack USB 3.0 support. Enabling this feature makes your USB 3.0 ports work like USB 2.0 ports when there is no USB 3.0 support. The EHCI Hand Off feature on older systems makes USB 2.0 ports work like USB 1.1 ports when there is no USB 2.0 support. If XHCI or EHCI Hand Off feature Auto mode or Auto Smart is an option, use these settings so the port will select the appropriate mode for you.

**FIGURE 18.4** USB Legacy mode and XHCI Hand Off BIOS/UEFI settings.

> **TIP**
>
> USB settings might be found in more than one of the following locations in UEFI/BIOS settings: integrated peripherals, security, onboard peripherals, and others.

## Trusted Platform Module Security Features

The Trusted Platform Module (*TPM*) is an encryption chip included in many Windows computers. The TPM is used to improve the function and security of cryptographic keys that are used to help protect a computer and its operating system.

The TPM can be built into the motherboard or can be retrofitted to a motherboard that has a TPM connector. TPM can also be built into firmware and is built into most recent AMD and Intel CPUs. However, TPM is typically disabled in BIOS/UEFI settings.

TPM version 2.0 is required for Windows 11 because it improves security over the older TPM 1.2 version supported in Windows 10. To enable TPM, open BIOS/UEFI settings and check the security menu for an entry called Advanced Security, Trusted Computing, or similar. A typical AMD setting (AMD fTPM) is shown in Figure 18.5 before and after being enabled. Enable the appropriate item and restart. You will not see the Trusted Computing options dialog until you reenter BIOS/UEFI settings.

> **NOTE**
>
> TPM is referred to by many different names: on Intel systems, it might be called Platform Trust Technologies (PTT) or Trusted Execution Technology. AMD typically calls it AMD fTPM, as shown in Figure 18.5.

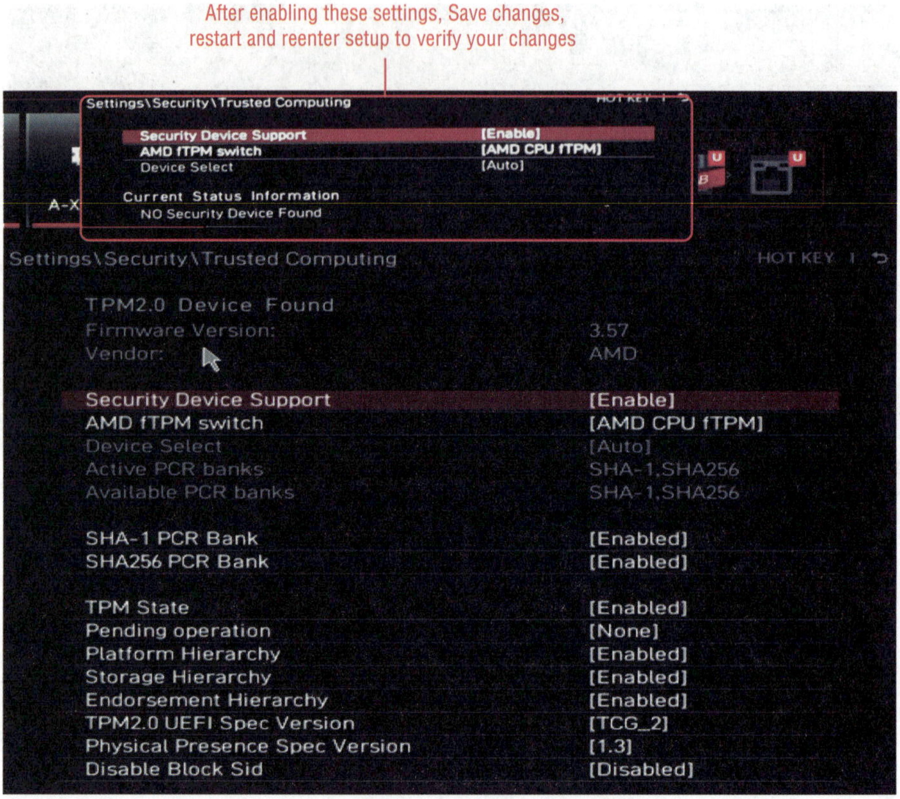

After enabling these settings, Save changes, restart and reenter setup to verify your changes

Settings\Security\Trusted Computing                    HOT KEY

Security Device Support                    [Enable]
AMD fTPM switch                           [AMD CPU fTPM]
Device Select                             [Auto]

Current Status Information
NO Security Device Found

A-X

Settings\Security\Trusted Computing                    HOT KEY

TPM2.0 Device Found
Firmware Version:                         3.57
Vendor:                                   AMD

Security Device Support                   [Enable]
AMD fTPM switch                           [AMD CPU fTPM]
Device Select                             [Auto]
Active PCR banks                          SHA-1,SHA256
Available PCR banks                       SHA-1,SHA256

SHA-1 PCR Bank                            [Enabled]
SHA256 PCR Bank                           [Enabled]

TPM State                                 [Enabled]
Pending operation                         [None]
Platform Hierarchy                        [Enabled]
Storage Hierarchy                         [Enabled]
Endorsement Hierarchy                     [Enabled]
TPM2.0 UEFI Spec Version                  [TCG_2]
Physical Presence Spec Version            [1.3]
Disable Block Sid                         [Disabled]

**FIGURE 18.5** **AMD fTPM before and after being enabled.**

## Fan Considerations

There are at least two types of fan connectors on the motherboard that are monitored by BIOS/UEFI settings: CPU fans and system fans. CPU fans have four wires because they use pulse width modulation (PWM). PWM fans can be turned on or off on demand as CPU temperature increases and decreases. In Figure 18.6, the CPU fan graph on the left shows the percentage of time the CPU fan runs based on the CPU core temperature.

Chassis (also known as CHA) fans use three wires. These fans can run at variable speeds on some systems by changing input voltage. In Figure 18.6, stats for each fan connector on the motherboard can be viewed separately. On other systems, all chassis fans are listed together.

## Secure Boot

Secure Boot is the default boot setting for systems with preinstalled Windows 8 and later installed. Secure Boot is designed to stop rootkits, a form of malware that hides in system firmware or startup files. When Secure Boot is enabled (it is usually enabled on systems

**FIGURE 18.6** CPU and Chassis fan displays on a typical desktop computer; the inset shows connectors on a typical motherboard.

with preinstalled Windows, but not on motherboards for system builders), it blocks rootkits but also blocks non-Windows operating systems.

Secure Boot is an issue if you need to install a non-Windows operating system, such as a Linux distro, on a system set up for Secure Boot. To disable Secure Boot in BIOS/UEFI settings, locate the Secure Boot setting (typically found in Windows Configuration or similar), and select Disabled. Save your changes and restart, and you can then install a non-Windows OS.

If you are installing Windows, improve security by enabling Secure Boot. It is required for Windows 11. If it was never enabled before, follow the prompts to install encryption keys and then enable it.

## Boot Password

A boot password (also known as a *user password*) can be used to help keep a system secure from unauthorized tampering when not in use. When this option is enabled, the user must provide the password configured by the tech who set up the computer to be able to start the computer. This option is typically located in the Security dialog.

Some systems, like the one shown in Figure 18.7, have three passwords: the Supervisor password prevents unauthorized users from accessing BIOS/UEFI settings; the User (boot) password; and the hard drive (HDD) password is designed to prevent unauthorized users from accessing the contents of the hard drive.

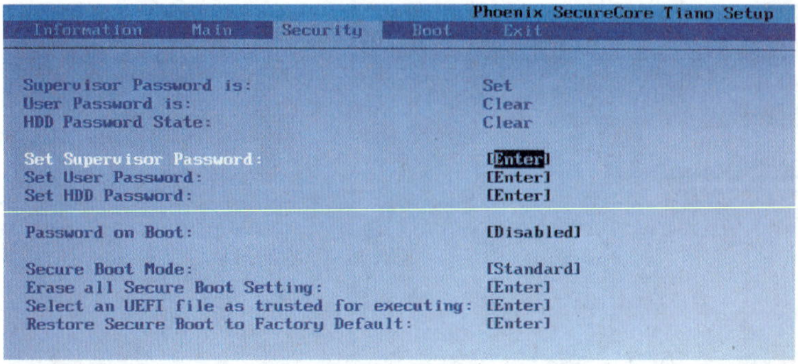

**FIGURE 18.7** A system with three passwords that can be enabled in BIOS/UEFI settings.

> **WARNING**
>
> HDD passwords can be easily defeated and should not be used to protect the contents of the drive. Instead, use BitLocker or a similar full-disk encryption product.

# ENCRYPTION

Encryption is designed to protect the contents of your computing device from being read by unauthorized users. Encryption can be performed at the operating system level with utilities such as BitLocker, at the application level with products such as PrettyGoodPrivacy (PGP), and at the hardware level with a TPM or a hardware security module.

## TPM

TPM version 2.0 is required by Windows 11 as part of its improved security. Before upgrading a Windows 10 system to Windows 11, you can download and run the Windows PC Health Check application. It will tell you if your system has TPM version 2 included and whether it's enabled. TPM should be enabled before enabling BitLocker full-disk encryption.

You can also check to see if you have TPM version 2.0 by searching for the Windows Security app, clicking Device Security, and clicking Security processor details. Figure 18.8 shows a typical report from an AMD system.

## Hardware Security Module

A hardware security module (*HSM*), like a TPM, is designed to encrypt information to protect it. An HSM, instead of being built into a system the way a TPM is, can be built into a separate device or can be incorporated into a PCIe card.

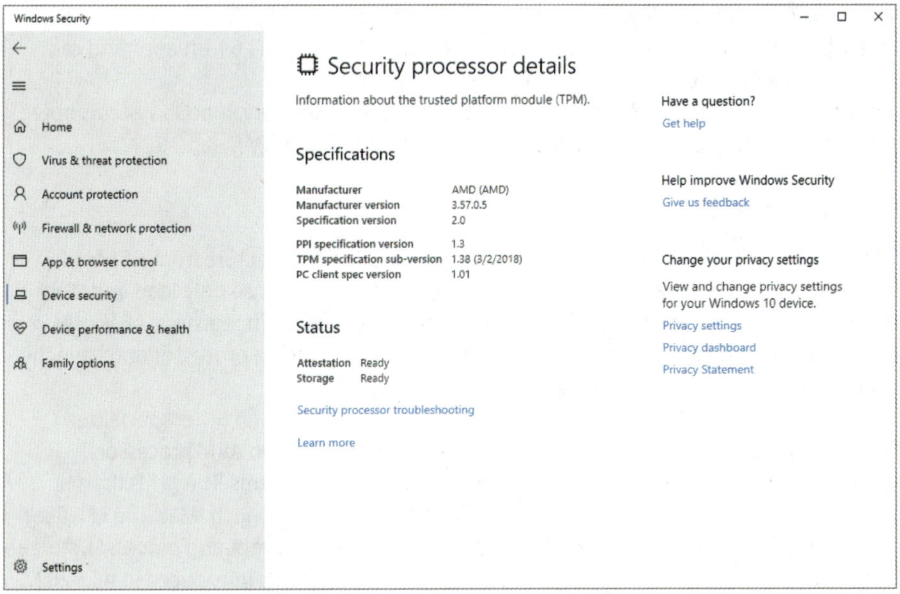

**FIGURE  18.8**  **An AMD system with TPM 2.0 enabled as reported by Security processor details.**

Typical uses for HSMs include managing secret keys used in encryption/decryption, preventing tampering with information, and accelerating cryptographic operations.

# CPU ARCHITECTURE

As a CompTIA A+ Certified technician, you may be called upon to help customers decide what types of systems should be selected for different purposes. The most fundamental choice to make is what CPU architecture should be used: ×64, ×86, or Advanced RISC Machine (ARM).

A central processing unit (*CPU*) is the most essential part of any computer. The CPU loads programs from RAM or storage, runs the instructions in those programs, and creates output. The CPU also receives user input and can send output to storage, printers, displays, or network destinations. CPU architecture refers to how the CPU is organized to perform work.

## x64/x86

Almost all of the computers that run Microsoft Windows today use ×64 architecture, which is based on ×86 architecture. Both of these processors use complex instruction set computing (CISC) designs. In CISC, a single command like MULT (multiply) actually has to perform several tasks, including getting values from their locations in memory, determining the product of those values, and storing the result in a specified memory location. ×86 processors (which run 32-bit and 16-bit applications) are limited to 4GB of RAM and have largely been replaced by ×64 processors, which can run 32-bit and 64-bit apps and can access virtually unlimited amounts of RAM.

Until recently, macOS systems also used ×64 processors. However, macOS systems now use a different architecture known as Advanced RISC Machine (ARM).

## Advanced RISC Machine

Advanced RISC Machine (*ARM*) uses a completely different architecture from ×86/×64 processors. ARM uses instructions that take only one clock cycle, use only load and store instructions to access memory, and perform all other operations in registers. ARM uses Reduced Instruction Set Computing (RISC) features to simplify the processor and have the program compiler do more of the work.

Originally, ARM processors were used in smartphones, tablets, and other specialized devices, including data centers. However, Apple has developed two ARM processors, M1 and M2, which are capable of running desktop operating systems. The M1 is used in recent Apple MacBook Air, 13-inch MacBook Pro, Mac Mini, and 24-inch iMac. The M1, like previous ARM chips, is an example of a system on a chip (SoC), combining processor, storage controller, graphics controller, image processor, and more. The M2, introduced in mid-2022, is much faster, more powerful, and has better power consumption than the M1.

Macs based on M1/M2 processors are not compatible with Intel-based macOS software, so be sure to check compatibility for customers with existing macOS systems.

## Single-Core and Multicore CPUs

A single-core CPU is designed to perform one set of tasks at a time. When a single-core CPU works on tasks that have more than one process, it uses concurrency, switching rapidly from one process to another until all of the tasks are completed.

To understand this, imagine that you need to push a car out of an intersection because it's out of gas. You push it a few feet and then adjust the steering wheel. You push it a few more feet, adjust the steering wheel again, and, eventually, you finish the job.

A multicore CPU has two or more CPU cores inside the CPU package. Each CPU core can work on different tasks (see the "Multithreading" section for details) at the same time.

To understand how multicore CPUs work, let's go back to our stalled car in the intersection. Imagine you have two people working to move the car: one to steer and the other to push (like a dual-core CPU). The car will be moved out of the way faster, and the more people (processor cores) available to push, the job will be even faster. The ability of a processor to perform multiple tasks (like steering and pushing a car) at the same time is called *parallel execution*.

If you must run two or more apps at the same time, such as an office suite's word processor and spreadsheet, or a photo editor and a sound editor, using a multicore CPU keeps the applications running faster and smoother than a single-core CPU would.

Although most games don't benefit from multicore CPUs, photo editing, video production, and sound editing apps are written to use the multiprocessing features of multicore CPUs. Originally, multicore CPU designs were limited to high-end processors introduced in the mid-2000s, but all CPUs made to run Windows, macOS, or Linux have been multicore for almost 10 years.

Table 18.1 compares the number of cores available in selected low-end, mid-range, and high-end desktop processors from AMD and Intel (laptop processors will vary) built from 2017-present.

**TABLE 18.1** Selected Recent AMD and Intel Multicore CPUs

| Manufacturer | Family | Model | CPU Cores | Number of Threads |
| --- | --- | --- | --- | --- |
| AMD | Ryzen 3 | 2200 | 4 | 4 |
| | Ryzen 5 | Pro 3600 | 6 | 12 |
| | Ryzen 7 | 5800 | 8 | 16 |
| | Ryzen 9 | 5950X | 16 | 32 |
| Intel | Pentium Gold | G7400T | 2 | 4 |
| | Core i3 | 7320 | 2 | 4 |
| | Core i5 | 10500 | 6 | 12 |
| | Core i7 | 11700 | 8 | 16 |
| | Core i9 | 12900 | 16* | 24 |

* 8 performance cores + 8 efficient cores

## Multithreading

In Table 18.1, you noticed that most of the listed processors can handle at least twice as many execution threads as their CPU core count. An execution thread can be a single program (such as a game) or a task in a productivity app, such as real-time word count in a word processor. The multithreading feature enables that same word processor to perform real-time spelling and grammar checking, pagination, and more at the same time. Web browsers also use multithreading to handle multiple tabs.

Intel introduced support for multithreading with a single processor core some years ago, calling it *hyperthreading* (HT Technology). As multicore processors were introduced, Intel used hyperthreading in multicore CPUs, and it's found in almost all Intel processors.

AMD calls its multithreading support *simultaneous multithreading* (SMT), and it is found in almost all recent AMD processors. Some UEFI/BIOS settings for AMD processors use the same *hyperthreading* term as Intel.

HT Technology and SMT are configured through the UEFI/BIOS settings dialogs.

### Virtualization

Virtualization enables a portion of a system's memory, processor, and storage resources to host another operating system, while the original OS is running. It's like having a Windows computer with a Linux computer inside it. Processors that have hardware support for virtualization enable the virtual machines they host to perform much faster. To learn more about virtualization, including BIOS/UEFI settings, see Chapter 23, "Virtualization."

# EXPANSION CARDS

Expansion cards enable desktop computers to act like computing's equivalent of Swiss Army knives: add a card to add more capabilities. The following sections cover the most common expansion cards: sound card, video card, capture card, and network interface card (NIC).

> **EXAM TIP**
>
> For the CompTIA A+ Certification Core 1 1101 exam, make sure you know the purposes of sound, video, capture, and NICs; how to change BIOS/UEFI settings when replacing on-board hardware; and how to recognize them.

### Sound Card

At one time, PCs didn't have onboard sound capabilities, so sound cards were developed to support games, presentations, audio playback, and video playback. However, for some years all PCs have had built-in stereo or surround audio. Buyers of sound cards now are looking for higher-quality sound, more connections to receivers, and better surround audio for gaming than what is provided with motherboard-based sound.

To add a sound card to an existing system, make sure there is a PCIe slot suitable for the card (PCIe ×1 or wider). The onboard audio should be disabled in BIOS/UEFI settings (Figure 18.9). If your system also has additional software installed to manage or configure the onboard sound, be sure to remove it using Settings or Control Panel.

Disconnect the cabling from the onboard audio jacks. Check the documentation for the new card to see when to install the drivers. Install the drivers and sound card per the instructions, and connect the speaker, line in, microphone, and so on, to the new card. Install any additional software and then test the card.

### Video Card

Video cards are required by some systems, but there are an increasing number of processors from both Intel and AMD that have built-in video support. However, if you need faster

3D performance for gaming or faster rendering photo/video work, you will want to install a discrete video card.

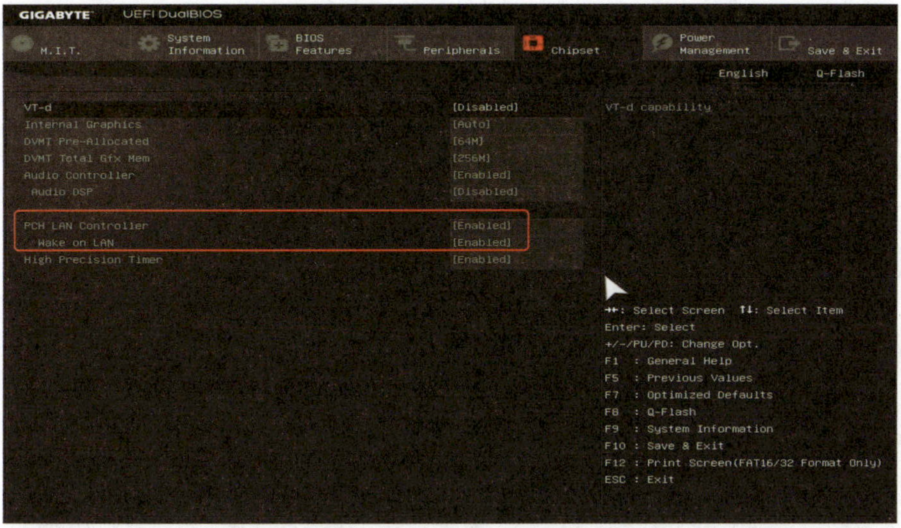

**FIGURE 18.9** Onboard sound before being disabled.

Before starting, make sure there is a PCIe ×16 slot available. It is not necessary to disable onboard video in BIOS/UEFI settings. However, it is advisable to do so after installing the new card as it might free up the RAM set aside for video support (see Figure 18.10).

Make sure the appropriate PCIe power connector is fastened to the card if it requires additional power.

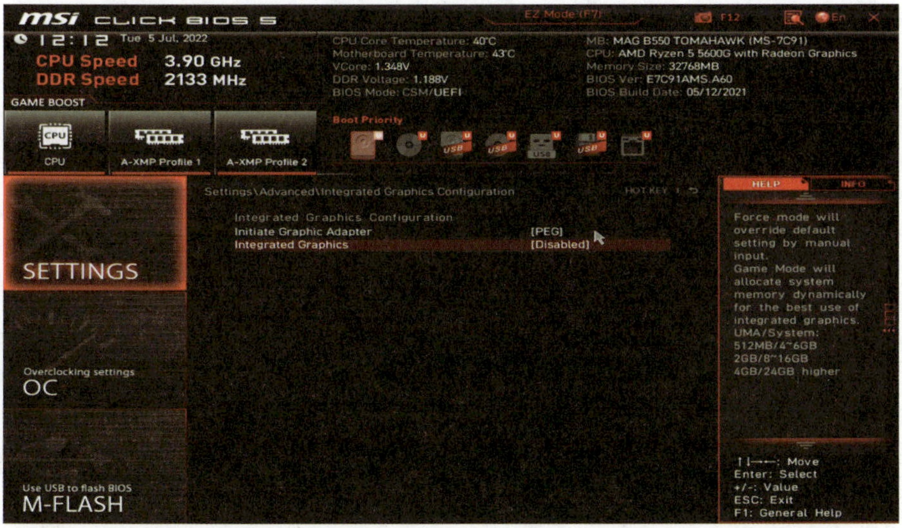

**FIGURE 18.10** Disabled onboard video.

## NIC

Almost all computers have at least one onboard network interface card (NIC) port. However, if a faster network connection is needed and a suitable PCIe slot is available, you can disable the onboard NIC after installing the new one (Figure 18.11). Typical NIC cards have Ethernet or fiber-optic ports; NICs made for wireless networking have one or more antennas.

**FIGURE 18.11** **Preparing to disable onboard NIC.**

## Capture Card

Capture cards make it easy to capture video from console games, other computers, and broadcast video sources as either still images or video clips. Although some capture cards are made for PCIe slots and other capture devices plug into USB 3.0 ports, there is no need to disable any onboard component to install a capture card. Be sure to install the driver software before installing the card or connecting the USB device; then install the capture software after the card or device has been connected and the system restarted.

## CERTMIKE EXAM ESSENTIALS

▶ Windows systems that use Secure Boot are protected against boot-time malware such as rootkits, but the price of extra security is a multistep process to get to BIOS/UEFI firmware settings.

▶ When you start working with a computer you're unfamiliar with, you should spend some time reviewing the BIOS/UEFI firmware options it provides and research settings you are unfamiliar with. This will help you solve problems with startup as well as issues that happen later.

▶ When you install expansion cards that replace onboard features, disabling the onboard features helps avoid configuration issues, but don't forget to remove drivers and supplemental apps made for the onboard feature you have disabled.

## Practice Question 1

You are helping a client troubleshoot a Windows 10 system that will not start from the system drive. After doing some research, you determine that the best course of action is to start the system from a diagnostic USB drive that contains a Linux distro. Which of the following BIOS/UEFI settings will make this EASIEST to do?

A. Change boot order

B. Enable TPM

C. Override boot order

D. Enable Secure Boot

## Practice Question 2

Your client wants to upgrade her fleet of Windows 10 PCs to run Windows 11. All of them were purchased with TPM installed. However, some are blocking upgrades to Windows 11. Which of the following could cause this issue? (Choose all that apply.)

A. TPM version installed on some systems is TPM 1.2.

B. TPM was not enabled on some systems.

C. Windows 10's TPM is not supported in Windows 11.

D. Secure Boot is not enabled on some systems.

## Practice Question 1 Explanation

This question is designed to test your real-world understanding of boot options. Let's evaluate these choices one at a time.

1. Option A (Change boot order) will work as it allows you to set the USB drive as the boot device. However, you will want to change it back to the normal boot order afterward, so it's not the easiest option.

2. Option B (Enable TPM) would prevent the Linux USB drive from starting unless it was created on the computer you need to diagnose. This is incorrect.

3. Option C (Override boot order) is a temporary change you make when you start the computer, sometimes even without going into BIOS/UEFI settings. There's no need to change the boot order back when you're done, so it's the EASIEST option.

4. Option D (Enable Secure Boot) would prevent the bootable Linux USB drive from booting, so it's also incorrect.

**Correct answer: C. Override boot order**

## Practice Question 2 Explanation

This question is designed to test your ability to understand the implications of TPM versions, Secure Boot, and Windows compatibility.

Let's evaluate these answers one at a time.

1. Option A (TPM version installed on some systems is TPM 1.2) is a possible reason for this issue. TPM 2.0 was released in 2019, and some systems prior to that support TPM 2.0. Depending upon the age of the Windows 10 computers, some of them might have the older, incompatible TPM 1.2 installed.

2. Option B (TPM was not enabled on some systems) could temporarily block the Windows 11 upgrade. However, by enabling TPM in BIOS/UEFI settings, you can determine whether or not the systems support TPM 2.0.

3. Option C (Windows 10's TPM is not supported in Windows 11) is incorrect because it contains two errors. TPM is built into system hardware, not Windows. Windows supports TPM if it's present, and a number of Windows 10 systems include TPM 2.0 support.

4. Option D (Secure Boot is not enabled on some systems) is another issue that must be addressed before upgrading to Windows 11. It can be addressed by making changes in BIOS/UEFI settings.

**Correct answers: A (TPM version installed on some systems is TPM 1.2), B (TPM was not enabled on some systems), D (Secure Boot is not enabled on some systems)**

# CHAPTER 19

# Power Supplies

*Core 1 Objective 3.5: Given a scenario, install or replace the appropriate power supply.*

**The** power supply is the unsung hero of a computer, keeping everything working. However, when the power supply fails, it's time to get a more powerful model. In this chapter, you learn the essential elements of Core 1, Objective 3.5, including the following:

▶ Input 110-120 VAC versus 220-240 VAC
▶ Output 3.3V versus 5V versus 12V
▶ 20-pin to 24-pin motherboard adapter
▶ Redundant power supply
▶ Modular power supply
▶ Wattage rating

## INPUT 110-120 VAC VS. 220-240 VAC

The purpose of a power supply unit (*PSU*) is to convert alternating current to direct current. *AC* (alternating current) is the power provided by the power company, and *DC* (direct current) is the power used by the motherboard and other components such as the CPU, ports, drives, fans, and other devices connected to it.

Most power supplies are designed to work with the 110-120 VAC input used in the United States and Canada as well as the 220-240 VAC input used by most of the rest of the world. Older power supplies use a sliding switch to manually select the voltage range (see Figure 19.1). However, current power supplies auto-switch as needed.

A *UPS* (uninterruptable power supply), which contains rechargeable batteries, can provide power to a computer and display for a short period of time in the event of a power failure to allow the system to be shut down,

Voltage selector switch set to 115 VAC

**FIGURE 19.1  A power supply with a manual voltage switch.**

What happens if you set the voltage selector at 220/240V and plug the power supply into the 110/120V outlet? This is a harmless error—the computer will not start. However, if you set the voltage selector at 110/120V and plug it into 220/240V, you will destroy the power supply and other components when you turn it on.

# OUTPUT 3.3V VS. 5V VS. 12V

A power supply converts high-voltage AC into low-voltage DC current at three levels.

▶ 3.3V (orange wires)
▶ 5V (red wires)
▶ 12V (yellow wires)

All three voltage levels are sent to the motherboard by the ATX 24-pin (in older power supplies, 20-pin) power connector shown in Figure 19.2. Black wires are used for ground, purple is +5V standby, green is PS on, blue wire for -12V, and the Power Good (PS) line is gray. Older power supplies also used a white wire for -5V.

Additional pins for 24-pin motherboard; don't use with 20-pin motherboard

**FIGURE 19.2**  **A 24-pin ATX power cable.**

Table 19.1 lists the additional power connectors and their uses.

**TABLE 19.1: POWER CONNECTORS AND USES**

| Connector | Form Factor | Voltages | Uses |
|-----------|-------------|----------|------|
| PCIe (see Figure 19.3) | 3×2 + 1×2 (8 pins total) (Older power supplies use 3×2 only) | 12V, ground | PCIe video cards, other PCIe cards; split design supports older video cards that use six pins only. |
| ATX12V (see Figure 19.3) | 2×2 (4 pins total) | 12V, ground | Older motherboards use this to supply additional 12V power. |
| EPS12V (see Figure 19.3) | 2×2 + 2×2 (8 pins total) | 12V, ground | Split design; use one set of four pins for motherboards with ATX12V connector. |
| SATA (see Figure 19.4) | 15×1 | 3.3V, 5V, 12V, ground | SATA drives; most SATA drives don't use 3.3V, so Molex can be adapted to SATA. |

| Connector | Form Factor | Voltages | Uses |
|-----------|-------------|----------|------|
| Molex (see Figure 19.4) | 4×1 | 5V, 12V, ground | PATA/IDE drives; can also be adapted to other devices. |
| Mini (Berg) (see Figure 19.5) | 4×1 | 5V, 12V, ground | Used for floppy drives; might not be present on newer power supplies. |

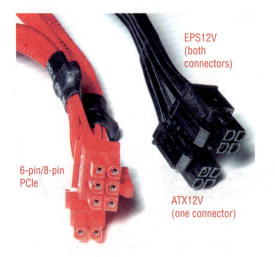

6-pin/8-pin PCIe

EPS12V (both connectors)

ATX12V (one connector)

**FIGURE 19.3** EPS12V, ATX12V, and PCIe power leads.

Molex

SATA

**FIGURE 19.4** Molex and SATA power leads.

**F I G U R E   1 9 . 5**   Mini (Berg) power lead.

# 20-PIN TO 24-PIN MOTHERBOARD ADAPTER

Older versions of the ATX power supply standard used a 20-pin connector from the power supply to the motherboard. However, the current standard uses a 24-pin connector. To enable a single power supply model to work with older and current motherboards, a couple of different methods have been used.

One method is the use of a 20-pin to 24-pin ATX power supply adapter (Figure 19.6). A user with a 20-pin power supply could plug it into the adapter, and the other end of the adapter would plug into the 24-pin motherboard. This method has been abandoned in favor of a 20+4-pin connector that will work on either type of motherboard without an adapter (refer to Figure 19.2).

Connects to 20-pin ATX power lead

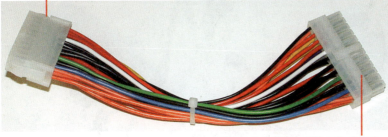

Connects to 24-pin ATX motherboard

**F I G U R E   1 9 . 6**   20 to 24-pin ATX power adapter.

# REDUNDANT POWER SUPPLY

A redundant power supply is two power supplies in one: the power supply fits into the same form factor as a normal power supply, but it has two connectors for AC power on the back side and two separate power modules inside. If one of the power supply modules fails, the second module takes over automatically. Some redundant power supplies have a handle on each module to make hot-swapping the failed module easier.

Redundant power supplies are typically found in both standard and rack-mount servers. However, some redundant power supplies are available for desktop tower PCs.

## MODULAR POWER SUPPLY

Traditional PC power supplies have all of the power cables for the motherboard, 12V additional power, drive power, and PCIe card power built into the unit (Figure 19.7).

**FIGURE 19.7**  A traditional (nonmodular) power supply.

If additional cables are needed for drives or other peripherals, existing connectors must be split, which can lead to additional points of failure, such as short-circuits or inadequate power to some internal devices.

Modular power supplies have removable cables for drives or PCIe cards, and some also have removable cables for the ATX, ATX12V/EPS12V motherboard power connectors. The builder can select the mix of power cables needed for a particular system's mix of drives, PCIe cards, and other devices (Figure 19.8).

**FIGURE 19.8  A fully modular power supply.**

# WATTAGE RATING

Wattage ratings for power supplies are calculated by multiplying the amperage rating (Amp) by the voltage rating. Add the various wattage ratings for the different voltages together to get the overall wattage rating for a power supply.

For example, a power supply supporting up to a 62Amp load at 12V DC uses 744 watts at full load. The 3.3V and 5V adds 130 watts at full load. This adds up to 874 watts. However, the power supply is rated at 750 watts (Figure 19.9). Rating the power supply primarily by its 12V wattage is typical with current higher-quality power supplies.

When you replace a power supply, especially if higher-wattage peripherals (PCIe cards, drives, CPU) have been installed, get a higher-wattage power supply with more 12V amperage available.

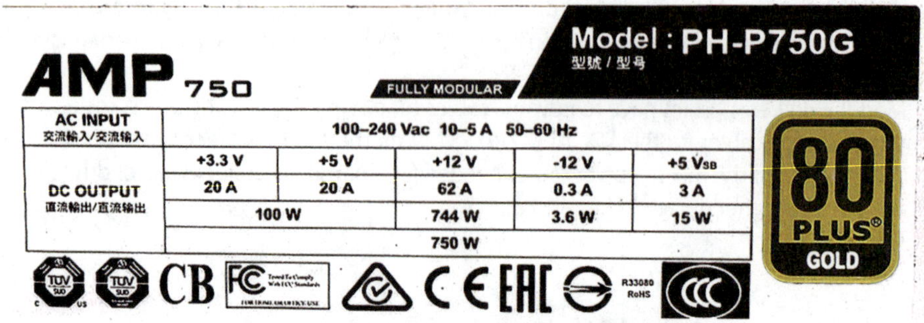

| AC INPUT<br>交流輸入/交流输入 | 100–240 Vac 10–5 A 50–60 Hz | | | | |
|---|---|---|---|---|---|
| | **+3.3 V** | **+5 V** | **+12 V** | **-12 V** | **+5 V$_{SB}$** |
| DC OUTPUT<br>直流輸出/直流输出 | 20 A | 20 A | 62 A | 0.3 A | 3 A |
| | 100 W | | 744 W | 3.6 W | 15 W |
| | 750 W | | | | |

**FIGURE 19.9** A high-quality 750-watt power supply.

# POWER SUPPLY REPLACEMENT PROCESS

To replace a power supply, take electrostatic discharge (ESD) precautions (use a wrist strap and a grounded work mat) and then follow this procedure:

1. Shut down the computer.
2. Turn off the power supply.
3. Unplug the AC power from power supply.
4. Open the case and disconnect all the power leads from the motherboard, drives, video cards, etc.
5. Locate the mounting screws holding power supply at rear of case (Figure 19.10) and remove. Retain for reuse.
6. Lift and slide the power supply out of the case.
7. Slide the new power supply into the case. Make sure the power supply's internal fan is oriented correctly per the case design.
8. Use the screws removed in step 5 to secure the power supply in place.
9. If modular or semimodular, connect the power leads as needed for the installed equipment.
10. Connect the power supply to the motherboard's main power lead and additional 12V lead.
11. Connect the power supply to the drives, PCIe cards, and other components as needed.
12. Close the case.
13. Connect the AC power to the power supply.
14. Turn on the power supply.
15. Restart the computer and test all the devices.

Power supply mounting screws

**FIGURE 19.10** A typical PC power supply and mounting screws.

## CERTMIKE EXAM ESSENTIALS

▶ Desktop power supplies are available in many wattage ratings and differ in other ways, including the number of internal device cables, support for PCIe video cards, and modular, semimodular, or nonmodular designs. This allows the builder to choose the best combination of features for a particular task.

▶ The most important component of the overall power in a modern power supply is the 12V amp rating. 12V is used for drives, PCIe video cards, processors, and the motherboard.

▶ Power supplies become less efficient over time, so a good strategy for upgrading a system for longer life is to look at replacing the power supply after three or four years.

## Practice Question 1

Your client has several four-year-old desktop PCs that are being upgraded with more powerful PCIe video cards and higher-performance CPUs. Both draw more power than the current components. The current power supply is a 550-watt power supply that provides 44Amps of 12V power (528 watts). Which of the following would provide at least 800 watts of 12V power and sell for the lowest price?

► Power Supply A: 58Amp 12V, $85

► Power Supply B: 70Amp 12V, $99

► Power Supply C: 64Amp 12V, $94

► Power Supply D: 78Amp 12V, $109

## Practice Question 2

You are preparing to install a new high-performance PCIe video card into a computer. Which of the following power leads are you most likely to need to connect to this card?

FIGURE 19.11 A

FIGURE 19.12 B

FIGURE 19.13 C

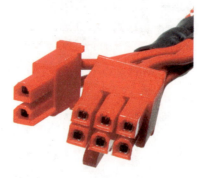

FIGURE 19.14 D

## Practice Question 1 Explanation

This question is designed to determine your ability to evaluate power supplies in terms of their specifications to solve a real-world problem.

Let's evaluate these choices one at a time.

1. Power Supply A provides 696 watts of 12V power (58Amp×12). This one does not provide enough power.

2. Power Supply B provides 840 watts of 12V power (70Amp×12). This unit meets the requirements and sells for $99.

3. Power Supply C provides 768 watts of 12V power (64Amp×12). This one does not provide enough power.

4. Power Supply D provides 936 watts of 12V power (78Amp×12). This one provides more than enough power, but at $109 it's $10 more than the competition. Power Supply B is the best choice for this client.

**Correct Answer: B. 70Amp 12V, $99**

## Practice Question 2 Explanation

This question is designed to test your knowledge of power supply connectors and their role in system upgrades.

Figure A is a SATA power cable. It powers SATA drives, so this answer is not correct.

Figure B is a Molex power cable. It is used for PATA/IDE drives and can be adapted to other uses. This answer is not correct.

Figure C is an EPS12V power cable. This provides additional 12V power to the motherboard. This answer is also not correct.

Figure D is the PCIe power cable. Use either the six-pin or eight pin (6+2) connector, depending upon the video card's requirements. This is the correct answer.

**Correct Answer: D. Figure D: PCIe power cable**

# CHAPTER 20

# Printer and Multifunction Device Configuration

## Core 1 Objective 3.6: Given a scenario, deploy and configure multifunction devices/ printers and settings.

***Printers*** and multifunction devices are among the most important peripherals in office of any size. The proper setup and configuration of both local and network types is essential to getting the most out of them. In this chapter, you will learn what you need to know about Core 1 Objective 3.6, including the following:

► **Properly Unboxing a Device—Setup Location Considerations**
► **Use Appropriate Drivers for a Given OS**
► **Device Connectivity**
► **Public/Shared Devices**
► **Configuration Settings**
► **Security**
► **Network Scan Services**
► **Automatic Document Feeder/Flatbed Scanner**

# PROPERLY UNBOXING A DEVICE—SETUP LOCATION CONSIDERATIONS

Printers and multifunction devices range in size from just slightly larger than a couple of reams of paper to behemoths that are almost as big as a kitchen range. Regardless of their size, there are several considerations to keep in mind when unboxing and setting them up.

Dedicated printers are becoming increasingly rare in the modern home, small office, or large office. Instead, the emphasis is on multifunction devices. A multifunction device (*MFD*) combines, at a minimum, an inkjet or laser printer and a flatbed scanner. Most also include an automatic document feeder for scanning and copy capabilities, and many also include fax capabilities. Another term for an MFD is *multifunction printer* or *multifunction peripheral* (*MFP*).

Departmental and enterprise-level MFDs also include or can be upgraded with paper-finishing features such as hole punching and stapling, and most also include support for secure printing because these devices are shared by multiple users.

## Safely Unboxing a Printer

Before you unbox a printer, keep in mind its size, weight, bulk, and the number of pieces in the box. A small laser or inkjet printer or MFD can be safely unboxed on a counter or sturdy desk. However, if it's more than 15 or 20 pounds or in a box that takes up most of the counter or table space available, consider unboxing it on the floor and then moving it into position. For departmental or enterprise printers or MFDs, consider using two or more people to safely unbox and position it, especially if the box is marked "team lift" or "heavy."

Don't drop or bang printers or MFDs around during or after installation. They have a lot of mechanical parts inside that may fail with careless handling.

## USB and Power Cable Considerations

If a printer or MFD will be connected directly to a computer via USB, make sure it is located within about 6 feet of the computer. Don't use a tape measure to figure this out. Instead, connect a 6-foot USB cable that matches the printer or MFD port to the USB port you want to use and make sure it will plug into the printer without straining the cable, damaging the USB port on the device, or becoming a tripping hazard.

> **TIP**
>
> USB cables longer than 6 feet might not be as reliable. If you must use a cable longer than 6–10 feet, consider using an active USB cable or use a network connection.

Make sure the printer or MFD is located within about 3 feet of an AC outlet or surge suppressor. Again, you don't want to stretch the power cable, put strain on the power plug on the device, or create a tripping hazard.

### Network Considerations

If the printer or MFD will be connected to a network via Ethernet, position the device as close as possible to an RJ-45 outlet on the network and use a suitable length of patch cable. Don't stretch the cable or put strain on the device's Ethernet port. Make sure the Ethernet patch cable is positioned so it's not a tripping hazard.

If the printer or MFD will be connected wirelessly, position it so it can receive the strongest wireless signal possible. If the signal is weak, consider installing a wireless repeater or using mesh networking to enable a strong signal to the device. Try to keep the device away from objects that could block the wireless signal.

### Other Considerations

When selecting a location for a printer or MFD, make sure there is adequate ventilation so the device won't overheat. Also, check temperature and humidity. If the air is too damp, print quality will suffer.

Make sure you can open the printer or MFD for paper loading, toner or ink replacement, and other maintenance tasks. If you need to move the printer or MFD to do any of these, try to find a better location.

> **EXAM TIP**
> When selecting a location for a printer or MFD, be mindful of its size, weight, proximity to USB or network connections, wireless network signal strength, humidity and temperature, and accessibility for paper and toner/ink replacement.

# USE APPROPRIATE DRIVERS FOR A GIVEN OS

A printer or MFD without drivers is an expensive paperweight! Although Microsoft Windows includes basic printer drives for some (mainly older) models, *basic* is the operational word here. MFDs using built-in Windows drivers might not have support for scanning, copying, or faxing. Inkjet printers might lack access to head cleaning or nozzle testing. So, be sure to download the latest drivers from the vendor website, and make sure you also download additional programs made for your printer.

### Printer Control Language vs. Postscript

*PCL* is short for Printer Control Language (also known as Printer Command Language), a page description language that defines fonts, color controls, objects, and other elements that make up a printed page. PCL was developed by Hewlett-Packard (HP) but is available on most non-Apple laser printers. The latest version is PCL 6.

Because PCL 6 uses a completely different way of controlling the printer than PCL 5, many vendors of PCL printers provide both PCL 6 and PCL 5 drivers. Which should you use? Use the PCL 6 drivers for better graphics and more font options, but if you have compatibility issues with some applications, use the PCL 5 drivers.

Although many printers use PCL, differences in the printer hardware resolution and other factors can make the same page look different on different printers. PCL is therefore device-dependent.

PostScript, unlike PCL, is a device-independent page description language. Although it was originally created for use with laser printers, PostScript can be used with any printer that has a PostScript driver. The current version of PostScript is PostScript 3.

If your printer or MFD has a PostScript option, here's how to decide if you need to install PostScript drivers or purchase the PostScript personality module:

> ▶ If you will be using the printer for text and basic graphics such as charting, line art, or photos, the standard printer language (usually PCL on laser printers) is fine.
> ▶ If you plan to use the printer for graphics arts and designs, you need PostScript.

**EXAM TIP**

PCL is used for document and other types of standard printing, while PostScript is used for more professional graphics printing.

# DEVICE CONNECTIVITY

Printers and MFDs can be connected to computers in three ways:

> ▶ USB
> ▶ Ethernet
> ▶ Wireless (Wi-Fi or Bluetooth)

**TIP**

Bluetooth printer interfacing is used by point-of-sale (POS) systems and by departmental or enterprise MFDs.

## USB

Almost all printers designed for direct connection to computers use USB 2.0 interfacing (see Figure 20.1). You can connect a USB printer to a USB 3.0 port, but the additional speed of USB 3.0 is not utilized.

If you have a choice between connecting a printer to a hub or connecting directly to a USB port on a computer, the port on the computer (root hub) is recommended.

**FIGURE 20.1** Ethernet (RJ-45) (top) and USB 2.0 (bottom) ports on a typical MFD.

## Ethernet

Almost all printers designed for network connection support Ethernet. To configure the printer for sharing via Ethernet, follow this basic procedure (the steps might be in a slightly different order):

1. Connect a CAT5e or CAT6 cable between the printer and the nearest RJ-45 jack.
2. Select Ethernet as the interface type on the printer.
3. Give the printer its network name.
4. Printers can receive an IP address from a router (if you select DHCP), or you can assign an IP address manually. If you choose to assign an address, make sure the IP address is in the same range as the rest of your devices and is not already in use.
5. Save and print out the configuration settings.

> **TIP**
>
> In large offices, Ethernet and Wi-Fi printers or MFDs are typically assigned static IP addresses so the device can be identified by its IP address and given a name (a process called *printer mapping*). If the printer is moved or gets a DHCP address that isn't mapped to local workstations, nobody can print.

### Wireless

To configure the printer or MFD for sharing via Wi-Fi, follow this basic procedure (the steps might be in a slightly different order):

1. Make sure you know the SSID and encryption key for the wireless network you want to use for the printer or MFD.
2. Select Wi-Fi (wireless) as the connection type (Figure 20.2).
3. Name the printer.
4. Enter the SSID.
5. Enter the encryption key.
6. Save and print the configuration settings.

**F I G U R E   2 0 . 2**  **Wireless configuration dialogs from a typical SOHO MFD (Epson ET-4750).**

# PUBLIC/SHARED DEVICES

There are two ways to add a printer to your network if it doesn't have onboard networking.

▶ Set up a direct connect printer as a share
▶ Set up a print server and connect the printer to it

## Printer Share

You can share a printer that is directly connected to your computer by enabling File And Printer Sharing in Windows. To enable it, follow these steps:

1. Search for *View Network Computers and Devices* and click it.
2. Click Network.
3. Click Network And Sharing Center.
4. From the Status (Network Status) dialog, click Network And Sharing Center.
5. Click Change Advanced Sharing Settings.
6. Click Private.
7. Make sure that Network Discovery and File And Printer Sharing are both turned on (Figure 20.3). If you make changes to either setting, click Save Changes.

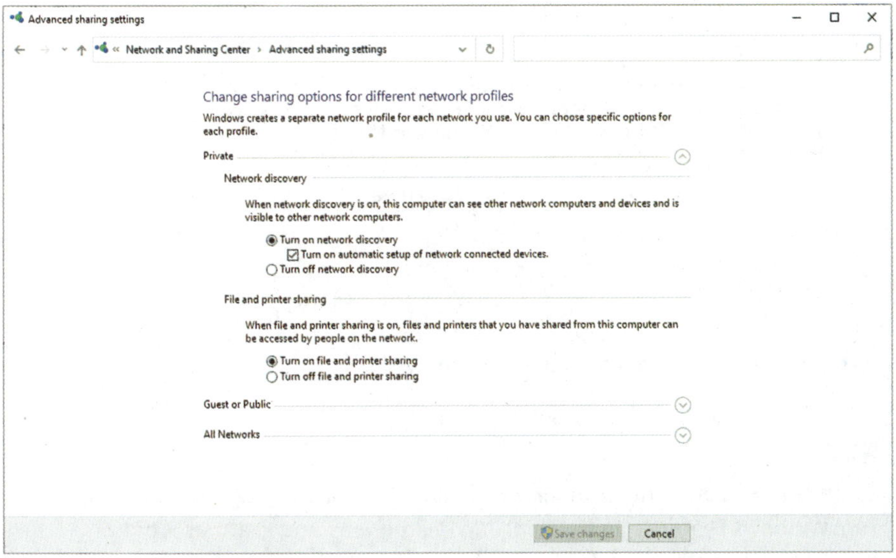

**FIGURE 20.3**  **Verifying that File And Printer Sharing and Network Discovery are enabled on a private network.**

Once File And Printer Sharing is enabled, follow these steps:

1. Open Settings ➤ Printers & Scanners.
2. Click your printer.
3. Click Manage.
4. Click Printer Properties.
5. Click Sharing.
6. Make sure Share This Printer is checked and Render Print Jobs On Client Computers are checked; change the printer name as desired (Figure 20.4).
7. Click Apply and then OK.

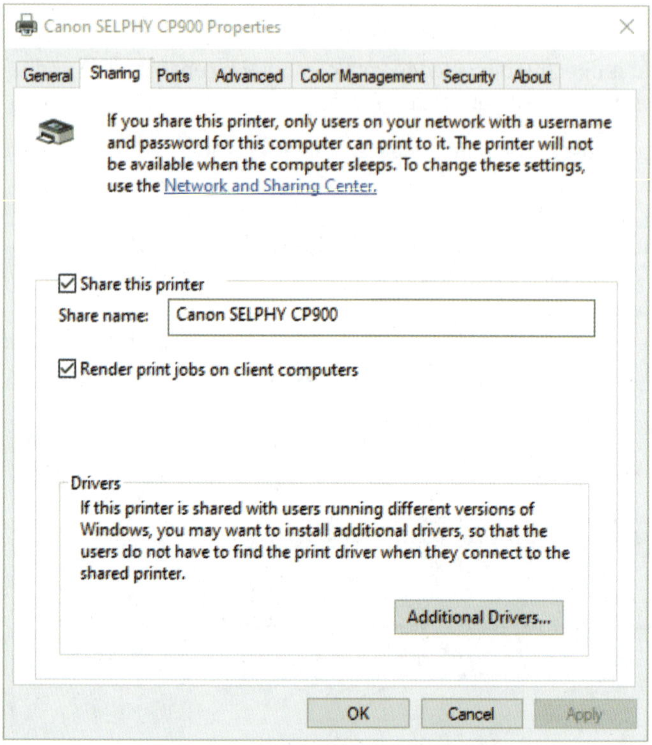

**FIGURE 20.4** Sharing a printer in Windows.

> **NOTE**
>
> To share a Windows printer or MFD with macOS or Linux computers, open the Turn Windows Features On Or Off dialog in Programs And Features (Control Panel), open the Print And Document Services category, and then check the LPD Print Service box. Click OK.
>
> To complete the process, have the administrator of the Windows computer add an account for each Linux or macOS user who needs to use the printer or MFD. To use the Windows printer or MFD, the Linux or macOS user must log into the Windows computer.

## Printer Mapping

After a printer has been shared, users need to connect to it, either by entering its IP address or by selecting the device sharing the printer and the name of the printer. This process is called *printer mapping*.

To connect to a printer via its IP address in Windows, follow this procedure:

1. Open Control Panel ➢ Devices And Printers ➢ Add A Printer.
2. Click The Printer That I Want Isn't Listed.
3. Click Add A Printer Using An IP Address Or Hostname and click Next.
4. Select TCP/IP Device from the Device Type menu.
5. Click the Hostname Or IP Address window and enter the printer's IP address.
6. Click Next.
7. If prompted, select the printer manufacturer and printer driver and click Next. If not listed, use Windows Update or Have Disk to install the printer.
8. Enter a name for the printer and click Next.
9. Select Do Not Share This Printer and click Next.
10. Click Print A Test Page and click Finish.

To connect to a printer shared by another device, browse to the computer with the shared printer in File Explorer, double-click the computer, and click the shared printer.

> **NOTE**
>
> To create a batch or script file that can be used to automatically log users into a shared printer, see `community.spiceworks.com/topic/2117417-need-a-batch-file-or-script-that-can-map-a-shared-printer-with-a-different-user`.

## Print Server

The term *print server* can refer to an Ethernet print server. This hardware device enables a printer or MFD without a network port to be added to an Ethernet network. Many of these also include Wi-Fi support. Check with the device manufacturer to determine whether a particular printer is compatible with a specific print server before purchasing one.

Another type of print server can be configured on Windows Server by installing the Print Management Server Role software. The server does not need to have any printers connected to it.

Print Management is also available on Windows Pro. Search for *printmanagement.msc* to start it. It's an optional feature in Windows 10 and 11, so it might need to be added.

> **NOTE**
>
> Learn more about the Windows Server version at `www.printeradmin.com/printer-management/print-management-console`. If you need to add Print Management to Windows 10 or 11, see `www.winhelponline.com/blog/restore-missing-print-management-console-windows-10`.

# CONFIGURATION SETTINGS

After a printer or MFD is installed, it's time to configure the software configuration settings in the printer driver. The most common settings and the ones you need to know for A+ certification are covered in the following sections.

To access these settings, open the Print dialog in your software program. Figure 20.5 shows a typical Print dialog from the OneNote for Windows 10 application. Note the More Settings link at the bottom of the dialog. Depending on the app, you might need to click a link like this to see all of the settings (Figure 20.6).

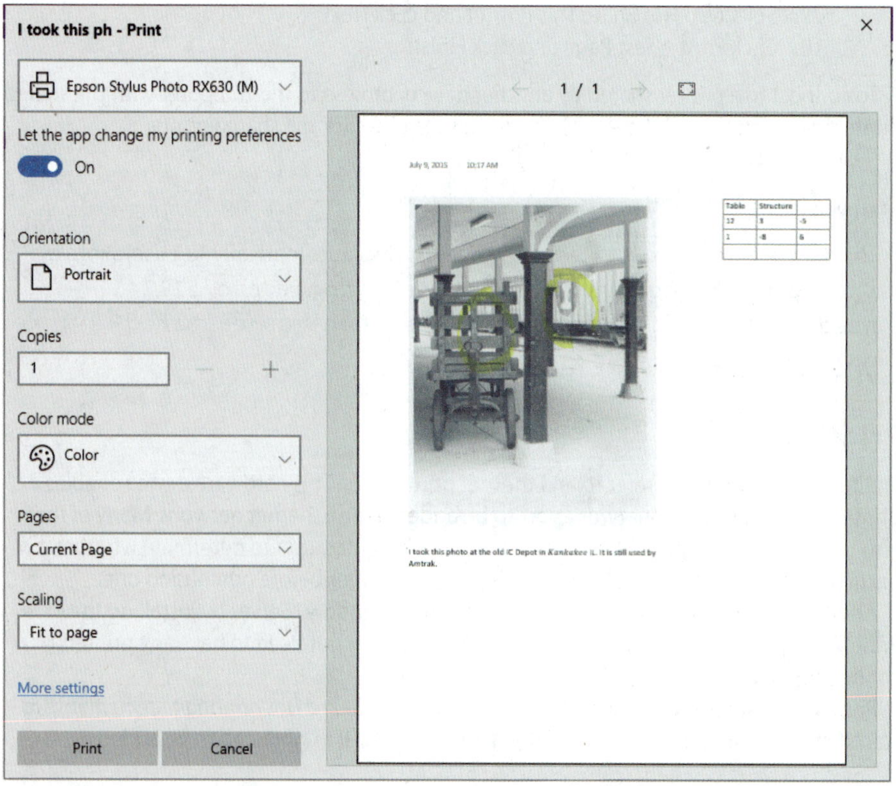

**FIGURE 20.5** A Microsoft OneNote for Windows 10 printer dialog.

## Orientation

Printers produce pages in one of two orientations: portrait (long side up) or landscape (short side up). The correct orientation might be set by the application, or it might need to be selected manually by the user. If the application has a Print Preview option, use it to make sure you have the correct orientation selected (refer to Figure 20.5).

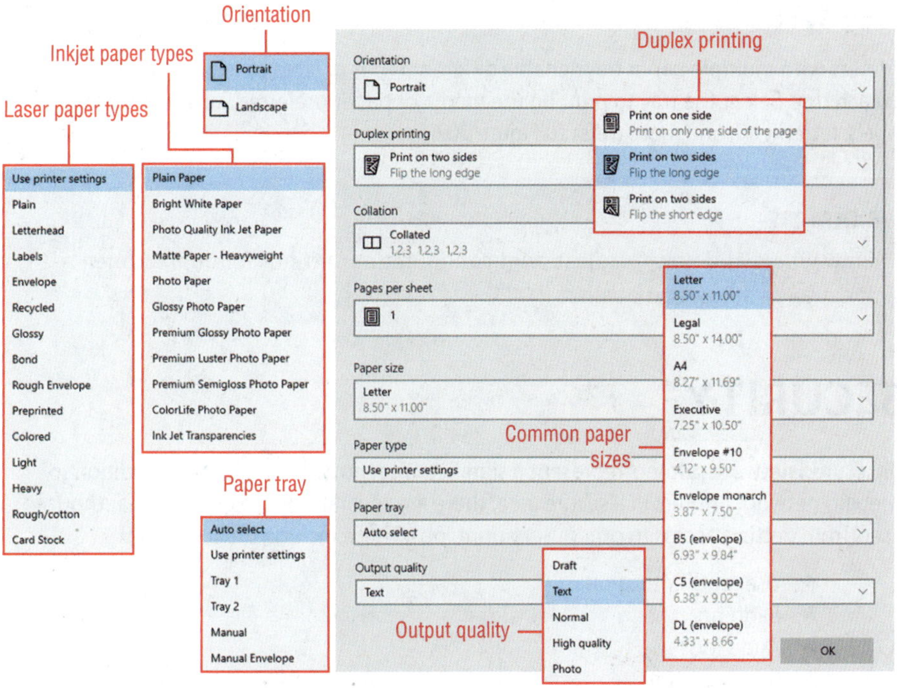

**FIGURE 20.6** Additional settings (not available on all printers).

## Duplex

Duplex (also known as double-sided printing) is available on some single-sided printers as well as those with a built-in duplexer (refer to Figure 20.6). If a single-sided printer has a duplex setting, it is used to properly position the paper for printing on the reverse side.

## Quality (and Paper Type)

Print quality is set in a variety of different ways. On typical inkjet printers, print quality has options for text and for various photo quality settings (refer to Figure 20.6). These settings optimize ink droplet size and the amount of ink used for the best results with the specified paper. Be sure to choose the correct paper type (refer to Figure 20.6) to avoid print quality problems with both laser and inkjet printers.

On laser printers, print quality is specified by resolution (DPI) and/or by selecting smoothing options. Dots per inch (DPI) is the measurement of the resolution of an image in print and on the screen. Typical laser printers and MFDs have a DPI of 300 or 600 dpi.

Accessing these options might require opening the Printer Preferences menu. If this menu is not available from the Print dialog, open Settings, go to the menu for printers, click the printer, and click the Print Preferences link. On some printers, installing more RAM enables higher-print resolutions or smoothing options to be selected.

### Tray Settings

Printers with multiple paper trays enable different types or sizes of paper and media to be in each tray. Select the tray to print on the media or paper preferred, such as envelopes, labels, letterhead, and more (refer to Figure 20.6).

---

**EXAM TIP**

Know where and how to adjust print configuration settings for duplex, orientation, tray settings, and quality.

---

# SECURITY

Unsecured network printers represent a significant security vulnerability. In addition to keeping network printers in a secure area, there are several ways to prevent unauthorized users from getting access to other users' print jobs. These include the following:

▶ User authentication
▶ Badging
▶ Audit logs
▶ Secured prints

### User Authentication

User authentication is a feature that permits only users registered on a specific printer or multifunction device to use it. After user authentication is configured, a user wanting to use the printer or MFD must log in to the printer with a valid username and password before printing can start. Depending upon the printer, the login might take place at the printer or remotely using a smart card or other login methods.

### Badging

Some printers and print management software permit the use of building access cards or smartphones with Bluetooth to enable you to print securely.

For a description of typical print management software that permits this type of secured printing, see www.papercut.com/blog/using-your-building-security-card-to-print-securely.

### Audit Logs

Some network-attached printers and MFDs have built-in audit logging capabilities. These must be enabled by the system administrator responsible for printer configuration.

Local printers or printers shared with the network can also log activity with Windows or with third-party software. To enable the Windows activity log for printer activities, follow this procedure:

1. Right-click the Start button and click Computer Management.
2. Click System Tools ➣ Event Viewer ➣ Applications And Services Logs ➣ Microsoft ➣ Windows ➣ PrintService.
3. To see installation or other admin activities, click Admin.
4. To enable logging of print jobs, right-click Operational and click Properties (Figure 20.7). Click Enable Logging and adjust the log size as desired (the default is 1028 KB).
5. Click Apply and then OK.

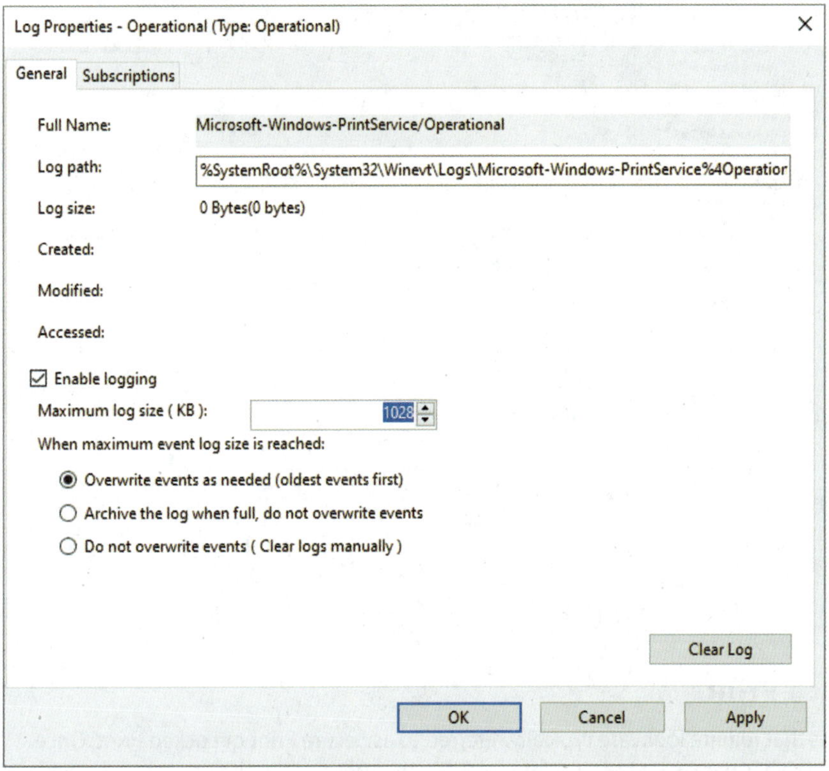

**FIGURE 20.7** Enabling PrintService ➣ Operational Print Logging.

To view the activity log, follow this procedure:

1. Open PrintService as described in the previous procedure.
2. Click Operational.
3. Look for Printing A Document in the Task Category. If you want to filter by event ID, it is 307. Figure 20.8 illustrates PrintService logging in the Operational category with the details for the print job (computer, user, time, and so on) listed on the General tab. The Details tab provides an XML view of the logged information.

**F I G U R E   2 0 . 8**   A logged print job.

> **NOTE**
>
> For additional information about print jobs, consider using third-party printer logging apps. A free app is available at www.papercut.com/products/free-software/print-logger.

## Secured Prints

Print jobs that require login are typically referred to as Secure Print or Locked Print. Once the print job has been sent to the printer or MFD, the user goes to the printer and is typically required to enter a passcode or PIN to retrieve the print job.

For examples of dialogs used by Canon, Ricoh, and Xerox printers that support Secure Print or Locked Print, see adminit.ucdavis.edu/tech-tips/how-secure-print.

> **EXAM TIP**
>
> Understand the importance of printer security and know how to implement user authentication, badging, audit logs, and secured prints.

# NETWORK SCAN SERVICES

Network scanning can be performed with most multifunction devices if they're connected to a network, either with a printer share or with their own onboard wired or wireless network connection.

## Email

You can scan documents to email with some scanners using a program provided by the scanner or multifunction device vendor. After the document is scanned, you can open your email client, and the document is attached to an email message.

With enterprise-level multifunction devices, the device has an embedded web server that is used to configure the email program. This type of device might use manually entered addresses or allow the user to choose addresses from a list.

## SMB

Some networked scanners and MFDs have the ability to send a scan made at the device directly to a printer using server message block (SMB), which uses TCP port 445.

See Chapter 6, "TCP/IP Ports and Protocols," to learn more about SMB and other network protocols.

Typically, enterprise and department-level devices need to be configured with specific users who can scan using SMB, and their computers need to have a specific folder created for use with SMB scanning.

Small business and home scanners with this capability feature a simplified setup that will scan to the selected user's Documents or Pictures folder after the appropriate software is installed.

## Cloud Services

Some networked scanners and MFDs can scan to cloud services. To use this feature, the user must install the appropriate software and configure the device to use the cloud service. Typical cloud services supported might include Google Drive, Dropbox, Evernote, and others. See the documentation for your scanner or MFD for details.

# AUTOMATIC DOCUMENT FEEDER/ FLATBED SCANNER

All except the most basic MFDs have both automatic document feeder (ADF) and flatbed scanning built in. An automatic document feeder (*ADF*) can accept one or more sheets of paper in a stack and feeds it past a fixed scanning window into an output tray.

ADFs work well for scanning standard-sized documents for copying or for converting into computer files. However, ADFs can jam if a mixture of paper sizes are fed into the tray or if the documents are bent, are of different thicknesses, or are slipperier than normal. These types of documents might not feed properly.

A flatbed scanning mechanism isn't as fast as an ADF as only one document at a time can be scanned or copied. However, a flatbed scanner can handle creased or folded original and books that will not fit into an ADF.

Some MFDs and scanners include OCR or ICR software. Optical character recognition (*OCR*) enables printed or typewritten text to be recognized and converted into editable PDF or popular document formats such as Microsoft Word.

Intelligent character recognition (*ICR*) goes a step beyond OCR by recognizing hand-written or hand-printed characters and converting them into text. This type of software is usually a part of document processing in banks, real estate, or other types of businesses in which handwritten documents are a major part of the workflow.

## CERTMIKE EXAM ESSENTIALS

▶ Printer or MFD setup starts with choosing a location that provides the power, accessibility, AC power, and network connections needed.

▶ Security features such as user authentication, Secure Print, or badging help prevent abuse and network attacks, while printer logging shows problems only after the fact.

▶ MFD scanners vary in their capabilities in part based on the software installed with them as well as their hardware features. Be sure to install the copy, fax, or network scanning features you need to make the most of these devices. Coverage of duplexing and ADF may show up on the exam.

## Practice Question 1

Your client has purchased an MFD but didn't use the software provided by the vendor to set up the device. Instead, he let Windows recognize the device and set it up. The copying feature doesn't work. What is the most likely place to start troubleshooting?

A. Test the scanner component.
B. Send back the MFD for replacement.
C. Install the software provided by the vendor.
D. Connect the printer to a USB port instead of the network.

## Practice Question 2

You are assisting a user with print quality issues on her inkjet printer. She is attempting to print photos on glossy paper, but the results are streaky and the paper has too much ink on it. Which two settings does she need to check?

A. Duplex
B. Quality
C. Tray
D. Paper type

## Practice Question 1 Explanation

This question is designed to test your real-world understanding of MFD and printer setup issues. Let's evaluate these choices one at a time.

1. Option A (Test the scanner component) ignores the limitations of Windows-included drivers. Many of these drivers can be used for printing, but not for other functions. This answer is incorrect.

2. Option B (Send the MFD back for replacement) is also incorrect. Without using a driver from the vendor, we don't know if the device is working correctly.

3. Option C (Install the software provided by the vendor) is the BEST answer. Start by installing the vendor-supplied software, and then try the copying feature.

4. Option D (Connect the printer to a USB port instead of the network) is incorrect. An MFD designed for network use can perform copying and other functions with either a network or USB connection if the vendor-supplied driver is used.

**Correct answer: C, Install the software provided by the vendor**

## Practice Question 2 Explanation

This question is designed to test your knowledge of Windows inkjet printer settings.

Let's evaluate these answers one at a time.

1. Option A (Duplex) is used to set up double-sided printing. Glossy paper is single-sided. This is not the right answer.

2. Option B (Quality) is one of the correct answers. Print quality should be set for a Photo setting (exact term depends upon the printer).

3. Option C (Tray) is used to select which paper tray is used. It has no effect on print quality. This is incorrect.

4. Option D (Paper type) is the other correct answer. The paper type setting needs to be matched to the actual paper type in use. The default is plain paper, which will not work well for printing photos.

**Correct answer: B, Quality, and D, Paper type**

# CHAPTER 21

# Printer Consumable Replacement

## *Core 1 Objective 3.7: Given a scenario, install and replace printer consumables.*

***Printers*** have a greater percentage of mechanical parts than just about any computing device. To keep them working reliably, periodic replacement of ink and toner is just one of the items on their maintenance schedule.

In this chapter, you will learn everything you need to know about A+ Core 1 Objective 3.7, including the following:

▶ **Laser**
▶ **Inkjet**
▶ **Thermal**
▶ **Impact**
▶ **3-D printer**

## LASER PRINTERS

A laser printer is a page printer. It receives data from a computer and converts the data into a pattern of dots that use electrostatic charges to attract toner. The toner is transferred by an imaging drum onto paper or other media and is heated to lock the image onto the media.

Laser printers are complex devices, and it's not surprising that they have a large number of consumables other than toner that might need to be replaced over their service life. Imaging components include the following:

- ▶ Imaging drum
- ▶ Fuser assembly
- ▶ Transfer belt
- ▶ Transfer roller

Paper handling components include the following:

- ▶ Pickup rollers
- ▶ Separation pads
- ▶ Duplexing assembly

But first, let's review the imaging process to see how these parts fit together.

## Laser Imaging Process

The CompTIA A+ imaging process involves these seven steps:

1. Processing
2. Charging
3. Exposing
4. Developing
5. Transferring
6. Fusing
7. Cleaning

This has traditionally been a focus of the exam.

> **EXAM TIP**
>
> Old versions of the exam covered a six-part laser printing process, omitting the processing step and making cleaning the first step. If you learned the old process, unlearn it. The seven-step process is the one to know!

### Processing
The printing process begins when the laser printer receives all of the page elements from the computer, including the page layout, fonts, text, and graphics. Its built-in rasterizer creates a page from this information and stores it in the printer's RAM.

### Charging
Charging refers to applying an electrical charge (-600V DC) to the imaging drum with a conditioning roller or primary corona wire.

### Exposing

Laser printers get their name from the laser beam that moves across the drum's surface and reduces the charge on the drum to -100V DC to create the image.

### Developing

In the developing process, toner is applied to the drum, but it sticks only to the portions of the drum where the charge was reduced by the laser in the exposing step.

### Transferring

To transfer the image from the drum to the paper, the paper receives a +600V DC charge and is moved past the drum. The toner on the drum is attracted to the paper, and after the toner is applied to the paper, a static eliminator strip cancels the paper's charge.

### Fusing

The fuser rollers heat the toner to about 350°F and melt it to the paper.

### Cleaning

To clean up the printer for the next page, a discharge lamp removes the image on the imaging drum, and the imaging drum's surface is scraped of excess toner. On a monochrome laser printer, the excess toner goes back into the drum, but a color laser printer dumps the excess toner into a waste toner container that must be emptied periodically.

## Laser Printer Imaging Components

The *imaging drum*, which transfers the image to paper, is an essential part of all laser printers. Depending upon the printer design, the imaging drum might also contain the toner (thus the term *toner cartridge*), or the toner and drum might be separate. An imaging drum has a specified life span based on page count. When the drum is nearing the end of its life span, it will warn the operator so the unit can be replaced. A toner cartridge that combines the imaging drum and toner cartridge must be replaced when the toner level is too low for good prints.

The *fuser assembly* is responsible for melting the toner to the paper to make a finished page. The fuser assembly can become dirty, leading to poor print quality, so it might be necessary to periodically wipe down the rollers after shutting down the printer and allowing the assembly to cool. If the fuser assembly stops working (fails to heat the paper), it needs to be replaced.

The *transfer belt* and *transfer roller* are used to transfer toner from the toner source to the paper. They need to be cleaned when print quality declines and replaced when they reach the end of their useful life.

## Laser Printer Paper Handling Components

Another source of trouble in a laser printer is paper handling, how paper is moved from the paper tray or manual feed through the printer until the page is printed and ejected.

Pickup rollers (Figure 21.1) are responsible for pulling paper from the paper tray or manual feed tray into the printer. Dirty rollers can cause creased paper, and worn rollers can cause paper jams.

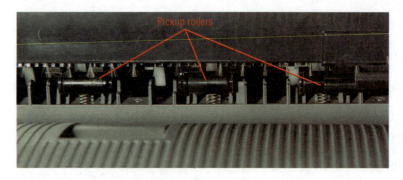

**FIGURE 21.1**   Pickup rollers in a typical laser printer.

The separation pad is used to assure that only one sheet of paper at a time is pulled into the printer. A worn separation pad allows multiple sheets of paper to be fed into the printer often resulting in paper jams.

Most printers today support double-sided printing, also known as *duplexing*. For duplexing to work, the duplexing assembly at the back of the printer has to pull the paper back through the printer after the front side is printed and reverse it so the back of the page is printed. When the duplex assembly is worn out, frequent paper jams will occur in the assembly.

## Laser Printer Maintenance

Like any mechanical device, laser printers require maintenance. Maintenance includes the regular replacement of consumables as well as the periodic replacement of parts that wear out and calibration to verify proper operation. The following sections cover the specific maintenance requirements for laser printers.

### Replace Toner

Laser printers rely on toner, but they vary widely in how toner is installed and located.

Many printers use a design that incorporates the toner and imaging drum. These toner cartridges make maintenance easier because a worn or damaged imaging drum is replaced as part of the toner replacement process.

Others use separate imaging drums and toner cartridges (Figure 21.2). Look for messages based on page count on the printer's front panel display to determine when it's time to replace the toner.

**FIGURE 21.2** Toner cartridge in a typical printer with a separate imaging drum.

## Apply Maintenance Kit

Laser printer maintenance kits are designed to replace the most common consumable parts other than toner. For example, an HP LaserJet maintenance kit typically contains an assortment like this:

▶ Fuser kit
▶ Toner collection unit
▶ Transfer belt unit
▶ Roller assembly
▶ Separation pad

Kits include parts made for a particular printer model and can be purchased from the printer vendor.

## Calibrate

Calibration is the process of making sure color laser printer print colors are aligned properly. The calibration process is run from the printer's control panel and takes several minutes. After the process is complete, print a test page to make sure the problem is solved.

## Clean

As discussed in previous sections, several laser printer components need to be cleaned. Parts such as fusers and rollers should be cleaned and the printer retested before replacing them. A toner vacuum (which is specially designed to capture toner powder) and an N95 or higher-rated face mask are recommended when cleaning laser printers.

# INKJET PRINTERS

Inkjet printers are character/line printers. They use tightly spaced groups of nozzles (one for each color) to print one line at a time of single characters or graphics up to the limit of the printhead matrix. Larger characters are created by printing a portion of the characters across the page, advancing the page to allow the printhead to print another portion of the characters, and so on until the entire line of characters is printed.

## Inkjet Components

The following are the essential components in an inkjet printer:

- ▶ Ink cartridges
- ▶ Printhead
- ▶ Roller
- ▶ Feeder
- ▶ Duplexing assembly
- ▶ Carriage belt

### Ink Cartridge and Printheads

Inkjet printers use at least one black ink (some also use an additional photo black) along with cyan, magenta, and yellow ink cartridges (Figure 21.3). Photo printers often have additional light colors to improve photo output. The ink cartridges are combined with the printheads on some printers, while others use separate ink cartridges and printheads. One of the most expensive liquids in the world per ounce is the ink in ink cartridges, so several vendors now make models that use refillable ink reservoirs (Figure 21.4).

**FIGURE 21.3**  Typical ink cartridges after installation.

**FIGURE 21.4  Ink levels in an inkjet printer with ink tanks.**

   Because of the way that inkjet printers combine inks to create printed output, almost all inkjet printers stop printing if one ink cartridge or reservoir runs out of ink. Monitoring ink levels is crucial to continued operation.

## Carriage Belt
The carriage belt (Figure 21.5) is used to move the printheads across the paper to create the image. If the carriage belt is damaged, the printer must be serviced or replaced.

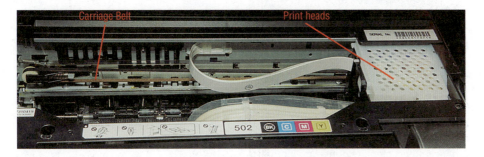

**FIGURE 21.5  Carriage belt and printheads in an inkjet printer with ink tanks.**

## Roller
Rollers are used to pull paper from the paper tray into the printer. When rollers become ink-covered, they can cause spots on printed output. Some printers have a built-in roller

cleaning routine, while others require you to clean the rollers manually. As with laser printers, worn-out rollers require replacement.

### Feeder

Inkjet printers can have straight-through paper feeds (feeding from the top) or bottom-mounted paper feeds that pull the paper in a C-shaped direction from the bottom of the printer. Keep the feeder free from dust and be sure to adjust the paper width in the feed tray when printing on narrow paper or envelopes.

### Duplexing Assembly

The duplexing assembly (Figure 21.6) is a common feature on both laser and inkjet printers. It is responsible for pulling a printed sheet back through the printer and flipping it so the back side can be printed. It can be removed to help clear out paper jams.

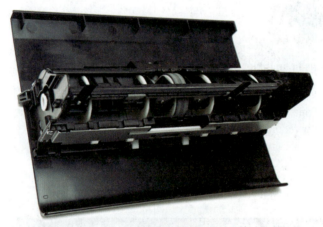

**FIGURE 21.6** A typical duplexing assembly after removal to clear a paper jam.

## Inkjet Maintenance

Because inkjet printers use liquid ink that can dry up and harden over time, inkjet printer maintenance focuses on keeping printheads clean. The following sections discuss this and other elements of inkjet printer maintenance.

### Clean Heads

Printers that are rarely used, and those that are turned off by removing power instead of by using the power switch on the printer, can have dirty printheads. These can lead to gaps in printing or, in extreme cases, no printing at all. Most inkjet printers have built-in cleaning processes that can be run from the printer's control panel or from the Maintenance menu available in the operating system's printer properties or preferences menu.

Use a nozzle check printout to look for gaps and then run the cleaning process. The clean heads process uses ink, so it's useful to have spare ink cartridges available. After cleaning, retry the nozzle check printout.

### Replace Cartridges

Replacing ink cartridges is one of the most common maintenance tasks. If your printer displays estimated ink levels, check them before starting a print job. The cartridge replacement process moves the printhead to a location where the ink cartridges can be removed. Make sure you follow the manufacturer's replacement process, including removing the protective tape from the new cartridge. After you replace the cartridges, the printer might ask you to confirm which cartridges have been replaced. At the end of the process, you should do a test print. Some printers will do this automatically, so have paper in the printer.

### Calibrate

Because inkjet printers form both text and graphics by printing bands of dots in a matrix, it's essential to have the printer line up each band with the preceding band. Otherwise, both text and graphics will be distorted.

The calibration process is needed more frequently with inkjet printers than with laser printers. Some manufacturers automatically run a calibration routine every time ink cartridges with integrated printheads are installed. Otherwise, calibration, sometimes referred to as *alignment*, can be run from the printer's control panel (Figure 21.7). In either case, make sure paper is installed in the printer so you can choose the best test sheet to finish the process.

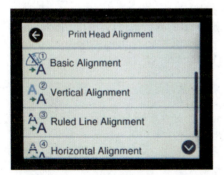

**FIGURE 21.7** Preparing to calibrate (align) an inkjet printer. (Source: Microsoft Corporation)

### Clear Jams

Inkjet printers can use various types of media, including standard printer/copy paper, labels, inkjet photo paper, and inkjet transparency media. To avoid jams, specify the type of paper being used for a print job and make sure the paper is properly aligned before inserting it.

If a jam takes place, check the printer control panel to see where the jam is located. Turn off the printer before removing the jam. If the media is torn, make sure there are no fragments left in the printer. If labels have come off a label sheet, make sure none of them are stuck inside the printer. If you need to remove the duplexer to clear the jam, make sure the duplexer is properly inserted afterward.

# THERMAL PRINTERS

Thermal printers use heat as part of the imaging process, and unlike laser or inkjet printers, they use specific paper. Thermal printers are frequently used as point-of-sale printers, which means they must be able to run reliably with little downtime.

The major components of a thermal printer include the following:

- ► Feed assembly
- ► Heating element
- ► Special thermal paper

## Feed Assembly, Heating Element

The feed assembly in a typical thermal printer holds a roll of paper and rollers. The paper is pulled past the heating element, which uses a full-width matrix printhead to place the text and image on the paper.

## Special Thermal Paper

Heat-sensitive paper, called *special thermal paper* on the CompTIA A+ Core 1 exam, is what is used in most thermal printers. Special thermal paper comes in many varieties, including different widths, colors, sticky back for use in shipping labels, and others. When ordering paper, be sure to know the specifications needed for the printer.

> **EXAM TIP**
>
> The current CompTIA A+ Core 1 exam no longer covers thermal printers that use heat-sensitive ribbons, but they are still in use. Be sure to use recommended paper types and compatible ribbons to assure good printer operation.

### Heat Sensitivity of Paper

There are two levels of heat sensitivity.

High-sensitivity paper requires less energy to create a receipt and is recommended for fast printing of ATM receipts, bar codes, and parking receipts. It produces a darker image.

Low-sensitivity paper is used for point-of-sale receipts and other applications in which speed is less important.

Check the specifications for a thermal printer to determine which heat sensitivity is recommended.

## Thermal Printer Maintenance

Thermal printer maintenance is simpler than with other types of printers, but a poorly maintained printer can be frustrating for shoppers who receive illegible or faded receipts. The following sections cover what is needed to keep them working.

### Replace Paper

The telltale magenta strip near the edge of the receipt is the end-of-paper indicator. When it appears, it's time to get another roll of paper and prepare for installation. Operators who don't properly advance the new paper roll past the cutter are likely to have paper jams.

### Clean Heating Element

To prevent gaps and spots on printouts, follow the vendor's recommendation to clean the heating element: a typical method is isopropyl alcohol applied with a cotton swab. Be aware that the heating element can be very hot.

### Remove Debris

Debris in the feed assembly or on the heating element needs to be removed to help ensure high-quality printouts. Some printers include a built-in cleaning cartridge. Be sure to replace the cleaning cartridge as recommended.

# IMPACT

Impact printers, once the mainstay of offices, are now relegated to warehouses, repair shops, and other less-than-pristine locations. If properly maintained, they can continue to print out multipart forms and reports. Their essential components include the following:

- ► Printhead
- ► Ribbon
- ► Tractor feed

## Printhead

Impact printers use dot-matrix printheads that contain 9, 18, and 24 thin wires that push on a ribbon to create an image on the paper. The printhead is moved back and forth across the paper by a carriage belt (Figure 21.8).

## Ribbon

An impact printer's ribbon is made of inked cloth and is inside a plastic cartridge. The pins in the printhead press on the ribbon against paper backed by a platen (rubber cylinder behind the paper) to form text and images. To avoid excessive wear, the ribbon inside the cartridge is advanced periodically during use.

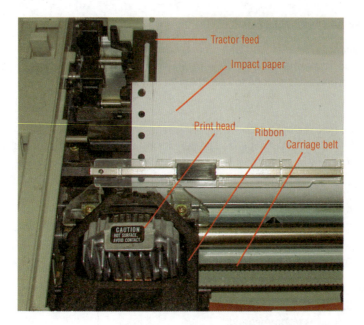

**FIGURE 21.8** The parts of a typical impact printer.

### Tractor Feed

A tractor-feed mechanism is used by almost all impact printers. It uses paper with removable perforated ends; the pins in the tractor feed go through the holes in the paper to push or pull the paper past the printhead.

### Impact Paper

Impact paper is typically tractor-feed paper, which is sold in boxes containing paper with perforations along the edges and at every page length. After printing, the edges are torn off along the feed perforations, and each page is torn off at the page perforation.

Some impact printers can also use single sheets of paper similar to laser or inkjet paper.

### Maintenance: Replace Ribbon, Replace Printhead, Replace Paper

Printhead replacement is expensive, and the best way to avoid it is to change ribbons when the printout becomes faint or the ribbon begins to fray.

If an impact printer begins to produce printouts with gaps in the letters, one of the pins in the printhead has become bent or broken. Stop using the printer and replace the printhead. If the printer has a platen, check it for cracks or hardening and replace it to help protect the next printhead you install.

Paper is also part of impact printer maintenance. Don't use paper that is partially torn off the tractor-feed edges, and be sure to adjust the head gap and tractor-feed width to match the paper or other media in use.

# 3-D PRINTERS

A 3-D (or 3D) printer turns a CAD drawing or digital 3-D model into a 3-D object. Some 3-D printers use a printhead that can "float" above the print bed, moving horizontally and vertically to build up the object layer by layer from various types of plastic or metal materials. Other types of 3-D printers use resin along with various types of light sources to create 3-D objects.

Typical 3-D printers have one or more of the following consumables that must be maintained to allow quality prototyping and production to occur:

- ▶ Filament
- ▶ Resin
- ▶ Print bed

> **NOTE**
>
> The consumables in this section are those used by the following types of 3-D printing:
>
> Fused deposition modeling (FDM) uses plastic or other types of filaments along with a print bed and is the lowest-cost 3-D printing technology.
>
> Stereolithography (SLA) uses resin along with a laser beam to create a 3-D object.
>
> Digital light processing (DLP) uses resin along with a digitally controlled light source.
>
> Liquid crystal display (LCD) uses resin along with UV light from an LCD display to create a 3-D object.

## Filament

The essential building block of 3-D printers using the FDM process is the filament, which is melted and extruded to create the 3-D object. Materials include the following:

- ▶ Thermoplastics (PLA, ABS, PETG)
- ▶ TPE (combines rubber and plastic)
- ▶ Nylon
- ▶ Wood
- ▶ Metal
- ▶ Carbon fiber
- ▶ Glass

Check the recommended filaments for the specific 3-D printer in use, the diameter required, and the settings recommended for the printer with a specific filament type.

### Print Bed

3-D FDM process printing uses a flat print bed to support the object while it is being printed. Print beds can be made of various materials, such as glass, metal, or acrylic plastic, and are sometimes covered with additional materials to improve adhesion of the project or to make removing the finished project easier.

### Resin

Printers that use a light source such as LCD, DLP, or laser use resin rather than filament. Resins are designed for specific light sources and tasks. Be sure to consult with the printer and resin vendor to choose the correct resin type for your printer and application.

---

## CERTMIKE EXAM ESSENTIALS

▶ All types of printers have consumables. The obvious consumables are paper, ink, toner, filament, and resin. However, maintenance items that wear out before a printer's life span is over are also considered consumables, such as fuser assembly, waste toner reservoir, and printheads.

▶ Regardless of the printer type, each model uses consumables made especially for that model or printer family. These may come from the original manufacturer or are manufactured to the same specifications.

▶ Using the right consumables helps make a printer last longer and produce higher-quality output with fewer failures along the way.

## Practice Question 1

Your client is experiencing a lot of poor-quality printouts from a laser printer. It prints pages on standard copy paper that look OK until they are picked up, and then the print falls off the page. The toner cartridge and imaging drum check out OK. Which other component is likely to be the cause of the problem?

A. The rasterizer that creates the page in the printer
B. Not enough memory in the printer
C. Paper loaded upside down
D. The fuser

## Practice Question 2

You have been asked to pick up some consumables for the office. The shopping list contains the following:

A. One spool each of TPA, ABS, and PETG filament in black, white, and blue
B. Cash register tape
C. Black ink cartridge

Choose the types of printers you are shopping for from the following list:

1. Laser

2. Inkjet

3. Impact

4. 3-D

5. Thermal

## Practice Question 1 Explanation

This question is designed to test your knowledge of parts in a laser printer and what they do.

Let's evaluate these choices one at a time.

Option A: If the rasterizer wasn't working, there would be garbage on the page, or nothing at all. This is incorrect.

Option B: A printer memory shortage would cause the printer to stop until the page was ejected. Only part of the page would be printed. This is not the problem either.

Option C: The photo paper has a right and wrong side, but not copy or laser paper. This is not the right answer.

Option D: The fuser is the cause of the problem. Its job is to melt the toner to the paper. If it fails, the toner stays on the paper but will fall off when the paper is picked up, or even blow off the paper if there's any air movement by the printer.

**Correct Answer: D. The fuser**

## Practice Question 2 Explanation

This question is designed to test your knowledge of printer types and their consumables.

Let's first look at the consumables list:

A: TPA, ABS, and PETG filament is used by option 4, 3-D printer. No other printer type uses filaments, so we know that you are shopping for a 3-D printer.

B: Cash register tape is used by option 5, thermal printer. No other printer type uses this type of media, so we can add thermal printers to the list.

C: Black ink cartridge is used by option 2, inkjet printer. No other printer type uses ink cartridges, so we also have an inkjet.

From the information provided, we can conclude that you are shopping for a 3-D printer, a thermal printer, and an inkjet printer. There is no evidence that you are shopping for a laser printer or an impact printer.

In the real world, you would need more information than this to make your purchases. But at least you know which types of consumables go with particular types of printers.

**Correct Answer: 2, 4, 5. Inkjet printer, 3-D printer, Thermal printer**

# PART IV

# Domain 4.0: Virtualization and Cloud Computing

**Chapter 22**   Cloud Computing
**Chapter 23**   Virtualization

Virtualization and Cloud Computing is the fourth domain of CompTIA's A+ Core 1 exam. In it, you'll learn how organizations use cloud computing to meet business requirements and the way that virtualization supports cloud computing. This domain has two objectives.

**4.1 Summarize cloud-computing concepts**

**4.2 Summarize aspects of client-side virtualization**

Questions from this domain make up 11 percent of the questions on the A+ Core 1 exam, so you should expect to see approximately 10 questions on your test covering the material in this part.

# Cloud Computing

## *Core 1 Objective 4.1: Summarize Cloud Computing Concepts (Models and Characteristics)*

*Cloud* computing is a hot topic in IT circles. While many users have worked with some forms of cloud computing, such as Gmail or OneDrive, many parts of it are still unfamiliar territory. The CompTIA A+ Certification Core 1 exam expects you to understand some basic concepts, and in this chapter you will learn what you need to know about the following topics from Objective 4.1 (the rest of the topics from Objective 4.1 are covered in Chapter 22):

▶ **Common cloud models**
▶ **Cloud characteristics**

## WHAT IS CLOUD COMPUTING?

Cloud computing is any computing service, from apps to storage to servers, that is available over the Internet in a shared manner. Cloud computing puts these and other resources in reach via your web browser. Thus, if you're away from your normal computing environment (on a business trip, vacation, or performing remote work) or if you work in the cloud, there's little if any difference in your work regardless of your physical location.

# CLOUD DEPLOYMENT MODELS

Cloud computing can be implemented in many ways. In this section, we look at how cloud services are provided through specific cloud models. The cloud deployment models describe who may access different types of cloud services. There are four options.

- ▶ Public cloud
- ▶ Private cloud
- ▶ Hybrid cloud
- ▶ Community cloud

## Public Cloud

Almost any computer user these days has used the public cloud. Do you use OneDrive, iCloud, or Dropbox? How about Zoom or Microsoft Teams? `Outlook.com` or Gmail? These are just a few examples of the public cloud. Public cloud services are owned by private organizations that make those services available to organizations or individuals who pay or sign up for it.

After subscribing to a public cloud service, you use your web browser from an Internet-connected location to use services on the public cloud.

## Private Cloud

A private cloud differs from a public cloud in two ways.

- ▶ Its services are available only to specified users.
- ▶ It might use a private network as well as public networks.

A private cloud may be secured differently than a public cloud because it can use corporate firewalls or internal hosting to protect sensitive information. Unlike a public cloud, however, a private cloud might not save as much money because it requires dedicated IT services and equipment to run the private network and onsite portions of the cloud.

## Hybrid Cloud

A hybrid cloud provides the best of both worlds: it combines public and private clouds. Hybrid clouds can be used in a variety of ways. For example, organizations can keep their most sensitive information on the private cloud and use the public cloud for less sensitive information; the public cloud can be used to provide additional capacity when the private cloud has reached its capacity.

## Community Cloud

A community cloud is basically a hybrid cloud that is used by multiple organizations that are working on a project together and benefit from a shared cloud platform, such as in these examples:

▶ Different government agencies with similar requirements or that share information with each other can use a community cloud.
▶ Public and private organizations working together to improve their city can use a community cloud.

## Cloud Service Categories

The next way we can describe cloud services is by what they actually do for their customers. We use the *as a service (aaS)* cloud computing service categories to describe the function of a cloud offering. The following are three popular *aaS* models:

▶ Software as a service (SaaS)
▶ Infrastructure as a service (IaaS)
▶ Platform as a service (PaaS)

## Software as a Service

For individuals and organizations that want to use software without installing it themselves, software as a service is ideal. *SaaS* provides cloud-based access to software on demand.

Gmail, Salesforce, Microsoft Office online, and many other popular cloud-based services fall into this category.

## Infrastructure as a Service

For organizations that need access to data center infrastructure on an on-demand basis, infrastructure as a service is ideal. *IaaS* provides cloud-based access to compute, storage, and networking resources on demand.

The user is responsible for providing apps, development tools, and whatever else is needed. Think of it as "you bring the brains and we'll rent you the tools." A few examples of IaaS providers include Amazon Web Services, Microsoft Azure, and Google Cloud.

## Platform as a Service

For organizations that want to develop software and run it on somebody else's hardware, platform as a service is ideal. *PaaS* provides cloud-based access to infrastructure (similar to IaaS) along with development and support tools needed to create, implement, and update software.

Amazon Web Services Elastic Beanstalk, Google App Engine, and Microsoft Azure Functions are a few of the many PaaS services in this category.

Figure 22.1 compares these *as a service* categories in terms of what the provider supplies and what the client supplies.

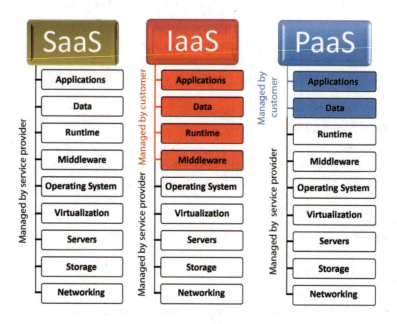

**FIGURE 22.1** Comparing SaaS, PaaS, and IaaS cloud service categories.

# CLOUD CHARACTERISTICS

What are some of the unique features of cloud computing? In this section, we discover five characteristics of cloud computing you should consider as you use the cloud.

### Shared Resources

The essence of cloud computing is shared resources. Need to bring on a new application server? Need more storage? Instead of buying or building infrastructure you might not need later, you can use the cloud. And, the resources you use in your time zone can be used by others in other time zones without interfering with your work.

### Metered Utilization

One common way cloud services are billed is with metered utilization. This is sometimes referred to as *pay as you go* because you are charged only for what you actually use. Think of it as a technology buffet where everything is on the menu, but you pay only for what winds up on your tray.

The alternative is subscription billing, in which an organization pays a flat fee for access to specified cloud service features. This method avoids price fluctuations but is less flexible if the organization's needs change frequently.

## Rapid Elasticity

Rapid elasticity means that cloud computing resources can be put into action quickly to meet high demand and can then be decommissioned when demand decreases. If you need this feature, make sure your plan supports it both technically and in terms of pricing.

## High Availability

High availability refers to the steps taken to assure that a computing activity doesn't go offline. In a noncloud environment, this would be achieved by having redundant servers, multiple network and online connections, and quick failover provisions. In a cloud environment using PaaS or IaaS, these are easier to achieve because you can provision your cloud resources with virtual clusters that provide the redundancy and multiple connections needed.

## File Synchronization

File synchronization, which enables files stored on different devices in different locations to keep up-to-date with each other, is another benefit of cloud computing. Services such as Microsoft OneDrive, Dropbox, Google Drive, and others enable people working remotely from home, while traveling, or in the office to have the same files available everywhere.

---

### CERTMIKE EXAM ESSENTIALS

▶ Make sure you understand the four cloud deployment models: public cloud, private cloud, hybrid cloud, and community cloud.

▶ Make sure you can distinguish between the major *as a service* categories (software as a service, platform as a service, and infrastructure as a service) and their features.

▶ Be sure you can define these five key cloud characteristics: shared resources, metered utilization, rapid elasticity, high availability, and file synchronization.

## Practice Question 1

Your client needs to scale up its current IT facilities to handle an expected rush of sales for its new electronic widget. It needs to handle global orders after the latest World of Widgets trade show using its existing software. Which of the following cloud service model types would best meet this need?

A. SaaS
B. Rapid elasticity
C. IaaS
D. PaaS

## Practice Question 2

Your company has just signed a contract with a cloud provider to enable field workers to automatically get updates to the current product catalog. Which cloud computing benefit will field workers be enjoying?

A. Rapid elasticity
B. File synchronization
C. Metered utilization
D. High availability

## Practice Question 1 Explanation

This question is designed to test your knowledge of the different cloud storage model categories and their capabilities to solve a real-world problem.

Let's evaluate these choices one at a time.

1. Option A, SaaS, would be appropriate if they had developed software they wanted to offer to the public for use online. That is not the goal. This suggestion is incorrect.

2. Option B, rapid elasticity, isn't about a type of cloud service model, but one of its benefits. This suggestion is incorrect.

3. Option C, IaaS, is the only one that matches the need to the appropriate cloud services. IaaS provides the infrastructure that our widget maker needs to be ready for more global sales.

4. Option D, PaaS, would be appropriate if the widget maker needed to develop software, but the software is ready. This is also incorrect.

**Correct Answer: C. IaaS**

## Practice Question 2 Explanation

This question is designed to test your knowledge of cloud computing characteristics and how they relate to real-world situations.

Let's evaluate these choices one at a time.

1. Option A, rapid elasticity, doesn't fit. If the sales force were going through rapid changes in size, this might be useful, but this characteristic has nothing to do with what the sales force is getting from the cloud. This is incorrect.

2. Option B, file synchronization, is exactly right. The field workers don't need to download new files and delete old files manually anymore. This is correct.

3. Option C, metered utilization, refers to how cloud services are purchased. The field workers don't need, or care, about this topic. It is incorrect.

4. Option D, high availability, refers to what's going on behind the scenes to make sure the product catalog is always available automatically. It is not a direct benefit. It is also incorrect.

**Correct Answer: B. File synchronization**

# Virtualization
## *Core 1 Objective 4.2: Summarize Aspects of Client-Side Virtualization.*

*Virtualization* has many uses for technicians, from technical support of older operating systems to creating safe spaces for experimenting with not-ready-for-prime-time apps. This chapter provides you with what you need to know about Core 1 Objective 4.2 including the following:

▶ **Purpose of virtual machines**
▶ **Resource requirements**
▶ **Security requirements**

## PURPOSE OF VIRTUAL MACHINES

What is a virtual machine (*VM*)? A virtual machine is a portion of a physical computer's resources (disk space, RAM, network, and so on) that is configured to act like a different computer. A VM can run a different operating system, run different applications, and connect to different networks than the physical computer that is hosting the VM. Figure 23.1 illustrates a nonvirtualized system.

Figure 23.2 illustrates two types of virtualization: Type 1 and Type 2. Typically, Type 2 virtualization is set up on desktop computers and small servers. Larger servers typically use Type 1.

Non-virtualized

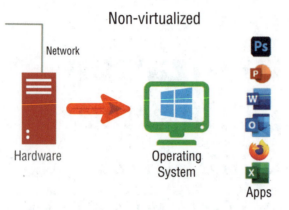

**FIGURE 23.1** **A nonvirtualized system.**

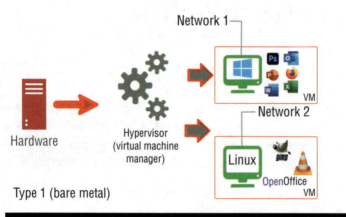

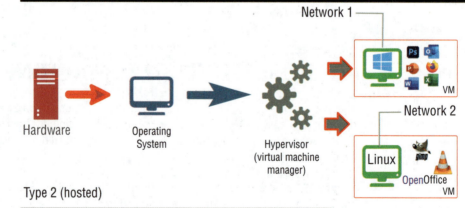

**FIGURE 23.2** **Type 1 and Type 2 virtualization compared.**

**NOTE**

There are two types of virtualization: Type 1 virtualization, also known as "bare metal," installs the virtual machine manager (VMM) on the hardware. The VMM then hosts virtual machines. Type 2 virtualization, or "hosted," installs the VMM on the operating system, which then hosts virtual machines. Type 1 is faster, but Type 2 is available to most users, with a number of popular VMMs being free, including Oracle VirtualBox and Microsoft Hyper-V among others.

The program used to create a virtual machine is called a *virtual machine manager* (VMM) or a *hypervisor*. The VMM is used to configure the VM by providing specified amounts of disk space and RAM; an operating system; extensions to enable easy sharing of the host PC's hardware and resources with the VM; and emulations of video, chipset, and network hardware (Figure 23.3).

**FIGURE 23.3**  Oracle VM VirtualBox configuring a VM for Windows 8.1.

A virtual machine is stored in a file that can be moved from location to location by copying or moving it.

## Sandbox

One of the reasons to create a virtual machine (VM) is to have a secure environment for running potentially dangerous apps or processes. A VM acts as a type of sandbox, meaning that an app that malfunctions or a process that could harm your computer inside the VM will affect only the virtual machine, not the physical computer.

## Test Development

Another reason to create a virtual machine is to have a safe environment for testing applications and processes. The sandbox analogy applies here as well: any problem with a pre-release application installed in the VM will affect only the VM, not the physical computer. Depending upon the exact failure, the solution for a crash inside the VM might be the same as when the app runs on a physical computer or might require changes to the VM configuration. In any event, you can continue to run your computer and other VMs while you work on the problem.

## Application Virtualization

One of the most important reasons to create a virtual machine is the ability to run the equivalent of an old computer or a different type of computer inside your current computer.

### Legacy Software/OS

Many years ago, I was working on a project that required me to run several different versions of Windows. Pre-virtualization, this required me to lug around three different computers! Thanks to virtualization, I can set up a different virtual machine for each version of Windows.

For example, assume that you are responsible for providing technical support for legacy versions of an application that run on older Windows versions. You can create a VM for each older Windows version, install the appropriate version of Windows, and install the appropriate version of the app into each VM you create. This is helpful because many apps work the way Microsoft Office does, not allowing you to have multiple versions installed on the same Windows installation.

Whether you are involved in tech support, playing retro games, or have other reasons to run old operating systems and old apps, virtualization is the answer.

### Cross-Platform Virtualization

Another important reason for virtualization is the ability to run a different operating system made for different hardware on your computer. When you set up a VM, you specify the operating system you will be installing. In Oracle VirtualBox, for example, you can choose from various flavors of Windows, Linux, macOS, and others. After you choose the type, you select the specific OS you plan to install (Figure 23.4).

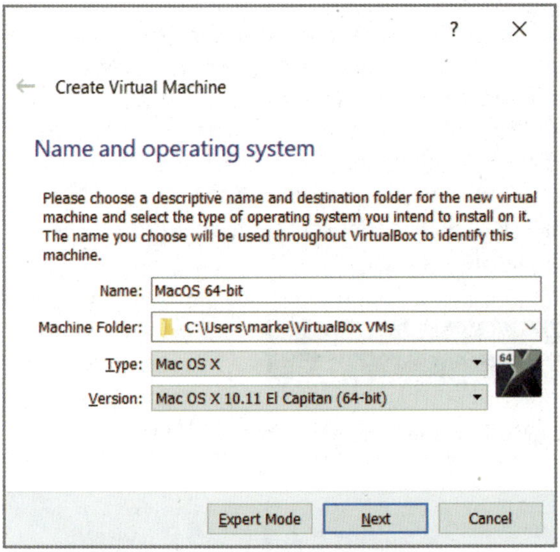

**FIGURE 23.4** Oracle VM VirtualBox creating a VM for running macOS.

**EXAM TIP**

Be sure you understand the purpose of virtualization, including sandbox, test development, and application virtualization, for the CompTIA A+ Certification Core 1 1101 exam.

# RESOURCE REQUIREMENTS

Virtualization has specific resource requirements that must be present on a computer that will be used to host virtual machines. These vary according to what type of virtualization is being used.

Type 1 and Type 2 virtualization use the VMM to create VMs on a single computer. The requirements for this type of virtualization include the following:

▶ Adequate RAM for each virtual machine as well as the host operating system (if Type 2 virtualization is being used). For example, if you are setting up a Windows 11 computer whose workload needs 8GB of RAM for Windows but will run two VMs that require 2GB and 4GB of RAM, respectively, you will need to have at least 14GB of RAM if both VMs are running at the same time. For type 1, add up the RAM requirements for the VMs you are creating and add the amount of RAM needed for the VMM. For example, if the VMM will create 8 virtual machines needing 4GB of RAM each (total 32GB) and the VMM itself uses 16GB, your computer would need 48GB of RAM.

▶ A processor with hardware assisted virtualization installed and enabled. Hardware assisted virtualization (*HAV*, sometimes called hardware virtual machine or HVM) is a processor feature that helps a VMM run VMs faster and with fewer demands on the host operating system. All Intel and AMD x64 processors have featured HAV for well over a decade. To enable it on an Intel CPU, enable Intel VT-x or VT-d in BIOS/UEFI settings. To enable it on an AMD CPU, enable AMD-V, SVM (secure virtual machine) mode, or AMD-Vi (Figure 23.5). Although some free VMMs don't require HAV, your system performance and VM performance is incredibly slow without it.

```
Intel VT-D Tech                              [Enabled]
Secure Virtual Machine:              YES
```

**FIGURE 23.5** Intel (top) and AMD (bottom) settings in typical UEFI system firmware.

> **NOTE**
>
> VT-d is a development of VT-x that allows the direct connection of devices such as PCIe network adapters to the hardware. It is useful more for server virtualization but is present in many desktops as well. AMD's equivalent is AMD-Vi.

While not required, it's highly recommended that the processor have a large number of execution threads. Given a choice between a faster processor with fewer execution threads (for example, a four-core processor with eight threads) and a slower processor with more execution threads (for example, an eight-core processor with 16 threads), go with more execution threads.

> **NOTE**
>
> Each execution thread in a processor can run processes or applications separately from other execution threads. All mid-range (Ryzen 5, Core i5) and high-end (Ryzen 7, Threadripper, Core i7, Core i9, Xeon) processors today support two threads per processor core (Intel systems with performance cores have two threads per core; efficiency cores have one thread per core).

Adequate hard drive space for each VM's virtual hard disk. A virtual hard disk is a file that is used to hold the VM's operating system, apps, and data files. VMMs recommend a virtual hard disk size based on typical usage factors for a VM running a particular operating system.

For example, Oracle VirtualBox version 6.x recommends the following amounts of RAM and disk space for some popular operating systems running in a VM (Table 23.1).

**TABLE 23.1** Oracle VirtualBox RAM and Virtual HD Recommendations

| VM Operating System | 32-Bit or 64-Bit | Recommended RAM | Recommended Virtual Hard Disk |
|---|---|---|---|
| Windows 7 | 32-bit | 1024MB (1GB) | 32GB |
| Windows 7 | 64-bit | 2048MB (2GB) | 32GB |
| Ubuntu Linux | 64-bit | 1024MB | 10GB |
| macOS El Capitan | 64-bit | 2048MB | 30GB |

A virtual disk image is the hard drive file that stores the virtual machine. When you create a VM and are asked how large you want to make your virtual hard disk, you are specifying the size of the VDI file. You can specify a fixed size, or you can specify a flexible size (dynamically allocated) that will expand as the VM requires up to the maximum size you specify (Figure 23.6).

**FIGURE 23.6** Creating a dynamically allocated virtual disk image during VM creation.

Downloadable virtual disk images are available in several formats including VDI (used by Oracle), VHD (virtual hard disk, used by many virtualization apps), VHDX (used by Microsoft Hyper-V), and VMDK (used by VMware). You can convert one type of disk image to another using tools built into some VMMs.

> **NOTE**
>
> A particular speed of network is not a requirement for a VMM, but the fastest, preferably wired, network connection available is recommended.

The last requirement is an operating system that can be installed in a VM. For permanent VMs, make sure you have an OS whose license permits it to be installed in a VM (this applies primarily to Microsoft Windows and macOS editions). For VMs used for testing, Microsoft offers preconfigured virtual disk images you can download that will run for a limited period of time. Most Linux distros have no installation restrictions on either physical computers or VMs.

> **EXAM TIP**
>
> For the Core 1 1101 exam, make sure you understand the essential resources needed for virtualization: CPU hardware support included and enabled in the BIOS/UEFI, lots of RAM, and a multicore CPU.

## Microsoft Hyper-V Requirements and Configuration

Microsoft Windows 10 and 11 Enterprise, Pro, and Education editions include Hyper-V virtualization. To use Hyper-V virtualization, the computer must have the following hardware features:

- ▶ 64-bit processor with Second Level Address Translation (SLAT)
- ▶ CPU support for VM Monitor Mode Extension (known as VT-c on Intel CPUs)
- ▶ At least 4GB of RAM

To determine if your CPU supports SLAT and VM Monitor Mode Extension, open a command prompt, enter the command `systeminfo.exe`, and look for memory size and the Hyper-V Requirements section (Figure 23.7). The computer shown in Figure 23.7 can run Hyper-V.

To set up Hyper-V virtualization, you must also configure Windows. Search for Windows Features, and click the matching Control Panel feature. Click Hyper-V to enable all Hyper-V features (Figure 23.8). Click OK, and reboot as prompted. When you restart, you can set up Hyper-V to create and host virtual machines.

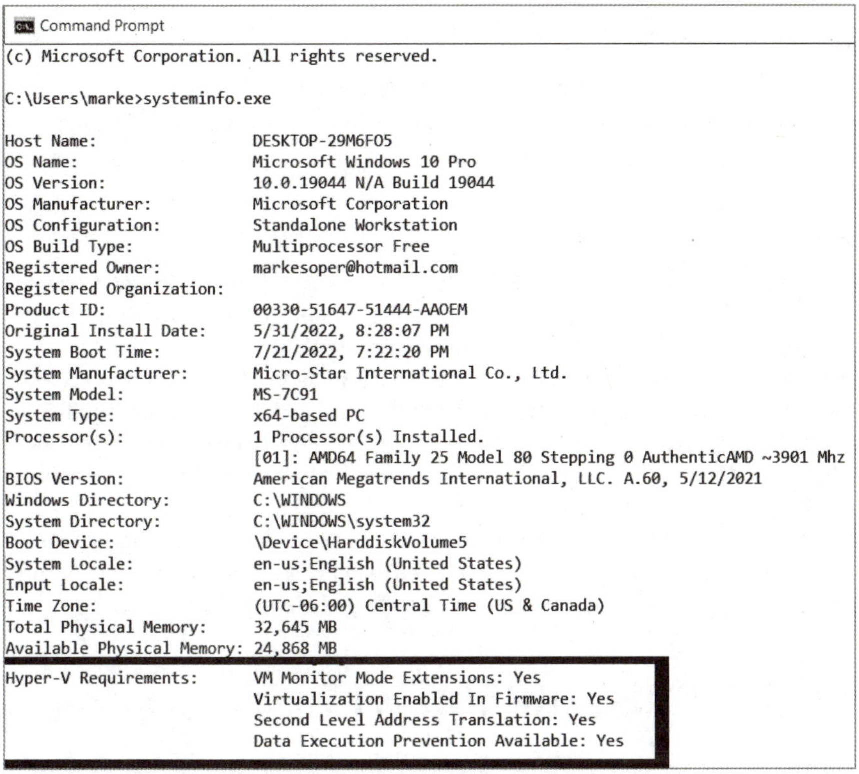
Command Prompt
(c) Microsoft Corporation. All rights reserved.
C:\Users\marke>systeminfo.exe
Host Name: DESKTOP-29M6F05
OS Name: Microsoft Windows 10 Pro
OS Version: 10.0.19044 N/A Build 19044
OS Manufacturer: Microsoft Corporation
OS Configuration: Standalone Workstation
OS Build Type: Multiprocessor Free
Registered Owner: markesoper@hotmail.com
Registered Organization:
Product ID: 00330-51647-51444-AAOEM
Original Install Date: 5/31/2022, 8:28:07 PM
System Boot Time: 7/21/2022, 7:22:20 PM
System Manufacturer: Micro-Star International Co., Ltd.
System Model: MS-7C91
System Type: x64-based PC
Processor(s): 1 Processor(s) Installed.
[01]: AMD64 Family 25 Model 80 Stepping 0 AuthenticAMD ~3901 Mhz
BIOS Version: American Megatrends International, LLC. A.60, 5/12/2021
Windows Directory: C:\WINDOWS
System Directory: C:\WINDOWS\system32
Boot Device: \Device\HarddiskVolume5
System Locale: en-us;English (United States)
Input Locale: en-us;English (United States)
Time Zone: (UTC-06:00) Central Time (US & Canada)
Total Physical Memory: 32,645 MB
Available Physical Memory: 24,868 MB
Hyper-V Requirements: VM Monitor Mode Extensions: Yes
Virtualization Enabled In Firmware: Yes
Second Level Address Translation: Yes
Data Execution Prevention Available: Yes

**FIGURE 23.7** This computer supports Hyper-V virtualization.

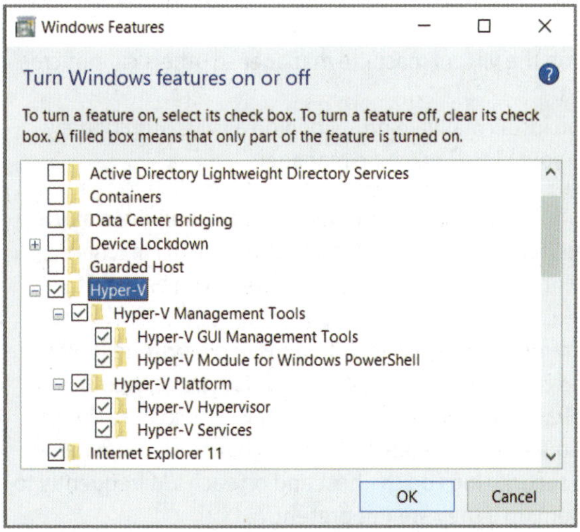
Windows Features
Turn Windows features on or off
To turn a feature on, select its check box. To turn a feature off, clear its check box. A filled box means that only part of the feature is turned on.
Active Directory Lightweight Directory Services
Containers
Data Center Bridging
Device Lockdown
Guarded Host
Hyper-V
Hyper-V Management Tools
Hyper-V GUI Management Tools
Hyper-V Module for Windows PowerShell
Hyper-V Platform
Hyper-V Hypervisor
Hyper-V Services
Internet Explorer 11
OK
Cancel

**FIGURE 23.8** Preparing to install Hyper-V features.

> **NOTE**
> To learn more about Hyper-V setup and use in Windows, see docs
> `.microsoft.com/en-us/virtualization/hyper-v-on-windows/`
> `quick-start/enable-hyper-v`.

### Desktop Virtualization

Desktop virtualization, also known as Virtual Desktop Infrastructure (VDI), is used to create a complete Windows desktop, including the operating system and apps, in a VM hosted on a server, and the server transmitting the VM to a device via a network.

So, instead of a user sitting down at a computer that is running a fast, multicore CPU with lots of RAM to use a VM, the user can be sitting at a low-powered PC (also known as a thin client), a tablet, a laptop, or even a smartphone to use a VM. The user interacts with the VM, and if the connection is fast enough, the experience is virtually identical to using a computer with a local operating system.

VDI on premise refers to a server on a LAN being used to provide VMs to clients on that LAN (Figure 23.9). VDI can also use cloud services, enabling VMs located hundreds or even thousands of miles away to be accessed by a wide variety of clients.

# SECURITY REQUIREMENTS

Virtual machines, like physical computers, are at risk from malware, attacks from external sources, and other threats. You need to protect the computer hosting your VMs. With a hosted (Type 2) VMM, protect the host operating system by using a strong password for login, installing anti-malware apps with real-time protection, setting up and maintaining a software firewall to block unwanted activities, and if multiple users are sharing a computer, make sure only administrators can run the virtual machine manager so others cannot create, alter, or destroy virtual machines.

To protect your VMs, make sure you install malware protection on all VMs. Additionally, use as many of these tips as apply to your virtual machine manager:

▶ Create a VM template, which has the OS, settings, and apps, and use it as a source for new VMs. This helps to minimize the use of the virtual machine console, which is a potential threat to a VM, as the console can be used to modify or delete a VM.

▶ When you set up a VM, remove unnecessary functions and hardware from the VM, such as screen savers, connections to optical and USB drives, web server functions, and so on. What is necessary to each VM may vary, so base this list on what the VM is configured to do. Protect VM virtual hard disks from being copied. Check logs and security logs on the host and on each VM frequently to check for threats; set them up if they are not present.

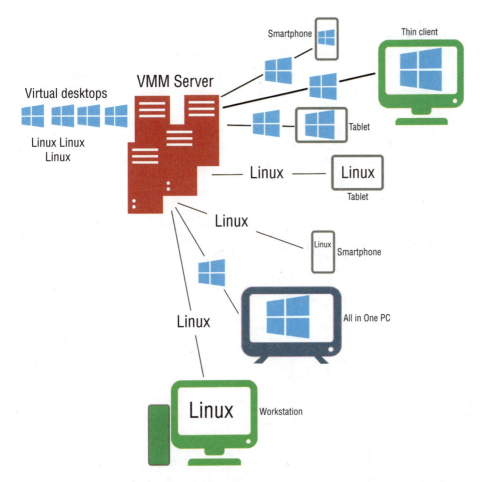

**FIGURE 23.9** Simplified diagram of a typical on-premises VDI environment.

## CERTMIKE EXAM ESSENTIALS

▶ Virtualization technology enables a single physical computer (desktop, laptop, or server) to act like two or more separate physical computers running different operating systems and different combinations of software.

▶ Virtualization has several purposes, including as a sandbox (protection of the host computer from malfunctioning apps), providing a safe environment for testing, application virtualization, and the ability to run legacy operating systems and apps for tech support or other purposes.

▶ Virtualization requires the host PC to have enough RAM and enough hard drive space to accommodate each VM that will be created.

## Practice Question 1

Your client is setting up an existing computer to be a virtual machine host for four 64-bit VMs, one running Windows 10, one running Windows 11, and two running Linux, all installed for testing purposes. Which of the following computers would be most suitable?

A.  Four-core, eight-thread 3GHz CPU with 16GB RAM, 4TB RAID 1 on Gigabit Ethernet

B.  Eight-core, eight-thread 4GHz CPU with 32GB RAM, 2TB SSD on Fast Ethernet

C.  Six-core, 12-thread 3.7 GHz CPU with 64GB RAM, 8TB RAID 1 on Wi-Fi 6

D.  Two-core, four-thread 2.5GHz CPU with 8GB RAM, 1TB on Wi-Fi 4.

## Practice Question 2

Your client is partway through setting up a VMM but is not sure if the CPU has hardware virtualization enabled. Which of the following BIOS/UEFI settings need to be enabled on an Intel CPU?

A.  VT-Q

B.  SVM

C.  Secure Boot

D.  VT-x

## Practice Question 1 Explanation

This question is designed to test your real-world understanding of VMM features. Let's evaluate these choices one at a time.

1. Option A (Four-core, eight-thread 3GHz CPU with 16GB RAM, 4TB RAID 1 on Gigabit Ethernet) offers enough space for testing and a fast network connection but is lacking in execution threads and adequate RAM for multiple 64-bit VMs.

2. Option B (Eight-core, eight-thread 4GHz CPU with 32GB RAM, 2TB SSD on Fast Ethernet) offers very fast storage and lots of RAM but lacks additional execution threads and is connected to an out-dated network.

3. Option C (Six-core, 12-thread 4.5GHz CPU with 64GB of RAM, 8TB RAID 1 on Wi-Fi 6) offers the largest number of processor threads, largest storage, largest amount of RAM, and very fast (although wireless) networking.

4. Option D (Two-core, four-thread 2.5GHz CPU with 1TB on Wi-Fi 4) is lacking processor threads, RAM, drive capacity, and network speed.

**Correct answer: C. Six-core, 12-thread 3.7GHz CPU with 64GB RAM, 8TB RAID 1 on Wi-Fi 6**

## Practice Question 2 Explanation

This question is designed to test your knowledge of computer configuration for virtualization.

Let's evaluate these answers one at a time.

1. Option A (VT-Q) is not an actual BIOS/UEFI setting. This is not the right answer.

2. Option B (SVM) is the configuration setting used for AMD processors, not Intel, so it is incorrect.

3. Option C (Secure Boot) is a requirement for installing Windows 11 on either an Intel or AMD processor, so it is incorrect.

4. Option D (VT-x) is the configuration setting needed for an Intel processor to enable hardware virtualization support.

**Correct answer: D. VT-x**

# PART V

# Domain 5.0: Hardware and Network Troubleshooting

Hardware and Network Troubleshooting is the fifth domain of CompTIA's A+ Core 1 exam. In this domain, you'll learn how technicians identify and resolve problems in support of end users. This domain has seven objectives.

5.1 **Given a scenario, apply the best practice methodology to resolve problems**

5.2 **Given a scenario, troubleshoot problems related to motherboards, RAM, CPU, and power**

5.3 **Given a scenario, troubleshoot and diagnose problems with storage drives and RAID arrays**

5.4 **Given a scenario, troubleshoot video, projector, and display issues**

5.5 **Given a scenario, troubleshoot common issues with mobile devices**

5.6 **Given a scenario, troubleshoot and resolve printer issues**

5.7 **Given a scenario, troubleshoot problems with wired and wireless networks**

Questions from this domain make up 29 percent of the questions on the A+ Core 1 exam, so you should expect to see approximately 26 questions on your test covering the material in this part.

# CHAPTER 24

# Troubleshooting Methodology

## Core 1 Objective 5.1: Given a scenario, apply the best practice methodology to resolve problems

**As** an IT professional, you'll often be called upon to troubleshoot issues that are causing problems for users or teams. Troubleshooting can be challenging because you're often trying to diagnose a problem that nobody else can figure out. But, personally, I find troubleshooting exhilarating! It's an opportunity to figure out a mystery and show off your IT skills. And when you solve the problem, you get to be the hero of the hour!

In this chapter, you'll learn everything you need to know about A+ Core 1 objective 5.1, including the following topics:

▶ **Always consider corporate policies, procedures, and impacts before implementing changes**

► **Identify the problem**
Gather information from the user, identify user changes, and, if applicable, perform backups before making changes
Inquire regarding environmental or infrastructure changes

► **Establish a theory of probable cause (question the obvious)**
If necessary, conduct external or internal research based on symptoms

► **Test the theory to determine the cause**
Once the theory is confirmed, determine next steps to resolve the problem
If the theory is not confirmed, re-establish a new theory or escalate

► **Establish a plan of action to resolve the problem and implement the solution**
Refer to the vendor's instructions for guidance

► **Verify full system functionality and, if applicable, implement preventive measures**

► **Document the findings, actions, and outcomes**

# TROUBLESHOOTING METHODOLOGY

Every troubleshooting situation is unique, but there are some basic steps that you can follow to conduct troubleshooting in an orderly manner that produces good results. CompTIA endorses the six-step troubleshooting process shown in Figure 24.1.

> **TIP**
>
> It is vital that you memorize the steps of the troubleshooting methodology shown in Figure 24.1. You will almost certainly find one or more questions on the exam asking you to evaluate a situation and identify the current step that a technician is following or the next step that they should take.

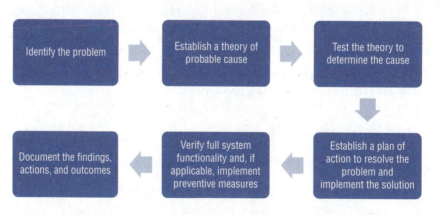

**FIGURE 24.1** CompTIA's six-step troubleshooting methodology.

Let's examine the process in more detail. We'll explain what occurs during each step and also walk through an example.

## Identify the Problem

The first thing that you need to do is identify the problem. Talk to the end user, figure out what issues they're experiencing, and identify the symptoms. For example, they might tell you that their network connection is slow or that they can't access a certain website. Gather as much information as you can and try to duplicate the problem. You'll want to replicate the user's experience so that you can help find the resolution. It's also a good idea during this phase to determine whether anything has recently changed on the user's system. When you question the user, be sure to ask them whether they've recently installed any new software, changed any components of their system, or made any other technology changes. At the same time, check with your colleagues to determine whether there were any environmental or infrastructure changes that might be contributing to the situation. Finally, before you move on, this is a good point to make backups of any data or configurations that might be affected by the troubleshooting process. That will give you the opportunity to roll back any changes that have unintended consequences.

Imagine that you're a desktop support technician and you are called to the desk of a user who is having trouble using a browser to access the Internet. When you first arrive, you should work to identify the problem. Here are some actions you might take:

▶ **Gather information** from the user and the system. Find out what the user is experiencing and examine the system's settings. You might learn that the user is seeing an error page no matter what website they try to visit.

▶ **Duplicate the problem** by trying to visit some websites yourself from the user's computer. You might also try visiting websites from other computers on the same network to identify whether the problem exists on only one system or whether it is network-wide.

▶ **Question the user** about any things they've tried to do to resolve the problem themselves. Have they tried restarting the computer or reseating the network cable?

▶ **Identify any symptoms** that might exist. Is this affecting only web traffic, or does the system appear to be completely disconnected from the network?

▶ **Determine whether anything has changed.** Ask the user when they last were able to use the Web and whether they or anyone else has installed any software or altered any settings since that last known good state.

The identification stage is crucial to the remainder of the troubleshooting process, as it ensures that you have all of the information you need to evaluate the situation.

## Establish a Theory

Once you've identified the problem, it's time to conduct some internal and external research based on the symptoms you're observing. If it's not a simple problem, you can go back to your own workspace and consult the references available to you. And yes, Googling things is absolutely fine! I often solve my own problems by searching on the Internet, so don't feel shy about doing that. Googling an error message often leads you directly to a page full of possible solutions. You should also visit the website for the vendor of the hardware or software involved in the problem. Vendors often have *knowledge bases (KBs)* that you can search for troubleshooting advice. Your own organization also likely has an internal KB that documents common issues found within the organization.

In the case of the user who can't access websites, you might consult the organization's knowledge base and discover that website connectivity issues are often the result of misconfigured proxy servers.

With this information in hand, establish a theory of the probable cause. That's a fancy way of saying that you should make an educated guess about what's wrong. You don't have to be correct the first time; you're just trying to identify what you think is the most likely cause of the problem. When you do this, you should question obvious assumptions and consider multiple problem-solving approaches to help you find the best idea. If you have other team members assisting you, it's OK to take a *divide-and-conquer* approach, letting different team members pursue different theories.

In the case of the user who can't access the Web, you might establish a theory of probable cause that the user's proxy settings are not correctly configured to use the organization's proxy servers.

## Test the Theory

Once you have a solid theory, you'll want to test that theory to see if it's correct, which helps you determine the root cause of the incident. If your theory holds up, then you can move forward with solving the problem. If your theory doesn't work out, just return to the previous step and start testing a new theory. If you are unable to establish a new theory, you may escalate the problem to a higher level of support.

To test your proxy server theory, you might examine the user's proxy settings and see if they match the organization's standard settings that you discovered in the knowledge base.

## Establish a Plan of Action to Resolve the Problem and Implement the Solution

After you determine the root cause of the incident, you can establish a plan of action to resolve the problem and identify any other effects that the problem may be having on this user or other users. This may include altering system or network settings, installing or removing software, reconfiguring devices, replacing hardware, or performing many other possible steps. Make sure that you refer to any instructions from vendors for guidance as you develop your plan.

If you discovered that the user's computer settings did not match the organization's standard proxy settings, you might then plan to reconfigure those settings to match the organization's standards. Before carrying out your plan, you should document the current settings so that you are able to undo any changes that you make if they are not successful.

If you're able to fix the problem yourself, you can implement the solution, or if you need help from other IT professionals, you can bring in other experts as needed. You might go through an iterative process of implementing several possible solutions. If that's the case, it's a good idea to completely implement and test one change and then undo that change if it didn't work before moving on to the next possibility. Making multiple changes at the same time increases the likelihood of new issues.

> **WARNING**
>
> When troubleshooting a problem, never forget that you are not working in isolation. You are part of a team that is part of a larger organization, and the steps you take may have unforeseen consequences on other users or departments. Always consider corporate policies, procedures, and impacts before implementing any changes.

After documenting the user's current proxy settings, you may then change the settings to match the organization's standard settings.

## Verify Functionality

Once you've implemented your solution, verify that the entire system is functioning normally and, if it makes sense, put preventive measures in place to prevent the problem from recurring for this user or affecting other users. You should test the new settings completely to ensure that you have not only fixed the problem but also that your solution did not cause new issues.

After changing the user's proxy settings, you should then attempt to visit a variety of internal and external websites to ensure that they were effective. If the user's system is not working properly, you will need to establish a new theory and repeat the trouble-shooting process.

## Document Your Work

Finally, the resolution of the problem isn't the last step in the process. You still have one more task to complete. Document your findings, lessons learned, actions, and outcomes. Documenting troubleshooting efforts isn't a very exciting part of our work, but it's important because it creates a record for other IT team members to follow if they experience similar issues. You're saving them the work of going through all the same troubleshooting steps that you just followed!

This may be as simple as updating the current incident details in your organization's incident tracking system. On the other hand, if you discovered new information during your troubleshooting that wasn't included in the knowledge base, this is a good time to document that information so that the next technician who encounters the problem may benefit from your discovery.

---

### CERTMIKE EXAM ESSENTIALS

▶ The CompTIA troubleshooting process consists of six steps.

1. Identify the problem.

2. Establish a theory of probable cause.

3. Test the theory to determine the cause.

4. Establish a plan of action to resolve the problem and implement the solution.

5. Verify full system functionality and, if applicable, implement preventive measures.

6. Document the findings, actions, and outcomes.

## Practice Question 1

You are working with a user who was experiencing an issue with displaying computer-aided design (CAD) graphics on her computer. You replaced her monitor and performed some tests that showed that the problem is resolved and the user has full system functionality. What should you do next?

A. Document your findings

B. Close the ticket

C. Conduct additional testing

D. Escalate to senior technicians

## Practice Question 2

You are helping a user troubleshoot a problem printing to a new all-in-one (AIO) device that was recently installed. The user is unable to print any documents to that printer but is able to print to other devices on the same network. You have researched the problem on the Internet and in your organization's knowledge base (KB), and that research is pointing you to several possible issues. You are working to identify which issue is the most likely culprit. What step are you taking in the troubleshooting process?

A. Verify full system functionality

B. Identify the problem

C. Implement the solution

D. Establish a theory

## Practice Question 1 Explanation

This is a straightforward question that is asking you to identify where you are in the troubleshooting process and determine the appropriate next step. If you consult the troubleshooting methodology in Figure 24.1, you'll discover that verifying full system functionality is the fifth step in the process.

1. Option A (Document your findings) is correct because that is the sixth step in the process. You should complete that documentation of findings/lessons learned, actions, and outcomes before closing out the case.

2. Option B (Close the ticket) is incorrect because you have not yet documented your findings and completed your work.

3. Option C (Conduct additional testing) is incorrect. There is no need for you to conduct any additional testing, as you have resolved the problem successfully.

4. Option D (Escalate to senior technicians) is incorrect. There is no need for you to escalate to a senior technician, as you have resolved the problem successfully.

**Correct Answer: A. Document your findings**

## Practice Question 2 Explanation

This question is also testing your familiarity with the CompTIA troubleshooting methodology shown in Figure 24.1. In this case, you must determine where you are in the troubleshooting process.

1. Option A (verify full system functionality) is incorrect. You do not yet know which issue you are solving, so it would be premature to verify full system functionality (step 5).

2. Option B (identify the problem) is incorrect. You have already identified the problem—the user is unable to print to the new all-in-one printer. That means that you have completed step 1, identifying the problem.

3. Option C (implement the solution) is incorrect. You do not yet know which issue you are solving, so it would be premature to implement a solution (step 4).

4. Option D (establish a theory) is correct because the question indicates that you have researched the problem and are trying to select the most likely issue. This activity is part of step 2 of the troubleshooting process, which is establishing a theory of probable cause.

**Correct Answer: D. Establish a theory**

# CHAPTER 25

# Troubleshooting Motherboards, RAM, CPU, and Power

## Core 1 Objective 5.2: Given a scenario, troubleshoot problems related to motherboards, RAM, CPU, and power.

**Motherboards,** RAM, CPU, and power problems can cripple a computer and also can mimic each other. In this chapter, you will learn what you need to know about Core 1 1101 objective 5.2, including the following:

▶ **Common symptoms**

## COMMON SYMPTOMS

One of the challenges in troubleshooting motherboards, RAM, CPU, and power is that a symptom can be caused by more than one problem. Keep the CompTIA A+ six-step troubleshooting methodology to resolve problems in mind as you study symptoms and solutions to help you choose the best one for a situation.

**EXAM TIP**

The six-step troubleshooting model is covered in detail in Chapter 24, "Troubleshooting Methodology," but here's a quick review to keep in mind for the Core 1 1101 exam: 1. Identify the problem. 2. Establish a theory of probable cause (question the obvious). 3. Test the theory to determine the cause. 4. Establish a plan of action to resolve the problem and implement the solution. 5. Verify full symptom functionality and, if applicable, implement preventive measures. 6. Document the findings, actions, and outcomes. **Always consider corporate policies, procedures, and impacts before implementing changes.**

# POWER-ON SELF-TEST BEEPS

The Power-on Self-Test (*POST*) is part of the BIOS/UEFI firmware that checks for serious (reduces system functionality) or fatal (prevents system from booting) errors during system startup.

Beep codes, in which the computer's onboard speaker beeps several times to indicate serious or fatal errors, are used by many desktop motherboards to indicate various types of system problems. Because of the wide variety of BIOS/UEFI firmware versions in use, your best resource for determining a particular computer's beep codes are the system or motherboard documentation. With many systems no longer having onboard speakers, the power LED may flash instead of, or in addition to, beep codes. See Table 25.1 for examples.

**TABLE 25.1   Example Beep Codes**

| Brand and Model | Beep Code or Power LED Code | Meaning |
|---|---|---|
| Dell Inspiron | 1 | BIOS/UEFI firmware failure |
| | 2 | No RAM memory detected |
| | 3 | Motherboard chipset component failure |
| | 4 | RAM failure |
| | 5 | RTC clock battery failure |
| | 6 | Video card/chip failure |
| | 7 | CPU failure |
| ASUS | 1 short beep | System boots normally |

| Brand and Model | Beep Code or Power LED Code | Meaning |
| --- | --- | --- |
| | 1 long, 2 short | Memory problems |
| | 1 long, 3 short | Video card problem, such as not enough power to card |
| | 1 long, 4 short | CPU fan error or CPU overheating |
| Gigabyte AMI BIOS | 1 short beep | Memory error |
| | 2 short beeps | Memory parity check error |
| | 3 short beeps | Memory error in first 64K |
| | 4 short beeps | RTC clock failure |
| | 5 short beeps | CPU error |
| | 6 short beeps | Keyboard error |
| | 7 short beeps | CPU error |
| | 8 short beeps | Graphics card error |
| | 9 short beeps | Memory error |
| | 10 short beeps | CMOS error (CMOS stores UEFI/BIOS firmware settings) |
| | 11 short beeps | CPU cache RAM error |

**NOTE**

Complimentary Metal-Oxide Semiconductor (*CMOS*) is a chip on the motherboard where UEFI/BIOS settings such as onboard drives, boot sequence, memory size and speeds, and other information is stored.

The graphics processing unit (*GPU*) is the technical name for a computer's graphics (video) chip. Most POST routines check for GPU issues and beep if the GPU is missing or defective.

Some systems use POST to indicate problems with the front-side bus (FSB), a term for the connection between the CPU and high-speed components such as RAM and the GPU. This type of system design is actually out-of-date, so this is used mainly on older systems.

Here's what to do if a beep or LED code indicates a system problem at power on:

▶ If a beep or LED code shows up at startup, look up the code and replace the item being referenced.

▶ Take ESD precautions (grounded work mat, wrist strap connected to the case), shut down the computer, and disconnect it from AC power.

▶ With memory errors, remove all but one module. Make sure it is plugged into the correct slot for one module.

▶ With graphics card errors, check power to the card. If the card is not properly connected to power, connect it to power. If the card is not properly seated in the PCIe slot, unscrew the card bracket(s), remove the card, and re-insert it.

▶ With CPU errors, make sure the CPU fan is properly plugged into the motherboard and that the fan spins. Check the CPU heat sink to make sure it is properly installed.

▶ With real-time clock (RTC) errors, check the RTC battery. Replace it if it is more than two to three years old or if it has signs of corrosion or leakage.

After making the appropriate changes, close up the system, remove your wrist strap, reconnect it to AC power, and restart the system.

> **EXAM TIP**
>
> For the 1101 Core 1 exam, don't worry about memorizing codes (there are too many!), but understand that beep codes indicate serious or fatal startup issues.

# PROPRIETARY CRASH SCREENS (BLUE SCREEN OF DEATH/PINWHEEL)

CompTIA uses the term *proprietary crash screen* to refer to a crash screen displayed by an operating system. When Windows cannot continue, PCs typically display a STOP error against a blue background (Figure 25.1). This is commonly called the Blue Screen of Death (*BSOD*). If the BSOD stays on the screen and has a QR code, you can use your smartphone's QR reader to connect to a website that explains the specific error or note the error message and look it up manually. Depending upon the system configuration, the system may restart after recording the BSOD data to a memory dump file, or you might be informed to restart the system yourself. Sometimes a BSOD is a one-time event (a glitch), but if it happens again, you should investigate it.

macOS displays a pinwheel, which resembles a spinning beach ball, in place of the normal macOS cursor, when it cannot continue. Figure 25.2 shows an enlarged version of the pinwheel.

To determine the cause of the pinwheel, search for *Console*. Open it, and select from Crash Reports, Spin Reports, and other types of reports and logs. Use this information to find the source of the problem.

Failed module

http://windows.com/stopcode

DRIVER_IRQL_NOT_LESS_OR_EQUAL

**FIGURE 25.1**  A typical Windows STOP error (Blue Screen of Death).

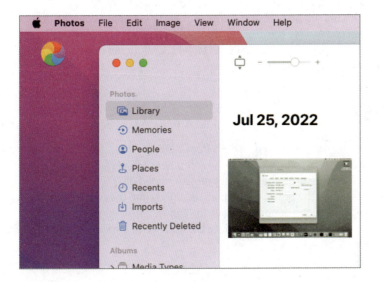

**FIGURE 25.2**  The macOS pinwheel.

These are some recommended solutions:

▶ Force Quit an app that is unresponsive. Click the Apple icon, click Force Quit, and select the app to close. Or, press the Command, Option, and Escape keys simultaneously to display the Force Quit menu.
▶ Run Disk Utility's First Aid application to fix disk errors.
▶ Remove unwanted apps and unneeded large data files from your system drive; copy data files to a USB or Thunderbolt drive and remove them from your system drive.
▶ Clean up the dynamic link editor cache (it helps apps use shared library files) by opening Terminal and entering this command

```
sudo update_dyld_shared_cache -force
```

Provide the administrator password as prompted.

## BLACK SCREEN

A black screen can have an obvious cause on a desktop computer: the display is turned off. However, there are many other causes.

On a laptop, the desktop might be using the external display instead of the built-in display. Use the appropriate function key or Fn+function key to switch back to the built-in display or mirror the displays.

Most monitors today have multiple connection options. Make sure the display cable is plugged into a working video port. For example, on a system with both integrated graphics and a video card, use the video card ports. Also, use the display's on-screen menu or on-screen display (OSD) to manually select the correct input if necessary.

On older laptop and desktop computers that use a fluorescent backlight, the inverter might have failed. Use a flashlight pointed at the display after the system has booted to see if the desktop is visible. If you can see the desktop, the inverter has failed. Because recent systems use LED or OLED displays that provide better screens, it might not make sense to service an older display or laptop that uses an inverter.

## NO POWER

No power prevents desktop computers and displays from starting. First, check the obvious. If the system or device was working previously, is the computer or display plugged into a working outlet or surge suppressor? Is the surge suppressor turned on?

If these check out, make sure the power cord is plugged tightly into the computer or display. If the cord is just barely long enough to make the connection, it might be damaged internally. Use a longer AC power cord or reduce the distance to the surge suppressor. Replace the power cable.

Check the circuit breaker. Depending upon how a building is wired, there might have been a localized problem that has caused power to be interrupted. Before resetting the breaker, try to determine what tripped it and work on a solution.

If the system was just built or serviced, check on these internal issues. One of the front-panel wire pairs that must be plugged into the motherboard is for the chassis power switch (Figure 25.3). If it is incorrectly plugged in or not plugged in at all, the system cannot start.

**FIGURE 25.3** A properly installed chassis power switch.

If the chassis power switch is properly wired, check the power leads from the power supply to the motherboard. Make sure the 20/24 pin main ATX and the 4-pin ATX12V or 8-pin EPS connectors are firmly plugged into the motherboard and locked into place.

The last thing to try is a power supply tester. You plug the power supply's 20/24-pin main ATX cable into the tester to make sure the power supply works. If it's dead, replace it with a unit that has a higher wattage rating and more 12V DC power.

# SLUGGISH PERFORMANCE

Sluggish system performance can be caused by a variety of issues. First, start by checking for malware. A malware scan can be run while other apps are running. If malware is detected, quarantine or delete it.

If no malware is detected or if removing it doesn't improve the problem, check CPU and system cooling. Many systems will reduce performance if the CPU or RAM is overheating.

Many systems lack sufficient cooling fans. If you use 3.5-inch or 2.5-inch HDD or SSD drives, consider adding a drive bay fan (Figure 25.4). These are powered by the motherboard using the SYS_FAN or similar connectors, which can also monitor their speed.

If the system was running properly with few apps open but becomes sluggish with more apps open, consider adding RAM. When a system runs short of physical RAM, it starts swapping data to and from a disk, which acts as virtual RAM. Especially if you are using a mechanical hard disk drive (HDD), this really slows down the system.

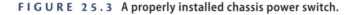

**F I G U R E   2 5 . 4**   Installing a drive bay fan in a typical desktop computer.

# OVERHEATING

An overheated system can cause system slowdowns or even shutdowns. First, see if adequate airflow is coming through the case. A system doesn't need to be as dirty as the one shown in Figure 25.5 to have overheat-related slowdowns and crashes. Keep exterior air intakes and outputs clean. If necessary, remove the front panel of the case to clean it.

In extreme cases, an overheated CPU will simply shut down the computer. However, it will probably run more slowly in the meantime. Use the system monitor or PC health feature in the BIOS/UEFI settings (when available) to check system temperature.

To see information reported by BIOS/UEFI firmware without restarting the computer, install a system monitoring app such as HWMonitor from CPUID (Figure 25.6).

If you are overclocking your system (running CPU, RAM, and motherboard timings at faster than normal speeds), this can cause a system to overheat if you are using stock cooling. Consider switching to a liquid CPU cooler (Figure 25.7) or RAM that has built-in heatsinks (Figure 25.8) to keep these parts cooler.

**FIGURE 25.5** An extremely dirty system with virtually no airflow.

An overheated GPU can cause corruption on the display screen. If the GPU fan(s) fail, the card can be damaged. Check for fan performance and GPU temperature using the monitor methods discussed earlier. Reducing or stopping overclocking can help an overheated GPU go back to normal temperatures.

| CPUID HWMonitor | | | | |
|---|---|---|---|---|

File  View  Tools  Help

| Sensor | Value | Min | Max | |
|---|---|---|---|---|
| DESKTOP-29M6FO5 | | | | |
| Micro-Star International Co. Lt... | | | | |
| Voltages | | | | |
| +12V | 12.144 V | 12.144 V | 12.144 V | |
| +5V | 5.050 V | 5.050 V | 5.050 V | |
| CPU NB/Soc | 0.798 V | 0.796 V | 0.798 V | |
| CPU VCORE | 1.350 V | 1.328 V | 1.362 V | |
| +3.3V | 3.324 V | 3.324 V | 3.328 V | |
| DRAM | 1.188 V | 1.188 V | 1.188 V | |
| CPU VDDP | 0.913 V | 0.913 V | 0.913 V | |
| Temperatures | | | | |
| CPU | 61.0 °C | 60.0 °C | 61.0 °C | |
| SYS | 43.0 °C | 43.0 °C | 43.0 °C | |
| MOS | 38.0 °C | 38.0 °C | 38.0 °C | |
| Chipset | 45.0 °C | 45.0 °C | 45.0 °C | |
| Socket | 40.0 °C | 38.0 °C | 40.0 °C | |
| PCIE_1 | 40.0 °C | 39.0 °C | 40.0 °C | |
| Fans | | | | |
| CPU | 2218 RPM | 2197 RPM | 2264 RPM | |
| SYS1 | 1048 RPM | 1032 RPM | 10176 RPM | |
| SYS4 | 1013 RPM | 1004 RPM | 1016 RPM | |
| Utilization | | | | |
| System Memory | 53.0 % | 51.0 % | 53.0 % | |
| AMD Ryzen 5 5600G | | | | |
| Voltages | | | | |
| CPU VDD | 1.381 V | 1.306 V | 1.381 V | |
| SoC VDD | 0.794 V | 0.794 V | 0.794 V | |
| VID (Max) | 1.356 V | 1.331 V | 1.387 V | |
| Temperatures | | | | |
| Package | 63.6 °C | 60.6 °C | 63.6 °C | |
| Cores (Max) | 61.2 °C | 54.3 °C | 61.2 °C | |
| L3 Cache | 51.6 °C | 49.1 °C | 51.6 °C | |
| GFX | 47.3 °C | 45.3 °C | 47.3 °C | |
| Powers | | | | |
| Package | 32.41 W | 26.71 W | 41.31 W | |
| Cores | 23.32 W | 5.55 W | 32.28 W | |
| L3 Cache | 1.30 W | 1.23 W | 1.44 W | |
| Currents | | | | |
| CPU VDD | 21.82 A | 18.71 A | 39.49 A | |

Ready                                                        NUM

**FIGURE 25.6** HWMonitor displays temperature, voltages, and fan speed for the CPU and other components.

# BURNING SMELL

A burning smell coming from your power supply indicates "It's dead, Jim!" There's no repairing it—get a new one with a higher wattage rating and especially more 12V DC power than the current one. Check the form factor (some replacement power supplies are larger than ATX standard dimensions), and if you're replacing a Dell power supply, find out if the computer uses a standard ATX power supply or a proprietary Dell version. Don't mix them up!

**FIGURE 25.7** A typical liquid cooling kit for Intel or AMD processors.

**FIGURE 25.8** A standard DDR4 DIMM (top) compared to a high-performance model with built-in heatsinks (bottom). (Source: top, Micron Technology, Inc.; bottom, Corsair)

Don't assume that replacing the power supply solves your problems. A blown power supply can also damage the motherboard, CPU, and RAM.

Bad capacitors on the motherboard or problems with other internal components can also cause burning smells (and even occasionally smoke). If you're not sure which component has the burning smell, take apart the system and move each component to another room. You should then be able to tell which one is up for replacement.

## CAPACITOR SWELLING

A capacitor stores an electric charge. They are quite common on motherboards and in other computer hardware. Older computers often used liquid-filled capacitors that would swell and leak (Figure 25.9).

**FIGURE 25.9** **Leaking, swollen capacitors compared to intact capacitors.**

Leaking or swollen capacitors can damage motherboards and other components and cause system lockups and crashes. Technicians faced with this problem can carefully cut the wire leads connecting a leaky capacitor to the motherboard and solder a solid capacitor with the same rating in its place. Most motherboard vendors now use solid capacitors to avoid this problem.

## INTERMITTENT SHUTDOWN

An intermittent system shutdown can be caused by an overheated CPU, by corrupt RAM, or by a power supply trying to provide more power than it was designed to do. Waiting for a few minutes for the computer to shut down and restarting it provides temporary relief until the problem occurs again. While the system is resting, check to make sure the power supply fan and case fans are turning and that air intake and exhaust openings are clean.

If you suspect the CPU is overheated, check the CPU temperature, check its fan for proper operation, and replace the fan with a higher-rated one or even liquid cooling if your system can use it.

To find corrupt RAM, run the Microsoft Windows Memory Diagnostic or a third-party utility such as MemTest86. If bad RAM is discovered, remove all but one DIMM or SO-DIMM and run the test again. Repeat until you find the defective memory module and replace it.

Use a power supply wattage calculator to determine the power supply wattage you need. If your power supply is too small, marginal, or several years old (power supplies lose efficiency over time), replace it with a power supply from a reliable manufacturer that meets or exceeds the recommended wattage.

# APPLICATION CRASHES

Application crashes can have many causes. Here are some issues to look for and suggested solutions.

If the application crashes after an upgrade to the application, the upgrade isn't compatible with your operating system or graphics drivers. If possible, roll back the application to the previous working version and check with the application vendor for a solution. The vendor might issue a replacement upgrade or advise you to upgrade your graphics driver.

If the application crashes after an upgrade to your operating system, the application isn't compatible with the operating system. See if an upgrade to the application is available. If not, use the Program Compatibility Troubleshooter in Windows or the Compatibility tab in an app's properties sheet (Figure 25.10) to see if the program will run with compatibility changes.

If the application crashes and no upgrades to the application or the operating system have happened, find out if the crash occurs only under certain circumstances, such as another app running at the same time or at a particular time of day. This can help determine possible causes. If there's no pattern to the application crashes, run an application repair process, usually available from the Apps menu in Settings. Click an app and click Modify or Repair to repair an app.

# GRINDING NOISE

A grinding noise coming from an HDD is a clear sign that the drive needs replacement. However, grinding noises coming from other sources such as the CPU fan or case fans indicate the fan bearings have failed. Replace the fan immediately! When you're shopping for a new case fan, look for fans using fluid or ball bearings. Low-cost sleeve bearings fail when the lubricant has dried up.

If the power supply fan starts grinding, replace the power supply. Resist the temptation to try swapping out just the fan. Components inside the power supply store potentially lethal levels of voltage for some time even when the power supply is turned off and disconnected from AC power.

Noise = failure = replacement!

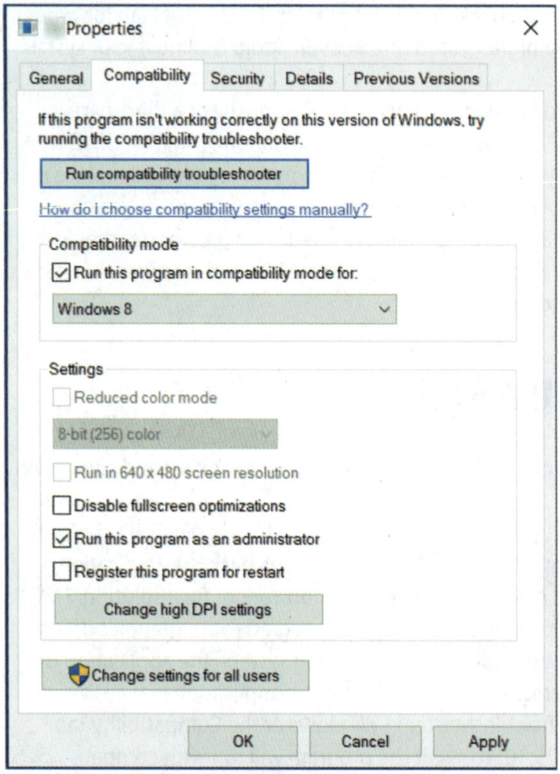

**FIGURE 25.10** The Compatibility tab for an app in Windows can be used to help a balky app to run correctly.

# INACCURATE SYSTEM DATE/TIME

Windows systems seldom have significant date and time problems. The real-time clock (RTC) battery on the motherboard along with the time synchronization feature in Windows help keep the on-screen clock on time.

To determine if the battery is failing, reset the date and time and note if the system starts losing time or if the system forgets its BIOS/UEFI settings. When the battery (typically a CR2032 or equivalent) fails, replace it and then reset the time in Settings and system settings with BIOS/UEFI settings. These batteries are also used in laptops (Figure 25.11).

**FIGURE 25.11** Replace the RTC battery on a desktop or laptop to solve a problem with inaccurate system date/time or lost system firmware settings.

**EXAM TIP**

The 1101 Core 1 exam will likely test your troubleshooting common symptoms knowledge gleaned from this chapter. Be sure you are familiar with all the topics covered related to motherboards, RAM, CPU, and power!

## CERTMIKE EXAM ESSENTIALS

▶ The Power-On-Self Test (POST) is a BIOS/UEFI firmware function performed when a system is powered on. It reports errors by means of beep codes, power LED flashes, or motherboard diagnostic lights.

▶ Windows Blue Screen of Death (BSOD) and macOS spinning pinwheel are proprietary crash screens caused by operating system, app, or hardware issues.

▶ Overheating can lead to sluggish system performance, complete system shutdown, operating system or app crashes, display corruption, and other problems. Cleaning air intakes, adding fans, checking for correct fan operation, and discontinuing overclocking will help prevent overheating.

▶ Problems such as inaccurate system date/time, grinding noise, and capacitor swelling are typically caused by defective hardware.

## Practice Question 1

Your client is experiencing frequent system crashes that happen with a mix of applications and tasks. An examination of the computer reveals that there are four possible causes:

A. Memory issues
B. Overdue application and operating system updates
C. Clogged air intakes
D. Power supply overloaded
E. The client is on a deadline (of course!). Which should you address FIRST?

## Practice Question 2

You are visiting a client when you notice a desktop computer in a nearby cubicle is making a grinding noise. You mention this problem to your client, and she asks you to take a look. After a quick look at the computer and reviewing the documentation, you realize that the grinding noise is coming from the bottom rear of the computer and that the computer uses an SSD for storage. Which of the following is the most likely source of the noise?

A. Case fan
B. Power supply fan
C. HDD
D. CPU fan

## Practice Question 1 Explanation

This question is designed to test your real-world understanding of system troubleshooting and priorities. Let's evaluate these choices one at a time.

1. Option A (memory issues) will take some time to resolve. Memory must be tested and possibly swapped out and replaced to isolate the problem. It's a possible cause, but not necessarily the first item to address.

2. Option B (overdue application and operating system updates) is troublesome from a security stand-point but is more likely if there was a pattern. This will also take some time to resolve and again might not be the actual cause of the problem.

3. Option C (clogged air intakes) can cause frequent system crashes because of overheating affecting memory contents, CPU performance, and GPU performance. Even if the clog is significant enough to require removing the front of the computer, this is the BEST answer because it must be done and won't take a lot of time.

4. Option D (power supply overloaded) is a possible solution, but it will require calculating the power load, comparing it to available power supplies, and ordering one if the power supply is inadequate. A power supply can't properly operate without adequate airflow, so this should not be the first item to address.

**Correct answer: C. Clogged air intakes**

## Practice Question 2 Explanation

This question is designed to test your ability to apply your knowledge of component locations and failures to narrow down possible noise sources.

Let's evaluate these answers one at a time.

1. Option A (case fan) is not likely on current systems. Older systems had a top-mounted power supply with a case fan mounted in the middle or the bottom of the rear of the case, but systems built in the last decade usually have bottom-mounted power supplies. This is not the best choice.

2. Option B (power supply fan) is the most likely source of the noise. On most systems, the power supply is located at the bottom rear of the case.

3. Option C (HDD) can be ruled out because this system uses an SSD drive for storage. SSD drives use high-speed nonvolatile memory rather than magnetic media and read-write heads, so there are no components capable of making a grinding noise.

4. Option D (CPU fan) is not possible because the CPU is located near the middle or top third of the mother-erboard, well away from the source of the noise.

**Correct answer: B. Power supply fan**

# CHAPTER 26

# Troubleshooting Storage

## Core 1 Objective 5.3: Given a scenario, troubleshoot and diagnose problems with storage drives and RAID arrays.

**Storage** drives and RAID arrays are among the most critical subsystems to troubleshoot and diagnose, because these locations contain the operating system and critical data. In this chapter, you will learn what you need to know to master Core, Objective 5.3, including the following:

▶ **Common symptoms and solutions**

## COMMON SYMPTOMS AND SOLUTIONS

The following sections help you discover the solutions to common symptoms that can affect mechanical drives and SSDs.

### Light-Emitting Diode Status Indicators

Desktop computers use *light-emitting diode (LED)* lamps to indicate drive activity and power. These small lights are located on the front or top of desktop computers.

Typical users don't pay much attention to these status indicators. The LED drive activity light usually flickers (indicating disk activity) during normal operation. However, if it stays on steadily, this may be an early indication of storage-related issues or misconfiguration.

### Drive Status LED Stays On Steadily as Soon as Computer Starts

If the drive status LED stays on steadily as soon as the computer starts, start by taking ESD precautions such as a wrist strap connected to the chassis. Next, shut down the system. Then, unplug it and open it. Now, check the connection of the drive activity LED on the motherboard.

If the drive status LED is connected to the power LED lead, the drive status LED will stay on all the time. Figure 26.1 shows how close the drive status and power LEDs are on a typical motherboard. They're easy to mix up.

**FIGURE 26.1** **A typical motherboard's drive activity (HDD) LED and power LED connectors.**

Plug the drive activity LED into the correct pins, making sure you match up positive (+) and negative (-) leads, and if other pins are misconnected or disconnected, plug them into the correct pins. Finally, close the system, restore power, and restart it. The drive activity LED light should blink during disk activity. Figure 26.2 illustrates a different system's front-panel wires after proper installation.

**FIGURE 26.2** **Correctly installed front-panel LED and other cables.**

If the drive activity LED works normally and then stays on, the computer might have locked up. Try opening the Start menu or Task Manager. If there is no response, the computer has locked up. Run drive and memory tests after restarting the computer to see if you can discover the underlying problems.

### Drive Status LED Blinking Frequently Under Heavy Loads

It's normal for the drive status LED to blink as the system is running, but if you see the light blinking much more frequently than usual and your system is running slowly, this could indicate that malware is slowing down your system by causing excessive disk access.

To get a good idea of drive performance, you can use the Drive Performance tab in Windows Task Manager. Start by right-clicking the Start menu and clicking Task Manager. Next, click the Performance tab and click C:. If the active time approaches 100 percent (Figure 26.3), no matter which apps are open, close Task Manager and check for malware.

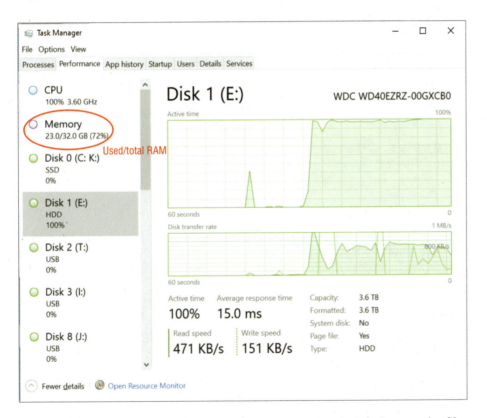

**FIGURE 26.3** **A data drive reaching 100 percent active time during complex file editing is normal, but a system drive staying near 100 percent even with little activity can spell trouble. (Source: Microsoft Corporation)**

If you suspect malware is slowing down your system, here's how to check for it. If you have antivirus or anti-malware installed, run a full system scan. If infected files are found, quarantine them and report them via the app's reporting features. Next, recheck drive performance. If active time is unchanged, use a different tool such as Malware Bytes to perform a second check.

Heavy disk activity can also be caused by a lack of system RAM. Ideally, a Windows system should have about 50 percent of its RAM available with a typical mix of apps available. Here's how to check. First, run Windows Task Manager, click Performance, and check the Used RAM amount highlighted in Figure 26.3. If Used RAM is consistently well over 50 percent, consider adding more RAM.

If your computer is using a mechanical drive (HDD) as a system drive, open File Explorer's This PC view and check the amount of free disk space for C: drive. If it is less than 15 percent free (Figure 26.4), the system will need to perform more disk access to create and use temporary files and will not be able to defragment files to make larger contiguous blocks of space. Use Windows Tools such as Disk Cleanup to remove unneeded system files. Remember, this step is not necessary for SSDs.

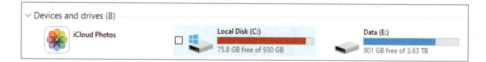

**FIGURE 26.4** **This system drive needs to free up about 75GB more space.** (Source: Microsoft Corporation)

## Grinding Noises

Grinding noises inside your system indicate serious mechanical problems. If the grinding noises are coming from a mechanical hard disk drive (HDD), the drive needs to be replaced immediately. This type of noise usually indicates that the read-write heads are coming into contact with the media.

In this situation, it may not be possible to retrieve data from the drive without sending it to a data recovery specialist that can replace the read/write heads. A data recovery specialist might not be able to recover the data either, depending upon the extent of damage.

Grinding noises may also be coming from the system fan. To determine if grinding noises come from a drive or a fan, shut down the system, unplug it from AC power, open the system, and disconnect the power leads from one drive. After reconnecting power and restarting the system, if the grinding noise is gone, then the drive is at fault, and you should replace it. Repeat this process for each drive if the computer has multiple internal drives. If the grinding noise persists after checking all drives, check fans that are part of the case and/or CPUs and replace any that have failed.

## Clicking Sound

Grinding noises are loud and obnoxious. However, a much quieter noise, a *clicking sound* coming from a mechanical drive, can also indicate a looming data disaster. The clicking sound is caused by repeated attempts to read a data sector. After a failed read, the head resets and attempts to read the data sector again. It might eventually succeed, or you might see a data error such as "Sector Not Found - Abort, Retry, or Fail?" on the screen.

Before tossing the drive, follow this procedure to see if your data can be salvaged. Open File Manager, click This PC, and right-click the drive where the clicking sound appears to originate. Click Properties, Tools, and Check (for Errors). Review any errors found and then try the operation again. If you have more than one mechanical drive, repeat the process with each one.

If the drive is still creating clicking sounds and slow disk access, create a full backup of the drive, determine the drive vendor, and run the vendor's own disk diagnostics using the most thorough test. This test could take several hours if the drive is working.

If the drive fails diagnostics, replace it. If it's in warranty, contact the vendor for an exchange.

## Bootable Device Not Found

When the computer can't find the boot drive, don't assume the drive is dead. The system might have "lost" the boot drive setting. Here's how to find out.

To begin with, restart the system and go into the BIOS/UEFI firmware setup dialog. Next, go to the Boot Order dialog. Make sure the boot drive is listed first or after an optical drive (Figure 26.5, Figure 26.6). If the boot drive is not listed first or second, change the boot order.

If the boot drive isn't listed at all, make sure all of the SATA drive ports are enabled. If some are disabled, enable them and see if your drive is available again. Save any changes you make and restart the system.

If the boot drive is still not listed, shut down the system, disconnect power, take ESD precautions, and open it up. Check power and data cable connections to the drive and data connections to the motherboard. Reconnect power and restart the system, returning to the BIOS/UEFI firmware setup. If the drive is still not listed, try connecting it to a different SATA port. If it still doesn't work, it's probably dead.

### EXAM TIP

On Windows 10 and 11 systems that use the default Secure Boot setting, the boot drive setting points to Windows Boot Manager (Figure 26.5) instead of a physical drive. If this setting is what you see but the system won't boot, you need to repair the boot settings. See "Repairing Windows Boot Settings" for details. Systems that don't use Secure Boot will list a physical drive instead (Figure 26.6).

**FIGURE 26.5** Windows Boot Manager is the default boot drive on a Windows system using Secure Boot. (Source: Microsoft Corporation)

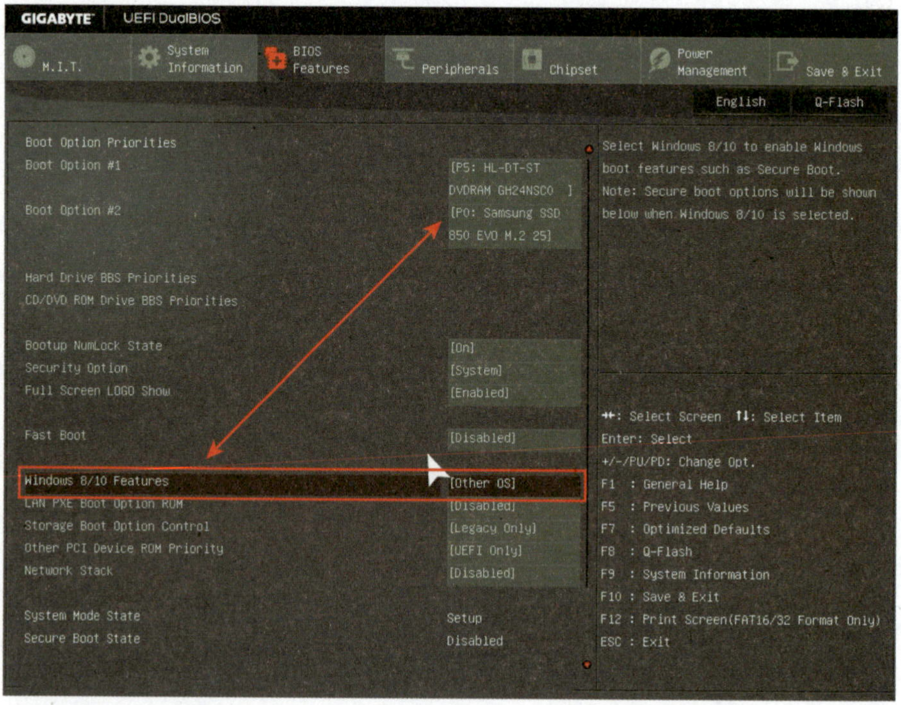

**FIGURE 26.6** A physical drive is the default boot drive on systems running Linux or Windows with Secure Boot disabled. (Source: GIGA-BYTE TECHNOLOGY CO., LTD.)

**TIP**

If a USB drive is listed first in the boot order and is connected, some systems won't boot if the drive isn't bootable. Disconnect a nonbootable USB drive and restart the system.

## Repairing Windows Boot Settings

If Windows 10/11's boot settings are causing boot errors, you may see messages such as "Operating System Missing," "Boot File or MBR Corrupted," or "Bootmgr Missing or Corrupted." To repair errors like this, follow these steps:

1. First, start the system from a Windows DVD or USB drive. When prompted to start the installation process, click Next.
2. Click Repair Your Computer. The Choose An Option menu appears.
3. Next, click Advanced Options from the Choose An Option menu. Click Command Prompt. When the command prompt appears, enter each of these commands, one at a time:

   ```
   Bootrec /fixmbr
   Bootrec /fixboot
   Bootrec /scanOS
   Bootrec /Rebuildbcd
   ```

4. To finish up, remove the bootable DVD or USB drive and restart.

## Data Loss/Corruption

Data loss and corruption is a serious issue that may indicate serious issues with your drive or other components in your computer. To help prevent problems, always shut down your operating system properly, not with the power switch on the PC!

If the system crashes, check your system and data drives for errors after you restart. In Windows, open each disk's properties sheet, click the Tools tab, and click Error Checking.

In macOS, open Finder, and select Disk Utility from the Applications/Utilities menu. Click the drive to repair, and then click First Aid.

In Linux, use FSCK (File System Check) on unmounted disks; to check the system disk, create a Live CD or USB Linux boot disk, use it to start your system, and run FSCK from there. Use vendor-supplied disk testing utilities for additional testing (if available).

If problems persist, think beyond the drive itself. Check data and power cables for damage or poor connections. If the system restarts frequently (which can cause data loss and corruption), test the power supply and RAM for errors and replace defective components. If the power supply and RAM check OK, but data errors persist, replace the drive.

> **EXAM TIP**
>
> Be familiar with troubleshooting common storage drive symptoms including the following:
>
> ▶ LED status indicators
>
> ▶ Grinding noises
>
> ▶ Clicking sounds
>
> ▶ Bootable device not found
>
> ▶ Data loss/corruption

## RAID Failure

RAID, covered in Chapter 16, uses two or more drives as a single logical drive to boost performance or reliability. RAID level 0 stripes data across two drives, while RAID level 1 mirrors the contents of one drive to another. RAID 5 uses three or more drives with parity information stored across all drives to enable a lost drive's contents to be recreated. RAID 10 combines striping and mirroring to provide high performance and protection against single-drive failure.

A *RAID failure* can be catastrophic or merely frustrating, depending upon the RAID type in use (see Table 26.1).

**T A B L E  26.1**  **RAID Failure**

| RAID Level | Number of Failed Drives | Result |
|:---:|:---:|---|
| 0 | 1 | Loss of all data. |
| 1 | 1 | The RAID array must be rebuilt from the remaining drive after a bad drive was replaced. |
| 5 | 1 | The RAID array must be rebuilt from remaining drives after a bad drive was replaced. |
| 10 | 1 | The RAID array must be rebuilt from the remaining drives after a bad drive was replaced. |

RAID failure isn't just caused by bad drives, however. It can also be caused by a RAID host adapter failure. If a RAID failure occurs, here's how to make sure you find the best solution.

First, record (using a digital camera or smartphone) all RAID error messages displayed by the operating system or the RAID host adapter. Next, shut down the system immediately.

Consult with the RAID vendor or a RAID data recovery expert to determine the cause of the RAID failure and whether the array should be rebuilt or if the data should be copied from the surviving members to a completely new drive not in the array. If a failed RAID host adapter is the cause, follow expert advice on acquiring a replacement, as different RAID card or motherboard chipset vendors' implementations of RAID are not interchangeable.

To prevent RAID failure, make sure you are using a UPS with a high-quality surge suppressor. Power spikes are a leading cause of RAID failure.

> **TIP**
>
> To learn more about RAID 0, 1, 5, and 10, see www.prepressure.com/
> library/technology/raid.

## Self-Monitoring, Analysis, and Reporting Technology Failure

It would be great if a drive would inform the user it was about to fail. That's what self-monitoring, analysis, and reporting technology (*S.M.A.R.T.*, or SMART) technology does. Built into SATA hard drives and SSDs as well as M.2 SSDs, SMART monitors a wide range of drive conditions to warn you of failure. SMART can be disabled in the system BIOS/UEFI firmware, so make sure it is enabled so you can get drive warnings.

A typical SMART error is displayed at boot time with text such as the following:

- ▶ Pri Master Hard Disk: S.M.A.R.T. Status Bad, Backup and Replace
- ▶ SMART Hard Disk Error
- ▶ The SMART hard disk check has detected an imminent failure
- ▶ Hard Disk 1 (301)

The problem with waiting for error messages like these is that they typically appear when a drive is in such bad condition that it fails before any backups can be made.

To get an early warning of SMART failures, use the following methods. You can run drive vendor-supplied disk diagnostics and view the SMART status (Figure 26.7). This method provides the most detail. Use tools built into the operating system to view SMART status; in Windows, open a command prompt in Administrator mode and enter the following command:

```
wmic diskdrive get model,status
```

This command is helpful if you have multiple drives, as it lists each SMART-enabled drive connected to your system and its status. If the Status column displays OK, the drive is working properly. Other status message such as bad, unknown, or caution indicate that SMART has detected drive problems.

In Linux, use the smartctl app, part of the smartmontools package, to run SMART tests and display results. See the MAN page for smartctl in your Linux distro for details. In macOS, smartctl can be used as well as commercial tools such as DriveDX to display SMART data.

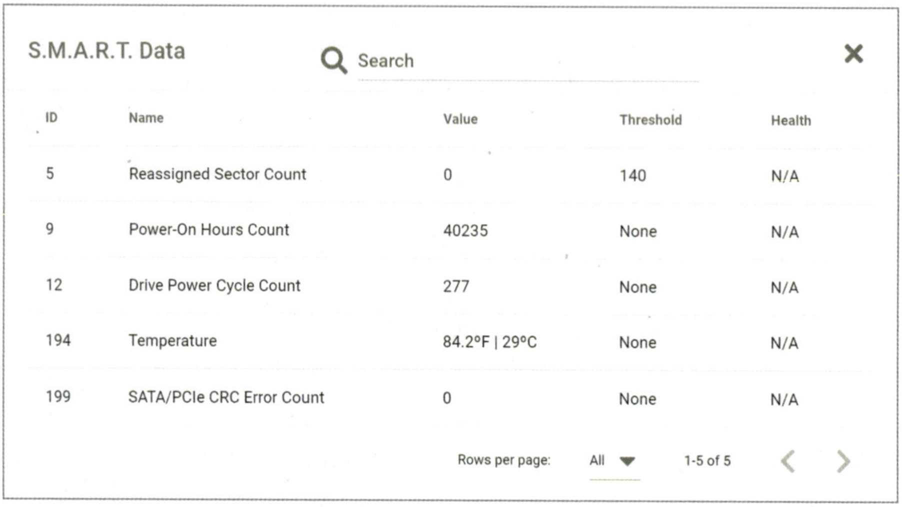

| S.M.A.R.T. Data | Q Search | | | ✕ |
|---|---|---|---|---|
| ID | Name | Value | Threshold | Health |
| 5 | Reassigned Sector Count | 0 | 140 | N/A |
| 9 | Power-On Hours Count | 40235 | None | N/A |
| 12 | Drive Power Cycle Count | 277 | None | N/A |
| 194 | Temperature | 84.2°F \| 29°C | None | N/A |
| 199 | SATA/PCIe CRC Error Count | 0 | None | N/A |

Rows per page:   All ▼   1-5 of 5   ‹   ›

**FIGURE 26.7** SMART data from a Western Digital SATA drive indicates no issues. (Source: Microsoft Corporation)

## Extended Read/Write Times

*Extended read/write times* are another sign of disk problems. If a disk takes much longer to read or write, it's time to use disk diagnostics and repair tools. First, use disk repair tools built into the operating system to repair disk errors. If the drive still has slow read/write times, use vendor-supplied disk diagnostics to clean up disk problems. Some of these can swap bad sectors for good sectors, so the drive might work better after using these apps.

Check for malware and remove it. Many types of malware can slow down a drive. If the problem began after installing new software, check the Startup folder in Windows for apps that might slow down the system. On a new system, remove unwanted third-party security and other apps.

## Input/Output Operations Per Second (IOPS)

*I/O* refers to input/output. The Input/Output Operations Per Second (*IOPS*) of your system and data drives measures how quickly these devices receive and send data. By measuring IOPS under normal operation, you can compare the results to results measured when the drives appear to be running more slowly.

> **NOTE**
>
> Relatively speaking, the slowest hard drives in a modern computer are mechanical drives using SATA. SSDs using SATA are much faster but are blown away by SSDs using the NVMe interface on M.2 slots or connected to PCIe v3 or faster expansion cards.

Although you can use built-in tools in Windows (Performance Monitor) and Linux (iotop) to measure activity, the interface is complex and requires some interpretation. For easy performance testing and results in IOPS or MBps, you can use CrystalDiskMark (Windows) and the similar KDiskMark (Linux) or AmorphosDiskMark (macOS).

Figure 26.8 shows you typical IOPS test results for a 5400rpm drive connected to a 6Gbps SATA interface. Figure 26.9 shows the same tests performed on a medium-performance SSD connected to a 6Gbps SATA interface. Note the extreme difference in speed for an SSD versus a mechanical drive though both are using the SATA interface.

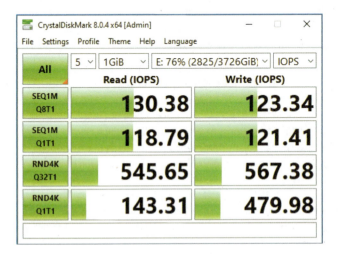

**FIGURE 26.8** CrystalDiskMark IOPS test of a 5400rpm SATA drive. (Source: Crystal Dew World [en])

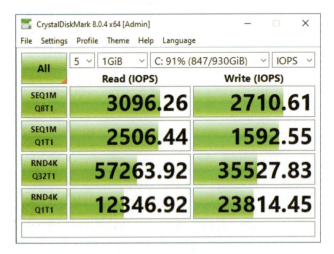

**FIGURE 26.9** CrystalDiskMark IOPS test of a typical SATA SSD drive. (Source: Crystal Dew World [en])

## Missing Drives in OS

When you connect a new SATA drive to a PC, it's not ready for use. Until it is prepared, the normal operating system (OS) features such as file management, file save, and file retrieve cannot be performed on that drive. Think of it as a raw device that must be "cooked" to be useful.

The process of making a hard drive (mechanical or SSD) ready for use has two parts: partitioning and formatting. Windows performs both steps in Disk Management. Before a new drive can be partitioned and formatted in Disk Management, Disk Management must initialize the drive. After initialization, you use Disk Management to select a drive type, specify a file system such as NTFS or exFAT, format the drive, and assign a drive letter (Figure 26.10).

If a drive is "missing" in File Manager, check the following:

1. Is it visible in Disk Management? If not, the drive might not be connected to power and data cables. Shut down the system if the drive is internal, check power and data cable connections to drive and motherboard, and try it again.

2. If an internal drive is connected to power and data cables but is still invisible in Disk Management, restart the computer, enter the BIOS/UEFI firmware setup program, and make sure the drive is detected. Some systems permit some SATA host adapter ports to be disabled. Enable all SATA ports, save changes, and restart.

3. If the drive is visible in Disk Management, review the partition type. If it is unallocated, partition it, set up a file system on each partition (if more than one is used), and format the partition(s). To make the drive visible in File Management, assign a drive letter to it.

4. If a drive has a non-Windows partition, that part of the drive will not be usable by Windows unless the partition is removed (which wipes out the data on that portion).

5. A drive with a damaged partition table or boot sector will no longer be visible in File Management. Use disk repair tools to attempt to make it visible again.

For Linux, check BIOS/UEFI firmware settings for internal drives, and verify proper mount location for drive. For macOS, make sure Finder is seeing the drive in its Sidebar: drag the drive icon into the Sidebar. If external drives are missing from the Sidebar, open Finder's Preferences and make sure External Drives are selected.

---

**EXAM TIP**

Make sure you understand the following objectives for the Core 1 exam:

▶ RAID failure

▶ Self-monitoring, analysis, and reporting technology (S.M.A.R.T.) failure

▶ Extended read/write times

▶ Input/output operations per second (IOPS)

▶ Missing drives in OS

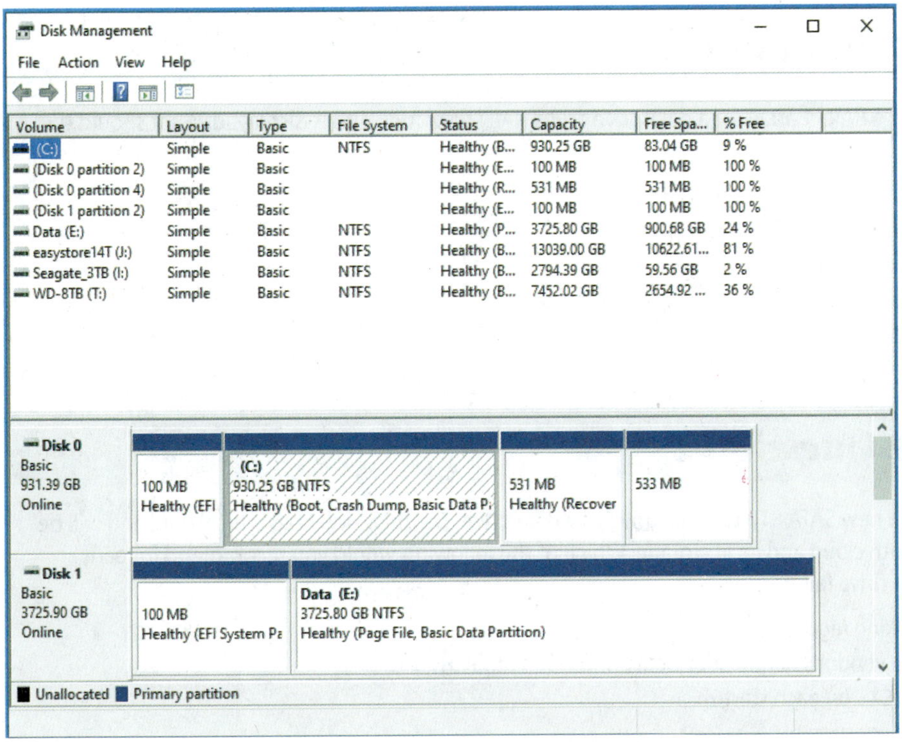

**FIGURE 26.10** Disk Management shows both partitions and assigned drive letters. (Source: Microsoft Corporation)

## CERTMIKE EXAM ESSENTIALS

▶ Although drive problems manifest themselves in many different ways, they have several fundamental causes. These include power and data cable issues, malware, damage to drive structures, operating system issues, and firmware issues.

▶ Before dismantling a computer to solve drive errors, check operating system and firmware settings and scan for malware.

▶ Knowing normal system behavior provides a technician with valuable insights in solving system problems.

▶ Performing disk performance tests on a system when it is running normally provides valuable baseline information that can be used for comparison when running the same tests on a system that is running slowly.

## Practice Question 1

Your client is using a RAID 1 array for a data drive and a RAID error message is displayed. What should the client do first?

A. Shut down the computer with the RAID array.
B. Restart the system to see if the error persists.
C. Replace the host adapter.
D. Capture all error messages from the operating system or RAID array.

## Practice Question 2

You are installing a new SATA 8TB internal drive as a data drive. The drive will hold critical data and will be backed up with both cloud and local storage. Which of the following would you recommend for early warning of SMART drive failure?

A. Run error-checking regularly.
B. Install the drive vendor's diagnostics utility and run it regularly.
C. Run `SMARTST.EXE` on each startup.
D. Replace the power supply.

## Practice Question 1 Explanation

This question is designed to test your knowledge of RAID troubleshooting.

Let's evaluate these choices one at a time.

Option A: Shut down the computer with the RAID array. This is a necessary part of solving the problem, but it should not happen first.

Option B: Restart the system to see if the error persists. This is a very dangerous response. Because RAID 1 uses mirroring, problems with one drive could be copied to the other, wiping out the data.

Option C: Replace the host adapter. This might be part of the solution, but until we know whether a drive or the host adapter has failed, this solution should not be tried first.

Option D: Capture all error messages from the operating system or RAID array. This is the best place to start, as these error messages can be helpful in determining where the failure has taken place. A smartphone camera (no flash, please!) is an easy way to capture these error messages and avoids the possibility of a failed screen capture overwriting important information.

**Correct Answer: D. Capture all error messages from the operating system or RAID array.**

## Practice Question 2 Explanation

This question is designed to test your knowledge of how to prevent problems with mass storage devices.

Let's evaluate these possibilities one at a time

Option A: Run error-checking regularly. While this is an excellent part of disk health, error checking does not detect or report SMART drive statistics.

Option B: Install the drive vendor's diagnostics utility and run it regularly. Unlike error-checking, these diagnostic utilities do check and display SMART diagnostic information, warning you in advance of potential failure. This is the BEST answer.

Option C: Run SMARTST.EXE on each startup. Unfortunately, this helpful utility doesn't exist.

Option D: Replace the power supply. A defective power supply can cause drive problems that can lead to SMART drive failure, but a power supply replacement needs to happen only if the power supply fails voltage or fan tests.

**Correct Answer: B. Install the drive vendor's diagnostics utility and run it regularly.**

# CHAPTER 27

# Troubleshooting Video

## *Core 1 Objective 5.4: Given a scenario, troubleshoot video, projector, and display issues.*

**Although** large-screen HDTVs with 4K and higher resolutions are taking over for projectors in both home and office environments, projectors are still king when it comes to portable display tasks. Add projectors to the challenge of video and display issues, and there are a lot of things to consider when what users are seeing isn't right. In this chapter, you will learn what you need to know to master Core 1, Objective 5.4, including the following:

▶ **Common symptoms and solutions**

## COMMON SYMPTOMS AND SOLUTIONS

Video, projector, and display subsystems share some problems and symptoms in common, while others are unique to the hardware. The following sections help you discover the solutions to these common symptoms.

## Incorrect Data Source

There's no picture on the display or projector? One common cause is that the incorrect data source has been selected. Most displays and projectors support two or more data sources. So, how do you determine this is the problem?

Check the following:

1. That power on display or projector is turned on. If it's turned on, continue with step 2.
2. Check the data cable connections to the computer and display or projector. What port is the data cable connected to?

The solution is to use the projector control or on-screen display on the display to select the correct data source (see Figure 27.1). You might want to tap the keyboard or move the mouse in case the display is asleep. When you see the desktop, you've solved the problem.

**FIGURE 27.1** **Selecting the correct data source. (Source: Microsoft Corporation)**

If your system has a secondary display but there's no picture, what do you try? First, open the Display properties sheet and make sure the secondary display is detected. Then, choose the way you want to you use the secondary display: use Mirrored (same image on both displays) or Extended Desktop (menu on primary display, more desktop on second display).

If you see "HDCP" on your screen instead of a video, it means that your video card or display doesn't support High Bandwidth Digital Content Protection (HDCP), a feature designed to prevent unauthorized copying of HD video content. If you encounter this when using an adapter from a DVI video card to an HDMI or DisplayPort display, the DVI port on the video card doesn't support HDCP. Upgrading your video card drivers might solve the problem, or you might need to use HDMI or DisplayPort cables without adapters. If you are connected to an HDTV, make sure you are using a port on the TV that supports HDCP.

## Physical Cabling Issues

Bad cables can cause all types of problems. Here are a few of them and their solutions. Symptoms such as off-color picture or no picture can be caused by the data cable not being properly attached to the computer, display, or projector.

To solve this problem, shut off the display or projector and the computer. Then, reattach the cable. Older cable types such as VGA or DVI use thumbscrews, so make sure they're tight. HDMI and its variants as well as microDisplayPort push into place. DisplayPort can be trickier: some push into place, but others use a push button to unlock the connector. Don't use the push button when it's present, and you can break the cable.

If you're using adapters, make sure the adapter physically and electronically supports both ends of the connection. For example, some DisplayPort implementations can't work with VGA monitors, while some HDMI ports must also connect to a USB 2.0 port to provide the necessary power to properly support a VGA monitor.

Turn on the power after reconnecting everything.

Cable damage is another cause of off-color or no picture. Check the cable connection for bent or damaged connectors, cracks, exposed wires, or frayed insulation. If the cable has damage, replace it.

If you have replaced a shorter cable with a longer cable and now there are problems, the new cable might be too long. Check the recommended cable length against the actual cable length. A cable that might work OK on a desktop computer might be too long to work on a laptop computer because of lower port power levels.

## Burned-Out Bulb

One of the reasons you won't see an image from your projector could be a burned-out bulb. Here's how to tell and how to prevent it.

If you don't see an image coming from the computer along with a hot smell coming from inside the projector, but the data source and the power are OK, check the projector bulb. If it's burned out, be sure to let the projector cool down before replacing the bulb. Always use the power button to shut down the projector, and don't unplug the projector until it has cooled down completely.

Be proactive, especially if you're a day or more away from getting a replacement if you need to order it: carry a spare bulb and make sure the bulb and the projector are protected against vibration. Check the cooling fan and filters to make sure they're working properly.

## Fuzzy Image

Maybe you don't need new glasses; it might be the projector or display! Here's how to find and fix this problem.

The first place to check for a fuzzy image is the projector lens. Use a step stool or ladder to safely reach the front of the projector.

If the front of the lens is dirty, make sure the projector is cool and get a microfiber cloth. Apply a small amount of lens fluid to the cloth and carefully wipe off the front of the lens until clean. Turn on the projector, project an image, and check the image quality.

Use the focus ring of the projector lens to adjust picture sharpness.

If the projected image or the image on a display is not sharp, the problem might be that the recommended resolution isn't being used. If possible, adjust the recommended resolution. In Windows, right-click the Desktop, select Properties, and click Display Settings. If the recommended resolution (Figure 27.2) is not highlighted, try to select it. If you are unable to select it, the projector or display doesn't support the recommended resolution. Use the highest resolution available.

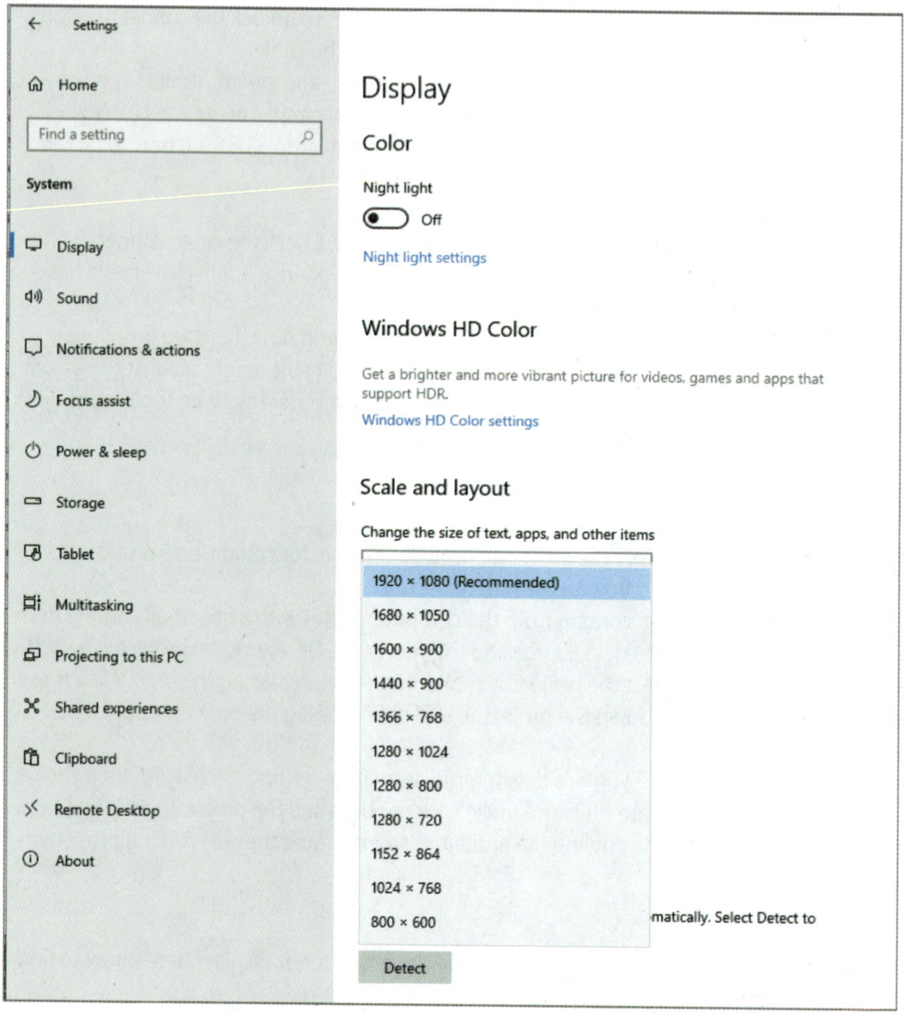

**FIGURE 27.2** This display is set to use the recommended resolution.
(Source: Microsoft Corporation)

Don't neglect dirty touchscreens on mobile devices, touchscreens, or two-in-one computers. Be sure to use only touchscreen-rated screen cleaner.

## Display Burn-In

Is your display "haunted" by on-screen "ghost" images of items previously on-screen that are still visible, such as logos, software menus, etc.? There might, repeat, might be a solution.

Image retention takes place because the same information was left on-screen for a long period of time. This can be repaired.

**EXAM TIP**

The exam likes to use *display burn-in* and *image retention* as synonymous, but in reality, true display burn-in is not repairable; the display must be replaced. The solutions in this section are for image retention. Both look similar, but the only way to tell which is which is to attempt solutions.

To get rid of image retention, try these solutions:

▶ Display an all-white or rapidly changing picture on an LCD or OLED screen for many hours (or days) to reverse the damage.

▶ You can create a white image with a photo editor and display it on-screen on minimal brightness but with the screen saver or blanking option turned off.

▶ You can also find YouTube videos you can play and some vendors sell DVDs or other media with patterns you can play that may solve the problem.

It's better to prevent image retention than to try to cure it afterward. So, what can you do? First, use screen blanking or a screen saver with motion to avoid the problem. Also, reduce screen brightness if you must leave a static image on-screen for long periods of time.

## Dead Pixels

If you see a black pixel that never changes color, it's a dead pixel. If you see a pixel that stays bright no matter what, it's a stuck pixel. What can you do about it?

First, see if the vendor will replace the monitor or display panel. Keep in mind that different vendors have different acceptable defect levels that must be exceeded before a panel is bad enough to warrant replacement.

Can't get a replacement? Visit the www.jscreenfix.com website and try its pixel fixer app (Figure 27.3). Drag the window over the affected screen area and wait about 10 minutes to see if the problem pixel(s) are working better.

**FIGURE 27.3** Using JScreenFix to try to repair a stuck or dead pixel. (Source: Microsoft Corporation)

## Flashing Screen

The only time the screen should be flashing is if you're watching a flashing video. Any other time, your users will be reaching for the pain reliever, followed by their smartphones to ask for help. Here's what to do!

If the entire screen is flashing or blinking, this can be caused by hardware problems or by video card drivers.

To get updated video card drivers, go to the GPU vendor and download the latest GPU driver for your graphics card or on-board graphics. Install the driver and restart the computer.

To determine if the problem is a bad or misinstalled graphics card, follow this procedure. Use a wrist strap to protect against ESD discharge. Turn off the system and disconnect it from power. Open the system and determine if the graphics card is properly seated. If not, disconnect data and PCIe power cables, remove the card from the slot (Figure 27.4), and replace in the slot. Make sure it is fully seated. Reconnect cables, repower system, and retry.

**FIGURE 27.4** A PCIe video card being removed from its expansion slot. When properly seated, the connectors on the card edge will not be visible.

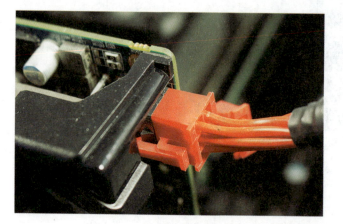

**FIGURE 27.5** Reconnecting the PCIe power cable to a PCIe video card.

If graphics card is properly seated, check the PCIe power cable connection to card. If not fully connected, detach the PCIe power cable and reconnect it. Make sure the cable connects to all leads on the card (Figure 27.5). Repower system and retry.

If the graphics are built into the motherboard, it's necessary to bypass them by using a graphics card. Here's how.

Use a wrist strap to protect against ESD discharge. Turn off the system and disconnect it from power. Install a video card into a PCIe ×16 slot. Connect the card to power and data cables. Reconnect the system to power and enter the BIOS/UEFI settings menu. Disable onboard graphics. After the system reboots, install drivers for the new video card. If the problem stops, the onboard graphics are defective. Continue to use the new video card or replace the motherboard.

## Incorrect Color Display

Is the white onscreen yellowish? Blue or red looking like purple? It's time to fix color problems. Causes (and solutions) vary with the display type.

With an LCD projector, there are three different LCD panels (red, green, and blue) inside the unit. If any of these get dusty or stop working, you can have color problems. While the unit is open, check the bulb, as a discolored bulb can cause bad color and is typically about to fail. Be sure to clean the filter too.

A DLP projector uses a color wheel and an array of micromirrors to make colors. If the wheel isn't moving, is faded, or is damaged, there's the cause. Repair or replace the unit.

A laptop uses a display ribbon cable that runs from the motherboard to the display panel. If the unit is dropped, the cable or panel might have been damaged. However, if the unit was serviced or upgraded, the cable might not have been properly secured afterward.

Any displays connected with external cables can have color problems if the cables are not properly secured. Check them.

VGA and DVI cables have exposed pins that are easy to bend or break. Check for problems. Keep in mind that some pins are missing on purpose, so don't panic.

Displays of all types have onscreen displays. Check for a color temperature setting in the onscreen display (Figure 27.6) or custom video driver. Adjust to taste (Figure 27.7).

## Audio Issues

It's supposed to be an exciting game, but without sound, it's boring. Whether you're trying to play a game, watch a movie, or chat, audio issues can ruin the experience. Let's find the problems and solve them!

No audio playback can have many causes. First, make sure the audio isn't muted: check the control on the Windows taskbar and make sure the mixer is set to the correct output. If no audio plays after connecting an HDMI or DisplayPort display, the mixer may have switched to that port for output. Switch it back to the correct speaker output.

If you can't pick up or record audio, make sure the microphone isn't muted and that the correct microphone is selected in the mixer.

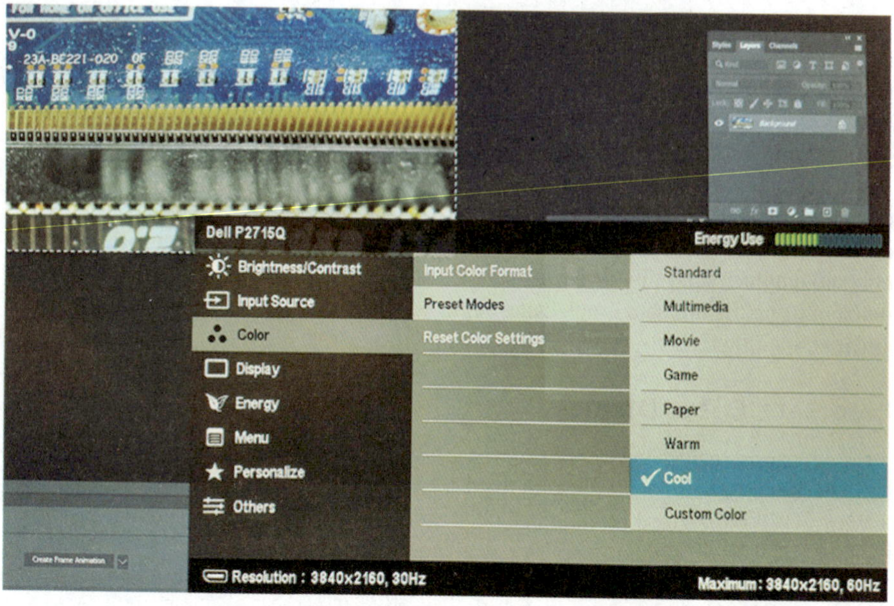

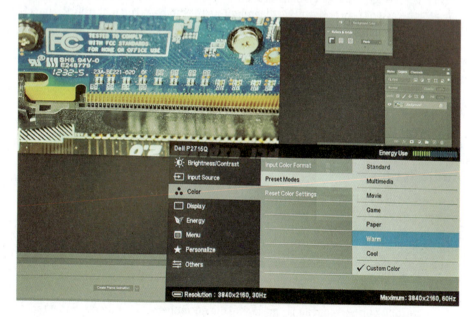

**FIGURE 27.6**  The Cool preset color mode on a Dell display. (Source: Microsoft Corporation)

**FIGURE 27.7**  Previewing the Warm preset color mode on a Dell display; note the difference in color from the previous example. (Source: Microsoft Corporation)

Incorrect cabling can cause problems in both playback and recording. If the microphone or webcam is USB, check the connection to the USB jack. If the jack is front-mounted, check the cable from the front-mounted jack to the motherboard.

Data cables that are 3.5mm have lots of potential problems because they can be plugged into the wrong jacks. The standard 3.5-inch color coding includes pink for microphones (mono line in), green (speaker or headphone out), and blue (stereo line in). Additional colors are used for surround audio. A lot of laptops now use a combined headset/microphone jack (Figure 27.8). If you mismatch these, you won't hear or record any audio unless you use an adapter.

**FIGURE 27.8** A three-ring (combined microphone/speaker or headset) jack at left compared to stereo microphone jack (center) and headphone jack (right).

Some computers feature SPDIF (also known as S/PDIF) digital audio for connections to home theater systems. If you're having problems, make sure the SPDIF audio cable is properly connected to both the receiver and PC and that SPDIF audio is selected as the output on the PC mixer and is selected as input on the receiver.

Distorted audio can have many causes, including having the volume on the receiver or speakers turned up higher than the PC volume settings, interference from nearby sources (move the devices or speakers), or outdated audio drivers (update the drivers).

## Dim Image

Is the picture from your projector or display too dark? Check these causes and solutions.

For displays and projectors, check the brightness setting. Depending upon the unit, there might be separate brightness and contrast settings or different custom settings (video, movie, text, presentation, vivid, and so on).

Use the special function keys to adjust the built-in screen's brightness on a laptop, two-in-one, or convertible unit.

Don't overlook the display drivers for your 3D graphics card. Both AMD and NVIDIA offer brightness and other gaming display tweaks.

As projector bulbs age, they can develop a coating inside the bulb that can reduce brightness. Replace the bulb to restore full brightness.

Remove dust from LCD screens, color wheel, lens, and other components to improve projection brightness.

Darken the room to help improve screen brightness.

## Intermittent Projector Shutdown

Projectors don't like overheating any more than you do. However, that's not the only reason a projector might shut itself down. If the projector has an auto standby mode, adjust the timing to prevent the projector from turning off while in use. Allow the projector to cool and shut it down before checking for dirty filters or clogged fan (both of these can lead to overheating-based shutdowns). Remove and reconnect the projector bulb to assure a solid connection.

### CERTMIKE EXAM ESSENTIALS

▶ Troubleshooting video, projector, and display issues can be challenging because of the different components involved, so use the "change one item at a time" methodology to solve problems. In other words, after determining the most likely cause of a problem, change that one item, and see if the problem is solved. If not, restore the original configuration and move to the next possible cause. Repeat until the problem is solved.

▶ The projector bulb can cause quite a few problems with projectors, so keeping it clean and properly ventilated is important to long life and reliable operation.

▶ When HDMI and DisplayPort video connections are in use, they are often configured as the primary audio connectors, disabling built-in, 3.5mm, or USB audio output. Be sure to check both audio and video mixer settings when HDMI or DisplayPort connections are in use.

## Practice Question 1

Your client occasionally uses an HDTV for classroom presentations. Normally everything works fine, but she has a new laptop and video cable, and when she connected it, there was no picture on the HDTV. Which of the following is the FIRST item to check?

A.  New laptop has defective video port.
B.  The video cable is defective.
C.  Mirroring was not enabled.
D.  The new laptop is using a different type of video cable.

## Practice Question 2

Your friend has frantically called you with a problem: he can't get his brand-new PCIe graphics card to display anything. He upgraded an older system and had problems connecting the PCIe power lead to the card. When you arrive, you discover that he has inserted a six-pin PCIe power cable into the card that takes eight pins. Which of the following should you look for FIRST?

A.  An eight-pin PCIe power cable
B.  An adapter to turn a drive power cable into a PCIe power cable
C.  A different slot for the PCIe card
D.  A replacement power supply

## Practice Question 1 Explanation

This question is designed to test your knowledge of display troubleshooting.

Let's evaluate these choices one at a time.

Option A: A new laptop could have a defective video port, but it should be tested to determine if this is the issue. Let's look at easier solutions first.

Option B: As with the first answer, a defective video cable is a possibility. However, it is not the easiest item to check.

Option C: Mirroring is a good way to use an additional display, but the user has never needed to select this option before. Something else is wrong.

Option D: Let's look at the video cable used by the new laptop and compare it to the old one. If the new laptop is using DisplayPort or miniDisplayPort and the old laptop used HDMI, the HDTV needs to have its video source set to match the new cable. This is the first possibility to check.

**Correct Answer: D. The new laptop is using a different type of video cable.**

## Practice Question 2 Explanation

This question is designed to test your knowledge of PCIe video cards and power requirements.

Let's evaluate these possibilities one at a time

Option A: An eight-pin PCIe power cable. The existing six-pin cable might actually have two additional pins that are on a separate wire bundle for use with both six-pin and eight-pin PCIe cards. If there isn't one present, it would be time to look for another solution. This is the first item to check.

Option B: Drive power to PCIe power adapter. These exist and are just a few dollars. Two cautions, however: you must use two Molex power connectors to provide power for an eight-pin PCIe card. If the power supply has a marginal amount of 12V power, it might make sense to replace the power supply instead.

Option C: Try a different slot. All PCIe slots for video cards provide the same amount of power, not enough for a card that has a power connector.

Option D: Replace the power supply. This might be necessary, but it's not the first thing to try.

**Correct Answer: A. An eight-pin PCIe power cable**

# CHAPTER 28

# Troubleshooting Mobile Devices

## Core 1 Objective 5.5: Given a scenario, troubleshoot common issues with mobile devices.

**Because** mobile devices spend a lot of time on the go, they are subject to specific problems related to battery care, connectivity, calibration, and physical damage. This chapter teaches you want you need to know about Core 1 Objective 5.5 including the following:

▶ **Common symptoms**

## COMMON SYMPTOMS

Mobile devices can have a number of issues. However, unlike computers, especially desktops, most mobile device problems require a trip to the repair shop. Use this section to help the mobile users you work with (including you!) to keep their devices out of trouble.

> **TIP**
> The symptoms in this chapter also include recommendations for preventing problems. Use them to keep your equipment from needing repair or replacement.

## Improper Charging

It's convenient to keep your smartphone or tablet plugged in all of the time, but it's not the best way to care for your device's battery. Mobile device vendors recommend that a charging level between 40 and 80 percent is ideal and that keeping it plugged in to a charger after it has reached a full charge can shorten the battery life of your mobile device.

As far as charging goes, many users plug their smartphones into standard USB ports for charging. Standard USB ports provide barely enough power to charge a phone slowly, and slow charging isn't good for a phone either.

It's much better to use an AC adapter made for the phone or tablet (either OEM or a reliable third-party). Chargers for multiple USB ports can save AC outlets. AC adapters for smartphones need to deliver at least 1 Amp to charge a phone and about 2.1 Amps to charge a tablet.

> **NOTE**
>
> Some desktop computers have high-amperage USB ports that can be used to fast charge mobile devices. Check the documentation for your computer for details.

You don't need to use an Apple-brand Lightning cable, but be aware that a true Lightning cable has special electronics in it for better charging. A cheap cable might not. Before purchasing a third-party cable, check reviews to find out if a particular cable is truly compatible.

During the connection with an AC adapter, a mobile device determines the charging rate. Sometimes the connection estimates a very long time (for example, four to five times longer than normal for the charge level needed). If this happens, disconnect the cable from the mobile device, wait a minute or two, check the AC adapter connection to the wall socket or surge suppressor, and try it again. Usually the estimated charging rate will return to normal. If not, change cables or change chargers.

## Poor Battery Health

If your brand-new mobile device could easily run for 24 to 36 hours without needing a charge, but a year or two later it barely makes it through the workday without a stop at the charging station, it may be suffering from poor battery health. This can be caused by improper charging, overheating, or a swollen battery (next section).

Some smartphones have a battery or battery and device maintenance menu that you can use to optimize battery life (Figure 28.1). To help improve battery life, enable the power saving feature in your mobile device. When enabled, your device will have a little dimmer screen and run a little more slowly, but the charge will last longer.

To keep your mobile device from running down as quickly, make sure you adjust the brightness to the current lighting conditions. I dislike the automatic brightness control (not bright enough for me), so it's up to me to turn down screen brightness when inside and up when outside. To conserve more power, disable or remove unnecessary features and apps. If you don't use an app or feature, consider it a candidate for removal.

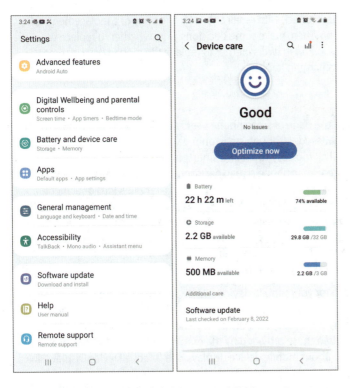

**FIGURE 28.1** Using the battery and device maintenance menu on a Samsung Android smartphone.

No matter how careful you are with charging, battery life tends to decline as a phone ages. Replacing the battery can help, but you need to weigh the potential improvement against what you would gain with a trade-in to a newer and more powerful device.

## Swollen Battery

A swollen battery is often the result of a mobile device being overcharged or left on in a hot, poorly ventilated environment. This is more serious than it might appear at first glance. If the back is no longer straight, the phone seems a little thicker in your hand, or the screen protector isn't fitting as well as it once was, your mobile device may have a swollen battery.

A swollen battery could be difficult to swap, and potentially dangerous if it starts to leak. Batteries in newer smartphones may have unusual shapes (for example, some vendors use a large L-shaped battery for some models). Most smartphones must be pried apart to perform a battery swap. Fortunately, many vendors of DIY battery replacements provide the tools needed.

If a lithium-ion battery leaks liquid or gas fumes near an ignition source, it could catch on fire. The safest way to deal with a swollen battery in a mobile device is to stop using it as soon as you notice the problem.

Don't turn it on or charge it. Check with repair shops for the price of a replacement battery including installation. Then, make some decisions: one, whether to replace the battery yourself or have a shop do it; two, whether to replace the mobile device; three, whether to practice better charging habits.

## Broken Screen

Broken screens have been the bane of smartphone users since the first smartphone hit the sidewalk and its screen shattered. Although smartphone vendors have adopted more and more durable glass, it's still all too easy to break a smartphone's screen.

The cost to repair a broken smartphone screen has risen sharply with more recent models. A leading third-party repair service can replace the screen on iPhone 8 Plus or earlier for less than $150. However, most of the iPhone X and newer phones can cost more than $400 at third-party repair shops, with Apple itself charging more than $320 for some of its latest models. Samsung's late-model Galaxy phones cost about $300 for screen repair at another leading third-party battery and phone repair chain.

To avoid these astronomical prices, we recommend the following:

▶ Buy insurance for your mobile device and be sure to compare not only the price of the insurance itself but also deductibles and number of replacements allowed. Many third-party insurers provide better coverage with lower (or no) deductibles than those provided by the mobile device vendors themselves. To learn more about mobile device displays, see "Mobile Device Displays" in Chapter 2.

▶ Use a protective case for the mobile device along with a highly durable cover glass for the screen. I have seen a cover glass look like a broken smartphone screen after the phone was run over by a car, but after the cover glass was removed, only the cover glass was shattered—the screen was still perfect!

## Poor/No Connectivity

Smartphones feature not only Wi-Fi and Bluetooth connectivity but also cellular connectivity. In spite of the huge increases in the number of signal towers and the efforts by the leading carriers to reduce dead zones, there are places where there is no connectivity at all or you're seeing only one or two bars. The following tips apply to both smartphones and tablets with cellular connectivity:

▶ If you're not moving, try changing the angle of your phone or hold it out the window. The car frame or nearby buildings could be blocking cellular signals.

▶ If you're moving, wait a couple of minutes to see if you drive out of the dead zone.

▶ Try restarting your smartphone. This step (much like restarting your PC or mac) can fix a lot of problems including connectivity.

▶ Install all updates provided by your cellular carrier.

▶ Turn on Airplane mode for a minute or two to disable cellular connectivity and then turn it off. Note that turning off Airplane mode restarts cellular service, but you will need to manually turn on Wi-Fi and Bluetooth with most mobile devices.

## Liquid Damage

Liquid damage is one of the worst things that can happen to a mobile device. Whether it fell into the swimming pool or took a trip through the washing machine, a wet phone is usually a dead phone. Smartphone and tablet vendors use liquid-reactive stickers inside their phones to see if a phone has been dunked. So, the odds of your getting the phone company to spring for a free replacement are about nil.

The proverbial zipper bag of rice treatment occasionally helps because rice absorbs moisture, and using silica gel packets provides better results. However, consider products such as the Bheestie Bag or Yikes! Phone and Tablet Rescue Pouch. These use water-absorbing materials that work better than rice or silica gel for drying out a smartphone or a tablet. Be sure to allow as many as three days for a complete dry-out and be sure to remove the case and the SIM card before trying to dry out your device.

For users who will be using smartphones around water, the best move is prevention—keeping phones protected from water and choosing phones or smartphone cases with IP68 water resistance.

For IP68-rated products, check with the vendor to see the maximum water depth the protection is rated for, as it varies with the phone. IP67 water resistance is good for up to 1 meter (3.3 feet). Note that mobile device vendors don't provide warranty coverage against water damage.

## Overheating

Every summer, there's usually a story or two about somebody baking cookies or pizza inside a hot car. They're funny but prove the point that the interior of a car in summer is a very hot place. Leaving your mobile device in a hot car also bakes it, but instead of delicious food, you have a device with a shortened lifespan—or one that might not work anymore.

Hot cars aren't the only place where a mobile device can overheat. Charging your phone in a closed purse, leaving it on in a coat or jacket pocket, or playing video while the battery is at 5 percent and charging are also effective. Cranking up the screen brightness, using your camera, and running games with intense graphics are three more ways that you can overheat the phone by pushing the device's processor and RAM to their limits.

Adequate ventilation, not using a phone or tablet when it's low on power and charging, and keeping it out of hot cars are good for your smartphone or tablet.

## Digitizer Issues

All smartphones and tablets have built-in touch screens. In addition to providing easy operation, the screen acts as a digitizer for your signature, photo edits, and much more. Digitizer problems are a big deal.

A damaged screen doesn't necessarily affect the digitizer, as the screen is the top layer, followed by the digitizer, and the display. That's why a smartphone or tablet with a cracked screen can still function.

To determine whether your device's digitizer has failed, see if it can detect your finger or stylus presses. If you have a drawing app on your device, select a drawing tool, touch the screen, and move around the screen to draw a shape. If the pen disappears at some part of the screen, the digitizer is not working.

Before assuming the digitizer has failed, make sure the screen is clean. Also, a poorly installed screen protector can cause digitizer problems, so make sure your screen protector is installed properly.

If a digitizer replacement kit is available for your smartphone or tablet, you can replace a bad digitizer yourself using tools similar to those you would use for replacing a cracked screen.

> **TIP**
>
> Typical tools used to fix mobile devices include nylon spudgers (used to pry apart cases); fine-tipped curved tweezers (used to remove small parts), small screw, star, and nut drivers; screen removal suction cups; and more. See `blog` `.repairdesk.co/2021/08/23/repair-tools-for-your-cell-` `phone-repair-business` for more information.

The process requires disassembling the device, removing the screen, and removing the digitizer layer. The digitizer layer is connected to the phone's mainboard, so those connections must be removed to enable the replacement to be installed.

## Cursor Drift/Touch Calibration

Cursor drift, when the mouse pointer or typing cursor moves across the screen by itself, is often a problem on laptops, convertibles, and two-in-one computers with touchpads. When you're typing on a device with a touchpad, it can be easy to bump the touchpad and move your cursor. On Windows systems, you can adjust the sensitivity of the touchpad. In Windows 10, open Settings ➢ Mouse & Touchpad. In Windows 11, open Settings ➢ Bluetooth & devices ➢ Touchpad. Depending upon the menu options listed, use a Medium or Long delay or a Medium Sensitivity or Low Sensitivity (Figure 28.2) setting to help reduce cursor drift due to accidental taps.

Cursor drift can also happen on systems that have no issues with accidental touchpad taps.

These are some recommended solutions for cursor drift:

▶ Sometimes additional driver entries can be found in Device Manager for a mouse or other pointing device. Disable additional driver entries to see if the cursor drift problem stops.

▶ Remove the battery from a wireless mouse and then reinstall it.

▶ If the mouse has custom driver software, uninstall it and use the standard Windows or macOS software driver. If you prefer the extra features of the custom driver software, check on an update from the vendor.

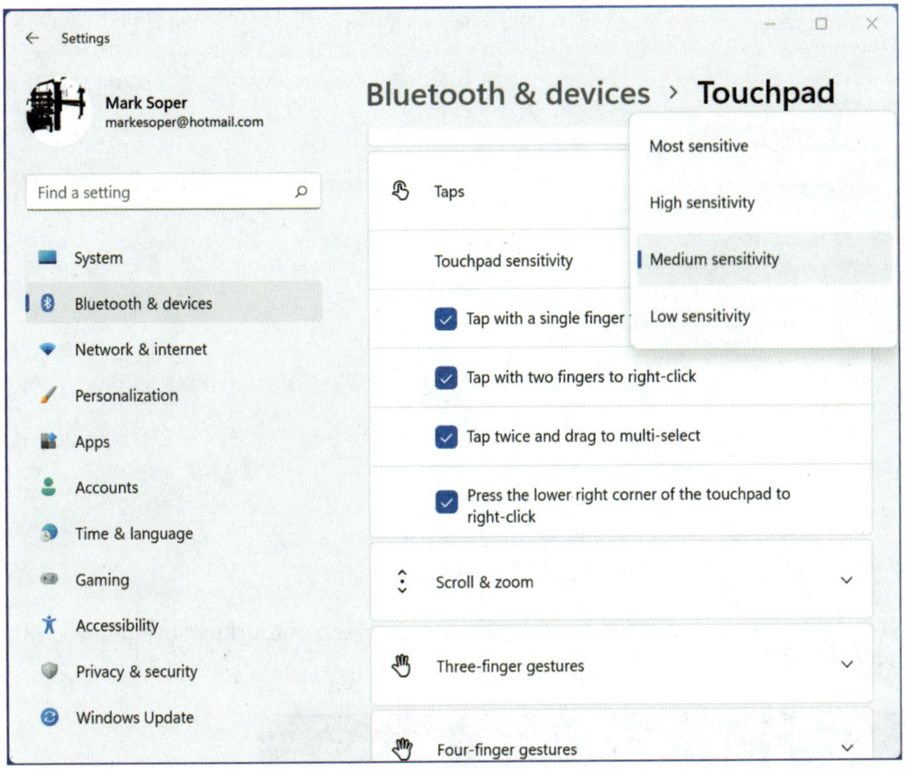

**FIGURE 28.2** **Using the Touchpad menu on Windows 11 to reduce touchpad sensitivity.**

▶ If the cursor drift is happening on a mouse that uses a smooth surface, put a mouse pad on the table and use it.

▶ Try plugging the mouse into a different USB port or into a USB hub instead of a port.

Touch calibration should be performed if the touchscreen is not properly detecting your taps. Windows 10 and 11 have built-in support for touch calibration. To run it, open Control Panel and search for Tablet. Click the link to Tablet PC Settings and click Calibrate (Figure 28.3). Select Touch Screen and follow the prompts to tap the screen markings as directed. Save settings when done.

If you're having problems with the touch pad on your Windows device, follow the same procedure to calibrate the touch pad. Just choose Touch Pad when prompted.

To calibrate the touch screen on an Android device, you will need to use a third-party app such as the RedPi Apps Touchscreen Calibration (Figure 28.4).

You can't calibrate the touchscreen on an iOS device yourself (that would require a trip to an Apple facility), but you can adjust touch sensitivity through Settings ➤ Accessibility ➤ Touch.

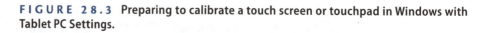

**FIGURE 28.3** **Preparing to calibrate a touch screen or touchpad in Windows with Tablet PC Settings.**

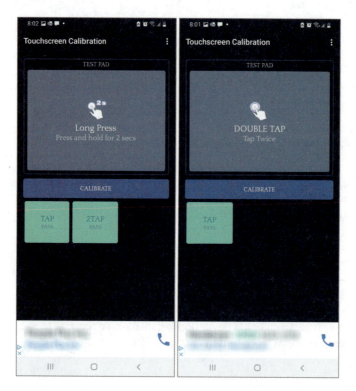

**FIGURE 28.4** **Calibrating an Android touch screen with the Touchscreen Calibration app.**

## Physically Damaged Ports

The use of nonkeyed cables on iPhones (Lightning or USB Type-C) and Android (USB Type-C) has helped to minimize the chances of ports being physically damaged by trying to force the charging cable into the smartphone the wrong way. However, smartphone ports can still be physically damaged by the port accumulating debris, by the cable breaking off in the port, or by drops and falls.

Before assuming that a charging port is damaged, take a close look at it. There might be dust and debris in the port that are preventing the phone from charging. Carefully use a tiny needle or pin to clear out debris and then check to see whether your phone charges.

A broken cable that is stuck in a smartphone port can be removed by using tweezers—ordinary eyebrow tweezers can work, but the very slender tweezers packed in mobile repair kits can get into tighter spaces. If the broken cable is removed, try a good cable to see if you can still charge the phone.

A broken charging port assembly can be replaced on most phones with less disassembly than is required for screen or digitizer replacement. However, note that newer phones are often glued together and require a heat pad or gun to enable the back or front of the phone to be removed. A charging port assembly replacement, even if a repair shop does it, is much less expensive than a screen or digitizer replacement.

To learn more about cables, see Chapter 3, "Mobile Device Ports and Accessories."

## Malware

Malware targets more than PCs running Windows; Android and iOS devices can also be targets, and unlike Windows, Android and iOS do not provide anti-malware apps as standard features. One benefit of running anti-malware apps on your mobile devices is to protect your computers from attack via your mobile device. The following precautions help to protect mobile, desktop, and laptop computers from attacks:

- ▶ Use trusted Internet search engines.
- ▶ Enable user authentication.
- ▶ Always run updates.
- ▶ Avoid public Wi-Fi.
- ▶ Use a virtual private network (VPN).
- ▶ Use a password manager.
- ▶ Enable remote lock.
- ▶ Set up and use cloud backups.
- ▶ Use mobile device management (MDM) and mobile application management (MAM).

Most major anti-malware vendors have free or paid mobile versions. Free versions typically lack real-time protection and other useful add-ons such as email protection or a VPN. Before purchasing one, try the free version (if available) or take advantage of trial offers.

**EXAM TIP**

The 1101 exam is likely to test your knowledge of troubleshooting mobile devices. Be prepared for questions related to poor battery health, swollen battery, broken screen, improper charging, poor/no connectivity, liquid damage, overheating, digitizer issues, physically damaged ports, malware, and cursor drift/touch calibration.

## CERTMIKE EXAM ESSENTIALS

▶ Power problems including improper charging, poor battery health, and swollen battery are often related to each other. Following proper charging procedures, using smartphone and tablet features to check on battery condition, and avoiding overcharging can help prevent these issues.

▶ Broken screens and digitizers can be expensive and difficult to repair for inexperienced users. Before making these repairs, it's important to determine the value of a repair (performed by yourself or a repair shop) versus phone replacement costs.

▶ Many of the problems in this chapter are best dealt with by preventing the problem to begin with; keeping devices from overheating, protecting them from water and impact damage, and protecting them from malware are three of those examples.

## Practice Question 1

Your client has just dunked their water-resistant smartphone in the deep end of the pool. After checking the specifications, your client remembers that the phone has an IP67 rating. Which of the following BEST describes your client's situation?

A. The phone will be fine.
B. The phone is ruined.
C. The phone should be dried out immediately.
D. The phone should be replaced under warranty.

## Practice Question 2

Your client is using a Windows computer with a touch screen that is not registering touches consistently. After verifying that the problem is the same whether or not a stylus is used, you recommend checking in which of the following locations in Control Panel or Settings for the calibration settings?

A. East of Access Center
B. Tablet PC Settings
C. Mouse
D. Pen and Touch

## Practice Question 1 Explanation

This question is designed to test your real-world understanding of smartphone troubleshooting. Let's evaluate these choices one at a time.

1. Option A (the phone will be fine) doesn't take into account the limitations of an IP67 rating. IP67 is designed to handle short-term water contact at depths up to 1 meter (about 3.3 feet). The deep end of the pool is anywhere from 5 to 10 feet or more. This answer is incorrect.

2. Option B (the phone is ruined) is likely, but should not be assumed. This answer is also incorrect.

3. Option C (the phone should be dried out immediately) is the BEST answer with any smartphone regardless of its water-resistance rating. The phone might survive if this action is taken immediately.

4. Option D (the phone should be replaced under warranty) is wrong for two reasons: water damage is not covered, and even if it were, the water depth is well beyond the phone's rating.

**Correct answer: C. The phone should be dried out immediately.**

## Practice Question 2 Explanation

This question is designed to test your knowledge of Windows touch screen troubleshooting steps.

Let's evaluate these answers one at a time.

1. Option A (Ease of Access Center) helps configure mouse and keyboard functions for easier operation by users with limited mobility or vision. This is not the right answer.

2. Option B (Tablet PC Settings), is the right choice for calibration, working with either touch screen or touch pad devices.

3. Option C (Mouse) is not correct as it is used to configure mouse pointer sizes, colors, and operation.

4. Option D (Pen and Touch) is not correct as it is used to configure stylus or pen equivalents to mouse controls.

**Correct answer: B. Tablet PC Settings**

# CHAPTER 29

# Troubleshooting Printers

## Core 1 Objective 5.6: Given a scenario, troubleshoot and resolve printer issues.

*Printers* and multifunction devices are among the most important peripherals in any office, from a tiny home office to an enterprise. In this chapter, you will learn what you need to master Core 1, Objective 5.6, including the following:

▶ Common symptoms

## COMMON SYMPTOMS AND SOLUTIONS

Printers and multifunction devices use a variety of technologies, including laser, inkjet, impact, thermal, and 3-D, and similar problems can have very different causes because of those technologies. This chapter provides common symptoms and solutions based on those technologies.

### Lines Down the Printed Pages

Lines down the printed page can happen with a variety of printer types and have a variety of causes.

### Laser

With a monochrome laser printer producing long lines down the printed page, check for damage to the imaging drum (including the drum built into a toner cartridge). If there is dirt on the surface of the drum, you can attempt to clean it. If that doesn't resolve the issue, replace the imaging drum.

With a laser printer (monochrome or color) producing long lines down the printed page, check for a dirty corona wire, dirty exit rollers, or dirty fuser rollers, and clean any dirty components.

With a color laser printer, check for damage to the fuser sleeve, debris in the transfer unit, or damage to the transfer unit. After inspecting these items, clean dirty items and replace defective or damaged items.

With a monochrome laser printer producing randomized short streaks down the printed page, check for low toner. When you replace the toner, be sure to shake it well before installation.

### Inkjet

With an inkjet printer producing randomized short streaks down the printed page, check for incorrect head gap setting for heavy print stock and adjust the head gap as needed. Dirty printheads and print rollers should be cleaned.

### Multifunction

With a multifunction device producing randomized short or long streaks down pages printed with copier function, check for dirt or debris on scanner glass or in automatic document feeder (ADF) feed mechanism. Clean the scanner glass or ADF feed mechanism.

## Garbled Print

Garbled printouts can happen with any type of printer but can have a variety of causes. Check for problems with data cables, such as data cables not firmly attached or damaged data cables. To replace cables, turn off computer and printer, and reattach and secure data cable at both computer and printer. After turning on the computer and printer, do a test print.

A corrupt or incorrect printer driver can also cause garbled print. To fix this problem, uninstall the printer driver, go to the vendor's website, and download/install latest printer driver for the operating system. Run a test print to see if the issue has been corrected.

## Toner Not Fusing to Paper

If laser printer toner falls off the paper as soon as the paper emerges from the printer, this is usually a sign of fuser failure. The fuser assembly is supposed to heat up the paper so the printed image stays on the paper. In this situation, you should repair or replace the fuser assembly.

## Paper Jams

The term *paper jam* can also refer to jams involving other types of printed media, including labels, envelopes, and transparencies. The following causes apply to laser, inkjet, thermal, and impact printers.

If paper or media is too thick for the printer's normal paper path, switch to a straight-through paper path instead of the normal curved paper path if possible.

Make sure paper is loaded properly into the printer; don't overload the paper tray or load misaligned sheets.

If paper or media gets stuck inside the printer, be sure to remove all traces and clean up any leftover adhesive from labels.

After changing ink cartridges, toner cartridges, or making other adjustments, be sure to close any access panels.

If paper is jammed in the duplex unit or it's not installed properly to begin with, remove it and check for damage to drive gears. Replace a damaged unit. Reinstall a working unit and make sure it is properly secured in place.

## Faded Print

Faded print problems can occur with laser, inkjet, thermal, and impact printers for a variety of reasons.

### Laser

With a monochrome or color laser printer producing faded print, check for toner-saving settings such as Economode, and change the print mode to normal. Add toner or replace the toner cartridge if toner-saving settings are not in use.

With a color laser producing faded print, check for problems with the toner belt, which carries each color of toner to the imaging drum. Clean the belt, and replace it if problems persist after cleaning.

### Inkjet

With an inkjet printer producing faded print, check for clogged printer nozzles. Use nozzle check to diagnose which nozzles are clogged, and then run nozzle/head cleaning routine; repeat until the nozzle check is OK. The nozzle check consumes ink, and you should be prepared to replace ink cartridges or refill ink reservoirs to help solve the problem.

### Thermal

With a thermal printer producing faded print, check for incorrectly installed or incompatible thermal printer ribbon or incompatible thermal paper. Replace them with compatible items.

Debris on thermal printhead can also cause faded print. Clean the printhead, and replace it if the problem persists.

### Impact

With an impact printer producing faded print, check for a dried-out ribbon. If the ribbon has an additional ink reservoir, activate it; otherwise, replace the ribbon.

If the printer produces faded print only on the upper part of each letter, the head gap is incorrect. Adjust the head gap to the appropriate setting for the paper/media installed.

## Incorrect Paper Size

When an inkjet, impact, or thermal printer attempts to print beyond the paper size, check the paper size and orientation settings in the printer driver. Make sure these are set correctly before starting a print job.

## Paper Not Feeding

When the paper won't feed into a printer that uses a paper tray, check the amount of paper in the tray. Make sure the paper is loaded so that it can be picked up by the paper feed mechanism. Also, check for worn-out paper feed rollers. Replace the rollers if it's cost-effective, or replace the printer itself.

When an impact printer with a tractor feed won't feed paper, make sure the perforated paper edges are properly engaged with the tractor-feed mechanism. Make sure the feed tension is correct to avoid tearing paper edges.

When an impact printer with single-sheet feed won't feed paper, make sure the printer has been switched to single-sheet feed mode.

## Multipage Misfeed

When a printer with a paper tray misfeeds two or more sheets at a time, check for damp paper. It will stick together, so replace the current paper with paper stored at proper temperatures and humidity, and fan the stack of paper before inserting it into paper tray.

If the paper appears to be OK, check the sheet separator in the printer. Replace it if it is worn.

## Multiple Prints Pending In Queue

When print jobs are sent to the printer but nothing comes out, check to see if the Windows print spooler has switched to offline mode. This can be caused by a paper jam or loss of network connection to a network-connected printer.

To control print jobs, open print queue from the Control Panel or Settings, open the Printer menu, and click Use Printer Offline (if checked) to release the print queue. To cancel a print job, right-click the print job and select Cancel Print. To cancel all print jobs, right-click Printer and select Cancel All Documents.

## Speckling on Printed Pages

Speckling on printed pages is caused by debris, ink, or dirt being in the wrong places at the wrong times.

With laser, inkjet, thermal, or impact printers, check for debris build-up inside printer. Clean the interior, including the paper tray, rollers, paper path, etc.

When speckling is visible on copier output with a multifunction printer, check for dirt or debris on the scanner glass or in the ADF scanner mechanism and remove it.

With a laser printer, check for leaking toner; replace the toner cartridge and clean up excess toner from inside the printer. Also check for a faulty or dirty photoconductor unit (which uses an electrical charge to create the image used for printing). If the printer uses a separate imaging drum, scratches on the unit can collect waste toner leading to specks; clean or replace the unit as needed.

With an inkjet printer, check for leaking ink cartridges. Replace the cartridges and clean the rollers and other interior components.

## Double/Echo Images on the Print

"Ghost" images (double images or echoes) on printouts left over from previous pages in the same print job or from previous print jobs with a laser printer can have many causes.

Measure the ghosting image and compare it to the circumference of the imaging drum. If the distance is the same, the imaging drum is not being cleaned properly by the discharge lamp due to the drum's reaching the end of its useful life. Replace the imaging drum or toner cartridge as applicable.

Dirty fuser rollers can leave an imprint of the previous print job on subsequent jobs. Clean them.

Damp toner or toner cartridge can cause ghosting. Replace toner with toner/toner cartridge that has been stored properly (see the recommendations on package). Check the temperature and humidity in the printer room and adjust if it's out of the recommended range.

Using paper/media not designed for laser printing can cause ghosting. Use the recommended paper/media. Make sure the paper/media setting is correct for the type in use.

## Incorrect Color Settings

Incorrect color settings are a waste of media, toner, or ink, depending upon the printer type. With any color printer, matching the onscreen colors with printed output is very helpful. If the colors onscreen don't match printed output, download the correct color profile settings for your monitor from the vendor; install the color profile into Color Management (Control Panel) by choosing Use My Settings For This Device.

### Color Laser and Inkjet

With a color laser or inkjet producing incorrect color output, check for incorrect color settings in the printer driver for the document or photo. Run color calibration and make sure the media type and print quality settings are set correctly.

Change the color management settings (turn off, if on; turn on, if off) and note which setting produces the best results for a particular application or type of document or image.

### Color Laser

Disable Economode or other toner-saving settings.

### Color Inkjet

For documents, use Standard print quality. For photos, use Photo or High or similar print-quality settings. Be sure to also match the paper type.

> **WARNING**
>
> With a color inkjet printer that uses ink tanks instead of ink cartridges, make sure the correct ink color is used to fill each reservoir. If the wrong color is in one or more tanks, follow the manufacturer's instructions for emptying (purging) the tanks and refill with the correct ink colors.

## Grinding Noise

Grinding noises coming from a printer are bad news because they indicate mechanical problems. The causes and solutions to grinding noises differ with the printer type.

### Laser

If a laser printer makes grinding noises during operation, check to see if the moving parts in the printer are stuck, jammed, or misaligned. To determine the source of noise, shut off the printer and wait for it to cool down. Then, open the printer to make the source of the noise accessible.

Remove the component (fuser assembly, imaging drum, etc.); when removing a component, check for damage to gears on the component or inside the printer. Check for debris from damage; replace the component and make sure it is tightly secured in place; loose components will cause damage over time.

### Inkjet

If an inkjet printer makes grinding noises during operation, check to see if moving parts in printer are stuck, jammed, or misaligned. To determine the source of noise, open the printer to make the source of the noise accessible. Check the play and movement of print-head, belt, paper feed, duplex unit, etc. When removing a component, check for damage to gears on the component or inside the printer. Check for debris from damage. Replace the component and make sure it is tightly secured in place; loose components will cause damage over time.

## Impact

If an impact printer makes grinding noises during operation, check to see if the moving parts in printer are stuck, jammed, or misaligned. To determine the source of noise, open the printer to make the source of the noise accessible. Check the play and movement of printhead, belt, tractor feed, single-sheet feed, etc. When removing a component, check for damage to gears on the component or inside the printer; check for debris from damage. Replace the component and make sure it is tightly secured in place; loose components will cause damage over time.

## Finishing Issues

Many office-grade network printers can staple or hole-punch printed output, making the production of a finished pamphlet or booklet easier. These features may be located inside the printer or in an external finisher attachment. When finishing features stop working, here's what to look for.

## Staple Jams

If a page or booklet stapling unit is not stapling and the unit has stopped, check for a jam caused by defective staples. Keep in mind that a page stapler puts the staple in the top corner of a stack of paper, while a booklet stapler puts two staples into a folded booklet.

Look for error codes on the printer to determine which unit has failed; open the correct access panel and remove the staple holder; flip open the end of the stapler holder and remove the jammed staples; flip closed the end of the stapler holder, verifying it is locked into place, and reinstall the holder; close the access door.

Another cause of staple jams is trying to staple too much paper. Don't exceed the paper weight or number of sheets recommended for stapling.

## Hole Punch

If the finishing unit is not punching holes in the correct location, check the hole punch settings. Make sure you have selected the correct page orientation before specifying hole punch locations. Upgrade the printer driver to the latest version.

## Incorrect Page Orientation

When a document is laid out in landscape mode, prints in portrait mode, or vice versa check for a mismatch between document layout and printer driver setting. Both should be set to the same settings. Otherwise, one overrides the other. Try this workaround if necessary: change the layout option in the printer driver from the correct to incorrect setting and then back again.

**EXAM TIP**

Expect to see questions relating to maintenance tips for printers. Here's a quick overview:

▶ **Laser:** Maintenance: Replace toner, apply maintenance kit, calibrate, clean

▶ **Inkjet:** Maintenance: Clean heads, replace cartridges, calibrate, clear jams

▶ **Thermal:** Maintenance: Replace paper, clean heating element, remove debris, check heat sensitivity of paper

▶ **Impact:** Maintenance: Replace ribbon, replace printhead, replace paper

▶ **3-D:** Filament, resin, print bed

## CERTMIKE EXAM ESSENTIALS

▶ When dealing with common printer problems, the first item to determine is the printer type. The same or similar symptoms often have drastically different causes depending on the printer type.

▶ If the temperature and humidity of the printer location and where supplies and paper are stored are beyond recommended ranges, print quality will be adversely affected with most types of printers.

▶ Printer driver settings may need to be changed when the paper type or location are changed or when problems are visible in the printed output.

## Practice Question 1

The laser printer in your office is making a grinding noise. What should you do FIRST?

A.  Shut down the printer.
B.  Listen to the printer to determine where the noise is coming from.
C.  Replace the imaging drum/toner cartridge.
D.  Replace the fuser assembly.

## Practice Question 2

Your client calls you because the multifunction device is producing speckled pages. Which question should you ask FIRST to help troubleshoot the problem?

A.  Are all printouts affected or only printouts made when copying a document?
B.  Is this a laser or inkjet device?
C.  How old is the toner cartridge or imaging drum?
D.  Does the printer use an ink cartridges or ink tanks?

## Practice Question 1 Explanation

This question is designed to test your knowledge of printer troubleshooting.

Let's evaluate these choices one at a time.

Option A: Shut down the printer. This is a necessary part of solving the problem, but it should not happen first.

Option B: Listen to the printer to determine where the noise is coming from. This answer affects what you do next. For example, noise from the rear of the printer suggests the fuser assembly, while noise in the front suggests paper feed or imaging drum. This is the BEST answer.

Option C: Replace the imaging drum/toner cartridge. This might be the solution, but without determining the source of the grinding noise, this should not be tried first.

Option D: Replace the fuser assembly. This might be the solution, but without determining the source of the grinding noise, this should not be tried first.

**Correct Answer: B. Listen to the printer.**

## Practice Question 2 Explanation

This question is designed to test your knowledge of how to troubleshoot multifunction devices.

Let's consider these options one at a time.

Option A: Are all printouts affected or only printouts made when copying a document? This should be the first question to ask because it determines what to check. If all printouts are affected, the next item to determine is the type of printer. If only copies are affected, the most likely cause is the scanner glass or ADF. This is the BEST question of those listed.

Option B: Is this a laser or inkjet device? This would be the first question to ask to troubleshoot a printer. However, because this is a multifunction device, it should be asked *after* determining which printouts are affected.

Option C: How old is the toner cartridge or imaging drum? This question could help determine the cause of the speckling, but it assumes the printer type and cause of the problem. It should not be asked first.

Option D: Does the printer use an ink cartridges or ink tanks? This question could help determine the cause of the speckling, but it assumes the printer type and cause of the problem. It should not be asked first.

**Correct Answer: A. Are all printouts affected or only printouts made when copying?**

# CHAPTER 30

# Troubleshooting Networks

## *Core 1 Objective 5.7: Given a scenario, troubleshoot problems with wired and wireless networks.*

**Wired** and wireless networks are essential parts of making computers and mobile devices work. When they stop working, everything stops. In this chapter, you will discover what you need to know about Core 1 Objective 5.7, including the following:

▶ **Common Symptoms**

## COMMON SYMPTOMS

Network problems disrupt both work and play more than ever as we depend upon networks to stay connected with the world. The following sections discuss common symptoms and provide solutions.

### Intermittent Wireless Connectivity

Wireless devices are convenient, but when they become unreliable because of intermittent connections, they become frustrating. Look for the issues discussed here.

Obstructions between your location and the router or access point can cause problems, especially with older (802.11a, b, and g) hardware. On a 2.4 GHz network (b, g, and n), change the wireless frequency channel to 1, 6, or 11 to minimize interference from other networks. Move to a different location if possible.

With a mobile device, try holding it at a different angle. If you're in a vehicle that's parked, open a window and hold your smartphone or tablet out of the window to improve signal strength.

On Windows 10/11, run the network adapter troubleshooter, available from the Update & Security menu in Settings (Windows 10) or System menu (Windows 11).

Also with Windows 10/11, disable the power management option to turn off your network adapter to save power. You can find this by opening Device Manager, opening the Network Adapters category, opening your network adapter, clicking the Power Management tab, and clearing the Allow the Computer To Turn Off This Device To Save Power. Click OK.

If you use a USB wireless adapter, connect it to an extension cable so you can more easily adjust its position.

If you use a PCIe or PCI card in a desktop computer with external antennas, change the position of the antennas to improve your connection or replace the standard antennas with antennas that are rated for better signal strength.

Check for other devices that might be interfering with your signal. If you are using 2.4 GHz signaling, check for baby monitors, old wireless phones, and microwave ovens. If you are using 5 GHz signaling, check for 5 GHz wireless phones. If possible, replace wireless phones with 6 GHz models to avoid this type of interference.

Set your router to use Auto instead of a fixed wireless channel, especially with 2.4 GHz signaling. Auto will change the channel if there is too much interference from other Wi-Fi devices.

In larger homes or offices, especially those with lots of obstructions, consider using mesh networking. With a mesh network, there are multiple access points that are connected to the wireless router and to each other with a dedicated signal, and the user enjoys a seamless transition between networks.

## Slow Network Speeds

Both wired and wireless network speeds have improved significantly over time, going from 10 Mbps to 10 Gbps (wired) and from 11 Mbps to 1 Gbps and faster (wireless). However, getting the fastest speeds from either type of network means that mix-and-match hardware needs to go.

On a wireless network, try to use only 802.11ac (Wi-Fi 5) and 802.11ax (Wi-Fi 6 or 6E) hardware. A wireless network that also has older network devices (802.11b, a, g, or n) on it must use slower signal rates to accommodate those standards.

In addition to slower signal rates, older wireless network hardware doesn't always support WPA2 or WPA3 encryption. If you have a mixture of devices that support different encryption standards on the same network, all of the devices must use whatever standard they have in common, such as WPA, which can also slow down newer, faster devices. For these reasons, use a separate wireless network (SSID) for 802.11n (2.4 GHz) and older standards.

On a wired network, mixing Gigabit Ethernet or 2.5 Gigabit Ethernet hardware with Fast Ethernet (100 Mbps) hardware will slow down the network to Fast Ethernet speeds. In addition to using Gigabit Ethernet or faster switches and routers, make sure the cabling is suitable for the network speed you want: CAT5e or CAT6 for Gigabit. CAT5e can also support 2.5 Gbps Ethernet up to 100 meters.

On Windows 10, a feature called Large Send Offload (LSO) is often enabled on wired Ethernet adapters. LSO is designed to improve network performance by changing how large files are sent. Unfortunately, many users find it actually slows down network performance. A good way to see if it affects network performance is to disable it if enabled or enable it if disabled. To see its current setting, open the entry for your network adapter in Control Panel, click the Advanced tab, and look at the Large Send Offload v2 (IPv4) and (IPv6) settings (Figure 30.1). On this system, both are enabled, so after checking network speed, try disabling both of them to see if upload performance improves.

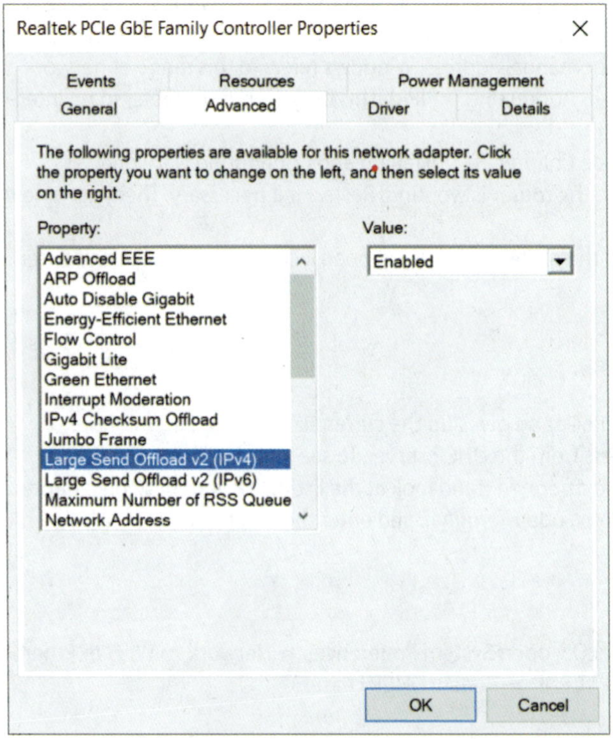

**FIGURE 30.1** Examining the current setting for IPv4 LSO.

**NOTE**

If you find that changing LSO settings improves upload performance, remember to make the change on other wired adapters on your network.

## Limited Connectivity

When you see "Limited Connectivity" next to a network connection, it's bad news for Internet users. It means the Internet, the network of networks, isn't there for that device. Here's why and what to do.

All devices on an IP network need an IP address to work. There are generally two places where you can get an IP address: a DHCP server or manually by configuring the setting through Network properties. A DHCP server on small networks is built into the router. Normally, when a network device connects to the network, the DHCP server assigns it an IP address. In a few seconds, the device is on the network, and if the network connects to the Internet, the Internet is available to that device.

However, if the DHCP server can't be reached or doesn't assign an IP address and there is no manual IP address assigned, the "Limited Connectivity" message or icon appears. Limited connectivity means that local networking, such as printing to a network printer or copying files between network clients, works, but nothing outside the local network is accessible. This is possible because Windows, macOS, and Linux assign IP addresses in the 169.254.x.x ranges when there is no DHCP or manual address. Windows refers to this range of network addresses as Automatic Private IP Addressing (APIPA). This range is not routable, so no Internet for you!

To learn more about APIPA, see Chapter 10, "Installing and Configuring Networks."

To fix the problem, make sure the router is working. Restart it if necessary. Then, get a new IP address.

To get a new IP address from the router in Windows, open a command prompt and enter these commands:

```
ipconfig /release
ipconfig /renew
```

The command `ipconfig /release` gives up the current IP address; `ipconfig /renew` asks for a new IP address from the DHCP server. To see whether a new IP address was assigned, use the command `ipconfig` and look at the listing for your network adapter.

To get a new IP address in Linux, open Terminal, and enter these commands:

```
sudo dhclient -r
sudo dhclient
```

To get a new IP address in macOS, open System Preferences ➢ Network ➢ Wi-Fi or Ethernet (as needed) ➢ Advanced ➢ TCP/IP ➢ Renew DHCP Lease.

## Jitter

Every network has *latency*, the amount of time between when a command is sent to the network and when a response is received from the network. Normally, latency on a given network is about the same amount of time. *Jitter* is the term for variations in latency.

Jitter is a big problem with VoIP, videoconferencing, and other situations in which it's vital that packets come through in the correct order.

To help prevent jitter, make sure that quality of service (QoS) is enabled for voice and video data. QoS gives priority to real-time communications.

QoS is enabled automatically in Windows 10. However, you can use the Group Policy Editor to configure QoS by making changes to the QoS Packet Scheduler located in Local Computer Policy ➤ Computer Configuration ➤ Administrative Templates.

On some routers, QoS settings can be optimized for games, media streaming, and web surfing. Enable the QoS media streaming setting in your router if available (Figure 30.2).

**FIGURE 30.2**  Selecting QoS settings suitable for VoIP and media streaming in an Asus router.

On a wired network, using cables that run faster than the minimum necessary for your network type can help reduce jitter. For example, use CAT6 or greater instead of CAT5e.

With wired or wireless networks, performing network-intensive activities such as updates or large file transfers at different times than videoconferencing or other audio/video traffic will help reduce jitter.

## High Latency

Different types of networks have different amounts of latency. Geosynchronous satellite Internet, because of the 22,000-mile trip a signal takes to the satellite and the 22,000-mile trip back for its response, has latency of around 600 ms, compared to 15–35ms for cable Internet. The shorter the latency, the better a particular Internet service is for gaming, videoconferencing, and streaming media services. When latency goes up even momentarily, it affects these services.

Some causes for higher-than-normal latency can include DNS server errors. Try changing your default DNS servers to the Google DNS servers 8.8.8.8 and 8.8.4.4 (IPv4); IPv6 Google DNS servers are 2001:4860:4860::8888 and 2001:4860:4860::8844.

To make this change in Windows, open Settings ➢ Network & Internet ➢ Status ➢ Change Adapter Options. Right-click your network adapter and select Properties. Highlight Internet Protocol Version 4 and click Properties. Click the radio button for Use The Following DNS Server Addresses and enter the IPv4 values given earlier. Click OK (see Figure 30.3).

If your network also uses IPv6, highlight Internet Protocol Version 6 and click Properties. Click the radio button for Use The Following DNS Server Addresses and enter the IPv6 values given earlier. Click OK.

**NOTE**

If you prefer non-Google DNS servers, see the list at `privacysavvy.com/security/business/best-free-public-dns-servers`.

If your system is low on RAM (for example, less than 8 GB for a system that uses office apps and web browsing or less than 16 GB for a system performing photo or video editing), add RAM.

Download only one item at a time and don't run a lot of apps that use network connections at the same time. For example, don't be surprised if downloading a big Windows or application patch while you are also streaming a movie in HD makes your movie stutter and your audio quality poor.

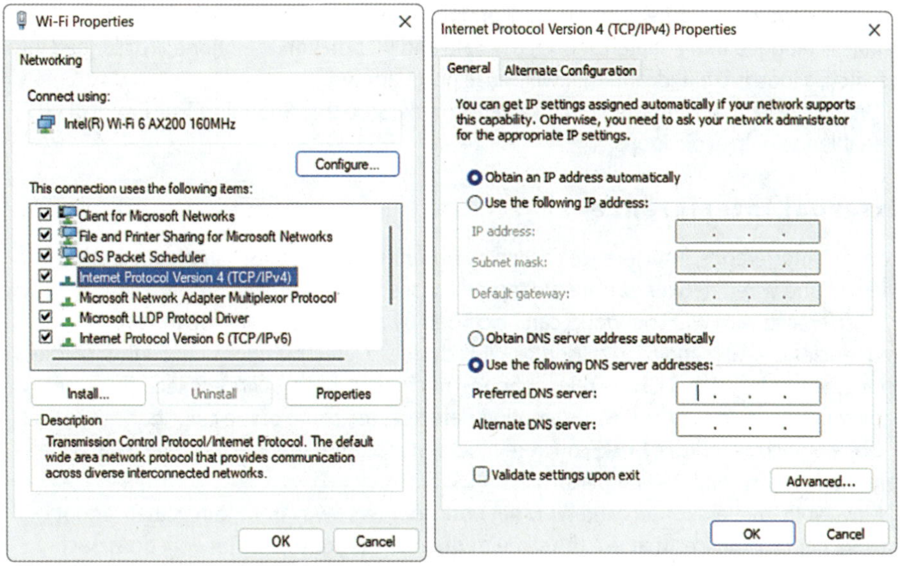

**FIGURE 30.3** Preparing to manually enter preferred DNS servers.

## Poor VoIP Quality

VoIP uses the Internet and a local area network (LAN) to deliver voice calls to telephones in both business and home environments. Problems with VoIP call quality can cause big problems for all users.

Problems such as jitter, lack of QoS settings for media streaming, and high latency have a particularly big impact on VoIP call quality. Deal with these issues as described in earlier sections of this chapter and you should see an improvement in your VoIP call quality.

To improve call quality further, check with your VoIP provider to see whether they can add a jitter buffer to your connection. A jitter buffer stores data packets temporarily and then feeds them to your VoIP connection in the correct order. The jitter buffer is added to your service by the vendor.

Try shutting down your router for about 20 seconds and then repowering it. Allow your wireless connections to be reestablished before using the network again.

If you are hearing echo, turn down the volume of your headphone or speakers to avoid your VoIP microphone from picking up the audio.

## Port Flapping

Port flapping is a problem on a switch port in which the port goes offline (down) and online (up) frequently over a time period of about 10 seconds. Bad cabling is a frequent cause of port flapping. A cable that has a bad crimp, a broken retaining clip, or a cracked connector should be replaced immediately. However, bad cables don't always look bad. Use a cable tester to check your cables.

If port flapping is happening with VoIP phones, make sure that only one jack on the phone is plugged into a switch. If both the data and PC ports on the phone are plugged into a switch, a loop is created, and that will cause port flapping.

On a network that is running Cisco switches, make sure that Spanning Tree Protocol (STP) is enabled to help avoid loops.

## External Interference

External interference, interference caused by non-network sources, can plague both wireless and wired networks. Here are typical causes and solutions.

Interference with Wi-Fi networks can be caused by any devices that use the same frequencies (2.4 GHz and 5 GHz) used by Wi-Fi devices. Defective fluorescent lights, cordless phone headsets, 2.4 or 5 GHz wireless phones, microwave ovens, wireless security cameras, baby monitors, two-way radios, and motion detectors are some of the culprits.

Objects such as mirrors, brick, concrete blocks, stucco, metal, water, and electrical panels can also interfere with Wi-Fi signals.

Move your wireless routers and Wi-Fi network adapters away from things that cannot be moved. Replace devices that use the same frequencies as your Wi-Fi network does, such as swapping out older cordless phone systems with DECT 6.0 (6 GHz) systems and 2.4 GHz wireless security cameras with 5.8 GHz models. Consider using Wi-Fi mesh networks to provide multiple routes to signals.

Wired networks can also run into interference problems. A problem called *cross talk* between the wires in a UTP cable means that a UTP cable can interfere with itself, or if several cables are bundled together, cross talk can take place between cables.

Switching from CAT5e to CAT6 or 6a cable, both of which have better cross talk prevention, can help improve network performance.

Because most wired networks used unshielded twisted-pair (UTP) wiring that has no shielding, external interference from power lines, fluorescent light fixtures, alarm systems, and elevators can cause problems leading to slow network performance due to repeated retries to send and receive signals.

Rerouting cables away from external interference sources helps a great deal. However, if this isn't possible, using shielded twisted pair (STP) cabling for interference-prone parts of the cable run will solve the problem. STP cable has a metal foil shield between the outer jacket and the TP wires. Keep in mind that STP cable is more expensive and stiffer than UTP cable and may need to be grounded.

**NOTE**

For a good discussion of the pros and cons of UTP and STP cable and when to use STP cable, see www.firefold.com/blogs/news/stp-vs-utp-cables-comparing-each-and-when-to-use-them.

## CERTMIKE EXAM ESSENTIALS

▶ Solving network problems requires familiarization with both operating system and hardware elements of networking. Changes in the configuration of both software and hardware are often necessary to solve problems.

▶ Interference can be a significant problem with the speed and reliability of both wired and wireless networks.

▶ Network changes such as moving to higher-rated cables, using mesh networking, and adjusting router and network adapter settings in the operating system are some of the methods used to improve network speed and reliability.

## Practice Question 1

Your client has a Gigabit Ethernet network that is connected using CAT5e cabling. Some of the network cabling is running close to a flickering fluorescent light fixture, and users are complaining about slow network performance. Which of the following should you try FIRST to improve performance?

A. Replace UTP cable with STP cable.
B. Replace STP cable with UTP cable.
C. Enable QoS in the router.
D. Repair the fluorescent light fixture.

## Practice Question 2

Your client's small-office network has limited connectivity. Which of the following router functions has stopped working?

A. QoS
B. LSO
C. DHCP
D. IPv4

## Practice Question 1 Explanation

This question is designed to test your real-world understanding of network troubleshooting. Let's evaluate these answers one at a time.

1. Option A (Replace UTP cable with STP cable) would probably solve the network problem but could be difficult and expensive to implement, depending upon how that segment of network is installed. It is also a workaround, because it doesn't address the most likely cause, the defective fluorescent light fixture. This is not the best answer.

2. Option B (Replace STP cable with UTP cable) won't help at all for two reasons. First, there is probably already UTP cable in place. Second, STP cable would block interference from the fluorescent fixture. This is a totally wrong answer.

3. Option C (Enable QoS in the router) is a completely useless setting for this problem. QoS helps prioritize certain types of traffic for better performance, but doesn't help with overall performance issues. This is not the right answer.

4. Option D (Repair the fluorescent light fixture) gets to the root of the problem as defective fluorescent light fixtures are known sources of interference. Fixing this problem might require only changing a tube or replacing a ballast and will also improve the light coming from the fixture. This is the FIRST fix to make.

**Correct answer: D, Repair the fluorescent light fixture**

## Practice Question 2 Explanation

This question is designed to test your knowledge of router troubleshooting. Let's evaluate these answers one at a time.

1. Option A (QoS) has nothing to do with connectivity. QoS is a router (and Windows) setting that improves performance for specified network traffic. This is an incorrect answer.

2. Option B (LSO) is designed to boost upload performance but is not a router configuration option. This is an incorrect answer.

3. Option C (DHCP) is correct because DHCP is a router function that provides IP addresses to computers and devices on the network. If DHCP stops working, devices cannot connect to the Internet.

4. Option D (IPv4) refers to the suite of Internet Protocol components used to connect to other computers and the Internet. If IPv4 had failed, there would be no connectivity at all. This is an incorrect answer.

**Correct answer: C, DHCP**

# INDEX

# ONLINE TEST BANK

To help you study for your CompTIA A+ Core 1 certification exam, register to gain one year of FREE access after activation to the online interactive test bank—included with your purchase of this book! All of the practice questions in this book are included in the online test bank so you can study in a timed and graded setting.

## REGISTER AND ACCESS THE ONLINE TEST BANK

To register your book and get access to the online test bank, follow these steps:

1. Go to www.wiley.com/go/sybextestprep. You'll see the **"How to Register Your Book for Online Access"** instructions.
2. Click "here to register" and then select your book from the list.
3. Complete the required registration information, including answering the security verification to prove book ownership. You will be emailed a pin code.
4. Follow the directions in the email or go to www.wiley.com/go/sybextestprep.
5. Find your book on that page and click the "Register or Login" link with it. Then enter the pin code you received and click the "Activate PIN" button.
6. On the Create an Account or Login page, enter your username and password, and click Login or, if you don't have an account already, create a new account.
7. At this point, you should be in the test bank site with your new test bank listed at the top of the page. If you do not see it there, please refresh the page or log out and log back in.